SELECTED PROSE OF LOUIS MacNEICE

Selected Prose of Louis MacNeice

Edited by
ALAN HEUSER

CLARENDON PRESS · OXFORD
1990

*This book has been printed digitally and produced in a standard design
in order to ensure its continuing availability*

OXFORD
UNIVERSITY PRESS

Great Clarendon Street, Oxford OX2 6DP

Oxford University Press is a department of the University of Oxford.
It furthers the University's objective of excellence in research, scholarship,
and education by publishing worldwide in

Oxford New York

Athens Auckland Bangkok Bogotá Buenos Aires Cape Town
Chennai Dar es Salaam Delhi Florence Hong Kong Istanbul Karachi
Kolkata Kuala Lumpur Madrid Melbourne Mexico City Mumbai Nairobi
Paris São Paulo Shanghai Singapore Taipei Tokyo Toronto Warsaw

with associated companies in Berlin Ibadan

Oxford is a registered trade mark of Oxford University Press
in the UK and in certain other countries

Published in the United States
by Oxford University Press Inc., New York

ISBN 0-19-818525-1

*Jacket illustration: Louis MacNiece in the
early 1960's (photographer unknown)*

To Liesel and John

Acknowledgements

ONCE again it is my purpose and pleasure to acknowledge personal and professional help in the work of this second volume of MacNeice's short prose. Thanks are due to the Humanities Research Committee of McGill University for an initial travel grant (1981); the Social Sciences and Humanities Research Council of Canada for a leave fellowship (1984–5) and two research grants (1982, 1985); McGill University for granting me sabbatical leave (1984–5) to complete the first volume, and David Williams, Chairman of the Department of English, for facilitating the enterprise. Research travel took me to the Humanities Research Center, Austin, Texas, to consult the Louis MacNeice Collection of Manuscripts there; to the Bodleian Library, Oxford, for their various collections of Louis MacNeice Papers; and to the BBC Written Archives Centre, Caversham Park, Reading, as well as to the British Library, the National Sound Archive, BBC libraries, all in London, and to The John Rylands University Library of Manchester.

For permission to publish Louis MacNeice's prose, grateful acknowledgement is made to his literary executor Jon Stallworthy, to Mrs Hedli MacNeice, Daniel MacNeice, and the MacNeice estate, as well as to the literary agents, David Higham Associates. For permission to quote from MacNeice's poetry in footnotes to both volumes, thanks are due to Faber and Faber, Ltd.

For primary materials, the bibliographies of MacNeice by William T. McKinnon (1970) and by C. M. Armitage and Neil Clark (1973), as well as the Auden bibliography by B. C. Bloomfield and Edward Mendelson (2nd edn, 1972), were a great help. These were supplemented by additional items of prose supplied by Professor Mendelson of Columbia University, as well as those items traced by Martin Lubowski of London, and more recently (1987–8) by Dr Peter McDonald of Pembroke College, Cambridge, and David Pascoe of Oriel College, Oxford. (Further details are to be found in 'Acknowledgements' to *Selected Literary Criticism of Louis MacNeice* (1987), vii–viii.) For photocopies of some of MacNeice's manuscripts and typescripts, I wish to thank Mrs Hedli MacNeice; Edna Longley of The Queen's University of Belfast; Cathy Henderson of the HRC, Austin, Texas. For photocopies of related materials and for help in tracing information, thanks are due to Kevin Andrews of Athens; John Burgass of Merton College Library; Robert M. Dunlop of Glasgow; A. J. Flavell of the Bodleian Library; Dr John Hoffmann of The Carl Sandburg Collection, The Library, University of Illinois; John Jordan of the BBC Written Archives Centre, Reading; Professor Edward Mendelson of Columbia University; Penelope Niven of Hendersonville, North Carolina; David Pascoe named above; Arnona Rudavsky of Hebrew Union College Library, Cincinnati; K. B. Shipp of the British Society of Perfumers; M. H. Sinnatt and Teresa E. Slowik of the Kennel Club, London; Jon Stallworthy of Wolfson College; Mrs Jean M. Stewart of St Nicholas' Parish Church, Carrickfergus.

Willing help was offered by the librarians of Broadcasting House, the BBC WAC, the Bodleian, and especially by the indispensable reference and inter-library loan librarians of McLennan Library, McGill University, as well as by my colleagues Abbott Conway, John Macnamara, and Archie Malloch. In addition to all of the above and those mentioned in 'Acknowledgements' to the first volume, for recent correspondence (1986–9) I am grateful to Christopher M. Armitage, North Callahan, Jasper Griffin, John R. Hilton (Laycock, Wiltshire), Mercy H. MacCann (Dungannon, Co. Tyrone), Graham Payn, James T. Maher, W. John Morgan (University of Nottingham), Brian Rust, the Rabbi Dr Jonathan Sacks, Sir Stephen Spender, David R. A. Thomson, Jonathan Vickers (National Sound Archive); John R. Whitehead (Munslow, Shropshire). For assistance in proof-reading and indexing, I have to thank Jake Brown.

Special thanks are due to Louis MacNeice's literary executor Jon Stallworthy (himself a practising poet) for advice, practical help, and a rare understanding, while for encouragement and support I owe the largest debt to my family, Margaret, Liesel, and John.

McGill University   A.H.
April 1989

Contents

Introduction

THIS book is the second volume of MacNeice's short prose writings long out of print, now (1990) selected and annotated for the general as well as the specialist reader. The first volume, *Selected Literary Criticism of Louis MacNeice* (1987), was intended to supplement MacNeice's three fine books of literary criticism, all certain to be in demand and kept in print.[1] That first volume was highly selective; not all or even most of MacNeice's numerous critical articles and reviews could be included; there was space for only a significant fraction, so reasonable discriminations and restrictive principles of selection had to be used. In this second volume, *Selected Prose of Louis MacNeice*, I have confined my choices to his short, self-contained prose dealing with matters other than the explicitly literary and critical, have been restrictive with articles of the early years 1929–39, but generous about inclusion for 1940–1 and 1948 onwards. There is, of course, still a good deal of literary interest in these pieces, for Louis MacNeice is a multi-dimensional writer who cannot be, refuses to be, pigeon-holed.

It may need emphasizing that this second volume does not incorporate any of MacNeice's prose books certain or likely to be kept in print.[2] The selection is wide-ranging and highly topical, dealing with ancient philosophy and contemporary history, with autobiography and travel, with reports of the Blitz, with matters of special interest to MacNeice—Irish, British, American, Hellenic, Indian—and with his favourite sport, rugby. All this may seem hit and miss, yet it has a logical and necessary coherence in MacNeice the man. The attempt has been made to represent him chronologically, in development, with many varied interests and vital affinities, from his

---

[1] *Modern Poetry: A Personal Essay* (1938; repr. with an introduction by Walter Allen, 1968), *The Poetry of W. B. Yeats* (1941; repr. with a foreword by Richard Ellmann, 1967), and *Varieties of Parable* [the Clark lectures 1963] (1965).

[2] *The Strings are False: An Unfinished Autobiography*, ed. E. R. Dodds (1965; repr. 1982), as an honest and exuberant account, and *Astrology* (printed once only in 1964), as a fascinating book of research, should both be kept in print.

majority at 21 to his premature death in 1963, nine days short
of his fifty-sixth birthday.

Louis MacNeice was not only an outstanding Irish poet and
pioneering BBC producer-playwright equipped with a rigorous
classical education (Sherborne, Marlborough, Oxford), but
also a Thirties poet equal or second only to Auden and a poet
who survived the Thirties with his credentials intact—as an
artist committed to the 'ordinary man' and writing for the
ordinary educated reader. Of course, he was committed also to
an Hellenic and pluralistic humanism[3] (rather than to Marxism,
Freudianism, or any recent ism), within limits to the British
empirical tradition, to his art—the poetic craft at hand from
early days, and eventually to the lively art of sound-broadcast-
ing. And he did all this with continuing respect for metaphysics
—though he soon came to prefer history to philosophy—and
with eventual distaste for the novel.[4] His development was
more than a gradual unfolding of his powers: wit and imagination, a scholar's bag of learning, Celtic humour, a love of saga,
fairy tale, and fantasy, a temperament haunted by dream,
nightmare, and life's losses. It was a development of widening
awareness and changing views (for instance, on Ireland and
Britain, and his relationship to them), of increasing refinement,
discretion, sophistication, as he expressed more and more not
only of the world around him but of his own lively and changing, private, inner world.

Travels outside Great Britain and Ireland took him not only
to continental Europe (Norway, France, Spain, Italy, Greece),
Iceland, and the USA, but also to south and south-east Asia
(India, Pakistan, Ceylon, Malaya), and Africa (Egypt and the
Sudan, Ghana, South Africa and Rhodesia). He reported in

[3] These terms, Hellenism, pluralism, humanism, are used here in reference not
only to *litterae humaniores*, but also to MacNeice's tendency to discount abstract
theorizing and to focus on discrete, concrete entities in flux, as he writes in his poem
'Plurality' of August 1940: *The Collected Poems of Louis MacNeice*, ed. E. R. Dodds
(1966, corr. 1979), 243–4, especially in the passage on 'Man is man . . .'

[4] Early on (*c*.1938) MacNeice turned away from prose fiction to poetry and play-
writing. His later article 'Is the Novel Dead? A Poet's View', *Observer* 8520 (19 Sept.
1954), confirms this distaste. The failure of his first, pseudonymous novel *Roundabout
Way* (1932) and of his two other early novels to be published, plus the immense
amount of hack-reviewing of largely hack fiction undertaken by MacNeice in 1935–7:
these things left their mark.

prose and verse on these places, many of them observed at critical moments in their history: Barcelona under siege before its fall; India and Pakistan during their transition to independence and partition; Athens immediately after the civil war in Greece; Egypt just before the Suez crisis; the Gold Coast at its transformation into Ghana; and so forth. Many of these travels were sponsored by the BBC for MacNeice to gather copy for radio programmes. In his later career, from 1947 on, he reported on the devolution of the British Empire into the Commonwealth;[5] and he would return to The George, or The Stag in London, or to The Pearl in Dublin (favourite pubs of his) to confide to cronies, laconically and enigmatically, insights into recent developments in history and art, into the makers, shakers, and breakers of lives and forms, though more often he would, just as naturally and enigmatically, keep his own counsel.

In the absence of a detailed and full-scale biography—presently being prepared by Jon Stallworthy (who is, after E. R. Dodds and D. M. Davin, MacNiece's third literary executor)—there are many details of the 'life' which could contribute to a volume of this kind, especially to explanatory notes; but it is not the business nor the mandate of this volume's editor to trace a total picture.[6] In the absence of an exhaustive bibliography,[7] there may be links in the chain of MacNeice's occasional prose which are missing in the corrected and slightly

---

[5] For a witty poem of the late 1950s on lecturers speaking anachronistically on British literature to colonials and foreigners, see his 'Old Masters Abroad': *Collected Poems*, 501.

[6] While waiting for Jon Stallworthy's full-scale life of MacNeice, the reader interested in his biography should look at MacNeice's own account in *Strings*, the memoirs in *Time Was Away: The World of Louis MacNeice*, ed. Terence Brown and Alec Reid (1974), Barbara Coulton's *Louis MacNeice in the BBC* (1980), William T. McKinnon's *Apollo's Blended Dream: A Study of the Poetry of Louis MacNeice* (1971), 3-38, and of course D. M. Davin's very useful summary in *DNB 1961-1970* (1981). See also relevant chapters in such books as Davin's *Closing Times* (1975), E. R. Dodds's *Missing Persons: An Autobiography* (1977), and Geoffrey Grigson's *Recollections Mainly of Writers and Artists* (1984).

[7] The bibliographies of MacNeice by William T. McKinnon (*Bulletin of Bibliography*, 1970) and C. M. Armitage and Neil Clark (*A Bibliography of the Works of Louis MacNeice*, 1973), the sources cited by Barbara Coulton (*Louis MacNeice in the BBC*, 1980), and the corrected 'Bibliography of Short Prose by Louis MacNeice' at the back of this volume, all require incorporation and expansion into a new and full bibliography.

extended Bibliography at the back of this volume.[8] What is offered, then, in this second volume of MacNeice's long-neglected prose, is a discontinuous, largely personal, social, and intellectual history—apart from literary criticism *per se*—wherein MacNeice in his usual, open, autobiographical way reveals a considerable amount about himself and his vital affinities. When he gave up a classical scholar's career for one of the lively arts, he was attracted both by doing something for his country in the war crisis and by the opportunities of writing and producing plays, adaptations, and features (radio documentaries) for a living, while continuing to write poetry in his remaining time. What is presented here is largely journalism which MacNeice never attempted to collect or select for publication; in his creative life it certainly would not have had priority. Yet it is a very useful and I think necessary part of the record in helping us to understand him and his original work in poetry and play-writing.

To clarify major phases in MacNeice's development, headings with dates are used in the pages of contents: five rough groupings—1929–36 (Oxford and Birmingham), 1937–9 (early London years), 1940–4 (war years), 1948–57 (a post-war decade), and 1958–63 (his last years). In the first phase at Oxford and Birmingham, MacNeice represents himself as a restless poet-scholar, academically preoccupied, a philosophic sceptic. The first article, 'Our God Bogus' (May 1929)—written shortly after the appearance of his first book of poetry (*Blind Fireworks*, March 1929)—is, however, more than a *jeu d'esprit* of scepticism, debunking fads of modern thought from the standpoint of a student of Greats. 'Poets and artists are much influenced by the latest ideas,' he admits, having disposed of Freud; and he goes on wittily to attack the extremes of mysticism, realism, scepticism itself, art for art's sake, transcendentalism, and the like. He takes his stand with those called eccentrics, modern poets (in this case, Cummings, the Sitwells, T. S. Eliot), in asserting an artistic and Hellenic humanism. In the

---

[8] Two of the notable gaps in this selection are 1930–3 and 1942–7: the former covering MacNeice's first marriage to Mary Ezra (before the arrival of his first child, Daniel, 1934); and the latter the period during and after World War II when the poet was absorbed in BBC war work and in his second marriage to the actress and singer Hedli Anderson (1942, with the birth of his second child, Corinna, 1943).

mid-1930s he extols two sceptics—Vilfredo Pareto the Italian sociologist (November 1935) and Lucretius the Roman philosopher-poet (May 1936)—but remains hesitant about going all the way with Pareto who 'openly sneers at theology and metaphysics'[9] and, while appreciating Lucretius' Epicureanism, cannot assent to E. E. Sikes's claim that 'the Epicurean religion . . . marks a distinct step in advance of the crude Hellenic thought'. It is a pity that MacNeice's preference for Aristotle over Plato cannot be explicitly represented from his early articles and reviews;[10] however, among my selections there are valuable and professional treatments of Platonism and Plato (October 1934, December 1935), demonstrating MacNeice's continuation of the Oxford idealism of the later 1920s in which he had been trained by Geoffrey Mure, a disciple of F. H. Bradley.

In his early London years (1936–9) after his divorce (November 1936), MacNeice—left with a very young son to be cared for —earned necessary money by busily teaching and busily writing, producing seven books and a veritable storm of journalism, much of it hack-reviewing of fiction. The opportunity is taken here to select from two of his books likely to remain out of print (*Minch* and *Zoo*, both published 1938), as well as from journalistic pieces. He was somehow in quest of another Celtic affinity —hence his two trips to the Hebrides in 1937—for he could not at first fully acknowledge his very real Irish identity, tangled as it was with Ulster. He was still the mischievous debunker—of recent prose stylists from Pater to Hemingway (see the playful parodies of 'Or One Might Write It So', from *Minch*, written August 1937)—and he emerged at the age of 30 from early snobbery to defend, in his own way, vulgarity (December 1937). Besides visits to Iceland (with Wystan Auden, August–September 1936) and to the Outer Hebrides (April and July 1937) which issued in two travel books (1937, 1938), he made two visits to Spain (with Anthony Blunt, Easter 1936; alone, December 1938–January 1939) before and during the Spanish Civil War, deliberately siding with the Loyalists in a brief state-

---

[9] Pareto's theory of 'residues' or quasi-instincts, which unconsciously and genetically determine human thoughts, appears to have left a strong mark on MacNeice: see, e.g., the poem 'Carrick Revisited', June 1945: *Collected Poems*, 224–5.

[10] MacNeice refers to Aristotle *en passant* in his article on vulgarity (Dec. 1937), in 'Wild and Domestic', para. 8 (*Zoo*, Nov. 1938), and elsewhere.

ment of support (December 1937), and reporting firsthand on the survival of the last government stronghold, Barcelona (January 1939), two months before the Fascist victory. In his descriptive book *Zoo* (November 1938) he engaged the reader in lifelike impressions of animals, especially showing an unsentimental appreciation of dogs as objectively 'something Other' ('Wild and Domestic'), and inserted 'A Personal Digression' on a trip back to Belfast which was mixed with reminiscences of earlier days. Now he began to swing back from youthful reaction against Ulster.

The early war years, 1940–1, constitute the pivot of MacNeice's development as man and writer. He spent ten months of 1940 in the USA[11]—a personal and academic visit prolonged by serious illness, a major operation for peritonitis— the time when he completed for American publication his *Poems 1925–1940* and continued to labour on his *Poetry of W. B. Yeats* (both February 1941), wrote a concise autobiographical sketch[12] and began his autobiography *The Strings are False*, all marking a summing-up of his life and art to date. His American experiences are partly recorded in a letter to Stephen Spender and in three articles (written summer 1940 to spring 1941); these are grouped together for the reader's convenience. Three of the four were written for Cyril Connolly's magazine *Horizon*, one for John Lehmann's *Penguin New Writing*. MacNeice now declared, 'I have never really thought of myself as British; if there is one country I feel at home in it is Eire'—December 1940 (April 1941); and, 'Born in Ireland of Irish parents, I have never felt properly "at home" in England, yet I can write here [England] better than in Ireland' (February 1941). MacNeice was forthright about the United States, but defensive about his friend Auden's decision to stay there, for MacNeice himself preferred 'at the moment' being 'in America to being in England'. However, after the Blitz began, he changed his mind and returned, casting in his lot with those braving the Battle of Britain. His account of the voyage home from New York to

[11] This was his second visit to America. MacNeice had been there on a brief lecture tour in spring 1939.

[12] For the American poet Stanley Kunitz's biographical dictionary of modern writers, *c*.1940 (1942), continued *c*.1953 (1955).

Liverpool through 'The Atlantic Tunnel'[13] vividly captured impressions of his old Irish cabin mate, of Canadian airmen, and of British seamen, survivors of the sunken HMS *Jervis Bay* (December 1940). He volunteered for the Royal Navy, but was rejected because of the after-effects of his serious operation; he then served as a London firewatcher in the Home Guard. The returned MacNeice found his English world in the war crisis 'more comprehensible' and hoped for a 'social revolution' which would preserve respect for the individual: 'When we come out of the tunnel we must still have faces—not masks.' In 'Traveller's Return' (February 1941) he continued his defence of British expatriate writers in America (especially Auden, George Barker, Ralph Bates): if they could write better in America than in England, they should be judged by that. 'Touching America' (March 1941) gave his personal view of the USA along with a summary journal of his ten months' stay —spring (teaching at Cornell University), summer (the Fall of France), and autumn (his hospitalization with peritonitis—'they thought I would die'; the presidential election campaign; war hysteria).[14] Some of this personal and social material was being revised 1940-1 for his 'unfinished autobiography', published posthumously as *The Strings are False* (1965).

In May 1941 MacNeice joined the features section (under Laurence Gilliam) of the BBC Drama and Features Department, though he had been writing features scripts for the BBC since February; his future course was set.[15] Five London Letters written during the Blitz for the left-wing New York magazine *Common Sense* (first half of 1941) and an article for *Picture Post* (May 1941)—six articles grouped together for the reader's convenience—gave firsthand details of civilian life in the midst of destruction, muddle, and death: from the German air raids and fire bombings to the governance of the country in crisis, from the Home Front (crowds sleeping in the tube stations, arrangements for the homeless, problems with the

[13] One of several verse memories of 1940-1, *Collected Poems*, 480-1.

[14] In this article he introduced a new word into the language: 'polylogue', cited in *OED2*.

[15] 'MacNeice continued his activities outside the BBC: he gave lectures and poetry readings, to the Poetry Society and to students; wrote articles; worked on film scripts for the Ministry of Information; produced a pamphlet on the American army': Coulton, *MacNeice*, 58.

food supply and with profiteering) to the Intellectual Front (the break-up of the leftist intelligentsia, the suppression of the *Daily Worker*, the 'People's Convention'), from the 'New Political Alignment' to the 'Anti-defeatism of the Man in the Street'. MacNeice debunked some common outside views of the Blitz: 'It is neither thrilling nor hell [to be in England in 1940–1] though it may have its moments of either. It is more of a Purgatory—routine, routine, routine, plenty to grumble at and plenty to admire, some moments of intense fear and hours and days, weeks and months, of waiting and working one's way not even to Heaven but a bit further up the spiral' (February 1941). He explained that popular ideas of the USA held by Britons and of the UK by Americans were 'quite fantastic': 'Neither the USA nor Great Britain is either a zoo or a museum or a midsummer night's dream; they are both just countries with a good deal in common and composed of individual human beings' (April 1941). MacNeice also reported that 'the feeling in Eire is now predominantly pro-British (though still opposed to participation in the War)' (May 1941). And MacNeice travelled to other cities such as Birmingham, Oxford, Plymouth; he did not confine his blitz reports entirely to London.

Two prose pieces placed at the end of the war section 1940–4, appear to be little known; they provide startling contrasts in content and in style. 'Broken Windows or Thinking Aloud' (written *c*.1941–2, but not published until 1988), a writer's testimonial, plain in style, incomplete, is thrust into short, quasi-poetic paragraphs, and witnesses to the integrity of art and artists during the 1939–45 war: in maintaining the freedom of the artist in a time of national crisis MacNeice has caught the tenor of Yeats's artistic pride and assumes he speaks for writers generally ('we', 'some of us'). 'Northern Ireland and Her People' (written *c*.1941–4, and first published herein), an insider's view of Ulster and Ulstermen, compact in style, stretches into long, deliberate paragraphs of exposition. It appears to be a commissioned piece, gives a sympathetic interpretation of Ulster's peculiarities, characterizes the Ulsterman beyond slogan words ('dour', 'bigot'), casts the subject in historical perspective to clarify rooted hostilities and differences between Unionists and Nationalists, Protestants and Catholics. When he wrote this piece MacNeice had changed his own attitude drastically: Ireland, Northern and Southern, need not be rejected or exorcized, as he had attempted in his love-hate poem 'Valediction' 1934 (1935), but could now be accepted in spite of 'troubles'; he would go on to discontent with Ireland's neutrality in the war,[16] and much later to clarify 'The Two Faces of Ireland' (September 1962), little suspecting the tragic violence to come after his death.

In the first years of the post-war decade 1947–57, when MacNeice travelled to India and Pakistan (1947), when he completed his *Collected Poems 1925–1948* (1949) marking the end of another period, when he co-translated Goethe's *Faust* with his friend Ernest Stahl in 1949 (1951; 1965) and then spent eighteen months working in Greece (1950–1), he launched a new phase in his development as a committed and professional artist.[17] In new 'non-literary' articles he displayed firsthand knowledge of Indian art and customs, Hindu, Buddhist, Muslim, Sikh (March 1948); put in a few good words for the Indian Civil Service at its best in the person of Malcolm Darling—though critical of Sir Malcolm's writing style (April 1949); yet all the time associated India with his native Ireland in being 'politics-ridden' and given over to 'the troubles' ('India at First Sight', 1949), 'a land of paradoxes' and extremes (March 1957). Among his writings on the subcontinent, MacNeice wrote in 1953 the commentary for the documentary *The Conquest of Everest* (a Countryman film, released by United Artists 1953–4).[18]

As for Greece, its classical, Byzantine, Turkish, 'Bavarian',

---

[16] See MacNeice's poem 'Neutrality', Sept. 1942, *Collected Poems*, 202–3.

[17] MacNeice's radio writing 1949–53 appears to have been so successful, especially in his verse translation and abridgement of Goethe's *Faust* 1 and 2 (written for broadcast, Oct.–Nov. 1949), that he was encouraged to write longer poems, clever but somewhat self-indulgent, largely for radio broadcast in the early fifties: six of his *Ten Burnt Offerings* (1952) written in Greece 1950–1 were broadcast Sept.–Nov. 1951; six instalments of his lengthy *Autumn Sequel* 1953 (1954), all of it in *terza rima*, were broadcast June–Aug. 1954: thus his three books of verse written 1949–53 may be considered as *tours de force* for radio or more simply as 'radio poetry'. Auden in introducing his *Selected Poems of Louis MacNeice* (Nov. 1964) detected 'a bad patch' in MacNeice's poetry of the early fifties; MacNeice himself reckoned 'This middle stretch | Of life is bad for poets' ('Day of Renewal', Sept. 1950, *Collected Poems*, 309).

[18] The film, photographed by Thomas Stobart and George W. Lowe, was narrated by Meredith Edwards. MacNeice referred to this venture in his *Autumn Sequel* iii. For reviews of this film, see *The Times*, 22 Oct. 1953, 7c; the *New York Times*, 10 Dec. 1953, 64: 4.

and modern phases were simultaneous presences for him in his long sojourn there: in Athens he served the British Institute and the British Council, presenting talks, arranging play-readings, producing Synge's *Playboy of the Western World*. He discovered and recorded traditional Byzantine music at the 'Wedding of Simon Karas' on Boxing Day 1950 in the old church at Daphni (September 1952). In early 1951 he met Henry Moore arriving in Greece for an exhibition of his work.[19] Three years later he showed unusually keen understanding of the history of Philhellenism (May 1954). When back in London he befriended George Seferis, the (then) greatest living Greek poet, Greek Ambassador in London 1957–62, who won the Nobel Prize for literature in 1963. Within a few years MacNeice was to discriminate clearly between Henry Miller's one-sided 'gush' about Greece in *The Colossus of Maroussi* and Kevin Andrews's sharp, realistic 'truth' in *The Flight of Ikaros* (March 1959). So both Greece and the Indian subcontinent provided MacNeice with enlargements of his sometimes contentious Irish and English worlds, as significant reference points as well as enlightenment for both his life and his art.

In addition to Celtic, Hellenic, and Indian subjects, Mac-Neice undertook to write a few general though modest statements about his artistic commitment. Two instalments of the series 'Notes on the Way' for *Time & Tide* (June–July 1952) present his reflections on recent art exhibitions he has seen in Paris and London—French Impressionist paintings, Byzantine mosaics—and make associations to India (the Indian bazaar, the Caves of Ajanta) and to medieval Europe. In searching for a conviction or a 'faith' which would hold true for the 'ordinary man', for the empiricist, as well as for the artist, he relies on an idea of craftsmanship close to the metaphysical—a confidence that in rendering 'sur-faces' he is showing 'faces' which have 'souls'. When confronted by the direct question of what he believed, he wrote as a professional and moral writer, not a metaphysician: 'What I do believe is that as a human being, it is my duty to make patterns and to contribute to order—good

---

[19] 'I remember Henry Moore arriving for the first time at Piraeus and saying something like: "This is a sculptor's country but it must be hell for painters."'— MacNeice's book review 'A Modern Odyssey' (Dec. 1960), in *Selected Literary Criticism of Louis MacNeice*, 222.

patterns and a good order' (1953): he was following in the steps
of Yeats in the construction of meaning, but without Yeats's
eccentric and elaborate system-building. If there was something
of the sly Celt and not-quite-forgotten Platonist in his claim of
'faces' which have 'souls', there was also a basic integrity and
modesty in his artistic commitment to 'good patterns and a
good order'.

In his last years, 1957–63, MacNeice came into his own.[20]
Awarded an honorary doctorate by The Queen's University of
Belfast, July 1957, and a CBE in the New Year's honours of
1958, then the first of two lectureships at Cambridge University
(1958; 1963), and invited to produce a *son et lumière* programme
for Cardiff Castle to celebrate the 1958 Festival of Wales, he
gained in authority and self-confidence in expressing to the
public his genuine Irish and Celtic identity—not only in under-
taking a good many reviews and assignments on and in Ireland,
but in showing enthusiasm for All Ireland rugby XVs at internationals; in these last years he wrote four rugby reports as well
as one on hurling and Gaelic football.[21] He recognized Celtic
territories as his own: in the Hebrides and the West of Ireland
where the legend of the seal continued to fascinate him (October
1954), in the story of Wales both mythic and historic (August
1958), in Irish heroism from the ancient warrior Cuchulain and
King Brian Boru to the modern rugby champion Kyle, in the
great modern tradition of spirited Irish writing from Yeats and
Joyce to Flann O'Brien to Samuel Beckett, Sam Thompson,
and Brendan Behan. The opening of a James Joyce museum
in the Martello tower at Sandycove, Dublin, June 1962 (the
fortieth anniversary of *Ulysses* and fifty-eighth of 'Bloomsday',
16 June 1904), was the occasion for an animated account of the

[20] MacNeice's verse became notably stronger, more self-assured, more compact,
from 1956–7 on; such concision was the reverse of his self-indulgent verse of the early
fifties. It may be noted that MacNeice was urged to try out TV work (April–Oct.
1958) but found it a medium hostile to his talents in sound. (However, he was assigned
to BBC-TV again in 1960.) This pressure certainly encouraged him in his decision to
go free-lance and to work only half-time for the BBC: see Coulton, *MacNeice*, 166, 175,
179–80.

[21] See MacNeice's sports articles (Jan. 1958, Feb. 1959, Jan. 1960, Feb. 1962,
June 1963). From school days at Sherborne and Marlborough MacNeice enjoyed such
sports and games as cricket, tennis, squash, rugby, draughts, and swimming. He
played tennis, regularly attended cricket matches, and followed rugby very closely,
especially rugby internationals.

'event' with all its international glitter and local Dublin gab: MacNeice remarked on the comic incongruities of a new fashion shop called the 'Anna Livia Boutique' and of a parade of models in costume, all 'with Joycean titles'—'never a dull garment'. President Kennedy's visit to Ireland in the next year brought MacNeice back to Dublin and Galway: as a good journalist he remarked upon the large security forces on duty, the great number of reporters, the elaborate decorations, the pub talk, the jokes, this 'sentimental visit: you can't have power politics all the time' (July 1963).

There were two autobiographical accounts in his last years: an astringent portrait of himself and of Oxford at the end of the 1920s ('When I Was Twenty-One', 1961) and an unscripted talk for his friend John Boyd at BBC Belfast, July 1963, on his indelible 'Childhood Memories' of Carrickfergus, including a lonely Puritan upbringing, his father's Church of St Nicholas, his reading 'a lot' in his father's library—very specific details, some published here for the first time (such as comments on the salt pier where William of Orange landed and on Carrickfergus Castle), for a few things of importance had been cut for posthumous publication (*Listener*, December 1963).

Over a hundred articles in my two volumes of selected prose trace a large, though clearly discontinuous, part of MacNeice's growth in life and art, at first hand and in his own words, apart from his development in poetry and drama. In the long run, the poetry and the plays (along with the criticism) are of chief interest. Louis MacNeice's literary career was naturally centred on creative writing: it is to the poems and the plays (a few for the stage, most for radio, one for television) that the reader will turn first and foremost for the pleasures of reading, listening, and reflecting. Yet, while MacNeice's poetry has been collected by E. R. Dodds (1966; corrected 1979), and recently selected and studied by Michael and Edna Longley in two Faber books (1988),[22] only one of MacNeice's plays—*The Dark Tower* (1947; 1964)—has been kept in print. It is to be hoped that the Oxford

[22] Moreover, not long ago, the young Irish poet Paul Muldoon edited *The Faber Book of Contemporary Irish Poetry* (1986) with a prologue drawn from a broadcast discussion between F. R. Higgins and Louis MacNeice, and featuring ten Irish poets since Yeats—with MacNeice granted more space (63 pages) than any other poet: this indicates MacNeice's current importance in 20th-c. Irish poetry as a vital link between Yeats and the new crop of Irish poets.

University Press in commissioning me to coedit with Dr Peter McDonald a short, popular selection of MacNeice's best plays will encourage the BBC or another enterprising organization to issue, on disc or in cassette, some of the surviving recordings of MacNeice's outstanding radio play-productions.

A Note on the Text

Because of the many varying house styles used over three decades (1929–63) and on both sides of the Atlantic by the journalistic and press editors of MacNeice's prose, it has been thought best to standardize (and, for a few American spellings, Anglicize) MacNeice's text according to current style: thus verbs and compounds ending in -ise have been altered, where appropriate, to end in -ize, Mr. changed to Mr, mediæval to medieval, and so on. The one exception is the word to-day, which was printed as such in the vast majority of instances. Also, short poems are given in roman type and inverted commas, instead of italics which are reserved for book-titles.

There are two further exceptions among the articles included: in the handwritten text of 'Broken Windows' ampersands have been retained, in order to give a better sense of the MacNeice holograph; in his final broadcast 'Autobiographical Talk: Childhood Memories' the transcription has been followed, with the presentation of hitherto-unpublished material within square brackets to indicate portions cut by the editor of *Listener*: it is hoped that this will give the reader some sense of MacNeice's speaking voice.

In footnotes, whenever two or more dates are cited together, dates of writing are given outside parentheses immediately after titles, whereas parentheses after titles of works and their dates of writing are reserved for dates of publication. Information in the footnotes—ranging from the commonplace to the out-of-the-way—is intended for the ordinary reader, not only the specialist. (Therefore, in many cases, the scholar need not consult footnotes.)

Our God Bogus[1]

Modern thought has got to the bottom of everything. We are singularly blessed; now we know what the world is like—it is a vast pressure of water on top of us and a blankness of mud below us and the danger of drowning and the nearness of octopuses. Modern thought has gone to the heart of the matter and has found not a heart of gold nor a heart of passion nor a heart even of candy, but a clammy mass of globular unpleasantness, a butcher's residue. Modern thought has explained everything excellently, has, in fact, unravelled everything; where there was, when we left the room, a completed woollen garment, we find when we return a tangle of separate strands, and instead of being angry we say what a clever kitten it is thus to reassert the fundamental elements of things and refute the fictitious simplicity of an artificial complexity.

The ingenuous illusion of disillusionment is very dear to us; and kittenish Mr Beverley Nichols has seen through everything except his own eyes; and it is certainly heroic to go round the world hitting corpses on the head with their own cradles.[2] You live on the surface, say the Quixotes of cynicism, and you are content so, but for us we must go deeper. Herr Freud[3] has leant us his diving suits or rather we borrowed them, and now we are going finally to get to the bottom of it. And so they get

[1] *Sir Galahad* 2 (14 May 1929), 3–4, in the second of only two issues of an undergraduate magazine edited by MacNeice, started by Aubrey Arthur Woolmer (1908–31) of Merton: John Hilton, 'Louis MacNeice at Marlborough and Oxford', app. B, *The Strings are False: An Unfinished Autobiography*, ed. E. R. Dodds (1965), 274, 280. 'Our God Bogus', a put-down of faddish modern ideas, was written while MacNeice was reading Greats (philosophy). It followed his first book of poetry, *Blind Fireworks* (March 1929).

[2] John Beverley Nichols (1898–1983), a spectacular predecessor of MacNeice at Marlborough and Oxford, had been president of the Oxford Union, editor of *Isis*, and founder-editor of *Oxford Outlook*. He became a journalist and popular novelist in the 1920s, wrote many topical books, and continued writing into old age. In *Are They the Same at Home?* (1927), 227–8, he paraded his 'pose' and 'flippancy' in the witty 'game of life' and declared English public life 'meaningless'. See obituary tribute in *The Times*, 17 Sept. 1983, 8g.

[3] MacNeice's scepticism about Sigmund Freud (1856–1939) distinguishes him sharply from W. H. Auden: see Auden's 'Psychology and Art To-day' in *The Arts To-day*, ed. Geoffrey Grigson (1935), reprinted in *The English Auden: Poems, Essays and Dramatic Writings*, ed. Edward Mendelson (1977), 332–42.

there, and as they have forgotten to leave anyone behind to pull them up again, they stay there; and indeed there is some finality about this.

Judging a lily by its roots, they defend themselves by the instance of the importance of roots afforded by the Irish potato famine in AD 1830.[4] It is as well to know that a thing has a root, but I suspected it all along. Hence I was not surprised by the discovery into concluding that the root is the only reality. Never having been a 'transcendentalist', never having thought that the flowers of art and religion had fallen from heaven and stuck in the ground like hairpins.

Poets and artists are much influenced by the latest ideas; so Euripides boosted the Sophists and Shelley was swept into enthusiasm by the claptrap of Godwin.[5] The garbage of popularized pseudo-scientific ideas is manure for works of art, but if applied too thickly it swamps them as theory swamped the cubists.[6] But poetry thrives on a moderate supply of monsters and falsehoods (e.g. the Elizabethan 'Machiavel').[7] Still we must not let these plethoric $\check{\epsilon}\nu\delta o\xi\alpha$[8] overpower us. To think of man as a puppet is a good change from thinking of him as a daemon, but our mantelpiece is getting overcrowded with disillusions and parodies. That is a good new housemaid of ours (we have had her thirty or forty years now). She made a good riddance of all the old junk ('the bower we shrined to Tennyson'),[9] oh, yes, gave us a sense of space. And the kids have had fun knocking down the strawman—

[4] Ironic, throwaway reference to one of the Irish famines common in the 19th c., but deliberately not to the 'Great Hunger' of 1845-9 which was one of the worst catastrophes of modern Irish history.

[5] Euripides, most 'modern' of the ancient Greek tragic dramatists, wrote in impassioned rhetoric (like that of the Sophists), while the Romantic poet P. B. Shelley was swept off his feet by the anarchical social theories of his father-in-law William Godwin (1756-1836).

[6] MacNeice, like Auden, disliked abstract art, which began with the artistic doctrine of Cubism 1907-14.

[7] The Machiavellian villain, though a distortion of Niccolò Machiavelli's doctrine of political power in *The Prince* (1532), was prevalent in Elizabethan drama, e.g. Shakespeare's *3 Henry VI* and John Webster's *The White Devil*.

[8] 'Matters of common opinion' (inconsistent with each other, so needing to be disentangled)—Aristotle, *Nicomachean Ethics* 1145[b]5 and 1145[b]8-20, in H. H. Joachim's *Commentary*, ed. D. A. Rees (1955), 219. Cf. Aristotle, *Rhetoric* 1355[a]17 and *Topics* 100[b]21. Joachim was Wykeham Professor of Logic at Oxford in MacNeice's time there.

[9] Thomas Hardy, 'An Ancient to Ancients' (1922), l. 36.

What's become of, if you please,
all the glory that or which was Greece
all the grandja that was dada?[10]

Theory begins by pointing out something which is unessential to art. We bow the head and eliminate that element (e.g. narrative content of a picture or metrical form of a poem); our art is now possibly one-sided, but still runs the risk of being art. But theory if it goes forward bravely will ban the other side also, and if the artist is still obedient he will eliminate this residue of the unessential and his art is now nothing. Here steps in the Hindoo mystic and applauds. For art was after all a very finite snare, a patch of colour, if of specially vivid colour, on the veil of Maya.[11]

Yet most of us lack the guts to be mystics; we are by our nature trimmers, descended from the neutral angels who were neither for God nor Lucifer. And so, though we cannot hope for any Platonic idea of colour, we go on daubing with our admittedly second-bests. We recognize the limitations and arbitrariness of our art. A bundle of unessentials, but not a mere bundle. It is the old sorites juggle—one by one the critic plucks away the hairs and Samson is left a bald-pate.[12]

The result is the sad disease of bogus-worship. Objective values are fictions for 'thine has a great hook-nose like thine'; and as for subjective . . . why then objectify? Fighting with bare fists on a non-existent stage against an opponent as unget-at-able as the Boyg in *Peer Gynt*,[13] the only logic is to throw up the sponge. Yet most of us go on talking about and enjoying and even producing art, but we let the world know that we do it with our tongue in our cheek.

10 Untraced; sounding like, but not by, Noël Coward; therefore, it is probably a leg-pull by MacNeice in parody of Edgar Allen Poe's poem 'To Helen' (1845), ll. 9-10.

11 *Maya*, the realm of real events as appearance, illusion, according to the Hindu Veda.

12 Questioning, cumulative logic (Delilah) can reduce philosophic strength (Samson) to impotence. Sorites: 'A series of propositions, in which the predicate of each is the subject of the next, the conclusion being formed of the first subject and the last predicate' ([Henry L.] Mansel) (*OED 2*); a 'sophism leading by gradual steps from truth to absurdity' (*COD*).

13 In Henrik Ibsen's epic verse drama *Peer Gynt* (1867), 2. 7, the young protagonist Peer challenges and fights an amorphous blob called the Boyg in vain; he is beaten; but at last the sound of church bells dissolves the Boyg, and he recovers.

Evolution and the 'nineties began it (not to go back to Protagoras)[14] and then there was Relativity and the Unconscious and the Great War and Homage to the Failures (in the Tchehov manner).[15] We found that the great roads of humanity were not eternal, not *per se* existent before and after; had been put together within history, were, in fact, mere conventions. And so the only realities were goat-paths. But for all that we went on walking the roads; but with our tongue in our cheek, remember.

Easily down-cast, over-ridden by scepticism. We are told 'The apple you are eating is mere appearance excepting the pips; *they* are the reality'; and the apple promptly loses its flavour for us. Yet we should have got past judging things by their cores or intestines or origins or atoms. We should say rather: 'No doubt you are right and those things are the real. So much the better for the apparent, the superficial, the conventional. Thank God Prometheus taught us to touch up nature.[16] Thank God for Make-Believe. Much good may your One-and-Only do you, but we shall play with our coloured bricks for ever.'

Art is necessarily conventional, superficial. To chew one's cud in the void may be ravishing, but is not art. The preachers of 'subjectivity' send one back to moo in long-abandoned meadows. To 'express oneself', what need one do but moo? The essence of art is that it expresses other people. Hence Tolstoy exalted 'infectiousness'[17] as the criterion of good art; but he had two fallacies, (1) that Humanity is the Masses and so the good of the masses is the good of humanity, (2) that people always (by some innate faculty) know their own good, so that it must be education which destroys this knowledge.

[14] (5th c. BC), first and most famous of the Sophists, friend of Pericles, known to Sophocles, but no works survive: see Plato's *Protagoras*. The starting-point of Protagoras's epistemology was 'man [i.e. a man, or men in their individual perceptions] is the measure of all things': Plato's *Theaetetus* 152A–B.

[15] Anton P. Chekhov (1860–1904), about whom MacNeice later wrote a radio play *Dr Chekhov* (6 Sept. 1941), revised as *Sunbeams in his Hat* (16 July 1944), collected in *The Dark Tower and Other Radio Scripts* (May 1947).

[16] In Greek myth the Titan Prometheus, maker of mankind from clay, introduced men to fire and many arts.

[17] In *What is Art?* (1898), Leo Tolstoy claimed that the highest (religious) art should 'infect' people with feelings of love of God and man: cf. MacNeice's *Selected Literary Criticism*, ed. Heuser (1987), 7 with n. 11.

I contend that art extends beyond the artist, the paradox being that by so doing it will support his inside (as a spider must have twigs to hang its fancies to). Poetry like that of Mr Robert McAlmon[18] and painting like that of the Surréalistes (see p. 23)[19] fail because they presuppose an autonomy of the individual artist. But it is a truism since Aristotle that a man is essentially other men.[20] And mere uttering is aphasia.[21]

Mr Hilton (see p. 12) says we are not to go back to the child and the primitive.[22] Yet science has been asserting the importance of the child and the primitive, and (closely connected with these) the 'subconscious'. And there is Matisse's famous remark that he was trying to paint like a child of 5.[23] Mr Eliot and Mr Wyndham Lewis made rallies for Reason and the White Daemon of Socrates, but both in their own works are largely irrational.[24] For the irrational must be kept under, but it must be *there* (like foundations); every work of art is a conflict as in every house the roof is fighting against the foundations. The poet must transcend but not exclude—*Here we go round the prickly pear.*[25]

We are at last ceasing to jettison everything in a passionate scepticism. This scepticism showed itself in 'Pure Form' (see

[18] Robert McAlmon (1896–1956), the expatriate American publisher, wrote minor free verse 1921–37: see his autobiography *Being Geniuses Together* (1938) and *McAlmon and the Lost Generation*, ed. R. E. Knoll (1962).

[19] In *Sir Galahad* 2 (14 May 1929), 23–4: Anthony Blunt's (1907–83) comment on the Surréalistes under the title 'Paris Exhibitions'.

[20] Aristotle, *Categories* 5, on substance.

[21] Cf. MacNeice's article 'Poetry To-day' (Sept. 1935), para. 8, in his *Selected Literary Criticism*, 13–14.

[22] In *Sir Galahad* 2, 12: John Hilton (1908–), 'On Putting Away Childish Things'.

[23] Untraced as Henri Matisse's (1869–1954) remark, although characteristic of him, for Matisse is quoted as saying, 'I want to recapture the freshness of vision . . . characteristic of extreme youth' (his *Retrospective Exhibition* [catalogue], at Philadelphia, 1948, p. 9). Paul Klee (1879–1940) was the chief exponent of the child cult in modern art, closely connected to primitivism and the subconscious: Robert Goldwater, *Primitivism in Modern Art*, rev. edn (1967), 192–215. Was MacNeice also thinking of the musical prodigy W. A. Mozart (1756–91) who began composing at the age of 5?

[24] Both T. S. Eliot (1888–1965) and Wyndham Lewis (1884–1957) employed restraining intellect to a notable degree in their discursive and critical prose, but in their imaginative writings followed intuition or instinct. Socrates' 'good spirit' was a preventative or restraining reason, some 'spiritual tact checking [him] from any act opposed to his true moral and intellectual interests': Paul Shorey, trans., *Plato's Republic*, 2 vols. (1956), ii. 52 n. 2 on 496c.

[25] T. S. Eliot, 'The Hollow Men' (1925), sect. 5, st. 1.

Clive Bell who had no use for 'Real Life') and in formlessness (which professed to be 'real life' put down on paper).[26] All which is vulgarly naïve, but tastes differ and 'Every Girl Her Own Kosmos' makes a tasteful New Year present. The English have always liked 'common sense'—facts which we can understand; but, as Hume showed, this leaves us paradoxically with nothing but feelings which we can't.[27] There is nothing for it but to be an idealist or a cow.

An idealist works within an outlook (as distinct from a chaos) which is his outer convention; his inner convention is what is usually called his 'form'; the two should be concentric. Robert Louis Stevenson set himself to learn polite writing; this was bogus.[28] For conventions are not rules of 'style', drawing-pins to fasten one's matter on the board. So we may ban the stylist (*qua* stylist). As we have banned the realist (*qua* realist). And the sceptic (*qua* sceptic). For all these are bogus. Whereas we are willing to admit ragamuffins like Mr Cummings (for there is form in his disintegration) and poseurs like the Sitwells (for there is method in their madness) and pedants like Mr Eliot (for there is life in his pedantry).[29] But the transcendentalists (*qua* transcendentalists—who went out when the sceptics came in) we shall not readmit them. But assert without blushing the Hellenic platitude 'Remember that thou art neither a beast nor a god but a man' (which means a bit of each).[30]

[26] The extremes of art-for-art's-sake ('pure form') and of 'naturalism' ('real life') as espoused respectively by the Bloomsbury Group of writers and artists (including Clive Bell, 1881–1964) and by Émile Zola (1840–1902).

[27] 'According to [David] Hume [1711–76], there are two possible grounds . . . of evaluation, utility and feeling, the one objective and subject to rational confirmation, the other subjective and personal. The objective standard, unfortunately, applies only to instrumental values and not to ultimate ends. However, the subjectivity of feelings is not cause for despair about achieving agreement on ethical judgments, since the sentiment that motivates them, the disinterested pleasure and approval that we feel in contemplating actions directed toward the welfare of others, is, for Hume, as for [Bishop Joseph] Butler [1692–1752], a universal tendency in human nature.' Raziel Abelson, 'Ethics, History of', *The Encyclopedia of Philosophy*, ed. Paul Edwards, 8 vols. (1967), iii. 93.

[28] Stevenson (1850–94) confessed that he began to write as a 'sedulous ape' to many other writers: 'A College Magazine', para. 2, in *Memories and Portraits* (1887).

[29] For E. E. Cummings, the Sitwells, and T. S. Eliot, see MacNeice's 'Poetry To-day', paras. 14–21, in his *Selected Literary Criticism*, 18–24.

[30] A commonplace, found in such writers as Aristotle (*Politics* 1. 2. 14, 1253ᵃ28) and St Augustine (*Homilies on the First Epistle of John* 8. 7–8). See Marcel Detienne, 'Entre bêtes et dieux', *Nouvelle revue de psychanalyse* 4 (1972), 230–46.

Our minds were given us to put things in and take things out of, but tub-thumpers and tub-dwellers both prefer them empty. Cynics and salvationists let us at last turn our backs on them, on the chorus of futile brass and on Diogenes trundling his tub;[31] while above them is the sky, being to one party a future and superior bandstand, to the other innumerable rows of asterisks prudently covering the bad language of the Absolute.

---

[31] Diogenes of Sinope (4th c. BC), nicknamed the 'dog-philosopher', prototype of the cynic, 'took for his abode the tub in the Metroön': Diogenes Laertius, *Lives of Eminent Philosophers* vi. 23, with trans. R. D. Hicks, 2 vols. (1925), ii. 25.

The Domain of Selfhood[1]

The Domain of Selfhood. By R. V. Feldman. (George Allen & Unwin. 10s. 6d. net.)

Mr Feldman writes as a Platonist within the Jewish tradition. He is not the first of his kind, as many Jews since Philo[2] have found the Platonic Ideas a sympathetic doctrine which they have rehabilitated in their own way. But Mr Feldman belongs to his time as well as to his race and the balanced stress of these two allegiances makes his book probably the first of its kind in English. It is therefore a pity that certain oddities of manner may discourage or deceive his readers; an excessive love of metaphor, an odd facetiousness, purple periods and journalistic tropes are naturally suspected by the orthodox philosophic reader and, what is more regrettable, tend to dissipate the argument. People may also cavil at his repertory of private terms though these, I think, are mostly legitimate; it is less confusing to use a new term than to use an old term in a new way. His eclecticism also I do not mind; it is a Jewish virtue and is in place in so personal a work. I regret, however, that in suggesting affinities he did not elaborate some of the more notable (e.g. with Kant).[3] But these criticisms touch on the outside. This book, which is Mr Feldman's first published work, is notable as another instance, but from a less usual angle, of the present reaction against dogmatic flux. His ethics, like any ethics which is to have drive, is frankly dualistic. Any tiro can spot a χωρισμός[4] but a χωρισμός is not a *reductio ad*

---

[1] *Criterion* 14: 54 (Oct. 1934), 160–3. Reginald Vivian Feldman (1904–69), MA of Christ Church, Oxford, came up in 1923. He also wrote *The Union of Prophetism and Philosophism in Maimonides* (1935). Clement C. J. Webb (1865–1954) wrote a foreword to *The Domain of Selfhood* (1934).

[2] Philo of Alexandria (*fl.* AD 40), a Greek-speaking Jewish philosopher who attempted to reconcile the Torah and Greek thought, is considered a forerunner of Christian theology. See his works, trans. F. H. Colson and G. H. Whitaker, 10 vols. (1929–42) (Loeb Classical Library).

[3] For Kant, see n. 16 below.

[4] 'Abstraction'.

absurdum; to consider it such is to be bullied by the Law of Sufficient Reason.[5]

It is notorious that in this age so many of the few saintly people are professedly anti-God. This has meant the divorce of morality from religion. The more consistent jettison morality also. A kingdom of ends will naturally have God as its king; vice versa where there is no king there will be no kingdom. If the cosmos is a mere self-expanding fieri[6] one's duty is merely to expand along with it; only you can hardly call that duty. Serious people now talk of an 'Experimental Ethics'[7] with all the stress on the experiment; for an analogy they refer to aesthetics, viz.—One cannot postulate goodness or badness; one can only feel one's way (as the artist is said to do) towards doing what is suited to the circumstances. But this fact that one has to feel one's way had not been ignored by the idealists; Plato, e.g., says that the individual soul μαντεύεται,[8] half sees what it wants to get at. But the bio-chemist (and too often his friend the psychologist) would have it that half-seeing is merely a species of blindness. Mr Feldman with refreshing effrontery gives the lie to these people. His belief (like theirs?) is in the end a matter of faith (above or below reason), a constitutional twist or slant. Thus he appeals to the argument from *Pazranut*, a Hebrew word 'denoting lavishness, grace, creative generosities. . . . The argument which proceeds from the existence of human endowments to the nature of the endower is typically

---

[5] Formulated by G. W. Leibniz, *Die philosophischen Schriften*, ed. C. J. Gerhardt, 1875–90, ii. 40; iv. 438; vii. 199, 309, 374. The 'principle of sufficient reason'—called a 'law' by Bertrand Russell in *A Critical Exposition of the Philosophy of Leibniz* (1900, 2nd edn 1937), 209–10 (a handbook which MacNeice may have used)—may be stated thus: that there is an adequate reason to account for the existence and nature of everything that could conceivably *not exist*, and that in each case the ultimate sufficient reason for such contingent 'truths of fact' depends on God's free choice. Russell expounded 'the law of sufficient reason' in chap. 3.

[6] A 'coming-into-being'; *in fieri*, 'in process of being made'. The astronomer Georges Lemaître (1894–1966) formulated in 1927 the big bang theory for the origin of 'the expanding universe', which physicist Sir Arthur (S.) Eddington (1882–1944) popularized in a small book of that title (1933).

[7] On application of the experimental method to ethical theory, see John Dewey, *Reconstruction in Philosophy* (1920), chap. 7 ('Reconstruction in Moral Conceptions'), and *The Quest for Certainty*, Gifford Lectures 1929 (1930), chap. 10 ('The Construction of Good'). In his just-published *Art as Experience* (1934), Dewey used a similar empirical approach to art.

[8] 'Intuits, surmises, presages', as in Plato, *Cratylus* 411B; *Republic* 349A; *et passim*.

(though not exclusively) Hebraic.'[9] At first sight this argument
is naïve and old fashioned; at second sight is not nearly so naïve
(because not nearly so narrow) as the argument of modern
physicists that God's way is the way of mathematics. As for the
charge of anthropomorphism, it is about time we remembered
that some degree of anthropomorphism is a practical necessity;
it is part of the falsification which we have to take for granted
when we use a human language. Anyone can pick holes in
anything that has ever been written about God. But many
people would sympathize with Mr Feldman when he argues
that it is more arrogant to dispense with God than to assume
him (even when one assumes him in one's own image). In Mr
Feldman's words 'To eliminate God is to treat human nature
as a greater mystery than it deserves'.

The central concept of *The Domain of Selfhood* is what Mr
Feldman calls Self-Respect. This is not to be confused with,
e.g., Butler's Self-Love.[10] The exact status of the Ideal Self[11]
which is the subject of Self-Respect I find very puzzling. Yet
I cannot deny its right to the name of Self; we therefore have
two kinds of Self and the relation between them is, of course,
open to all the quips of sceptical monism. This brings us back
to the accepted gulf between Actuality and Value. Mr Feldman
makes an important distinction between primary and secondary
value and opportunely maintains that 'Platonic dualism does
not devaluate actuality and history'. This is a good flat contradiction of the popular view of Plato; it is more than can be said,
e.g., of Bradley's Absolute-ex-machina.[12] I am sorry that,
while on this point, Mr Feldman did not reply to Gentile, who,
attacking the Platonic and Aristotelian standpoint, misrepres-
ents(?) it as based on the principle of non-contradiction.[13]
Gentile's Eternal Present makes an excellent foil to the Platonic
Ideas:[14] it would be impressive to uncover a latent Gentile
within Plato and Aristotle themselves.

[9] Feldman, pt. 1, suppl. B, 55–6.

[10] Bishop Joseph Butler (1692–1752) refuted the complacency of self-interest or self-
love in 'Of the Nature of Virtue' appended to *The Analogy of Religion* (1736).

[11] Feldman, pt. 1, sect. 2. 48–53.

[12] F. H. Bradley, *Appearance and Reality* (1893), Bk. 2, on the Absolute.

[13] Giovanni Gentile, *The Theory of Mind as Pure Act*, trans. H. W. Carr (1922),
chap. 4, 43 ff.

[14] Ibid., chap. 10, 153.

The Ideal Self for Mr Feldman is something between God and Man, 'a tertium quid or angel'. He denies that it is an hypothesis (he does not tolerate the circularity of the Als Ob.).[15] Again daringly reactionary, he correlates Self-Respect with Pity. This is characteristic of his humane Hebraism, as is also the fact that instead of stressing the wire-drawn concepts of conscience and duty he prefers to focus on what he calls the ultimate Vocative, the thou-thou relation between Man and God. This switch-over from Plato to the Psalmist enables us to assess Mr Feldman's peculiar position. He looks forward explicitly to 'a syncretism of the spirit of Plato with the spirit of the prophets'. With the objection that syncretism is bad philosophy I somewhat sympathize. I feel that philosophy, like other products, has certain advantages when it is superficially parochial (e.g. the beauty of the Categorical Imperative was conditioned by a German sectarian upbringing).[16] But we cannot demand this local factor in a Jewish thinker. When Mr Feldman writes his promised critique of the Jewish Medieval Philosophers, it is to be hoped that he will show how far Jewish thought is homogeneous, and will assess the relative strength, in their tradition, of Platonism and Pantheism (it being sometimes said that Hebraism is typically pantheistic, with the corollary that Spinoza is a typical Hebrew). A dialectic of Judaism would be very valuable as a corrective to those who find in the Jews a perfect subject for crude generalization. Mr Feldman has still most of his work to do, but *The Domain of Selfhood* is a sincere and interesting document.

15 'As if'. John Hilton notes that at Oxford MacNeice read with interest Hans Vaihinger's *The Philosophy of 'As if'* (1924): MacNeice, *Strings*, 283.

16 Immanuel Kant (1724–1804), reared in the Lutheran-Pietist truths of simplicity and obedience to the moral law, and reflecting upon the writings of Christian Wolff and G. W. Leibniz, expounded his doctrine of the 'categorical imperative' or unconditional moral law in *Grundlegung zur Metaphysik der Sitten* (1785; *Foundations of the Metaphysics of Morals*), sect. 2: 'Act as if the maxim of thy action were to become by thy will a universal law of nature'—*Kant's Critique of Practical Reason and Other Works on the Theory of Ethics*, trans. T. K. Abbott, 6th edn (1909), 39.

Charlatan-Chasing:
How We Live and How We Think

A WORLD-FAMOUS BOOK TRANSLATED[1]
The Mind and Society. By Vilfredo Pareto. Edited by Arthur
Livingston. (Jonathan Cape. £4 4s. 4 vols.)

Vilfredo Pareto was born in 1848. Following in the steps of his
father, an engineer, he had jobs successively on the railway in
Rome and as superintendent of iron mines belonging to the
Banca Nazionale of Florence. These facts throw some light on
his hard-headedness and distaste for metaphysics. Metaphysics
is no use for banking, mining, or railways. In 1894 Pareto was
appointed to the chair of political economy at Lausanne. In
1916 appeared the first edition of his magnum opus, the *Trattato
di sociologia generale,* which is now published in an English translation as *The Mind and Society.*

America has for some time had her Pareto experts, but then
in America each university has one or more professional soci-
ologists. Mr Arthur Livingston has done a noble piece of work
in introducing Pareto to the English; he has been twelve years
preparing this excellent edition.[2] Croce we know and Gentile
we know; to these rather heady thinkers Pareto will act as an
excellent, if bitter, antidote.

The *Trattato* is a holocaust of a book, sustained with fiery
intensity through four volumes (in English) and two thousand
pages. It sets out to be a purely experimental sociology after the

[1] *Morning Post*, 15 Nov. 1935, 6. Vilfredo Pareto (1848–1923), *The Mind and Society*
(*Trattato di sociologia generale* [1916], 2nd edn 1923), trans. Andrew Bongiorno, Arthur
Livingston, James H. Rogers, ed. Livingston, 4 vols. (1935). This treatise 'is the most
elaborate statement of [the materialist school of sociology] . . . Men act first and then
think of reasons for their action only afterward. These reasons he [Pareto] calls
"derivations" because they are derived from . . . the "residues," or quasi instincts,
which in fact determine human modes of conduct and through them, human modes of
thought as well.'—Werner Stark, 'Sociology of Knowledge', *Encyclopedia of Philosophy*,
vii. 476. MacNeice refers to *The Mind and Society* in *Zoo* (Nov. 1938), 73.
[2] Arthur Livingston (1883–1944), Professor of Romance Languages at Columbia
University, was an American Italianist and prolific translator.

fashion of chemistry or physics, essentially non-metaphysical, confined to the realm of experience. The method is the inductive method. Hypotheses are to be used as in science. By successive stages we shall approximate to truth, not hoping for more than an asymptote.

Pareto is no preacher or missionary; at least he tries not to be. He is, in his own phrase, merely a logico-experimental thinker. Any ulterior motive would falsify his inquiries. There is, he says, very little genuine logico-experimental thinking. What is put forward as such is a mere varnish of logic used to cover up those instincts or sentiments which really govern human conduct. Such pseudo-logical masks Pareto calls 'derivations'; the sentiments which they mask are 'residues'. I wonder at times if some parts of Pareto's own argument would not fall in the category of derivations. Witness his suspicious fervour on matters of sex, prohibition, St Francis of Assisi.[3]

He is not, perhaps, as broadminded as he would make out. At the beginning of his work he makes the admirable profession that he is going to use one method to one end and the admirable admission that he will be thereby limited to one sphere out of several. Thus he will be able to combat the theologian when the latter meets him on his own ground and attempts a scientific discussion; he will not be able to combat the theologian *qua* theologian. But Pareto does not remain humble. Throughout the book he openly sneers at theology and metaphysics.[4]

His highhandedness we can forgive him. After all, that is his personality (irony: he tried so hard to be impersonal). His book is extraordinarily good reading, and many will welcome his diagrams and algebraic use of letters. There are hosts of footnotes, and one cannot always see the wood for the trees. Mr Aldous Huxley has called this book a museum of human stupidity.[5] Though again it is not always stupidity. The

[3] Pareto's 'fervour' in these matters may be seen in his extensive and elaborate footnotes to sects. 1324–96 and 1800–17.

[4] Pareto's attack on metaphysics and theology is particularly strong in vol. iii, 'Sentiments in Thinking (Theory of Derivations)', sects. 1402, 1419, *et passim*.

[5] Aldous Huxley—who had referred to the Italian *Trattato* as 'a superb piece of work' (introduction to his *Proper Studies* [1927], xviii)—wrote a favourable book review of the English translation entitled 'Pareto's Museum of Human Stupidity, With the Face of Confucius and the Fierce Irony of Voltaire', *New York Herald Tribune Books*, 9 June 1935, 1–2.

lawyer, philosopher, and priest may think they are acting through and for science, but often the cause and end of their action is Art. Pareto makes little allowance for Art. It is lost among the residues.[6] He does, however, allow that the social utility of a theory or institution cannot be correlated with its scientific truth.[7] This should also apply to the aesthetic value of a theory.

Pareto's scepticism should be tonic at the present moment, when the Nazis and Marxists are trotting round their hashed-up Hegel, when 'Science', as Mr Yeats has said, is the religion of the suburbs,[8] when the Church is flirting with worlds which do not belong to it,[9] when Bergson begins to gush about asceticism,[10] and when Jung gives the soft hand to palmistry.[11] The intellectuals and the reformers are betraying us with their optimism.

One of Pareto's most charming polemical tricks is to take and clap together the hands of two apparent opponents—Spencer and Comte, Salomon Reinach and Father Lagrange, Rousseau

[6] Only brief mention of art is made among such matters as obscene paintings, sculptures, romances, and fabliaux, in sects. 1380, 1381 n. 4 (p. 863).

[7] See sects. 14, 72–4, 843–4, 2340–52.

[8] 'Science—opium of the suburbs', *Fighting the Waves*, in *Wheels and Butterflies* (1934), collected in *Explorations* (1962), 377 (see also 'Pages from a Diary in 1930', *Explorations*, 340): cf. MacNeice, *The Poetry of W. B. Yeats* (1941; 1967), 58. MacNeice is mixing Yeats's saying with the one by Karl Marx, 'Religion . . . is the opium of the people' (introduction to *Critique of the Hegelian Philosophy of Right*, 1843–4), which Yeats was challenging.

[9] In the 1920s and 1930s the Papacy entered the political arena by signing a series of Lateran Accords with Italy and concordats with many European countries (notably in 1933 with Germany under Hitler—in order to define the position of the Roman Catholic Church in Germany), but these were widely interpreted as compromises with dictatorial regimes, Fascism and Nazism. There were anti-Roman-Catholic riots in Belfast at the end of July 1935.

[10] Henri Bergson, *Two Sources of Morality and Religion* (1932), chap. 4, 251, 267.

[11] 'It appears safer for us to proceed from the outer world inward, from the known to the unknown, from the body to the mind [psyche]. Therefore all attempts at characterology have started from the outside world. . . . To the same class of interpretations from outward signs belong palmistry, Gall's phrenology, Lavater's study of physiognomy, and, more recently, graphology, Kretschmer's physiological types and Rorschach's klexographic method [reading of meaningless blotches in personality testing].'—C. G. Jung, *Modern Man in Search of a Soul*, trans. W. S. Dell and Cary F. Baynes (1931, 1933), chap. 4 ('A Psychological Theory of Types'), 86. (See *The Collected Works of C. G. Jung*, ed. Herbert Read and R. F. C. Hull, 18 vols., Bollingen Series 20. vi: *Psychological Types* [1971], app. 3, 525.) Jung had just delivered the Tavistock Lectures in London, 30 Sept.–4 Oct. 1935: *Analytical Psychology: Its Theory and Practice*, ed. Mary Barker and Margaret Chase (1936; rev. R. F. C. Hull, 1968), in which dream-analysis is discussed.

and Hobbes.[12] He never falls from the arms of the Whites into those of the Blacks. The mid-Victorians who explained everything by 'origins' are in his eyes 'merely replacing one metaphysics by another'.[13] He likes to show (a) that two people, e.g. Diogenes and a Capuchin friar, are given to explaining what is essentially the same by very different 'derivations',[14] and (b) that the same man will make use of opposite derivations simultaneously.[15]

Pareto with his hatred and contempt for Hegel and Plato would presumably have banned the application to himself of the word 'dialectic', but in a limited sense 'dialectic' describes very well his treatment of history.[16] In his classification of 'residues' he distinguishes two most important classes—Class I, the 'instinct for combinations', Class II, the instinct of 'group-persistence'. These represent, to put it very simply, the urge to try something new and the urge to stick to what is familiar. These two sets of residues can be complementary or antagonistic. The undulations of history are explained by the battle and balance between them. Thus in recent times Class I residues finding an outlet in Science reached a peak about 1860–70. At the beginning of this century there was a fraction in favour of group-persistences—Nationalists, Catholics, etc.

It is said that Pareto is claimed as an apostle of Fascism.[17] Certainly he disapproves, and shrewdly criticizes, 'the Socialist religion' and its wider genus, 'the democrat's religion', while he approves of the use of force. And he has a good word for Machiavelli and Bismarck.[18] There are many passages, how-

12 Herbert Spencer (1820–1903) and Auguste Comte (1798–1857): *Mind and Society*, sects. 283–95; Salomon Reinach (1858–1932) and Father Marie-Joseph Lagrange (1855–1938): sects. 383–99; Jean-Jacques Rousseau (1712–78) and Thomas Hobbes (1588–1679): sect. 1507.

13 Sect. 1402: 'merely replacing one metaphysic with another, explaining the better known by the less known, and facts susceptible of direct observation by fancies which . . . could not be proved'.

14 Sect. 1802.

15 Pro-contra: sects. 587–8, 871–3, especially 1416. 4: 'From the logical standpoint two contradictory propositions cannot hold side by side. From the standpoint of non-scientific derivations two apparently contradictory propositions can very well stand together in one individual, one mind.'

16 Theory of historical cycles: sects. 2330 ff., 2387–9.

17 e.g. A. G. Keller, 'Pareto', *Yale Review* 24: 4 (June 1935), 824–8, quoted Mussolini on Pareto: 'He was my teacher' (828).

18 Niccolò Machiavelli (1469–1527) and Otto von Bismarck (1815–98): sect. 2553, II-γ (p. 1865).

ever, which would offend any good Fascist. Read page 626, and compare the situation in Abyssinia.[19]

[19] Sect. 1050 (p. 626): 'With a hypocrisy truly admirable, these blessed civilized peoples [Europeans] claim to be acting for the good of their subject races in oppressing and exterminating them.' Cf. the Italian invasion of Abyssinia without declaration of war, 3 Oct. 1935, and the declaration of the League of Nations branding Italy as aggressor.

Plato and Platonists[1]

Plato's Thought. By G. M. A. Grube. (Methuen. 12*s.* 6*d.*)
Plato. By Vladimir Solovyev. (Stanley Nott. 5*s.*)

There are two types of Platonist—those who try to present Plato as he was and those who try to exploit him for their own crusades and platforms. Professor Grube belongs to the first type, Vladimir Solovyev to the second.

Professor Grube's book is a very good summary, under eight headings, of Plato's thought. The best book on Plato in English is probably Professor A. E. Taylor's *Plato,*[2] but the ordinary educated reader, who is not a classical scholar or a professional philosopher, is likely to find it rather sticky reading; the arrangement of the book dialogue by dialogue, though according to the best traditions of empiricist science, is a little tedious and in places the reader will not see the wood of general principles for the trees of erudition. The English translation of Constantin Ritter's condensed summary[3] is also not too easily digestible and contains some disputable assertions and too many modern analogies. Professor Grube on the other hand is concise, clear, and candid. And he does not set out to humble the reader in advance like one very eminent Platonist who wrote that a man could not hope to understand Greek philosophy unless he first understood the technicalities of the Greek lyre.[4]

[1] *Spectator* 155: 5608 (20 Dec. 1935), 1037-8. George Grube (1899-1982), Professor of Classics at Trinity College, Toronto, 1931-70, a leading member of the Co-operative Commonwealth Federation and editor of the *Canadian Forum* 1937-41, was a frequent translator of classics: obit. in the *Toronto Star*, 15 Dec. 1982, A 19. Vladimir Solov'ev (1853-1900) was a Russian philosopher, religious thinker, poet, and literary critic. His short book *Plato* was translated by Richard Gill, with a Note on Solov'ev by Janko Lavrin and a portrait by Nora Lavrin (1935). Three months earlier MacNeice had reviewed Solov'ev's book in the *Morning Post*, 20 Sept. 1935, 14.

[2] Alfred Edward Taylor (1896-1945), *Plato: The Man and His Work*, 3rd edn rev. (1929), commended by Grube, preface, op. cit., vii. There were four editions of Taylor's book in his lifetime, and three posthumously.

[3] Constantin Ritter, *The Essence of Plato's Philosophy*, trans. Adam Alles (1933) of *Kerngedanken der platonischen Philosophie*, mentioned by Grube, preface, x.

[4] Untraced. However, Pythagoras (who deeply influenced Plato) closely compared

Though Professor Grube treats Plato's thought under specific headings—Pleasure, The Gods, Statecraft, &c.[5]—he does not in the least neglect chronology or write, as so many do, as if there was one all-embracing Platonic creed which Plato was born with and died with. Witness his excellent chapter on the Nature of the Soul, where he points out that the treatment of the soul in the *Phaedo* is 'Plato's first word, not his last'.[6] Anyone who has ever had to write an essay on the soul in Plato will know how terribly tempting it is to take the extremist version of the *Phaedo* as final and build upon it, or against it, a dashing piece of polemic. There are other common misapprehensions which Professor Grube corrects, e.g. as to Plato's views on pleasure and on democracy. He has the courage moreover to disassociate Plato from monotheism—'It is characteristic of Plato to express the divine principle as both a unity, and a plurality, for he was a Greek and a pagan. . . .'[7]

'It must be said that the tragedy of Plato's life had not only a terrible beginning, but also a lamentable ending, just as should happen in a true tragedy . . . Like Shakespeare's Hamlet, he did not marry his Ophelia; she was drowned.'[8] This is a different tone from Professor Grube's; this is platonizing *à la Russe*. M. Janko Lavrin tells us all we need to know (for our purpose) about Vladimir Solovyev, the author of these words, in an introductory note to the translation of Solovyev's little monograph on Plato. Solovyev (1853–1900) ranked among his countrymen as a philosopher though his chronic eclecticism might lose him that title in England or Germany. It is typical of the man that he supported a reunion of the Catholic and Russian churches. He believed, in M. Lavrin's words, that the only hope for philosophy lay 'in that *integral knowledge* (as he calls it) which ought to synthesize our Western empirical and rational cognition with the intuition of the East, the truth of

---

musical intervals (on the lyre's strings) with mathematical numbers, and both with cosmic principles. Could there have been a story (comical?) about a 'very eminent Platonist' to this effect at Oxford in the 1920s? Or is MacNeice 'showing off'?

[5] Chaps. 2, 5, 8, etc.
[6] Chap. 4, 129.
[7] Chap. 5, 170.
[8] Solov'ev, *Plato*, 50.

science and philosophy with that of religion; and all of them again with active living.'[9]

Solovyev's essay on Plato centres round Socrates. Plato's business was to carry on the Socratic mission of love, so his two central dialogues are for Solovyev the *Phaedrus* and *Symposium*, while his epistemological works, for instance, are mere inhuman trifling. Helped by vague chronology, dogmatic romanticism, and the lack of a sense of humour, Solovyev outlines Plato's decline and fall. From the conception of Eros, which was his zenith, Plato lapsed to the 'useless' Utopianism of the *Republic*. Worse than this, he went on to flirt with practical polities in the affair with Dionysus the Elder. And then—'just as should happen in a true tragedy'—he wrote the *Laws*. The *Laws* (for another view see Professor Grube) 'is not a forgetting but a direct renouncement of Socrates and his philosophy. . . . What a profound and tragic catastrophe, how complete the moral fall!'[10] Solovyev concludes with a Christian moral—'Socrates by his noble death exhausted the moral power of purely human wisdom, and reached its limits.'[11] Socrates, that is, made clear the necessity for Christ. We have heard that before, but where does Plato come in? Solovyev tells us, though in other words— Plato is his master's posthumous Judas.

---

[9] Lavrin, 'A Note on Vladimir Solovyev', ibid. 6–7.
[10] Ibid. 80–1.
[11] Ibid. 82–3.

The Passionate Unbeliever[1]

Lucretius, Poet and Philosopher. By E. E. Sikes. (Cambridge University Press. 7s. 6d.)

Mr Sikes's new book is a sympathetic and well-balanced study of Lucretius, whom he champions without, as advocates often do, falling into exaggerations corresponding to those of the adversary. Epicureanism has often been attacked as worthless materialism. In order to prove that it is not worthless it is not necessary to deny that it is materialism. Patin's brilliant phrase, *l'anti-Lucrèce chez Lucrèce*,[2] can be worked too hard. It is safer, as Mr Sikes does, to point out the clashes between Lucretius as poet and Lucretius as philosopher than to maintain that Lucretius was really a God-fearing man, one of the Elect without knowing it.

Mr Sikes begins his indication by very properly objecting to the aspersions thrown on Lucretius by believers in 'pure poetry'.[3] In perhaps the majority of poets didacticism is present, if in varying degrees, and it is impossible to decide at what degree didacticism is to be disallowed. Poetry and philosophy do not always work together in harmony but they are not diametrically opposed to each other. Mr Sikes discusses in two several chapters, while admitting that the two things cannot really be separated, the 'Genius' and the 'Art' of Lucretius.[4] The truth is that Lucretius' Epicureanism flows over both categories; he was naturally adapted to this creed, but the creed

---

[1] *Spectator* 156: 5628 (8 May 1936), 846. Edward Ernest Sikes (1867–1940), Fellow of St John's College, Cambridge, was an editor of Greek texts, the author of *The Greek View of Poetry* (1931), and a contributor to *Encyclopaedia Britannica* and *Cambridge Ancient History*.

[2] Guy Patin (1601–72), the French doctor and writer, was celebrated for his *Lettres* (1692, 1695, 1718). Here his *Études sur la poésie latine*, chap. 7, were cited by Sikes, 19: 'It is this side of Lucretius [i.e. Epicureanism] that the great French critic, Patin, emphasised in the pregnant phrase *l'anti-Lucrèce chez Lucrèce*. Writing as a Catholic for Catholics, he drew attention to the poet's unconscious inconsistency . . . (for and against 'the existence of a Deity'); again cited by Sikes, 131, 134.

[3] Ibid. 3.

[4] Ibid., chaps. 1, 2.

was also the mode which he deliberately employed in order to systematize his world (and his world involved his poetry). The creed itself is treated very fairly by Mr Sikes. Indeed it is in its favour that he makes the one overstatement which I noticed in this book—'the Epicurean religion—in my opinion—marks a distinct step in advance of the crude Hellenic thought'.[5] This is downright but at the same time vague. What is meant by 'the crude Hellenic thought'? The thought of Pythagoras, Plato, and the tragedians? Or does Mr Sikes mean the thought not of the thinkers but of the men in the street? In the one case his tribute is excessive and false, in the other it is scarcely a tribute. But Mr Sikes is, of course, perfectly justified in maintaining that Epicureanism was not so mean or so silly as Macaulay, for example, represented it.[6] He compares it impartially with Stoicism. It is absurd, as he points out, to impute pessimism to the Epicureans rather than the Stoics—'the chief source of Stoic gloom lay in their determinism'.[7] On the other hand, the Stoics score in virtue of their altruism. Epicurus 'failed to account for any altruistic sentiments'.[8] Pity was left unexplained. Yet there is plenty of pity in Lucretius, and that is one of his significant inconsistencies.

Mr Sikes even puts in a word for the notorious atomic swerve —the rather pathetic Epicurean attempt to save Free Will— and for the Epicurean gods, objects, as he points out, of an almost aesthetic reverence rather than masters to be feared and pandered to. And while in no way neglecting Lucretius' debt to Epicurus, he rightly points out that in his enthusiasm for physics (knowledge for knowledge's sake) Lucretius 'seems to revert, in spirit, to Democritus or—we should rather say—to Empedocles'.[9] He shows his discrimination further in commenting on Lucretius' not too consistent accounts of prehistory—Lucretius was 'a true, mediating, Epicurean. On the

---

[5] Ibid. 68–9.

[6] Thomas Babington, Lord Macaulay (1800–59), referred to both Epicureanism and Stoicism as 'a garrulous, declaiming, canting, wrangling philosophy' in 'Lord Bacon' (1837), *Literary and Historical Essays Contributed to The Edinburgh Review* (1923), pt. 1, 370. Sikes, 161, refers to Macaulay's censure of Epicureanism as 'the silliest and meanest of all systems of natural and moral philosophy'.

[7] Sikes, 141.

[8] Ibid. 171.

[9] Ibid. 92.

one hand he is under no illusion as to primitive innocence . . .
he has no belief in the noble Savage. On the other hand he had
little respect for the noble Roman.'[10] A further example of Mr
Sikes's moderate and qualified criticism: Epicurean anthropo-
logy, he maintains, is the one branch of their science which has
stood the test of time. But, he hastens to add, not in its entirety.
The Epicurean version of the Social Contract is not valid. Here
'Epicurus failed, as so often, to profit by the teaching of
Aristotle'.[11]

This book should be an excellent introduction to Lucretius,
but those who know their author well should also benefit from
this very neat and unpretentious survey of the man, his gifts,
and his premisses.

[10] Ibid. 158.
[11] Ibid. 167.

The Hebrides:
A Tripper's Commentary[1]

I paid two visits this year—in April and July—to the Outer
Islands of the Hebrides. Before visiting them I had not realized
that nearly all the islanders speak Gaelic and that their
language is integral to their life. Owing to my ignorance of
their language I was unable to become intimate with the lives of
the people. I write about them therefore as a tripper who was
disappointed and tantalized by the islands and seduced by
them only to be reminded that on that soil he will always be an
outsider. I doubt if I shall visit the Western Islands again.

Apart from my sentimental reluctance to be an outsider I do
not wish to visit them again because they are in a decline.
London also is in a decline but there I feel that I am present at
a family sickbed—if not indeed a family deathbed. By blood
I may be nearer to a Hebridean than to a Cockney, but my
whole upbringing has alienated me from that natural (some
will call it primitive) culture which in the British Isles today is
only found on the Celtic or backward fringes. I went to the
Hebrides partly hoping to find that blood was thicker than
ink—that the Celt in me would be drawn to the surface by the
magnetism of his fellows. This was a sentimental and futile
hope. Once, sitting by a river drinking beer with some Lewismen while one of them sang a love-song in Gaelic, I felt
strongly that I belonged to these people and that, for all I
cared, London could sink in the mud. But the conviction of
alcohol does not last.

An island means isolation: the words are the same. We
expect in an island to meet with insular vices. What is shocking
is to find an island invaded by the vices of the mainland. The

[1] *Listener* 18: 456 (6 Oct. 1937), 718–20. Cf. *I Crossed the Minch*, with 8 drawings by
Nancy Sharp, written August 1937 (pub. April 1938), chap. 1 ('Introductory'), from
which this article was excerpted, cut, and edited by the literary editor J. R. Ackerley
(1896–1967) for the *Listener*, where it was published with 3 photographs (not in the
book) and a drawing. Among the cuts were a few mildly leftist comments and a
concluding imaginative dialogue.

Hebrides are now being invaded by commerce, which means that they are falling to the foreigner. This process may be inevitable but I should prefer to watch it somewhere where it is further advanced, where differences of wealth are of long standing and where, though the primitive culture has gone, a sophisticated culture has succeeded it. More than one generation is required before a man can be a capitalist with grace.

I have heard of a small crofter who cornered the local tweed industry. This was not a nice Arnold Bennett romance of the Poor Boy making good.[2] The Poor Boy made twenty thousand but the community which gave rise to him and his family is losing independence and character. A hundred and sixty looms in two small villages work for this man alone. The hundred and sixty families who used to make their tweed independently are now bound by contract to him; the manner of their work, the amount of their output, are imposed upon them from outside. They all use mechanical steel looms which turn out at least twice the amount of cloth in the time but not such a good cloth as the wooden hand-loom. The wool comes to them from the factories ready dyed and all that they have to do is the weaving. The crofters no longer spin or dye the wool and, when it is woven, they no longer waulk[3] the tweed. The decay of these arts means the disappearance of the songs which attended them —the spinning songs and waulking songs. It means, more widely, a great lessening of the worker's pride in his work. Quantity has ousted quality.

The tradition in the islands is that a man lives on his land but by what he gets out of the sea. In the eyes of the world, however, the fisherman-crofter is superannuated. And the world sends up its trawlers to sweep the fish out of the Minch. The islanders of Lewis defeated the efforts of those who wanted them to sacrifice their traditions for an organized commercial prosperity. But it is easier to defeat someone who attends to you, than someone who ignores you. The world is going to kill the last of the Celts by ignoring them.

When I first visited the islands, I was impertinent enough to

[2] (E.) Arnold Bennett (1867–1931), the English novelist.
[3] 'To subject (woollen cloth) to the operation of beating or pressing (together with other processes, as moistening and heating), in order to cause felting of the fibres and consequent shrinkage and thickening': *OED2*, 'Walk', *v*.[2].

resent what I considered the dourness of many of the inhabitants. Most English visitors are sure to be equally impertinent. The natives will not welcome you enthusiastically. They will be polite, considerate, and hospitable, but they will be able to get along better without you than with you; they have not yet acquired the Blackpool mentality. The seventh Duke of Argyll,[4] in a pamphlet (1883) defending his management of his estate in the island of Tiree, looked forward to the day when the place would be a paradise for visitors and properly equipped with golf courses.

Question: Where will the natives be then, poor things?
Answer: Oh, they will be the caddies.

The Hebrideans are slow of movement, like most peasants and fishermen. But they are not slow of speech or mind as the visitor thinks who can only speak to them in English. Most of them pick their way uncomfortably through English, slowly and heavily, without much expression. But listen to them speaking Gaelic and you will notice that they speak with fire, speed, and dramatic variety. In the same way when dealing with a foreigner they appear very undemonstrative but I have seen them greet their own near neighbours with a warmth of handclasping and kissing which we reserve for our relations back from the tropics. In many of them their religion, especially the Free Church brand, has cramped their vitality.[5] But a friend of mind who comes from Lewis, tells me that in the typical Lewisman Presbyterianism and 'Scottish' respectability are only skin-deep. Apply whisky and you will notice the resurgence of the Catholic and the Celt.

Most books about the Highlands and Islands steep the landscape in uncontrolled purples and golds and sentimentalize the people. From what I have seen on my two visits, the landscape of the Outer Islands is not unusually rich or varied in colour and the people lack that more blatant surface-charm or glamour—that sugared folkiness—which we are led to expect in out-of-the-way places by travelogues and geographical magazines. Nor

---

[4] John Douglas Edward Henry (Campbell), 7th Duke of Argyll, Lord Sundridge (1777–1847): *The Complete Peerage*.

[5] '*The Free Church (Kirk) of Scotland*: the organization formed by the ministers who seceded from the established Presbyterian Church in 1843': *OED2*.

are the Hebrideans good-looking. Their facial expression is more pleasing than that of the Lowland Scot but, like most Scots, their features are raw and imperfect. Some of the older women have a massive facial dignity due to prominent cheekbones and years of manual work. A few have a Madonna-like beauty but the Madonna quality is usually lost by a disproportionate length of chin and by the fact that they have ceased wearing the head-shawl. The landscape also would be more striking if there were more whins, as there are in Ireland, but whins are discouraged as the sheep tend to get caught in them. Wild flowers are plentiful in July. Not being a flower-lover proper I preferred the larger effects—emerald strips of oats coiling on the hills like snakes or a three-acre meadow purple with wild geraniums.

Most visitors to the Hebrides comment pityingly on the inertia of the inhabitants who refuse to develop their land scientifically or to apply modern methods of agriculture. But science presupposes a special education and modern methods presuppose a great deal of money. Or do you expect that a crofter who finds it difficult to pay a rent of two pounds a year will be able to get a steam tractor on credit and pay for it out of his profits? And in many parts of the Hebrides it is doubtful whether modern methods would be applicable. No machine could tackle the rugged slopes which are turned by hand into 'lazy-beds'.[6]

I could not bear, in the fishing-hotels, hearing people patronize the improvident natives whose lakes and rivers they were plundering. Yet it must be admitted that the islanders, like the Southern Irish, show a disregard for time and for penny-in-the-slot efficiency. When I visited the annual sports at Barra in Lewis an hour seemed regularly to elapse between one event and the next. And at some places the cows are not milked before ten in the morning. There is a charming little poem directed at this trait of the Highlanders:

> O that the peats might cut themselves
> And the fish jump on the shore,
> That I might lie upon my bed
> And sleep for evermore!

[6] Potato patches: see *OED* 2.

It is perhaps fairer to take these lines as the expression of that dream of a Schlaraffenland[7] which is proper to all who work upon the land. Many people in the Outer Islands are Scottish Nationalists. I had always laughed at Scottish Nationalism as a precious affectation of bright young men with a distaste for real politics, but in the islands the concept has more meaning than it has in Edinburgh. Scotland as a whole will never regain a vital self-consciousness of her unity and individuality, but such a thing is still just possible for the Gaelic-speaking islands as a group in separation from the mainland. Their traditional language needs no artificial cultivation; their population is small enough to allow of a genuine community feeling; their social life is still homogeneous (though commercialization may soon drive rifts through it); lastly the sea still separates them from their neighbours. In the words of Aeschylus: 'There is the sea and who shall drain it dry?'[8]

It would be absurd to suggest that the Hebrides should attempt to be self-supporting—economically independent. (No one, as far as I know, has yet introduced there the bogey of beet-sugar with its accompanying chorus of rats.) Some compromise, however, should be possible which would preserve the islands' social and cultural independence. Economically they should be allowed to adjust themselves to their bigger neighbours without kowtowing to them. I do not for a moment suggest that, in order to retain their language and community feeling, they should deliberately refuse the advantages of modernization. I met some Lewismen who deplored the recent establishment of 'bus services. Obviously when a Lewisman can get from Uig to Ness any day of the week in two or three hours by 'bus, the old differences between the Ness man and the Uig man will become much less marked and a certain amount that is locally of value will be lost. These local differences are much less important than what they have in common or than what the inhabitants of the whole group of islands have in common and in contrast to most Scotsmen on the mainland. Some day it may be a good thing that the Hebrideans should

---

[7] Cockaigne, fool's paradise, land of milk and honey where one may live in idle luxury.

[8] The original Greek is quoted in *Minch*, 10: ἔστιν θάλασσα, τίς δὲ νιν κατασβέσει.

lose their language and be in every way amalgamated with the rest of Scotland or (as the case may be) with all the English-speaking races of the world. But that day is not yet. The ill-effects of rapid anglicization can be seen in the town of Stornoway. The crofter comes to town to swap his traditional rhythm and routine for the fussy mentality of Glasgow and the jazzy culture of an English public library.

The Hebrides today do not suffer from poverty. As a crofter in Lewis said to me: 'You can't really say in a crofting community that people are *hard up.*' And if one man in a village finds it hard to get enough to eat, his neighbours will help him out. At the same time unemployment and unsatisfactory conditions of labour are impoverishing the people spiritually. And while neither the over-population of Lewis nor the under-population of Skye presents a rural Utopia, I have my doubts also about the Gaelic communities overseas.

For two centuries the natives of the Hebrides have been encouraged to emigrate, often by the false promises of hypocrite landlords. Dr Johnson, in 1773, deplored the wholesale emigration which was then going on from the islands: 'It may be thought that they are happier by the change; but they are not happy as a nation, for they are a nation no longer. As they contribute not to the prosperity of any community, they must want that security, that dignity, that happiness, whatever it be, which a prosperous community throws back upon individuals.'[9]

---

[9] Samuel Johnson (1709–84), *A Journey* [1773] *to the Western Islands of Scotland* (1775), ed. with Boswell's *Journal of a Tour to the Hebrides* (3 edns 1785–6) by R. W. Chapman (1924, 1970), 119.

Or One Might Write It So[1]

WALTER PATER: As the traveller first approached that long line of the islands which taken collectively and by that easy synopsis of the popular imagination, an imagination which in its instinctive short cuts where science would take longer detours often attains a beauty of expression more proper to what philosophers call the coherence theory of truth than to that other, the correspondence theory, were called long since the Long Island and still are called so to-day, he felt come over his mind like a flush upon the skin the sudden excitement not untempered by sadness of the approaching *Terra Incognita*. There came before his eyes the marshalled army of the drifters, among which the steamers had all but superseded the sailing craft, but it was not in a manner of speaking his eyes which saw them; he felt them rather with that sixth mysterious sense which is lodged below the nape of the neck. It seemed to him then pondering as he did the all but imponderable quintessence of a special locality, so important to a man of his sensibility though drawn as fine and subtly as a spider's web draped on an Ionic capital, that this world which he had travelled so long and with a so often disappointed ardour, had now little more to offer. Leaning his hands on the rail of the incoming steamer, but withdrawn in his mind into that *adyton*[2] which philology tells us is a place not to be entered of the spirit, he said to himself *Ave Ave—age jam meorum finis amorum*;[3] he had not asked for this but he was glad that it had come to him.

---

[1] *I Crossed the Minch*, (see prev. chap., n. 1), chap. 13, 177–93. Here MacNeice successfully parodies 5 well-known prose stylists and their characteristic subjects: (1) Walter H. Pater (1839–94)—precious elaborations on beauty with learned tags; (2) D. H. Lawrence (1885–1930)—sensitive female 'blood'-consciousness; (3) Ernest Hemingway (1899–1961)—the laboured simplicities of an economic style; (4) W. B. Yeats (1865–1939)—pompous elaborations, aristocratic pose, nationalistic and 'mystic' eccentricities; (5) faceless (a-n-other) detective fiction—slick realism, with a mixture of true and false clues, leading to a trick denouement.

[2] 'Not to be entered'; innermost sacred part of a temple: *OED2*.

[3] Horace, *Odes* 4. 11. 31–2: 'Come along then, last of my loves'—used much later by MacNeice as epigraph to his poetry book *Solstices* (March 1961).

D. H. LAWRENCE: She walked slowly along the road from Barvas to Ness. There were no trees, so she could not observe the sexual shapes of their vegetation, but the sun shining upon the moors assured her that all was not lost. The peewits kept crying, crying, as they chivvied each other with an interminable vivacity. The life of the peewits was a life which was not hers but it was a life akin to hers, a succession of white-hot pinpricks on the dark lining of her senses. Suddenly she saw two crofters engaged in peat-cutting. One of them stood in the ditch and cut the peats with deft strokes of an instrument, the other man received the peats and piled them up in a wall as if they were sandbags. The crofters did not look at her but she knew that they sensed her presence. Though their backs were towards her she knew that they knew she was there. They knew it not with their minds but deep down somewhere in the darkness below the diaphragm. A great joy filled her that the crofters should know she was there even though they turned their backs to her. The soft fresh cakes of peat, fleshly as the thighs of a mulatto woman, called to her like notes of music. As the first crofter cut each peat from the earth it was like a note on the piano. And as the second crofter took the peat-cake from him, took it from its dark bed amid the tacit womb-wisdom of the earth, and placed it on the top of the pile in the hungry glare of the sun, it was like another note on the piano but a note higher up the scale and sustained with a fiercer intensity. Then as she looked at the crofters she felt afraid. She felt afraid that they might suddenly turn and look at her not with their diaphragms but with the intolerable male questioning of their eyes. The crofters were part of the landscape but she was something alien to the landscape. She knew that she was something alien, her flesh contained an alloy, she was something newer and inferior. If the crofters turned and looked at her, it would be as if the whole long sea of the peat moors were to turn round and challenge her presence and tell her she had no right to be there. Ah, but she had a right, she thought, reassured by the crying of the peewits. The shadows of the peewits chivvied each other on the road. They chivvied each other, the peewits, they turned in their tracks in the air, then they came down again low—low and low as if to whisper a message in her ear. She knew in her blood the burden of the message of the peewits and a new self sprang up in her. Not the self which she had brought with her from Glasgow but a new self and yet an older than any of the selves which she had known. A great joy rang through her blood like massed bands and she thought 'I am as old as the crofters. I am only twenty-two in years but I am old with the wisdom of the earth. I am old like the peat which has lain beneath the surface for centuries. I am only waiting like the peat for someone to bring me to the surface, with kind ferocious hands to cut me in blocks and lay me in a pile in the sun.' She began to feel a terrible assurance, an assurance that nothing would stop her, that she would always now get what she wanted, infused with the wisdom of the earth, with the quickness and fullness of the earth that cannot be exhausted. She took the little ordnance map from her pocket and smelled it gently. There was no need to open it or look at it. She knew where she was going. With proud female steps she walked towards Ness like a swallow flying north in the spring.

ERNEST HEMINGWAY: A man knocked at the door of the Black House.[4] Nobody answered. The man opened the door and went into the byre. He went through the byre into the living-room. There were four men in the living-room and a woman. The room was full of smoke.

'May I sit down?' he asked them.

The men and the woman said nothing.

He took a box that was lying on its side. He turned the box up on end and sat on the end of the box.

'I would like a drink,' he said.

'Aye,' one of the men said.

'I would like a drink,' he said.

The woman looked at him and got up. She took a broken cup down from the dresser. She took a jug off the dresser and poured water from the jug into the cup. She gave him the cup and sat down again in her chair. The chair had a castor missing.

He tasted the water and put the cup down on the floor.

'I would like a drink,' he said.

The woman shrugged her shoulders.

'I would like a drink,' he said.

4 'A turf house . . . built of unmortared stone, found esp. in north-western Scotland and the Hebrides': *OED2*.

A cat came into the room from the bedroom at the other side. It walked across the room on four legs.

'I would like a drink,' it said.

'Aye,' one of the men said.

The woman got up and took down a saucer from the dresser. She opened a drawer in the dresser and took out a bottle of milk. She poured the milk into the saucer. She put the saucer down on the floor.

The cat came and looked at the saucer. Then it dipped its head and began drinking. It drank as if it was thirsty.

The man who had come in got up.

'I must go now,' he said.

He put his hands in his pockets and opened the door with his knee. He went out into the rain. The rain was raining.

'What the hell,' he said. 'What the hell.'

W. B. YEATS: One day I came to the village of Sorisdale.[5] I remember that I did not know where I was walking as my mind at that time was much occupied with religious and other problems. In Sorisdale I met an old man who looked like George Mair[6] but without Mair's vulgar insouciance and he told me some old legends dating from before the Norse Invasion. He spoke in Gaelic with which I was not acquainted, and owing perhaps to this or to some other reason I only partly understood him. I have often wondered since whether he was not pulling my leg. He told me that the sea lay down beyond the village and when I raised my eyes I saw that this was so. Presently an old woman came out from a white-washed house, and when she had looked at me for some time went back into the house and shut the door. I have no doubt that she thought I was one of the other-dwellers and that her shutting of the door was an instance of that atavism so common among Celtic peoples. It was not surprising that she was afraid of me, for at that time I had not been able to have my hair cut as there was no photo-

---

[5] A fictive place-name (based on life as a 'vale of tears'), mimicking the trisyllabic pattern of Yeats's Innisfree.

[6] George Herbert Mair (1887–1926), the distinguished English journalist, assistant director on the League of Nations Secretariat 1919–26, had married in 1911 the Irish actress 'Maire O'Neill' (Molly Allgood, 1887–1952)—a member of the Abbey Theatre company, the former fiancée of John M. Synge, and creatrix of the part of Pegeen Mike in Synge's *The Playboy of the Western World* (1907).

grapher on the island, and my eyes, as is common with persons on the verge of a trance, were enlarged like the eyes of a *revenant*. I felt, as I looked at the shut door, that if I had more courage or a greater conviction of my importance, I would knock at the door and ask the old woman some questions, but instead of doing this I turned round to walk back to my hotel, or rather, for all our actions are accomplished on two planes at once, to regain that equilibrium of spirit which human contacts disturb. I have often wondered since, when waking from sleep in the Reading Room of the British Museum, whether that old woman was really all that she seemed, or whether, when she shut the door, she did not retire into a more elemental chamber than the living room of her cottage. Such a question cannot be definitely answered though I have no doubt, since talking it over with an old man in Merrion Square[7] who had once had tea with Parnell, that such a removal from the material plane to the psychic is as easily accomplished as the changing of gears on a car. The universe has seemed to me at moments like a series of Chinese boxes which we undo from the inside outwards. This was also the conception of the yogis and can be found in a modern guise in the poems of Lady Flora Barsac.[8] When I stayed in her house in Hampshire, she showed me a poem which she had written with a wild goose quill and it seemed to me to be more profound, more exquisite, than the other poems of our century.

A. N. OTHER: All the time I sat in the *Loch Ness* I was thinking of the bridge below the scree. It was the first time I had come in direct contact with a murder. What alarmed me more was the thought of coming in contact with the murderer.

I took a stroll round the decks and carefully scrutinized the passengers. One of them was probably the murderer and that one knew my identity though I was unaware of his. There was an old man in a deer-stalker hat with a lump on the back of his

---

[7] Fashionable area near Trinity College and directly opposite the National Gallery, Dublin, where Oscar Wilde, Joseph Sheridan Le Fanu, and Daniel O'Connell once lived: Irish Tourist Board, *Official Guide* [to] *Dublin* (recent, n.d.), 34.

[8] An invented personage, probably patterned after Yeats's friend Lady Dorothy Wellesley, Duchess of Wellington (1889–1956), the English poet. MacNeice had reviewed her poetry in *Oxford Outlook*, June 1931. See Yeats's *Letters on Poetry* to her (1940).

neck. He was English and therefore suspect, for it was unlikely that any islander should have been concerned to kill that unknown little stranger, Dr Fifield.[9] The murder, it was admitted, could not have been from motives of robbery as a wallet containing £20 in notes had been found upon the corpse.

I looked round for other strangers but the only other passenger apparently who was not Scottish, was a Jewish-looking lady, rather flamboyantly handsome, with eyes like great black stones and fingers covered with rings. Having a good sense of smell I noticed that she was using the new scent, 'Ne Plus Ultra'.[10]

I returned to my deck-chair and sat looking moodily at the Minch. I could not get out of my mind the dreary picture of the scree with the tiny bridge below it and that odd little figure standing on the parapet, taking photographs apparently of nothing. I had passed him at half-past three on that sodden and desolate afternoon (what an afternoon to take photographs!) and the murder apparently had taken place ten minutes later as the watch on the dead man's wrist had stopped at 3.41, owing no doubt to one of the blows from the sledge-hammer.

It would have looked very suspicious for me but my action in at once calling the police as soon as I saw the news in the paper next morning over at Kyle[11] must have completely proved to them my innocence. But they insisted that I should return at once to Stornoway as I was the only person who had seen the murdered man within three hours before the murder. They were especially interested in the fact that when I had approached Dr Fifield he had jumped over the parapet of the bridge and skulked in the bed of the burn till I had gone by. One of the most curious points in the case was that they had been unable to find his camera, which must therefore presumably have been

[9] An invented personage, but just possibly referring to Lionel Richard Fifield, FRCS (1898–1928), a consulting surgeon of the London Hospital who had been fatally injured in a motor accident in London, 20 March 1928: obit. in *The Times*, 22 March 1928, 21a; inquest report, ibid., 24 March, 11e.

[10] MacNeice was fond of scent: cf. *Autumn Journal* 1938 (1939) iv. 17–18: *Collected Poems*, ed. E. R. Dodds (1966, corr. 1979), 107. 'Ne Plus Ultra' is fictive and ironic; but it may possibly also refer to part of the advertising for the perfume 'Joy', introduced 1935 by the famous fashion designer Jean Patou (1887–1936) of Paris. Then (the 1930s) 'Joy' was the most expensive perfume in the world.

[11] Kyle of Lochalsh, SW Ross and Cromarty—the terminal of the car ferry to Kyleakin, Isle of Skye.

taken by the murderer. They asked me over the 'phone what sort of camera it was and I said that I could not see accurately at the distance but that it was a small pocket camera and being a VPK owner myself I should guess it was a VPK.[12]

A bell on the *Loch Ness* rang for the second supper. So harassed was I by my thoughts that I could not remember whether I had eaten the first supper but I went down nevertheless, thinking it was well to err on the safe side and that I should need to stoke up my system in preparation for the gruelling business of the morrow. It is an odd thing but even in ordinary life I often forget if I have had a meal or not. My family have always thought me terribly absent-minded and indeed there are whole half hours here and there in my life which I have been quite unable to account for.

I ate my supper with my eyes bowed on my plate; my thoughts were too unpleasant to make ordinary frivolous conversation. But raising my eyes to help myself to some salad I saw looking into mine those of the Jewish lady. Her black eyes were like holes into nothingness and from that moment I was sure of her identity.

Why the police should be so certain that the murderer (or murderess) should intend to trail me back to Stornoway and endanger herself by revisiting the scene of her crime I was in considerable doubt, but I supposed it was to sabotage my evidence which she might think sufficient to hang her. I could not see myself that it was sufficient to hang anybody but no doubt the mere facts of time and place would, when fitted together in their jig-saw, provide a clue which at the moment I at least could not see.

The Jewish lady having finished her supper lit a Russian cigarette. I could see that her hand was shaking. No wonder, I thought, but all the same a cold shudder ran down my back and I wondered if she had a revolver in that capacious though elegant handbag. Thinking of revolvers the thought struck me with astonishment that a woman should commit a murder with a sledge-hammer, but looking at her again I saw that she had powerful shoulders, while at the same time I remembered the frail proportions of Dr Fifield, and as I pondered the matter it

[12] Vest pocket Kodak.

all became clear to me as day. When I had approached Dr Fifield he had jumped down over the bridge and disappeared from my sight in the bed of the burn. *But he had not been the only person in the bed of the burn.* There, crouching against the bridge where she could not be seen from the road, must have been this woman dressed from the Rue de la Paix[13] and holding the sledge-hammer in her gloved but relentless hands.

At Stornoway I was met on the quay by the Police Commissioner, who asked me to have finished breakfast by half-past eight on the following morning and to be ready to go out to the scene of the crime. 'Did you see anyone suspicious on the boat?' he asked. 'Yes,' I said and I described the Jewish lady to him. 'There she goes now,' I said as she passed us wonderfully poised and leaving behind her a waft of 'Ne Plus Ultra'.

'As I expected,' said the Commissioner, and taking out his pocket-book handed me a small photograph. 'Found on the body,' he said. It was a photo of the Jewish lady—an extremely good likeness.

'Wife, or mistress?' I asked.

'Not wife,' said the Commissioner. 'Dr Fifield, we find, was not married.'

'Well, was this woman staying with him on the island?'

'No, as far as we can ascertain. Dr Fifield, you know, was camping, but we have made enquiries in the district and no one admits to having seen any woman about. We have also made enquiries from the purser and stewards on the *Loch Ness* but, as bad luck would have it, a whole party of German Jewesses visited the island last week and returned immediately. About a dozen of them, so it was no good asking if there was a Jewess on board.'

'Yes,' I said, 'I saw 'em on the boat to Kyle. I suppose she was there, too.'

'Luck for her!' he said. 'What about a drink?'

'Mine's a Haig,'[14] I said.

I slept surprisingly well and met the Police Commissioner in the lobby of my hotel at half-past eight next morning. Hardly

---

[13] Fashionable shopping district, on the rive droite, Paris, between the place de l'Opéra and the place Vendôme.

[14] Haig & Haig, the Scotch whisky.

anyone in the hotel was up for the islanders are notoriously late risers.

'Had a good breakfast?' he said.

'Yes, thanks,' I said.

'Bacon and eggs, I suppose?' he said. 'They don't go in much for variety.'

I thought hard and couldn't remember if it was bacon and eggs or not. In fact I couldn't remember what I had eaten at all.

'Have you got a camera with you?' he asked, 'I should like you to take a snap or two of how Dr Fifield was standing when you last saw him. I'll represent Dr Fifield.'

'I'll get my camera,' I said. 'I nearly always carry it but I happen to have packed it in my suit-case.' I went upstairs, disinterred my VPK from among my shirts and collars and rejoining the Commissioner we both climbed into his smart little Hillman Minx and rattled out by Stornoway Castle and into the moors.

After about twenty minutes I began to feel extraordinarily empty. Good gracious me, I thought, I don't believe I had my breakfast after all.

Coming round the corner of the hill from which the little bridge was visible, the Commissioner stopped the car and we proceeded to walk forward the remaining hundred yards from the corner of the hill to the bridge. About forty yards short of the bridge there was a heap of stones on the right side of the road. The islanders are always on the point of repairing their roads.

'Ah,' I said, 'that's where I noticed the sledge-hammer.'

'What? The sledge-hammer was there when you passed?'

'Yes. It was lying on the top of the heap.'

'Then,' said the Commissioner, 'that will not fit in with your theory' (for we had discussed my theory in the car) 'that when Dr Fifield jumped down over the bridge, the murderer or murderess was already waiting for him there with the sledge-hammer in her hand.'

'No,' I said.

'That leaves', said the Commissioner, 'two alternatives—either that the murderer had a second hammer in his hand, which seems unlikely and further no such hammer has been found, or that after you had passed the bridge, he or she went back to this heap and fetched the hammer which you saw. I suppose you didn't turn round once you had passed the bridge?'

'Oh, yes,' I said, 'I turned round once or twice during the next ten minutes. I wanted to see if Fifield would come up again from under the bridge.'

'And you saw nobody, man or woman, on the road?'

'Not a soul.'

'You remember that the murder was committed ten minutes after you passed? And that Fifield's body was found in the bed of the burn?'

'Yes,' I said.

'Why, by the way,' said the Commissioner, 'if you were so interested in Fifield, didn't you look for him while you were passing over the bridge?'

'I suppose,' I said, 'I thought he was relieving himself.'

'How do you mean you suppose? Do you actually remember thinking that?'

'I can't remember, but that seems likely to have been what I would think.'

'Pity you aren't more precise,' said the Commissioner who was getting steadily more morose. 'Now we will go on to the bridge.'

We examined the bridge thoroughly and the bed of the burn beneath it. The soft ground by the burn was covered with foot-prints. 'Most of these were left by my men yesterday,' said the Commissioner. 'Darn nuisance the way they blunder about. The foot-prints tell me one thing, however.'

'What?'

'There's been no woman down here lately. There's not a single woman's foot-print in the lot.'

'That's odd,' I said.

'Hm,' said the Commissioner, 'now we'll take those photos. I shall be Dr Fifield.'

I took my VPK and saw that I had only two snaps left to take.

'Hell,' said the Commissioner. 'You might have brought an extra film.'

'Sorry,' I said, 'that's my memory again.'

'Well, we'll do what we can,' he said. 'Place me as Fifield was standing when you first came round the hill.'

I made him get up on the parapet of the bridge and hold his notebook in his hands as if it was a camera. Then I withdrew a little distance and photographed him.

'And how was he standing when you reached the heap of stones?'

'He went on standing like that,' I said.

'Just like that?'

'Yes, just like that, I think.'

'All right. Then all you can do is to photograph me from the other side.'

I did so.

'Now', said the Commissioner, 'we'll develop these at once.'

'In Stornoway?' I said.

'No. We'll do it on the spot. I have my reasons for this. Here is everything you will want. Now you see that sheiling over there? You can use it for a dark room.'

Dictatorial these chaps are, I thought. I filled a can with water from the burn and carrying my materials stumped up a marshy knoll and crawled on hands and knees into the sheiling. The doorway of the sheiling was less than three foot high and, as the roof was in unusually good preservation, the interior was almost dark. The floor was covered with rabbit droppings. I hung my coat across the doorway to make the darkness complete and set to my work. I laid the pan of developing liquid on the small ridge of turfs which supports the bed when the sheiling is in use, and slipped in the film. The Commissioner had provided a red lantern. A thorough chap, I thought. I could hear him moving about outside.

After a minute or two I took up my light and glanced at the films to see how they were progressing. I had little interest in any of the eight pictures on the strip. Not counting the last two which I had just taken of the Commissioner, they consisted entirely of snaps of the herring fleet at Stornoway and of women gutting the herrings on the quays.

Or, at least, I thought they did but when I glanced at the film lying in the developing pan, I dimly saw that those pictures were a different lot. There was the Commissioner all right but who was that woman at the other end of the strip who had been taken three times over. She was dressed in white and taken with a racket on a tennis court. I never took *those* snaps in Stornoway, I thought.

The middle sections of the strip were so dark that I could see nothing. They looked as if they would not come out. I put down the red lamp and sat tailor-wise on the ground racking my brains to explain the mystery of the film. Suddenly I got up and looked again. Yes, that was the woman all right. It was the Jewish woman who had travelled with me on the *Loch Ness*.

I leaned against the wall with sudden dizziness as the whole thing dawned on me. This was not my film and the camera was not my camera. It was the dead man's camera and *he* had taken the photos of this woman who had subsequently murdered him. She must certainly, I thought, have been his mistress and the motive therefore must have been jealousy.

But how had the dead man's camera got into my suit-case so that I had mistaken it for mine?

I thought very hard of the events on the day of the murder and wondered if, when I passed the bridge, I could absent-mindedly have pocketed the dead man's camera, supposing it had been lying on the top of the parapet. I have always been very absent-minded.

I heard the Commissioner moving outside the sheiling and called out to him—'I say. Something very odd has happened.' But the Commissioner did not answer.

I got up to go out to him, then remembered my business and took another look at the film. Ah, something was showing in the middle section after all. This will have been one of the snaps he took in the rain. Maybe the snap he was taking when I came round the corner of the hill.

It was. There was the ugly scree, the road coming round the corner, and there was myself on the road just having rounded the hill.

This was Snap Number Five. Numbers Seven and Eight were of the Commissioner. Number Six was very obscure. I did not remember having seen Fifield take a second photo, but evidently he had taken one more before he was murdered. It was very important that I should see the details of this photo.

I moved the pan a little and watched the film steadily, and steadily before my eyes the picture came into being. This was the snap of a man at three yards' range—a man with a sledge-hammer in his hand. I could not see his face but his whole bearing was demoniac. I looked from Number Six to Number Five and comparing the figures realized that the man was myself.

In a panic I dived for the doorway of the sheiling and, brushing aside my coat which hung over it, began scrambling out like an animal when I realized that against the sky a gun pointed downwards at my head. As the gun roared and I fell half out of the sheiling, I noticed that the smoking gun was held in the hand of a woman. I passed to unconsciousness in the odour of 'Ne Plus Ultra'.

The doctors say that I am very unlikely to recover. If I do recover, I shall certainly be put in an asylum. The world cannot tolerate people who are absent-minded and commit murders during their moments of absence.

As for the Jewish lady, far from having murdered Dr Fifield, she had come back in order to avenge him.

Statement on the Spanish War[1]

I support the Valencia Government in Spain. Normally I would only support a cause because I hoped to get something out of it. Here the reason is stronger; if this cause is lost, nobody with civilized values may be able to get anything out of anything.

[1] *Authors take sides on the Spanish War* (London: Left Review, Dec. 1937), unpaginated. The Left Review was founded by (Sir) Victor Gollancz (1893–1967), for whom see MacNeice's *Selected Literary Criticism*, 91–2. The question, 'Are you for, or against, the legal Government and the People of Republican Spain?', during the Spanish Civil War (1936–9), was signed in Paris, June 1937, by e.g. Louis Aragon, W. H. Auden, José Bergamin, Jean Richard Bloch, Nancy Cunard, Brian Howard, Heinrich Mann, Ivor Montagu, Pablo Neruda, Ramón Sender, Stephen Spender, and Tristan Tzara. For the Government were 127 writers including MacNeice (making his most politically committed statement to that date), Auden, Samuel Beckett, C. Day-Lewis, Stephen Spender; neutral (taking the Ivory Tower position) were 16; against, only 5. A copy of this booklet is in the HRC, Austin, Texas.

In Defence of Vulgarity[1]

The word vulgar originally meant common—that is, belonging to the crowd. Both common and vulgar are nowadays used disparagingly. This implies contempt for the crowd—and the distressing thing is that the crowd themselves also use the words contemptuously. Because, unfortunately, nobody wants to admit that he is merely a bit of a crowd: the crowd are always the other people.

I knew a charlady in Birmingham[2] who never went to the excellent suburban cinema at her door, but always took half-an-hour's tram ride to the centre of the town—to see exactly the same film in an almost identical cinema—because, she said, there was much more class in the audience. The charlady spent an hour in a tram to avoid sitting with people who were vulgar. This in itself, some people might think, was an instance of vulgarity on her part. In fact, if we examine behaviour which we find vulgar, we shall quite often discover that it arose from a desire to avoid vulgarity.

All of us seem vulgar to someone. I will give you some specimens now of my own vulgarity. But first a generalization. Most kinds of vulgarity consist of doing something to excess—not knowing where to stop, you might put it. It isn't surprising that the Greeks—who never stopped saying one ought to know where to stop—had a word for vulgarity.[3] For my own part, though my job is lecturing about the Greeks,[4] I have two traditions behind me which encourage me to rush into very un-Greek extremes or excesses. First of all, I am an Irishman, and

---

[1] *Listener* 18: 468 (29 Dec. 1937), 1407-8, one of a broadcast series on the BBC National programme, which also included Auden's 'In Defence of Gossip', ibid. 18: 467 (22 Dec. 1937), 1371-2.

[2] In 1930-6 MacNeice, then lecturer in Classics at Birmingham University, was living with his first wife Mary Ezra 'in a converted stables on the south, the genteel, side of Birmingham': *Strings*, 130.

[3] βαναυσία, 'habits of a mere artisan, vulgarity, bad taste': Aristotle, *Nicomachean Ethics* 2. 7. 6, 4. 2. 4 (1107^{b}19, 1122^{a}30); cf. 7. 1. 2 (1145^{a}24), where Aristotle associates θηριωσία (bestiality) with κακία (vice) and ἀκρασία (incontinence).

[4] In 1936-9 MacNeice was lecturer of Greek at Bedford College for Women, University of London.

the Irish are notorious for not knowing where to stop, either in conversation or in action. (By the way, many of the Irish think the English vulgar, and vice versa.) Secondly, I am a writer in the English language, and English literature is notorious for its lack of classical shape, its uncontrolled irrelevances.

Now the ways in which you can be vulgar are in conversation, in recreation, in the way you decorate your house, in the arts, in the soul, and in your personal appearance. I plead guilty to certain vulgarities in each of these matters. I suppose it is generally agreed that you are vulgar if you wear loud colours or use much make-up or jewellery. There is, by the way, an odd minority view held by some especially refined people, that it is vulgar to wear clothes all of which match each other exactly. But we cannot discuss that now. Personally, I like to wear bright colours on occasions, and I like women as a rule to use plenty of make-up and also scent. I wonder if you have noticed the very unfair distinction that is usually drawn between cheap scent and expensive scent. Obviously scent and make-up are just forms of self-advertisement, like the peacock's tail or the mandrill's cheek-pouches. Self-advertisement of this kind is conditioned by practical considerations. I would think it very wrong to call the mandrill vulgar because he can't afford the feathers of the peacock.

Then take conversation. For centuries, in fact since the days of Aristotle, it has been thought vulgar to have a loud voice, to talk a lot about oneself, to make risky jokes, and to monopolize the conversation. It is particularly vulgar to talk about one's money—whether one has lots of it, and boasts about it, or is broke and says so. Now I myself cannot see why a man should not talk about his money. Everybody is interested in everybody else's finances, and it seems hypocrisy to hush the subject up in the drawing room—as if bank balances were found under gooseberry bushes. As for talking about oneself in general—to make good conversation one has got to speak about what one knows something about, and there are very few people who aren't better up in themselves than in international affairs, or the private lives of the great, or the weather we are likely to have on Boxing Day. I know several young women whose schooldays were ruined because when they arrived at their school and behaved like normal human beings, they were told that it is vulgar to be demonstrative. In the same way it is generally considered vulgar in England to show that you enjoy your food, or to be volubly grateful when someone gives you a present, and of course it is still more vulgar to praise up a present which you are giving to somebody else—though why we should want to seem only to give our friends worthless things, I'm sure I can't understand. I dislike mock modesty—we get any amount of this in England—and I should welcome a little Latin ostentation to counterbalance it.[5]

Then where recreation is concerned, it seems to be only the very expensive sports, like polo or real-tennis, that escape the charge of vulgarity. Most highbrows consider golf vulgar. Rugger fans consider soccer vulgar—because it is a game for the masses who eat and drink on the stands and hoot at the referee. And of course we constantly hear people say how vulgar the cinema is. One of the most concentrated kinds of snobbery is what you find flourishing in film societies.[6] The film snob goes to the pictures—not that he *calls* them the pictures—for the ideas and the photography, particularly in films German or Russian. The man-in-the-street and his young woman go to a film to see the stars, and to be excited by the story and to enjoy the good looks of their favourite heroes and heroines. Here I'm all with the man-in-the-street. I look on the cinema as a frivolity.[7] I don't want to be very serious and intense about it. I have no aspirations to become a connoisseur of the camera. I don't want to go to films to get a criticism of life. I like best very slick films made at Hollywood, and I like to see them from a plush seat in an old-fashioned, vulgar, heavily ornamented cinema, redolent of scent and cigarette smoke. And while I am

---

[5] For a well-known example of 'Latin ostentation', see Cicero, *Epistolae ad Atticum* (*Letters to Atticus*), 5. 8. 1: '*multorum annorum ostentationes meas nunc in discrimen esse aductas*', 'that my many years' boastful promises [of able administration] are now brought to the test'.

[6] The Film Society, London (1925–39), founded 'to promote the intellectual respectability of the cinema', especially championing German expressionist, Russian, and other avant-garde films, 'was regarded with some hostility by the trade who, rightly, saw its existence as an implicit criticism of current exhibition policy': *The Oxford Companion to Film*, ed. Liz-Anne Bawden (1976), 250. For the London Film Society programme 1937-8, see *The Times*, 6 Nov. 1937, 10a.

[7] 'If I want entertainment I go to the cinema': MacNeice, 'The Play and the Audience' (1938), para. 2, in his *Selected Literary Criticism*, 87. Cf. remarks on going to the theatre in both articles.

on the subject of entertainment, I may say that when I can afford it, I like to go to the theatre in a white tie—and further, if I could afford it I should like to sit in a box, and I should like first to have dined on oysters and champagne. I know that people who write books about wine say that champagne is a vulgar drink, and that many people say that one only likes caviare because it is expensive. There may be quite a lot in this; but I am willing to admit that the extra expense gives me an extra thrill, and one which I am not ashamed of. By the way, I also like eating in the street.

Now to come to decoration. What is called simple good taste scares me. I don't like too much fitness-for-purpose—what is called functionalism.[8] I like to have a knob on my fireplace just because it is amusing to have a knob, and not because if I press a button it turns into an ashtray. No, I don't care for simple lines, or natural colouring on curtains or chair covers, or pastel shades on the walls, or steel furniture, or woodwork with no carvings on it. I get tired of blank spaces, and often find myself yearning for wallpaper instead of distemper. And once the wallpaper is there I should like to have it covered with roses. And like some other people, I find it easier to work in a room which is definitely over-decorated. When it comes to cars, I dislike streamlining, and when it comes to gardens I like to have a garden bursting with gaudy flowers[9]—not one of your neat geometrical patterns of single, refined specimens.

Now a word about art. I am all against the rarefying effects of good taste, and have no sympathy with the idea that artists are people who should not soil their fingers with life.[10] I don't

---

[8] A major principle of modern architecture and design (especially furniture), that form should follow from purpose or function, that materials should not be forced into decoration—according to the German architect Walter A. Gropius (1883–1969), founder of The Bauhaus, and the Swiss architect Le Corbusier (Charles-Edouard Jeanneret, 1887–1965). In partnership with Maxwell Fry in England 1934–7, Gropius designed some striking buildings, especially Village College at Impington, Cambridgeshire (1936), before leaving for the USA. See Alberto Busignani, *Gropius* (1973), 42 (illus.), 94 (biblio.). Le Corbusier followed the dictum, 'a house is a machine for living' (1920).

[9] Cf. 'Letter to Auden' (Nov. 1937), para. 7, n. 7, in MacNeice's *Selected Literary Criticism*, 84.

[10] MacNeice's *Modern Poetry* (Nov. 1938) was a manifesto for 'impure' art, for poetry close to and mixed with ordinary life: 'My own prejudice . . . is in favour of poets whose worlds are not too esoteric' (chap. 11, 198).

agree that the style is the man.[11] I always feel a vulgar curiosity to know what the man is talking about. In the case of pictures, I take a vulgar interest in their subject.[12] In the case of music, I have a vulgar preference for something with a tune. The plays I like best are a sort of mixture *à la* Shakespeare—comic relief sticking out in the middle of tragedy, rant, jokes for the groundlings, and slapstick.[13] Then I am very fond of the music-hall and the circus,[14] and I am quite fascinated by virtuosos, people who show off, and in the same way I like virtuosos in private life. At school I heartily admired the boys who mimicked their masters—though such mimicry is undoubtedly not in the best of taste, besides being bad for discipline. If I were a conjurer, I should like to start doing tricks in railway carriages, though I suppose that would not be in very good taste either.

I am afraid that all these vulgarities that I have been talking about derive from what some people still call the soul.[15] Some souls are essentially vulgar—all in favour of cutting a dash regardless of good taste. Or sometimes they claim to be a sort of good taste unto themselves. Vulgarity is asserting oneself outside one's own sphere, when one is not qualified to do so. But we may be excused, I feel, in these days of specialization from always having to stick in our own spheres. The business man, the bank clerk, and shop girl all have to have their Saturday nights. The strain of routine has got to be relieved by some—perhaps rather irresponsible—bravado. Of course,

[11] Comte G. L. L. de Buffon (1707–88), *Discours sur le Style* (1753), para. 15: '*Ces choses sont hors de l'homme, le style est l'homme même*': 'These things [subject matter] are external to the man; style is the very man.'

[12] Cf. 'Subject in Modern Poetry' (Dec. 1936), in MacNeice's *Selected Literary Criticism*, 57–74.

[13] Of the many sources for classic and neo-classic decorum or propriety (πρέπον, in Aristotle's *Rhetoric* 3. 7. 1–2), Horace's *Ars Poetica* (*Epistula ad Pisones*), ll. 86–92, distinguishing comic from tragic modes, was probably most in MacNeice's mind here: the principle became a neo-classic doctrine after Boileau's *Art poétique* (1674).

[14] Cf. MacNeice's 1937 poems 'Circus' and 'Bagpipe Music': *Collected Poems*, 92–4, 96–7.

[15] Aristotle defined ψυχή (soul) as 'the primary actuality of a natural body which potentially has life' (*De anima*, 412ª27–8) and based his treatise of the virtues on a study of the human soul (*Nicomachean Ethics* 1. 8, 1102ª4–1103ª11): cf. n. 3 above. But the influential French philosopher René Descartes (1596–1650) asserted that 'our [human] soul is in its nature entirely independent of the body [mechanical]': *Discours de la méthode* (1637), pt. 5, final para. ('*que la nôtre [l'âme humaine] est d'une nature entièrement indépendente du corps*').

people with perfect taste don't have to blow their own trumpets; everybody is looking at them already. All of us like to be looked at because otherwise we feel lonely—and hence the majority of us just have to blow our own trumpets. It may not be music, but at least it is self-assertion. Self-assertion more often than not is vulgar, but a live and vulgar dog who keeps on barking is better than a dead lion, however dignified.

Wild and Domestic[1]

Many people take to animals to escape from human beings—
but often, it turns out, because they find the animals so human.
Others, of whom I am one, find animals a delightful change
just because they are not human and never can be. They are
extraordinary and beautiful phenomena—things which move
about on legs (in many cases at least) as we do, but which are
for ever essentially different from us.

I even feel this with my dog ('O Sacrilege', you will say,
thinking of the Dog's Prayer[2] and how they can speak with
their eyes). When I am alone with my dog (I go on obstinately,
closing my ears to vituperation)—when I am alone with my dog,
there are not two of us. There is myself—and something Other.
It gives me a pleasant feeling of power, even of black magic, to
be able to order this Other about and give it food which it
actually eats. The dog, as we have domesticated him, is in a
sense our creation, a toy, an art-object. We play Pygmalion
with him and he comes to life.

A friend of mine, who deplored the keeping of dogs, said
after all what about half-wits; we don't buy a half-wit and keep
him in the drawing-room, seven-and-six a week for his food
and seven-and-six a year for his licence, and then when he
learns to shut the door or to beg, tell all our friends with a smile
that he's nearly human. The answer to this argument is that
half-wits are rarely beautiful and, further, they are not for sale;
if they were, no doubt somebody would buy one.

My friend was right, however, in objecting to our anthropomorphism. And if we must think of animals as human beings,
it is easiest to think of them—or at least of those in menageries—

[1] MacNeice, *Zoo*, illus. Nancy Sharp (Nov. 1938), chap. 4, 64–76.
[2] 'A Dog's Prayer' was a sentimental verse by Fay Inchfawn—published as a
valentine postcard on the Inchfawn series no. 1253–6, about 1928: 'Oh, Master, you
can surely see | All that you do is wise to me. | Success may crown your dearest plan |
Yet love you more I never can. | And though you miserably fail | No change knows
my delighted tail. | I watch your eye, your lip, your hand, | Trying your thought to
understand. | Within my heart one earnest plea— | Where you are, let me always be.'
Louis MacNeice was never a member of the Kennel Club.

as half-wits or lunatics—some, the big cats and apes, as manic depressives; some—the smaller monkeys and parrots—as paranoiacs; but most of them as schizophrenes, cut off from what we call actuality not only by their bars, but by the final glass barrier of their eyes.

When we talk about them, of course, we often have to speak *as if* they were human because the words with which we must describe them are themselves tainted with humanity. Many of their actions are superficially so like ours that we can only describe them in terms of our own actions. The first great thing that we obviously have in common with animals is the impulse to go on living. But it is quite a different thing for a creature with Reason to want to live from what it is for a creature without it. That is why human beings can commit suicide and animals can't.

I am sceptical then when human beings begin envying animals, witness Walt Whitman who thought he could turn and live with them—

> They do not sweat and whine about their condition,
> They do not lie awake in the dark and weep for their sins,
> They do not make me sick discussing their duty to God,
> Not one is dissatisfied, not one is demented with the mania of owning things,
> Not one kneels to another, nor to his kind that lived thousands of years ago,
> Not one is respectable or unhappy over the whole earth.[3]

Whitman is quite right, they don't, but how would Whitman have liked it if he had found himself an animal and deprived of the gift of the gab? Man is an unhappy animal and one that can talk. If he was not unhappy he would have nothing to talk about. But if he had nothing to talk about, he would be unhappy. (Sort that out for yourselves.)

A friend of mine gives me a recent example of pseudo-philosophy *re* animals.[4] He was bathing last week from a graveyard on the Severn in company with a Gloucestershire parson, his daughters, and dog. The dog barked when the daughters went

---

[3] Walt Whitman (1819–92), 'Song of Myself', sect. 32, st. 2.
[4] Probably Graham Shepard (1907–43): see n. 7 of 'London Letter [2]' (March 1941) below.

into the water. My friend commented on the dog's concern for the daughters and the parson, speaking with authority, for he swam in churchyard waters, said: 'Children and dogs give you your faith.'

To turn to the Greeks who would have thought Whitman a monster and the parson in the Severn crazy, Plato said that it is the top part of the soul which makes the man,[5] and Aristotle said that the human soul is not vegetative soul (the characteristic of plants) *plus* appetitive soul (the characteristic of beasts), *plus* rational soul, but that the addition of this third element, far from being mere addition, suffuses and transforms the other elements under it.[6] The spiritual chemistry of the whole undergoes a conclusive change. For example, a house without a roof is not, properly speaking, a house. Animals are—from our point of view—like houses which have never had roofs. All animals, therefore, are from our point of view anomalies.

I enjoy looking at animals, therefore, not because they are like me, but because they are different—even more different than my sleeping self is from my waking self. I can never have a good look at my sleeping self, but I can go one better and have a good look at an animal. I can admire in him that freedom from pros and cons to which in my waking life I myself can never attain (even supposing I wanted to). And I myself, when I look at an animal in the Zoo, am not responsible for him, cannot communicate with him, do not envy him. How few human beings does one meet on these terms.

I started going to the Zoo this summer after I had moved house to within earshot of it. For a year and a half I had lived in Hampstead,[7] with a garden of my own—roses, syringa, woodpigeons, and owls. I now found I should probably have no more garden. The lists of the house agents appalled me. The house agencies were ruled by a pompous and hygienic *Zeitgeist*. Brochures of mansion flats called me to the 'Art of Gracious Living', or the 'Most Thoughtful Flats in London'. In disgust I decided I would be neither Thoughtful nor Gracious; I would live somewhere dank, inconvenient, insanitary. But my desire

[5] Plato, *Phaedrus*, 245–6.

[6] Aristotle, *De anima* 2. 2, 413^{b}11–33.

[7] 4a Keats Grove, London, NW3, a garden flat rented from Geoffrey Grigson: see Grigson, *Recollections* (1984), 74.

for comfort made me compromise. Stream-lined efficiency is sinister because things do exactly what they are meant to do and leave no trail behind them; how much less real cars have become since they purified their exhausts. Still, up to a point one wants one's house to be tractable just as one would rather have a car than a bicycle. (Talking of cars, of course, their functionalism is largely hooey; the bonnet would be better behind and stream-lining makes no difference to speed under speeds of eighty miles an hour.) So I took an upper maisonette looking over Primrose Hill.[8]

Trees in front and a view to Highgate behind but no garden. It occurred to me that I was very near the Zoo. The Zoo would do for my garden. I should be able to drop into the Zoo for a coffee, look at one animal and come out again. I should never again be in the position of having to 'do' the Zoo. Doing anything kills it.

While I was between house and house I cherished this prospect. I would not take over the Zoo until I had taken over my flat. But my anticipations were pleasant for I have always fancied wild animals.

My crush on wild animals began when I was very small. My favourite book was *Cassell's Natural History*, a large Mid-Victorian work in two volumes, heavy to lift, illustrated with engravings which are so much more romantic than photographs.[9] This book had the charm of its period, being long-winded, discursive, and moralistic, full of quotations from the poets and curious anecdotes. The first section, on the Primates, had an alarming series of illustrations of brains and skeletons; many of the skeletons were climbing up trees. Many of the pictures were action pictures; there was one called 'The Lion, the Tiger, and the Jaguar', where these three animals were engaged in a three-some battle in the jungle, regardless of the fact that there is no jungle in the world which contains all three species. On the other hand there were some very sumptuous still lifes, such as an almost full-page engraving entitled 'Food of American Monkeys'. Every so often there was a coloured

---

[8] 16a Primrose Hill Road, London, NW3, an upper maisonette of 5 sunny rooms: see MacNeice's letter of 10 April 1938 to Mrs E. R. Dodds, Bodleian Library.

[9] *Cassell's Natural History*, ed. P[eter] M[artin] D[uncan], illus., 2 vols. (1876–82; many other edns).

plate—a naked man playing with a squirrel (must have been Adam), a collection of angora cats among green and purple cushions, wolves with red mouths and red eyes and almost Walt Disney teeth.

The same naïve romance of Natural History is to be found in some of the paintings of the Douanier Rousseau who, having been sent to Mexico on military service by Napoleon III,[10] retained ever after a vision of elegantly plaited jungle where idyllic monkeys lunch on full-moon fruits and striped tigers walk delicately through foliage cut like metal-work. For all these *paysages exotiques*, however overcrowded, have the tidiness of a *petit bourgeois* parlour—the palm-leaves are just so, the lion must stay on the mantelpiece.

I cannot remember if the first Zoo I visited was Dublin or London. I know that the first monkey I saw was an organ-grinder's monkey in Ireland scooping for pennies in a gutter of Irish mud. There was also a stuffed monkey which an old lady kept in her parlour and to which at the age of eight I wrote an ode, beginning:

> O monkey though now thou art stuffed
> Thou hast very often roughed
> A night out in the wild forest. . . .[11]

I went to the Zoo in Dublin at the same time as my father went to the General Synod of the Church of Ireland.

The Dublin Zoo is in Phoenix Park. Founded in 1830, it was the first place in Europe where they bred lions. The lions—though this is difficult to believe—were said to like the climate. As far as I can remember, the Dublin lions disappointed me, looked a shade moth-eaten. Many years afterwards I went to the Dublin Zoo after a rough crossing and, still rocking on my feet, watched a keeper spraying the feet of an elephant who had

---

[10] Henri Rousseau (1844–1910), the 'primitive' French painter noted for his childlike, ideographic style, was later, as a former 'customshouse officer' called *le douanier*. During a 4-year term of military service entirely in France, he heard fascinating stories—from soldiers who had survived the French expedition to Mexico (1862–5) in support of Emperor Maximilian—of exotic subtropical landscapes, which became one of his major themes: *Encyclopaedia Britannica*, 15th edn, 30 vols. (1974, 1984), Macropaedia xv. 1169. (Napoleon III or Louis-Napoléon, 1808–73, was emperor of France 1852–70.)

[11] 'An Ode to a Stuffed Monkey': *Strings*, 59.

foot-rot—bantering him in a brogue for the diversion of the visitors. I remember a common donkey in a heavily barred cage marked 'This Animal is Dangerous', and several cages which were empty, overgrown with grass like the drives up to the Irish Big Houses. When I left Phoenix Park the streets were crowded with beasts going to a cattle fair—squealing of pigs, smell of cow-dung and shag—and some children were sitting in the gutter making dung pies. Dublin has such a strongly physical presence, even in its brick and stone, that a zoo seems hardly necessary.

A town where I really welcomed the Zoo was Edinburgh. I stayed in Edinburgh in my early 'teens with my family and even then realized that the place was dead. Edinburgh is far deader than Dublin. I became depressed by the shadow of Edinburgh Castle and by the architectural freaks—the Scott Memorial[12] and the Parthenon on the Calton Hill.[13] So every morning I used to go out by tram to the Zoo. The Edinburgh Zoo lies on the slope of a hill looking to the sun, and I climbed from beast to beast in a kind of make-believe Pilgrim's Progress. I seem to remember parrots perched in the open air among bright red flowers. I re-visited this Zoo last year and found it still delightful; it now contains the finest artificial tiger-pit in Europe.

While I was at school at Marlborough my father had a curate who was Anglo-Catholic[14] (an unheard-of-thing in our parish) and, also unheard of, zoo-crazy. He lived in a shack which was really a soldier's home and built there a huge rabbit house, pasted round inside with photographs of lions. He always winced when he saw closely mown grass because he considered it an outrage against Nature. He read detective stories all night, smoked cigarettes incessantly, bought a motor-bicycle he couldn't ride, and told the old ladies of the parish that there

[12] 'An 1844 Gothic spire, 200 feet high, that rises above a statue of Sir Walter Scott and his hound, Maida': *Encyclopaedia Britannica*, ed. cit., Macropaedia vi. 306.

[13] (William Henry) Playfair's Parthenon, on Calton Hill at the east end of Princes Street, was an unfinished project, a Temple of Minerva for the National Monument: '12 stark columns, standing like a ruin from some vanished Aegean civilization', launched in 1822 'as a memorial to Scots who served in the Napoleonic Wars but tagged "Scotland's Pride and Poverty" when the money ran out in 1830': ibid. vi. 307.

[14] The Revd Thomas Bloomer was at Carrickfergus Parish Church (St Nicholas) 1918–22.

was nothing to touch a black panther. He and I used to take in fortnightly instalments a work called *Hutchinson's Animals of All Countries*[15]—a characterless work when compared with *Cassell's Natural History*.

When the curate left I knew no one who was really a zoo-fan, so I fell back on household cats, for my family had no dog. Every house, I think, should have a cat, for then you can be sure there will be at least one thing in the house that knows how to use its limbs. Our cats had suffered from a crazy cook who wore false pearls and thought the cats would die if they crossed the backyard wall. I had to wait for a really responsive cat until I had a house of my own.

My cat was short-haired ginger and I got him when he was very small; his ears were so out of proportion that he seemed to be swinging between them. His paws were like melting butter, he had a bird-like chirp and he responded to the word 'Milk'. When he grew up he used to bring live mice into my bed. He was very sexy in spring (I should never have dreamed of having him neutered, though cat-lovers say it is cruel to leave a cat male) and used to begin his serenades inside the house. We would then open the bedroom window and he would walk out, still singing, along the horizontal branch of a pear tree and, still singing, would descend its trunk and go far across the garden and over a high brick wall.

A little later, while in the same house (it was in Birmingham), I bought an Old English Sheepdog puppy, having been assured by its breeder that it would be no trouble to groom. This, like most things told one by dog-breeders, was untrue. As she grew bigger—and she grew very fast—her coat got shaggier and her feet more cart-horse and, as she lolloped more than cart-horses do, her mud-displacement was immense. And there was nothing she liked better than rolling in any kind of mess. The most astonishing thing about a sheepdog is that it has an expression—or rather that it has several. How this is possible through all that mass of hair I do not profess to understand.

At the same time, for contrast, we had a pug. The pug in my opinion is far the most elegant and characterful of toy-dogs.

---

[15] By Frank Finn, Martin A. C. Hinton, *et al.*, 50 pts. in 4 vols. (1923-5)—disappointing because the illustrations were 'characterless' photographs, not lively engravings as in *Cassell's*.

This was a very small bitch, a pure apricot fawn, with enormous lustrous eyes. Contrary to pug tradition she refused to get
fat, was extremely neurotic and would pirouette for hours
when excited, her tongue hanging out and her eyes popping to
bursting-point. We used to polish her with a hand-glove and
take her to shows; she did very well at Cruft's.[16]

The English dog show is the sort of thing Pareto ought to
have put in his footnotes to *The Mind and Society*, these footnotes
being, as Aldous Huxley said of them, a museum of human
folly.[17] No foreigner who wants to see the crazy English at their
ripest can afford to miss a big dog show. Hardly anywhere else
can you pick up with so little effort such gems of impossible
logic or blatant but unconscious egotism—Love me, love my
dog and hate everybody else's. It is a sheer delight to walk
through these great draughty halls, which dog papers always
call venues, and listen to the air ricochetting with virulence and
vanity.

The first time I showed, it was my sheepdog. I had hardly
ever seen any full-grown show sheepdogs and she turned out to
be half their size—'very poor bone', the judge said, wrinkling
her nose. (The show Old English Sheepdog weighs over a
hundred pounds; pity the sheep if there were any.) My sheepdog and I sat on the bench next to a working-man, who was
next to a titled lady whose dogs had a 'play-attic'. Her dog had
beaten his. 'The old bitch', he kept saying, 'what do you
expect? Army of men to brush them for her'. And his anger
puffing to Heaven blended with a cloud of French chalk as his
dog got up lumberingly and shook itself.

The personnel of a dog show is paradoxical. The toy department offers you six-foot Sapphos in breeches and hard-bitten
men who might be champions at billiards. Whereas the St
Bernards and Great Danes have often drawn tiny sentimental
old ladies with game legs who feed their pets upon bull's-eyes.

The dog show is a medium for the most arrogant self-

---

[16] Charles Cruft (1852–1938), 'the founder and organizer of Cruft's Dog Show', at
the Royal Agricultural Hall, during the second week in Feb. since 1890, 'the greatest
annual event of its kind in the world', 'open to all breeds': obit. in *The Times*, 12 Sept.
1938, 14d; tribute, ibid., 19 Sept., 8d.

[17] See MacNeice's review 'Charlatan-Chasing' (Nov. 1935) above with n. 5 on
Huxley. For MacNeice's notice of a dog show, see 'With the Kennel Club', *Night and
Day* 1: 16 (14 Oct. 1937), 40.

expression, the most decadent kind of virtuosity. Nearly all these dogs are artificial products of the fancies, artificially bred and artificially trimmed. I do not myself deplore their fancy breeding. Dogs lead such artificial lives that they may as well look artificial into the bargain. All I would ask is that they should keep their breeds differentiated. It is a great bore when all the other terriers begin to look like Airedales. And it is a shame to prune Kerry Blues of their magnificent coats.

A good example is the Sealyham. The Sealyham, say the older breeders, is becoming a sissy—no good for badger. But few serious badger-hunters are going to bother to chalk up their dogs for a parade at Olympia or the Bingley Hall or Belle Vue Gardens.[18] These parades are held to gratify the suburban dog-owners of England who know nothing about badgers and whose dogs would be too many in number to loose on all the badgers there are. What does matter is not that the selective breeding of Sealyhams has made them less badger-worthy, but that when a Sealyham gets too narrow in the head he loses his expression of *bonhomie*.

After my sheepdog I got a Borzoi bitch with Mythe blood in her but, alas, without the Mythe profile (the Mythe profile, one of the triumphs of breeding for a special feature, is so convex that it is almost the arc of a circle). This bitch, whom I still have, is so silly that it is almost as good as keeping a wild animal. She does no tricks, and is an incorrigible thief. Her eyes are neither human nor doggy, but like the eyes of a film star. She has no traffic sense. When she lies on the floor she is almost as flat as a mat. Though six years old, she has never been mated. I tend to agree with my friends who think this wicked. All animals should have experience of sexual inter-course. It is only human beings who can appreciate the rarefied self-indulgence of asceticism.[19]

Four years ago I also bought a bull mastiff bitch puppy (I prefer bitches for entirely sentimental reasons), a suet-pudding fawn with a black mask. She got dysentery, which led to a

[18] Olympia, Kensington; Bingley Hall, Birmingham; Belle Vue Gardens, Manchester—all General Championship Shows. Olympia was the site of Cruft's Dog Show. Bingley Hall was that of the oldest dog show in the world. Belle Vue Gardens was that of 'the Northern Classic' (i.e. Manchester Championship Show).

[19] Cf. MacNeice's comments on a Christian hermit and sex in para. 2 (with n. 6) of his review 'Modern Writers and Beliefs' (May 1935), *Selected Literary Criticism*, 5.

complete nervous collapse and eventually to paralysis, when she had to be destroyed. It was horrifying, but rather fascinating to notice that when she was already almost imbecile, she retained her reflexes of obedience and with crippled legs and almost sightless eyes would hobble after one when ordered to. Another feature, also horrifying and fascinating, was that till the end she retained her appetite, eating huge quantities of eggs in accordance with the vet's instructions. I found that the vet seemed to regard her disease as a kind of naughtiness. 'Give her no water,' he said, 'it's nonsense the way dogs always want to drink water. My dogs are the same, but I break them of it. It's just a bad habit.'

It is sentimental and misleading to say that a dog is the best companion. It is like saying that the best wine is non-alcoholic. A companion is someone who talks to one and/or to whom one talks on the understanding that one is understood. But at certain moments I prefer a dog to a companion as I might prefer a book, a landscape, or a cigar. For the top part of my soul, the contemplative aesthetic part, a dog is an excellent object for contemplation. Meanwhile, the lower parts of my soul, human though they are because they are never quit of the top part, can enjoy a sort of make-believe animal communion with the authentic animal on the mat.

A dog is an excellent thing to feel with one's hands. I nearly always want to feel things which I admire, for instance, statues (not that I often admire statues), and it is infuriating in a sunset or in the moon that one cannot lay one's hands on them. Of things to feel the best are those which are alive or which have been alive. Hence the appeal of furs as a dress for women. But no woman in a fur is as good—that is aesthetically—as the animal itself in it. The animal knows how to carry it.

I will go then, I said, to the Zoo which is going to be my garden and look at fur in action. But I had not yet moved into my flat. First I had to go over to Ireland. At the risk of appearing egotistical or irrelevant, I will recount this week-end in Ireland because it seems to me a sample. I am talking about the Zoo, and the Zoo has two million annual visitors. All these two million have intricate family backgrounds, a background which is with them in all their hours of recreation. As they pad round the macadam from bears to monkeys they are trailing clouds of history. My Irish week-end will give you a sample of typical personal history. This sample involves a recantation, a modification of attitude, a putting aside of snobbery.[20] That also is relevant to my purpose for no one who goes to the Zoo must go as a snob.

[20] Cf. MacNeice's earlier admission to being 'both a money snob and a class snob' in 'Dialogue with My Guardian Angel' in *Minch*, chap. 9 (written in Aug. 1937); there has thus been an important personal change in 1937–8.

A Personal Digression[1]

The week-end was all sunshine. I could not remember Belfast like this, and the continuous sunshine delighted but outraged me. My conception of Belfast, built up since early childhood, demanded that it should always be grey, wet, repellent and its inhabitants dour, rude, and callous. This conception had already been shaken last night in the boat-train from London; a Belfast man sitting opposite me at dinner was nice to my little boy,[2] said: 'A child should live a life like an animal till it's five.' This did not seem true to type. Belfast men were expected to be sadists whose only jokes are gruesome—*D'ye know what I saw yesterday—a boot floating down the river? There's nothing much in that. Nothing much in it! There was a leg in it.*

Breakfast in my family's house[3] was as ample as always. The same porridge on the side table—each one helping himself—the same breakfast service, the same triangular loaves of shaggy bread. But the house was not the same. Since living for twenty years in an ordinary little house at Carrickfergus, ten miles down the lough (running the gauntlet daily of factory hooters), and before coming to this large, ugly, but comfortable mansion on the Malone Road, my family had spent three years in a Queen Anne house at Waterford.[4] This break had upset my view of the Black North.

I have always had what may well be a proper dislike and disapproval of the North of Ireland, but largely, as I find on analysis, for improper—i.e. subjective—reasons. A harassed and dubious childhood under the hand of a well-meaning but

---

[1] *Zoo* (Nov. 1938), chap. 5, 78–86. An earlier draft of this chapter, an article entitled 'Recantation' (but virtually the same except that, in the book, two paras. were added at the end of chap. 5), was published in *The Honest Ulsterman*, Louis MacNeice Number, no. 73 (Sept. 1983), 4–9.

[2] Daniel MacNeice, born mid-May 1934.

[3] Bishop's House, Malone Road, Belfast—home of his father the Rt. Revd John Frederick MacNeice (1866–1942), Bishop of Down and Connor and Dromore 1934–42.

[4] Bishopsgrove, Waterford—home of his father when Bishop of Cashel and Waterford 1931–4.

barbarous mother's help from County Armagh[5] led me to think of the North of Ireland as prison and the South as a land of escape. Many nightmares, boxes on the ears, a rasping voice of disapproval, a monotonous daily walk to a crossroads called Mile Bush, sodden haycocks, fear of hell-fire, my father's indigestion—these things, with on the other side my father's Home Rule sympathies and the music of his brogue, bred in me an almost fanatical hatred for Ulster. When I went to bed as a child I was told: 'You don't know where you'll wake up.' When I ran in the garden I was told that running was bad for the heart. Everything had its sinister aspect—milk shrinks the stomach, lemon thins the blood. Against my will I was always given sugar in my tea. The North was tyranny.

When I was older and went to school in England[6] my dislike of the North was maintained. At school I felt among my equals, but when I came home I belonged nowhere. There was a great gulf between myself and the bare-foot boys in the streets. When I passed the men who stood most of the day, spitting, at the corners, I imagined that they were spitting at me. (I was the rector's son; they must think that I too disapproved of their swearing and censured the porter on their breath.) A perpetual embarrassment; I was the rector's son.[7]

As for the gentry I did not like them. They were patronizing and snobbish, and it seemed to me, hostile. Hostile because they idolized the military and my father was a clergyman and a pacifist, because they were ardent Unionists, and my father was a Home Ruler.[8] This hostility I almost certainly exaggerated. They no doubt thought of me as a shy and gauche little boy, who being forbidden to play games on Sundays or bathe at the pier, was not over-good company for their own children. I still think, however, that the Ulster gentry are an inferior species. They lack the traditions and easy individuality of the southern Anglo-Irish landowners; comparatively new to their class, they have to keep proving that they are at home in it. A few may try to ape the *bonhomie* of the South, but most of them

---

[5] Miss MacCready, called Miss Craig in *Strings*, 41–59. See Elizabeth, Lady Nicholson, 'Trees Were Green', in *Time Was Away*, 12.

[6] Sherborne Preparatory School for Boys, Dorset, 1917–21.

[7] Cf. 'Carrickfergus' (1937), l. 17: *Collected Poems*, 69–70.

[8] Cf. 'My father was one of the very few Church of Ireland clergymen to be a Home Ruler': *Strings*, 223.

set out to be more English than the English. All the boys go to English public schools and any daughter is a failure who fails to marry a soldier.

I had only been back to the North twice in the last seven years. During most of that time I had lived in Birmingham and now, on this lucid week-end, I compared these two industrial cities and found that Belfast was, if only for the moment, preferable. The voices of Birmingham are flat, dreary, 'with the salt left out of the soup', as someone said to me. The voices of Belfast are harsh and to an English ear unintelligible, but one feels personality behind them. A harsh personality, but something at least to rely on.

Then Belfast has hills around it and shipworks. The town itself is built on mud, resting on thirty-foot piles, but it is at least a town in a significant position—commanding Belfast Lough. Whereas Birmingham commands nothing. Looking up from the tramway junction I saw the Cave Hill blocking the end of the street. And my family's house lay under the Black Mountain—not black, but a luminous grey-blue. There was no speck of wetness on the streets. The macabre elements seemed to have vanished—no El Greco faces under shawls, no torn feet of newsboys leaping on racing trams.

The house was full of azaleas and the long greenhouse of geraniums. Built in the last century by a tea merchant, it was a hideous house, but very comfortable—run by five maids who slept in a wing over the garage. The walls stiff with heavy anaglypta wallpapers,[9] plaster vine-leaves grossly choking the cornices. The wooden panelling on the stairs ended at the turn to the second floor.

On these stairs, gloomy between dark walls under a stained-glass window, hung small engravings—the Bishops of Down and Connor, the Bishops of Dromore. Dr Percy of *Percy's Reliques*, in turban and bands,[10] Dr Dickson with powdered hair and beau's eyebrows,[11] Henry Leslie in a short beard and a ruff.[12] In the dining-room were oil portraits in heavy gilt

---

[9] 'A special type of thick embossed wallpaper': *OED2*.

[10] Thomas Percy (1729–1811), Bishop of Dromore, editor of *Reliques of Ancient English Poetry*, 3 vols. (1765; numerous later edns): for this and other bishops cited in nn. 12–15, see *DNB* and *British Library Catalogue*.

[11] William Dickson (1745–1804), Bishop of Down and Dromore.

[12] Henry Leslie (1580–1661), successively Bishop of Connor and Down, and Bishop of Meath, author of *The Martyrdome of King Charles* (1649).

mitre-topped frames. Dr Hutchinson, of the early eighteenth century, self-possessed, in a heavy wig to his shoulders, a man who knew the world.[13] Next to him Robert Knox of the middle nineteenth, youthful, poetic à la Romantic Revival, floating in lawn sleeves.[14] Over the mantelpiece Jeremy Taylor, moon-faced, quill in effeminate hand, sensitively self-conscious.[15]

In the afternoon we drove through County Down. Ballyna-hinch, Dundrum, Newcastle—drab rows of houses of dun-coloured or slate-coloured stucco. To tea with two elderly ladies under the Mourne Mountains. The spring had pampered their garden. All the trees were blossoming six weeks early—syringa, rhododendron, cherry. Enormous rooks exploded out of the tree-tops. Of six adults at tea three were deaf.

We drove back with the sun sinking on our left. The country was extravagant with gorse as if a child had got loose with the paints. Gorse all over the fields and sprawling on the dykes. Rough stone walls dodged their way up the mountain. A hillside under plough was deeply fluted with shadows. The pairs of fat white gateposts with cone tops showed the small fields of small farmers. Brown hens ran through a field, their combs like moving poppies. Then Belfast again, swans on the Lagan,[16] and home towards the Black Mountain, now a battleship grey, by a road called Chlorine Gardens.

On Sunday morning my father went off to preach at Bally-mena and I went with my stepmother[17] to morning service in the cathedral. Looking at the strictly vertical worshippers in front of me—women's hats level as inverted pudding basins, men's bald patches, red ears, gold spectacle clasps clamping the ears behind, I felt myself again a schoolboy, not at my ease, standing with my hands together and my elbows pressing on my hips, catching solitary phrases—the sea is His and He made it—remembering that it was in this cathedral that my

---

13 Francis Hutchinson (1660–1739), Bishop of Down and Connor, author of *A Short View of the Pretended Spirit of Prophecy* (1708).

14 Robert Bent Knox (1808–93), successively Bishop of Down, Connor, and Dromore, and Archbishop of Armagh, author of *The Irish Church* (1867).

15 Jeremy Taylor (1617–67), Bishop of Down and Connor, and administrator of Dromore, author of *Holy Living* and *Holy Dying* (1650–1).

16 River flowing past Dromore and Lisburn to Belfast Lough at Belfast.

17 Georgina Beatrice Greer (1872–1956), married MacNeice's father 1917.

father scandalized Belfast; he had refused to allow the Union Jack to be hung over Carson's tomb in perpetuity.[18]

Religion in Ireland is, as everyone knows, still a positive influence and still inextricably fused with social life and politics. Few of the Protestants or Presbyterians can see the Cross merely as a cross. Like a man looking into the sun through half-shut eyes, they see it shoot out rays, blossom in the Union Jack. And the Son of God goes forth to war in orange.

Idling in the house on Sunday afternoon, eating chocolates from a box which had been a Christmas present, I noticed that though the house was a different house, the creation of the tea-merchant with his Victorian ideal of taste imposed on posterity (a front door with polished granite pillars and Corinthian capitals: radiators throughout), my family had brought with them so much of the bric-à-brac of years that I still felt, as on my earlier visits to Waterford or Carrickfergus, suspended in a world without progress—eating chocolates left over from Christmas. Here were the same mats, only a little shabbier, floating at anchor in the passages, never quite level with the walls; here were the 'Grecian' black marble clocks, the same blue twine-box on the hall-table (which had cost, no doubt, ninepence but had survived since I could remember), the oil-paintings of the Shamrock Girl and the Cockle Gatherers, the small teak elephants from missionary exhibitions, the little calendars hanging in the lavatories on electric light switches, the solid pond of books of scriptural commentary, the flotsam of occasional literature. The old drawing-room carpet had gone to a top-floor bedroom. Glass cases contained presentation silver teapots, sea-shells, family photographs. In most of the rooms the blinds were drawn against the sun.

In this context I had to admit that I was not in touch with the North of Ireland or with Belfast. Who was I to condemn them? I was insulated with comfort and private memories. It was very possible that Ulstermen were bigots, sadists, witch-doctors, morons. I had seen their Twelfths of July. But I had always

---

[18] Sir Edward (Henry) Carson, Baron Carson of Duncairn (1854–1935), leader of the Ulster Unionists 1911–21, to whose 'courage . . . and capacity . . . Ulster owes her existence': Douglas L. Savory, *DNB 1931–1940*, 151. See *Strings*, 71, 78, and Terence Brown, 'Father and Son', *Time Was Away*, 22–3.

dramatized them into the Enemy. They were not really grandiose monsters. If they were lost, they were lost with a small 'l'.

When I was a little boy and my sister and I had to go to Belfast, we would sit in the train returning home, swinging our legs and chanting 'Belfast! Belfast! The city of smoke and dust!' Belfast was essentially evil—largely because it was new. Living in a town of Norman remains, I had held the doctrine that oldness was in itself a merit and new things *ipso facto* bad. This doctrine I no longer hold, so I must absolve Belfast on that score. For the rest I consider that Belfast politics are deplorable and the outlook of her citizens much too narrow. But that is not good enough reason for hating her citizens. If I hate, I only make them more hateable. And even if I had adequate grounds for hating them, I still ought to make sure that I am not hating them mainly because I identify them with the nightmares of my childhood.

The boat for Heysham left at 9.45 on Sunday night. A row of girls on the deck was singing 'When Irish eyes are smiling'. And before the gangway was loosened Lord Craigavon[19] came on board. The eyes continued smiling and we left for England. One must not dislike people, I thought, because they are intransigent. For that would be only playing their own game.

The night was full of stars and a moon two-thirds full sat steadily above the funnel. Not having yet reached its brilliance it showed its features clearly, resembling the death mask of Dean Swift.[20] The water was still and, as the boat moved gently out, a dark lead expanse, but lustrous, widened between the boat and the quay. The lights on the quay-side sheds were reflected in the water, but each reflection appeared to be two lights rather than one. From the Lagan bridge behind us the lamps plunged organ-pipe reflections deep into the river. The

---

[19] James Craig, the 1st Viscount Craigavon of Stormont, Co. Down (1871–1940), the chief lieutenant of the Ulster leader Sir Edward Carson, and Prime Minister of Northern Ireland 1922–40.

[20] Jonathan Swift (1667–1745), Dean of St Patrick's Cathedral, Dublin, the great Irish patriot and satirist. Swift's death-mask to which MacNeice refers here in 1938 was, in fact, a fabricated plaster head, an inferior specimen deposited in Trinity College, Dublin, and discounted by Sir Leslie Stephen: *DNB* xix. 222. However, T[homas] G[eorge] Wilson has since demonstrated the obscure survival of the original genuine mask: 'A Hitherto Undescribed Death-Mask of Dean Swift': *Journal of The Royal Society of Antiquaries of Ireland* 81 (1951), 107–14, with fig. 2.

boat moved in its sleep. Gliding on a narrow channel through a jungle of steel.

As we went faster, crinkling the water a little, the reflections squirmed like tadpoles, the double reflections from the sheds regularly and quietly somersaulting. Two cranes facing each other conferred darkly. In the widening channel the lines of reflected lights behind us stretched in uncertain alleys like the lines of floating corks set out for swimmers. A black motor-boat cutting across them threw out shooting stars behind it. A buoy skated rapidly backwards winking periodically red. Then the cranes and quays fell away and the channel opened into the lough—a single line of lights on each side—like a man stretching his arms and drawing a breath. Cassiopeia was tilted in her deck-chair over Antrim; Arcturus over Down.

I went into the smoke-room (the whole boat was luxuriously appointed). To-morrow I shall be back in London, visiting a house-agent. It was he, himself an Irishman from Limerick, who said to me two days ago: 'The Englishman is bigger. He doesn't let things upset him so.' Yes, I thought, the Irishman, like the elephant, never forgets; it is time that I forgot my nightmares. Before going to bed I went out again on deck. The night was cold and clouding; the moon had a slight aura. On our right the Copelands lighthouse[21] swept its light at intervals from west to east as if shooing us away from our country.

[21] At SE entrance to Belfast Lough.

To-day in Barcelona[1]

I was in Barcelona from December 29th till January 9th. The most surprising things I saw were on January 9th—in Toulouse, where I landed by 'plane from Spain: food in the shops and on stalls in the streets, drink in the cafés, well-clad people, the street-lamps lit. It only takes one ten days to find these things surprising.

I had arrived in Barcelona after dark, the streets like limbo but crowded. A feeling of thousands of people circulating round one in the night. That is one thing there is plenty of here—human beings; two and a half millions now against one million before. These people's lives have become very much simplified and assimilated to one another; the topics of conversation are few and universal, money has lost its diversifying force, and everyone, one feels, is by necessity in the same boat. For this reason one feels very much at home in the dark streets of Barcelona. There may be bitter dissensions among the politicians, but the people in the streets, one feels, have become a family party—or, if you prefer it, are in on the same racket—united by material necessities, by hunger, by the fear of sudden death which enhances the values of life. I have never been anywhere where these values were so patent. It would be difficult to be a Hamlet in Barcelona.

The shops are ghosts of shops, only open in the morning, the counters and shelves bare, one object every two yards. The cafés are ghosts of cafés—no coffee, beer, spirits, or wine, people making do with coloured water which is called lemonade or with terribly degraded vermouth (yet in one café there was a string quartet). They close at nine and the chairs are piled on the tables. But the people, though thin and often ill, are far

---

[1] *Spectator* 162: 5769 (20 Jan. 1939), 84–5. Cf. MacNeice's concise verse account in *Autumn Journal*, xxiii (*Collected Poems*, 148–50), and his extensive prose account in *Strings*, chap. 35, 176–96. This was MacNeice's second visit to Spain (his first had been at Easter 1936). Barcelona, the main centre of Republican strength, was under attack in the Spanish Civil War, July 1936–Jan. 1939, when its fall led to the Republican government's final surrender, March 1939.

from being ghosts of people. Facts in a city at war are necessarily uncertain; how can one know the truth about the Front or unravel the paradoxical knots of Spanish party politics or sort out truth from propaganda? One fact, however, is as clear— and as refreshing—as daylight: the extraordinary morale of these people—their courage, good-humour, and generosity.

Their strength, of course, can also be their weakness. Optimism on the Government side has already meant several gains for Franco.[2] Again, while a people must obviously adapt themselves to war conditions, it does not seem altogether desirable that war should become quite so much a habit as it has in Barcelona; one feels the people have almost forgotten about peace and might not know what to do with it if it came. Yet without this confidence and this adaptation to circumstances, Barcelona no doubt would have already given way to Goliath. Her people are essentially non-defeatist; no one this New Year admitted for a moment that Franco's present offensive[3] might succeed. I saw a new *comedor*[4] for children in an industrial district, which is being converted from a theatre and adjacent cinema.

In this, once the great city of cafés and taxis, you now have to get about by walking. And instead of cocktails and seven-course meals there are food-queues, rationing of acorns, a ladleful of lentils for dinner. By ordinary people food cannot be bought though it can be obtained by barter: soap, flints, and tobacco are among the best currencies. (I am told that Arabs come into the port and sell soap at 250 pesetas a kilo.) In my hotel[5] (where the bombing commissions stay) we had a privileged access to food—at fancy prices: a dish of chickpeas at 30 to 40 pesetas, horse and chopped swedes at 45, fried sprats (a very rare delicacy) at 60. (A superintendent of a *comedor* gets 400

---

[2] The Republican attack in the Battle of Ebro River, July–Nov. 1938, was met by relentless Nationalist air attacks and counter-attacks on the ground—directed by General Don Francisco Franco Bahamonde (1892–1975). After the International Brigades were withdrawn, a Nationalist counter-offensive beginning 30 Oct. crushed the Army of the Ebro by 18 Nov. See Brigadier Peter Young, *A Dictionary of Battles 1816–1976* (1977), 556–7.

[3] General Franco launched a massive new offensive in Catalonia, 23 Dec. 1938; on 26 Jan. 1939 his troops captured Barcelona with minimal resistance. See ibid. 555; but NB some of the year dates in Young are misprints.

[4] Dining hall; idiomatic for 'soup kitchen'.

[5] The Ritz: *Strings*, 179–80.

pesetas a month salary.) People's rations[6] at the moment (they are always decreasing) are as follows:—Bread: 150 grammes per day except on Sundays. Chickpeas (100gr.) and peas (50) on one ticket, but you only get these once a week or maybe once a month. Oil: ¼ litre, but they have had none now for three months and then it was like machine oil. They have had no fish on ration tickets for two months, no meat for one month. Those who, instead of having ration-cards go to the *comedores*, seem to me to be better off, because at any rate they know what they will get. And the children are considered first; for all that their diet is causing a vast increase in rickets and in skin diseases such as scabies. I should add that the people who work in the *comedores* seem invariably good-humoured, kindly, and strictly conscientious.

In these extremities statistics are more important than impressions, but here are some snippets from my visit. *The crowing of cocks*:[7] most characteristic sound in Barcelona (as if you were to hear cocks in Piccadilly). Lots of people keep hens or rabbits on their window balconies. *Lack of tobacco*: to give a man a cigarette is to give him the Kingdom of Heaven; I gave a Spaniard three cigarettes one night, and next day he sent me in return a hunk of dry bread wrapped in paper. *Refugee colonies*: often in converted convents, beds in the gloom under towering Gothic arches, old women with eye diseases making jokes about Mr Chamberlain, the children doing eurhythmics.[8] *Schools*: shortage of teachers, but the children clean (though washed in cold water) and happy, the walls often decorated with figures from Walt Disney—the Big Bad Wolf representing Fascism—or with Popeye the Sailor knocking Mussolini for a loop.[9] All the children seem to be natural artists; in some schools they still print their own poems and lino-cuts.

Air raids: The siren is like the voice of a lost soul, but the anti-aircraft defence is beautiful both to hear and to see—balls of

---

[6] For what follows cf. 'some facts about rationing', ibid. 188.

[7] Cf. *Autumn Journal*, xxiii. 44–5, 116 (end line) (*Collected Poems*, 149–50), and *Strings*, 181.

[8] Cf. *Strings*, 183; similar comparisons in subsequent notes. (Arthur) Neville Chamberlain's (1869–1940) efforts for 'peace in our time' had culminated in the notorious Munich Pact with Hitler (Sept. 1938) and in the resultant partition of Czechoslovakia.

[9] *Strings*, 182–3.

cottonwool floating high in the blue day, or white flashes at night.[10] The searchlights also are beautiful, and the red tracer bullets floating in chains gently, almost ineptly, upwards like decorations at a fair. After the raid on the centre on New Year's Eve the streets were heaped with powdered glass, and crowds collected to look at a spatter of black blood-spots fifteen feet high on a wall. During an alarm in Tarragona four girls romped down the square with their arms round each other's necks.[11] *Ruins*: near the cathedral a house six storeys high, its face and floors torn away; on the top storey a plate-rack fixed to the wall with all its plates unbroken and a shelf with two unbroken bottles.[12] The district to the side of the port, Barceloneta, has been evacuated; all the streets are rubble, and all the houses like skulls.[13] *Irony*: the Banco de Vizcaya still announces stock market prices for July 17th, 1936, and the chemists sell cures for obesity. *Recreation*: every Friday afternoon a crack orchestral concert, well attended, in the enormous Teatro di Liceo; the theatres and cinemas all running; a newsreel showing a fashionable dog show in Moscow. And people still playing pelota.[14] But the Zoo is macabre—a polar bear 99 per cent. dead, a kangaroo eating dead leaves.

In the Barcelona airport I met an American seaman, an ex-member of the International Brigade, short, square, and tough, with a face like a gangster.[15] On his lapel he wore the insignia of all the Government parties—to create good feeling, he said. He expressed the greatest admiration for the Spaniards—even, in spite of what some people say, as soldiers. I shared his admiration and, as I flew down from the Pyrenees to a country where money still goes, I felt that my descent into this respectable landscape was not only a descent in metres but also a step down in the world.

[10] Ibid. 184–5.
[11] Ibid. 193–4.
[12] Ibid. 183–4.
[13] Ibid. 184.
[14] Ibid. 189; *Autumn Journal* xxiii. 35 (*Collected Poems*, 149).
[15] *Strings*, 195–6.

Autobiographical Sketch[1]

Born in Belfast. Both parents Irish, from Connemara. Father (Rt Revd John Frederick MacNeice) now Protestant Bishop of Down, Connor, and Dromore; mother Elizabeth Margaret Clesham MacNeice.[2] Sent to Marlborough School, in England, 1917.[3] Read classics and philosophy at Oxford, 1926–30; Merton College. First in 'Greats'. 1930, married Giovanna Marie Thérèse Ezra, and appointed lecturer in classics at the University of Birmingham. Held this post till 1936, when appointed lecturer in Greek at Bedford College for Women in the University of London. Think the present English system of teaching the classics is bad. One son;[4] marriage dissolved 1936. 1940, special lecturer in English for the spring semester at Cornell University.

At various periods have done a lot of book-reviewing, etc. Contributed to most of the English periodicals, e.g. the *Spectator*, the *New Statesman and Nation*, the *Morning Post*, *New Writing*, the *London Mercury*, the *Criterion*, the *Times Literary Supplement*.[5]

Influences: at Oxford, T. S. Eliot, James Joyce, D. H. Lawrence, sundry philosophers (have long ago ceased reading philosophy). Nowadays prefer history, biography, statistics. Rarely read novels. Consider the world's greatest novel is Tolstoy's *War and Peace*. Wrote three novels in my early twenties—all bad.[6]

---

[1] *Twentieth Century Authors: A Biographical Dictionary of Modern Literature*, ed. Stanley J. Kunitz and Howard Haycraft (1942), 888–9. The entry is preceded by 'MAC NEICE, LOUIS (September 12, 1907–   ), Irish poet, writes:', and is accompanied by a small photo of the poet.

[2] The Rt. Revd J. F. MacNeice (1866–1942); E. M. Clesham (1866–1914). Entries for the bishop in *Who's Who* are spelled 'McNeice', to show his solidarity with all-Ireland, against Partition.

[3] Year when MacNeice was sent to Sherborne School for Boys, Dorset; he entered Marlborough in 1921.

[4] Dan[iel], born mid-May 1934.

[5] Articles and reviews in the first six periodicals; no articles or reviews discovered, unsigned, in *TLS*: possibly letters?

[6] *Roundabout Way* (1932) by pseud. 'Louis Malone', followed by the unpublished 'The F. Vet [Family Vet?]' and another also unpublished: see E. R. Dodds's notes to MacNeice's *Strings*, 143. No manuscripts of the last two early novels survive.

Politics: distrust all parties but consider capitalism must go. Visited Barcelona, New Year's Eve 1939,[7] and hold that in the Spanish Civil War the balance of right was certainly on the side of the Republican Government: the situation, however, much more complex than represented in the English press. Am opposed to Partition in Ireland.[8] Would normally vote Labour in England, but think the Labour Party won't get anywhere till they have got rid of their reactionary leaders.

Have been connected with the English Group Theatre in London, who produced my translation of the *Agamemnon* of Aeschylus (1936) and my bad experimental play, *Out of the Picture*.[9] Am now writing a trilogy of one-act plays, possibly for the Abbey Theatre, Dublin.[10] Think the London West End stage is moribund.

Forthcoming works include a new book of poems; *The Roman Smile* (literary criticism); a verse translation of the *Hippolytus* of Euripides, and a quasi-autobiographical book.[11] Have also, in addition to my own books, contributed articles to various books of literary criticism. Most of my books have been published in America.[12]

Continuation[13]

1941—joined the staff of the BBC[14] as script-writer and producer and have remained in this position till now, except for

[7] See his article 'To-day in Barcelona' (Jan. 1939), above.

[8] In this Irish position MacNeice was in agreement with his father; see n. 2 above.

[9] *Agamemnon* (pub. Oct. 1936) was performed 1 and 8 Nov. 1936; *Out of the Picture* (pub. June 1937), 5 and 12 Dec. 1937—both at the Westminster Theatre, London.

[10] These short plays do not appear to be extant.

[11] 'The Roman Smile', an unpublished work on Latin humour, is extant as a long typescript of 11 chaps. MacNeice's verse translation of the first chorus from Euripides' *Hippolytus* was published in *Poetry* (Poetry London) 2 (April 1939) [8–9], unpaginated; the rest of the verse translation was not made, at least has not survived. The 'quasi-autobiographical book' was published posthumously by E. R. Dodds as *The Strings are False: An Unfinished Autobiography* [1907–1940] (1965).

[12] The above sketch is followed by two brief paras. of editorial comment and a brief bibliography.

[13] Continuation of autobiographical sketch in *Twentieth Century Authors: First Supplement: A Biographical Dictionary of Modern Literature*, ed. Stanley J. Kunitz and Vineta Colby (Sept. 1955), 624–5, accompanied by two paras. of comment and a brief bibliography of additional works.

[14] May 1941.

an eighteen-month secondment 1950–1 to the British Council
as Director of the British Institute in Athens. Based in London
during World War II. Since then have made quite a few visits
abroad—to France, Norway, Italy, and India.

American Letter[1]

Dear Stephen,[2]

Just had your letter. I never wrote you my little synopsis of what America thinks about the war as I don't know what America thinks and, if I did, I couldn't synopt it. It is a truism, of course, that nearly all Americans want to stay out of it just as people want the weather to be fine; they know, however, that war is as arbitrary as weather and that, whether Mahomet wants it or not, this is a world where the mountains come knocking at his door. I met one professor who thought that if the Pope and Roosevelt got together they could fix up everything beautifully. On the whole, however, the most lively comments I have heard were from non-Americans. From Liam O'Flaherty,[3] for instance, who spent a lunch-hour in New York lambasting Ralph Bates[4] (Bates, as you probably know, outraged his old comrades by denouncing the Russo-German pact and the Soviet invasion of Finland).[5] O'Flaherty, who, like many Irish revolutionaries, wears a veneer of would-be

[1] *Horizon* 1: 7 (July 1940), 462, 464.

[2] Sir Stephen (Harold) Spender (1909–), the poet-friend of Auden and MacNeice. (See MacNeice's review of Spender's *The Destructive Element* (May 1935) in his *Selected Literary Criticism*, 4–7.) MacNeice wrote this letter from Cornell University, Ithaca, NY, where he was teaching poetry for the Easter semester 1940: *Strings*, chap. 2, 23 ff.

[3] Liam O'Flaherty (1896–1984)—the novelist and short-story writer from Aran, Ireland, the author of *The Informer* (1925; film by John Ford 1935) and of *Famine* (1937), a foundation member of the Irish Academy of Letters—arrived in New York City on 8 Feb. 1940: see *New York Times*, 9 Feb. 1940, 8c. O'Flaherty was a republican who supported Irish neutrality in World War 2; he spent the war years in Connecticut, the Caribbean, and South America: see Paul A. Doyle, *Liam O'Flaherty* (1971), 14.

[4] Ralph Bates (1899–), the English writer who had taken an active part in Republican politics in Spain 1930–7, appeared to turn his back on his old comrades in his article 'Disaster in Finland', *New Republic* 101: 1306 (13 Dec. 1939), 221–5, exposing the Russian and German *realpolitik* of invasion. Bates became Professor Emeritus of Literature, New York University.

[5] The USSR and Germany signed a non-aggression pact (23 Aug. 1939) before invading and dividing Poland in Sept. On 30 Nov. 1939 the USSR invaded Finland which repulsed attacks, until a new and massive Russian offensive launched on 1 Feb. 1940 crushed the Finns by 12 March: see Peter Young, *A Dictionary of Battles 1816–1976* (1977), 516–17, 458–9.

sense over a welter of violent, anarchic impulse, said the Russo-German pact was one of the best things that had ever happened; it had cleared the Pinks out of politics.

When we landed in New York,[6] there was ice on the quays and the sky was a candid blue like the eyes of a frigid woman. New York[7]—or, at least, Manhattan—is not only remote from Europe, it is remote from the rest of America. A paradise for escapists—provided they have money. Nickel after nickel into slot after slot, ice-cube after ice-cube into drink after drink, cataracts of peanuts and a labyrinth of lights, chromium, glass, reinforced concrete, every so often a shop being picketed and nobody caring, salacious ads, window-dressing virtuosity, queues in the cold for a doss-house in the Bowery, the electric eels in the Battery aquarium lighting up crimson bulbs, the black church moored at the end of Wall Street—a miniature doom, shoes being shined in every gap in hustle and the ambulance cars screaming. My second night on shore I dreamed I was on a steamer, one among other steamers running amok, a Gaderene stampede through a yellow boiling sea that was full of pylons, all the boats converging, bound to collide; for some reason I liked it.[8]

Last week I flew from New York to Chicago and back.[9] Much of the American landscape being dull from the train, I was astonished by its elegance from the air. Elegance is the word for it—enormous plains of beautifully inlaid rectangles, the grain running different ways, walnut, satinwood, or oatcake, the whole of it tortoise-shelled with copses and shadows of clouds; here and there were little lakes nailed down on the top of the ground like strips of canvas; khaki or bile-green rivers; the cities a mere encrustation limpeted on to a sublimely indifferent continent.[10] On American Airlines they pet you and pamper you, give you scrambled eggs among the clouds, and strawberries and cream, and tell you statistics, but you cannot, with this endless land below you, avoid a beautiful feeling of

---

6 End of Jan. 1940: *Strings*, 21. Cf. para. 1 of 'Touching America' (March 1941) below.

7 Cf. description in *Strings*, chap. 2, 23.

8 Cf. ibid., chap. 1, 21–2.

9 Cf. ibid., chap. 2, 25–6.

10 The same as 'Enormous plains . . . indifferent continent', loc. cit.

futility, of fresh clean scepticism about humanity in general; the elections of Republicans and Democrats, the squabbles of the AFL and the CIO[11] dwindle to a lottery in an ant heap; even if there were war down there on the plains of Indiana, it would just be one more ingredient in the pattern of a sliding map.

This thought of the irrelevance of one part of life to another reminds me of Auden's poem, 'Musée des Beaux Arts'.[12] I don't know that I can tell you where Auden is getting to, but it seems to me he has made this important discovery—that life is false to formula. I hear people are still fussing in England about the ethics of his migration to America. Why bother? The explanation he gave me seems reasonable enough—that an artist ought either to live where he has live roots or where he has no roots at all; that in England to-day the artist feels essentially lonely, twisted in dying roots, always in opposition to a group; that in America he is just as lonely, but so, says Auden, is everybody else; with 140 million lonelies milling around him he need not waste his time either in conforming or rebelling. Whether Americans would agree with this account of their country or not, the argument is valid for Auden. It is no question of *il gran rifiuto*;[13] he feels he can work better here than in Europe, and that is all there is to it.

Speaking for myself, I must say that at the moment I prefer being in America to being in England. Over here, as in England, there has been a great split on the Left and the high-minded keep on throwing mud at each other. Whether the intelligentsia at the moment can directly affect public affairs to any extent seems to me doubtful. What they ought to do is reassess their position *as intellectuals*; it is worth while remembering that there are more than the two alternatives of the Ivory Tower and the political tub.[14] If you come to analyse it, public-mindedness itself can be a form of escapism. I don't think for a moment that we should go all private; what I do

---

[11] The American Federation of Labor and the Committee (later, Congress) of Industrial Organizations.

[12] A poem of Dec. 1938: *The English Auden*, ed. Mendelson (1977), 237.

[13] 'The great refusal': Dante, *Inferno*, iii. 60 (i.e. abdication of responsibility). Cf. MacNeice's *Selected Literary Criticism*, 5, n. 3.

[14] Alternatives: escapism v. propaganda, or art for art's sake v. political commitment.

think is that we have been much too naïve about politics. Perhaps we all need a dose of the desert, and perhaps that is just what we shall get, whether we want it or not.

There is a theory that when one gets over here one can see things in perspective; I don't find that myself, am still desperately out of focus. The trouble is—and, of course, this is a truism—that life can't be dissociated from value. It's no good being a neo-Epicurean; the pig's paradise is only open to pigs. Man *is* a political animal, unfortunately, and one can't live either in a sty or a 'plane for ever.

Louis MacNeice

Ithaca, New York.

The Way We Live Now[1]

There was snow on the pier-roofs as we moved down the Hudson, the surface of the water was roughcast lead, the air was a grey mist, but the scrolls of smoke from the tugs were the purest white. Huge lettering on the quays of Manhattan called you to Miami Cruises. Passing the Battery, I looked with nostalgia at the Wall Street cluster of buildings, pattern of green and white and dull red and terra cotta; there were big pinheads of light already in the skyscraper windows. Brooklyn Bridge swung round into view (so long ago—last week—I had walked home over it at midnight) and then came the Statue of Liberty all dressed up for a charade; we could see her after Manhattan itself was lost. It was dark early: the closed deck was a black corridor—not even the glow of a cigarette. This is the tunnel between two worlds; this is the chrysalis, Lethe.

I shared a cabin with an Irishman who after twenty years was going back to County Cavan; 'Belonging to a neutral country,' he said, 'I can look at this war from an impartial angle.' He slept in his woollen underclothes with his rosary beside him. There were other Irish on board—a poor old woman with a parchment scalp who never could find the electric light switch in her cabin; a big old man with a bog-trotter's face who liked the drink; a dark, tough man without any surplus flesh who had come over to America in 1913. He had been a miner in California, Nevada, and Montana—money about in those days, but the States will never be no good no more. Too many population. You wouldn't believe him the money he had made to lose at poker; took a week off, lost all his wages in Reno. He didn't like Germans—the most domineering race on earth, bull-headed sons of bitches; he knew, he had worked with a German. Real son of a bitch and, like all them Germans, mad.

[1] *Penguin New Writing* 5 (April 1941), 9–14, the fourth in a series of this title; written early Dec. 1940 as stated in para. 1 (MacNeice returned to England, 9 Dec. 1940). Other contributors to this series (Jan. 1941–April 1942) included B. L. Coombes, Willy Goldman, John Sommerfield, V. S. Pritchett, Gordon Jeffery, Leonard York, Donald Swanson, Keith Vaughan. Cf. *Strings*, 17–18.

Crazy about beer, a suicide finally, shot his wife first. But he liked Italians—always very decent, always put a bottle of wine on the table for you. Good in business, too—always try again each time they go bankrupt. But not La Guardia, he didn't like La Guardia—La Guardia's a nigger-lover.[2] And he didn't like the WPA[3] or the Unions. The Unions were the God-damnedest bunch of racketeers in the States; working man can't bring up his family with all the dues he has to pay to the Unions—Social Security and the rest of it.

Faces were dour on board. The most colourful figure was a dwarf—presumably from the World's Fair—who wore a bow tie and an orange shirt and had blond brilliantined hair; sitting in an armchair dangling his tiny legs in perfectly creased trousers he had the impassivity of a Buddha but a business man's puckers round his eyes. The best-dressed figure was a dark-haired, rich young man travelling first who had the long, narrow face of a villain in traditional melodrama. He bought me a drink—'Here's Fun'—and talked about night clubs— 'You know the West End of London as well as I do'—and about Mexico, 'Ooh, the girl-friends!' I preferred two collarless seamen, travelling as passengers, who had a long, long conversation comparing their bouts of malaria. And an old ex-seaman who, after leaving the Navy, had gone on the music halls— Hippodrome in Birmingham, Empire in Belfast—dancing on a table in roller-skates; he had just had all his teeth out, so his conversation was nothing but 'Oh . . . ah . . .'

I had been ten months in the USA, during which time England—for me—had become *Terra Incognita*. The lurid technique of the American radio and press had hidden all Europe in an aura of death; at the same time I could not imagine this death—it was just not compatible with the college students or the New York intellectuals or anyone else I met in America; if this death were real, the Americans before my eyes could not be real too. By autumn I had reached a point where, though England had not regained its reality, my Americans had begun to lose theirs. Therefore to enter the Atlantic tunnel was to

[2] Fiorello H. La Guardia (1882–1947), 'the little flower', the flamboyant and popular reform Mayor of New York City 1933–45.

[3] Work Projects Administration, instituted 1935 to operate public works projects for unemployed persons.

leave a growing unreality for an unreality which I hoped would vanish when I met it; otherwise my return would be—what some of my friends in America considered it anyway—a mere adventure in nihilism. But the answer was not to be Nil, as I realized on the boat the moment I found myself among Lancashire, Glasgow, and Cockney voices. All saying 'bloody'; Americans do not say 'bloody'.

Suddenly one day—maybe a day, maybe a week, maybe a month after embarkation—we called at a one-eyed port which was God knows where and took on board two hundred Canadian airmen and a batch of British seamen, survivors from the Jervis Bay.[4] Transformation scene. The beer-queue blocked the third class lounge. Someone was at the piano picking out 'Land of Hope and Glory' with one finger while someone else played 'Mother Machree' on a mouth-organ. The airmen, with schoolboy complexions and schoolboy spirits, fooled with the electric fans. The bog-trotting Irishman, who had gone ashore and got two bottles of whiskey, came into my cabin very drunk and leaned over me as I was trying to write. 'That's a terrible long sentence for a young man to write. Where's your full stops? Where's your apostrophe esses?' He fumbled a knotty finger over the page and great drops of spittle fell and blurred my writing: he had teeth—and yellow ones at that—only on one side of his mouth. 'I'm only an old dumb Irishman bedamn but I know me apostrophe esses.' I shied away from the fall of spittle; the great drunk finger continued to wander over the manuscript. 'Ye're a decent young man, ye're deep as Hell's Gates, but'—oh, what a reek of whiskey—'grammar is grammar.'

Monotonous days; boat-drill and two sittings for meals; the food was poor and owing to breakages in rough weather, there was a shortage of glasses. Also a shortage of matches; we spent a considerable time getting lights from each other. Some Canadian volunteer members of the YMCA organized a sing-song—'Let's have some of that bar-room harmony. Sing as if you were gargling your throat with Listerine.' The ratings from the Jervis Bay, wearing mourning for their ship, played

---

[4] The armed merchant cruiser HMS *Jervis Bay* was sunk 5 Nov. 1940 while protecting a convoy against the German pocket battleship KM *Admiral Scheer*. For an eyewitness account of the sinking, see Calum Macneil in *The War at Sea: The British Navy during World War II* ed. John Winton (1967), 77–84.

ping-pong or cards with each other but did not talk much; they had escaped on a raft, up to their waists in water, all were washed off several times, scrambled back, two of them died. I heard someone pumping one of the survivors—a stout, red-faced seaman from Manchester who had a fleshy jowl, boils on his face, tattoo marks on his arms, a child's eyes. 'I've read about your wonderful experience,' etc. 'Reading about it's better'n experiencing it.' He relit his pipe and said nothing more.

The airmen, most of whom were wireless operators or ground staff, were all very young. One of them talked to me enthusiastically about the great Canadian flying school at Calgary—tiro flying over the prairies and advanced flying over the Rockies. He talked about fighter planes in exactly the same manner that a car-lover talks about cars—'a lovely job of work'. For the War itself he expressed no enthusiasm; that was a job of work too, but not a lovely one.

The last three nights or so of the voyage we were told to sleep in our clothes. I had an argument with my cabin-mate who objected to my taking off my shoes: 'What will the people say if you go down into the life-boat in your dirty feet?' I changed the subject and talked about Ireland but that was equally delicate. 'You know they've got no conscription in the North? You know who they've got to thank for that? Sure, it's Dev.[5] Dev. and none other. And you know, if they brought in conscription, who it is they'd conscript? The Unionists? Not at all. All them fellows been clamouring for years about their loyalty to the Empire, the day they bring in conscription, they'll all turn around and have two left feet.'

Then one day there were half a dozen young porpoises hurdling the waves in formation and, immediately afterwards, a Coastal Patrol plane. We are nearly there, boys, back in the mythical country. The dwarf has changed his shirt to a vivid green. The purser will change your American money into English. I had forgotten the heaviness of coppers.

[5] Eamon de Valera (1882–1975), President of the Irish Republic 1921–2, President of the Executive Council of the Free State 1932–7, Prime Minister and President of the Republic 1937–48, 1951–4, 1957–73. 'Britain heeded his protest, against the extension of conscription to Northern Ireland, when he claimed that the nationalist minority [there] would not tolerate it': D. J. Hickey and J. E. Doherty, *A Dictionary of Irish History since 1800* (1980), 125.

Next morning they 'hung out the washing' from the mast-
head, but we dropped anchor some miles out from the mouth of
the Mersey and stayed there another day. The boat was nearly
out of liquor, but a dagoish young man managed to get drunk
and played the accordion for two hours brilliantly. I slept
badly; it was almost like going to be married.

'The Mersey Docks,' read out a Canadian as we edged in to
the quay, 'The *Mersey* Docks'—a long ironic drawl on the word
'Mersey'. And it certainly was a dirty day—a wad of wet
brown mist on a shabby city. 'Christ, what a country!' But all
the same we have made it, we have got through the tunnel and
come up out of it intact. So what?

So this: I have never really thought of myself as British; if
there is one country I feel at home in, it is Eire. As a place
to live in or write in I prefer the USA to England and New
York to London. But I am glad to be back in England and,
in particular, in London. Because London since the Blitz has
become more comprehensible. Because this great dirty, slovenly,
sprawling city is a visible and tangible symbol of freedom; it
has not been centralized, organized, rationalized, dehumanized
into a streamlined ad for the cult of the State. Because there is
just a chance that the other tunnel we are in at the moment
may lead us up into a more concrete kind of socialism, which
will not substitute for a ruling caste of money a caste of political
power-addicts, of blinkered doctrinaires, of pseudo-Marxist
bureaucrats. The typical Englishman contains, paradoxically,
an anarchist; this can be seen from English poetry. Any social
revolution which is to suit this country must take account of
that anarchist. The notorious defects of the English are at least
the defects of a people who respect the individual human being.
A world view? All right, we need a world view (we can't be
mere empiricists for ever) but the world is made of human
beings. Any ideology which ignores the individual human being
is ripe for the scrap-heap. For the sake of Man we must
have an economic programme—but only for the sake of Man
and that means men and that means not Citizens 7601, 7602,
etc.,[6] but Tom, Dick, and Harry. When we come out of the
tunnel we must still have faces—not masks.

[6] Cf. Auden's poem 'The Unknown Citizen (To JS/07/M/378 . . .)', March 1939:
Collected Poems, ed. Mendelson (1976), 201.

Traveller's Return[1]

'From America no traveller returns,' so Mr Connolly wrote in his Comment in the December number of *Horizon*.[2] Having ignored this a priori truth by landing in this country on December 9th after ten months in the USA, I am surprised to find how many people ask bitterly after those other British writers who are still in America. When people over here talk about these expatriates, more often than not their acrimony equals their ignorance. As an ex-expatriate, therefore, I am about to discuss this subject under a handicap; I have seen it from both sides of the Atlantic.

While I was in America I felt a very long way from Europe, though not so far away as I felt during the autumn of 1939 in Ireland. You cannot forget the War in America (it is the chief subject of conversation), but you cannot visualize it. I could visualize it myself so long as the 'Sitzkrieg'[3] persisted, and during that period I had no wish to return to a Chamberlain's England, where my fellow-writers were sitting around not writing. From June on I wished to return, not because I thought I could be more *useful* in England than in America, but because I wanted to see these things for myself. My chief motive thus being vulgar curiosity, my second motive was no less egotistical: I thought that if I stayed another year out of England I should have to stay out for good, having missed so much history, lost touch.

These two motives of mine seem to me valid for me, but they are not *generally* valid. If an expatriate writer is free from vulgar curiosity and does not wish to keep 'in touch' with England (and such a wish is not a moral axiom), what other reasons are there why he should return? Three possible reasons: (1) Because

---

[1] *Horizon* 3: 14 (Feb. 1941), 110–17.

[2] Cyril (Vernon) Connolly (1903–74), the English author, journalist, and founder-editor of *Horizon*, 1939–50; see his Comment in *Horizon* 3: 12 (Dec. 1940), 281: 'From America no travellers return, no American letters get written, and to ask for them is like dropping pebbles down a well. This is regrettable, for *Horizon* has suspended judgement on the expatriates.'

[3] The 'phoney war' of 1939–40, before the blitz[krieg] of 1940–1.

he could be more useful in England. (2) Because in England he would become a better writer or a better person, or both. (3) Patriotism and/or homesickness.

(1) If an expatriate writer happened, say, to be a highly skilled engineer, he might be more useful to Britain as an engineer than he would be to the USA or the world as a writer. But none of the expatriates we are discussing has any such technical qualifications; the only thing they can do particularly well is to write. Would they be useful to Britain to-day *qua* writers? Any more use, that is, than they are while they reside in America? It is more than doubtful. A writer in England now can either sink his gifts in some form of propaganda work, at which he is not necessarily better than Tom, Dick, or Harry, or he can continue to survive as a free lance whom no one has time to attend to, or he can give up his profession of writing for the amateurdom of National Service. Usefulness? That is a conception which has never been commensurable with art; even the use of commercial or of propaganda art is hard to assess. Some writers of the Left in England regret that their late colleagues have not returned in order to be flaming torches. But are they, who have stayed over here, doing much flaming themselves? I will return to this point.

(2) The argument that a British-born writer by being in England now would better himself as a writer or as a person, or as both, is a good deal more plausible and may be true for certain individuals. But you cannot generalize. A minority of writers—like Malraux and Hemingway—seem to thrive *qua* writers on scenes of violence and suffering,[4] but none of the British expatriates belongs to this minority. War again brings out in many people certain virtues—notably courage and patience and, to a less degree, generosity—which had not before been apparent, but as these virtues, with the exception of generosity, are not particularly necessary to a writer; a writer, by having them forced upon him, may become in a sense a

---

[4] The French novelist and art critic André Malraux (1901–76) fought in China in the 1920s, as a Loyalist in the Spanish Civil War, and distinguished himself as a Resistance hero in World War II; out of these experiences he wrote novels on revolutionary themes. The American novelist Ernest Hemingway (1899–1961) took some part in the two world wars, as ambulance driver and war correspondent respectively, as well as supporting the Republicans in the Spanish Civil War; he wrote many tales of violent action—on war, bull-fighting, big-game hunting, etc.

better person while becoming an inferior, less productive or unproductive artist. If that is so—but again each case must be judged individually—his advance as a person must be balanced against his decline as an artist. On a long-term view it is not axiomatic either that war improves everyone—or most people —morally, or that a writer who has become, say, courageous and patient in his life but whose art is lapsing, is in the proper (objective) sense of the word a *better* man than a writer who is not practising courage or patience, but is getting on with his job.

(3) Patriotism or homesickness? Though patriotism includes a sentimental, as it were a family, feeling for place, we can distinguish the ethical motive from the sentimental. At certain times in certain countries there has been a moral urgency to be patriotic when the actual or ideal policy of a man's nation has been a *sine qua non* for his conscience. But to-day patriotism, in so far as it means subordination to a specifically national policy, is superannuated. This war, we assume, is not being fought— not by most of us—for any merely national end; we are fighting it, primarily and clearly, for our lives, and secondarily, and, alas! vaguely, for a new international order. How does this affect the expatriates? They need not at the moment fight for their lives. Will they contribute less to a new international order by living in a country where they are not nationals (a country, by the way, at least no less committed than Great Britain to internationalism)? As for homesickness, if anyone goes home because he is homesick, that is sympathetic, but it is not *ipso facto* a sign of strength; it might be a sign of weakness. Just as Action at All Costs is sometimes a sign of weakness; we have heard of 'escaping to the Front'.

When I first reached England I was asked if I had read Stephen Spender's attack on the expatriates. Later I was asked if I had read his defence of them. So I got hold of his 'Letter to a Colleague in America' in the *New Statesman and Nation*, of November 16th, which both my questioners referred to.[5] It was not stated *which* colleague he was addressing—and that makes some difference—but I received the impression that Mr Spender, while carefully conceding that 'if you can preserve the sense of

---

[5] *New Statesman and Nation* 20: 508 (16 Nov. 1940), 490.

the "time in London", then you are in a privileged position',
was in fact suspecting the worst. His letter, especially by
contrast with the press-gang attitude of others who have
touched this subject, was sensitive, imaginative, and tolerant,
but it struck me as inconsistent, indeed, as woolly. He writes:
'I know *as well as you must do* [italics mine] that there is no
possibility of running away from a fate which affects the whole
world,' but later—and this time the tone implies that 'I' know
it better than 'you' do—he writes that people 'cannot escape
into an entirely new and less disturbing series of events, not
even in Hollywood'. As he was writing to someone who was in
Hollywood, and as he immediately followed this remark with
aspersions on yoga and a 'philosophy of life' (presumably of the
bogus Southern Californian brand),[6] I took him to mean that
his addressee *was* trying to 'escape' into an entirely new and
less disturbing series of events. Mr Spender tells me he did not
mean this', but there are other people who mean it and say it.
And it may be true of *some* of the expatriates that they are trying
to put the clock back, but it is a black lie if applied to all of
them. Nor is it true of most Americans though Mr Spender
implies (or doesn't he?—read it for yourself) that the whole
country is backward, still living in the days before Munich. We
might remember too that there are people also over here—from
Colney Hatch to the War Office, from the *Daily Express* to the
People's Convention[7]—whose clocks, it seems, have stopped.

Mr Spender, in his letter, made a great to-do with time and
place. 'It is hardly a question', he writes, 'of *where* you are at
all, but *when*,' yet he goes on to subordinate the *when* to the
where, at least by implication, like this: X, an English writer,
is living in America, and America, because of geography, is
behind the times, therefore X, *because* he is in America, is also
behind the times. 'The only question worth asking', he goes on,
'about Auden, Isherwood, Heard, Aldous Huxley, MacNeice,
etc. [is] not whether they have run away on this particular

---

[6] The English writers Aldous Huxley and Gerald Heard (1889–1971) settled in
California in 1937, partly on a spiritual quest. W. H. Auden (1907–73) and
Christopher Isherwood (1901–86) came to New York in Jan. 1939, the latter going on
to California; apparently Spender was addressing this last writer and friend as 'a
colleague'.

[7] Colney Hatch: Middlesex district with large mental hospital; People's Convention: Communist organization.

occasion, but whether they think that there is a chance of
escaping from this history altogether.' As Mr Spender does not
answer this question, we cannot say we have been hit. Speaking for myself, I would deny that the possibility of such an
escape ever occurred to me. America (I am not speaking of
Hollywood, which may be a world to itself) is not a sound-
proof room. Nor are Americans politically anaesthetized. If
some Americans, like some Englishmen, are still pre-Munich,
other Americans, like other Englishmen, were post-Munich
before Munich happened. If Mr Spender *will* use this tricky
time-and-place relativism he must avoid even the suggestion of
downright generalizations. Anyway, to adopt his relativism for
a moment, I suspect him of wishing to repeople England with
pre-Munich Audens and Isherwoods. It was only before Munich
that this pair attempted the role of the Flaming Torch (a role,
in my opinion, to which neither was very well suited), and it
was before Munich that they wrote *On the Frontier*, their last
play, their most directly political—and also their worst—work.[8]

'But Auden and Isherwood', people say, 'were always
preaching the fight against Fascism.' So what? I had many
conversations with Auden this autumn, and he still is anti-
Fascist, but he is no longer in any way a 'fellow traveller'; since
getting off that particular train, he had decided—as he told me
in March 1939—that it was not his job to be a crusader, that
this was a thing everyone must decide for himself, but that, in
his opinion, most writers falsified their work and themselves
when they took a direct part in politics, and that the political
end itself, however good, could not be much assisted by art or
artists so falsified. Auden, that is, had repudiated propaganda.

'Well, he needn't preach or flame, but he ought at least to
come back.' Why? The answer too often is jealousy or spite—
'If I am under bombs, why the hell shouldn't X be too?' But
you can't conduct an argument by means of white feathers or
raspberries. War makes people so illogical. *If* you disapprove of
the expatriates being in America in wartime, you should have
disapproved of their settling there in peacetime, you should
have made a row when they first took out their papers.

<hr />

[8] See MacNeice's review of this play (Nov. 1938) in his *Selected Literary Criticism*,
101–3.

Some people do go so far. It is argued by extremists, most of whom have never crossed the Atlantic, that no Englishman— no English writer anyway—'can' change countries like this; it was all right, perhaps, for Henry James and Eliot to come this way, but no English writer can go that way and get away with it. This looks to me like sheer nonsense. Of course, it is hard to write where you have no 'roots', but because it is hard it may be all the more worth doing. We have had plenty of 'rooted' writing; the individual artist may have soon to dispense with 'roots' (in this narrower, local sense), just as the world must sooner or later dispense with national sovereignty. This question of roots is a question of degree: few of us believe the diehards who think you must stick to your own parish, fewer of us than formerly think that it is good for a small country like Ireland to attempt a cultural autarchy.

This reminds me; I can give myself as an example of uprootability. Born in Ireland of Irish parents, I have never felt properly 'at home' in England, yet I can write here better than in Ireland. In America I feel rather more at home than in England (America has more of Ireland in it), but I am not sure how well I could work if I settled there permanently. If I were sure on this point—as some of the expatriates are sure—it would only have been sensible of me to stay there. Many people in England, the war apart, are astonished that anyone can consider such a migration. Their astonishment is due to that anti-American prejudice which, like the corresponding anti-British prejudice among Americans, is founded on childish misconceptions and leads to a misunderstanding which is not only childish but dangerous. Dangerous especially now. If the two countries were more pervious to each other, it would not only reinvigorate the culture of both, it would ensure the existence of both. That two or three gifted English writers should be now living in the USA is at least one kind of much-needed *rapprochement*.

In the long run a writer must be judged by what he writes. The British expatriates, with the exception of Isherwood, whose books have always appeared after intervals of apparent inactivity, are still at least writing. Let us look at their more recent publications.

From Los Angeles come *After Many a Summer*, by Aldous

Huxley, and *The Creed of Christ*, by Gerald Heard,[9] each of which is a logical development from its author's long-established premises and appears neither better nor worse for his change of domicile. I myself hate the Huxley novel and deplore the Heard *Weltanschauung*, but I cannot see that they would write either better or worse if they moved back to England. And I cannot see that England would gain from the physical presence of either (England can get all they can give by reading their works), whereas they, by returning, might inconvenience both themselves and us; this is no place for either the museum mind or the yogi. But it is good to know that the Heard-Huxley firm can continue in business somewhere.

In New York are Auden, George Barker, Ralph Bates.[10] Barker has not been there long enough to publish a book, but it is probable that poetry of his kind (and it is silly to expect a war to produce mutations of kind) would not develop any better for his being in England; the chief difference is that there he may write more. Barker was never a Flaming Torch, and his sensitive, introspective, romantic, rather woozy talent is not the kind that requires a contact with mud and blood. As far as being 'of use' to his country goes, he will—paradoxically—be of more use to this country when writing as a free lance in America than when he was representing the British Council in a farcical attempt to preserve a cultural liaison with Japan.[11]

Bates, at one time a staunch supporter of the Third International, has settled in the USA and is continuing to write novels and stories which, apart from their other merits, are valuable social history.[12] 'Well, why can't he do his social history over here? There is lots of opportunity here.' Lots of opportunity for some; you must consider Bates's background.

---

[9] Huxley's *After Many a Summer* (1939); Heard's *The Creed of Christ: An Interpretation of the Lord's Prayer* (1941).

[10] George Granville Barker (1913–) came to New York 1940, visited California, and returned to England 1943. Ralph Bates came to New York 1937 on a lecture tour after fighting for the Loyalists in Spain. He became Adjunct Professor of Literature, New York University 1948–68, and then Professor Emeritus.

[11] Barker was Professor of English Literature at the Imperial Tohoku University, Japan, 1939.

[12] Bates was Captain in the Spanish Loyalist Army and in the International Brigade, Madrid sector, 1936–7, then settled in the USA 1937. He produced some good novels like *The Olive Field* (1936), but nothing after 1949–50.

Like many other writers of the Left, he has had to recant a
policy to which he had committed himself wholeheartedly; his
recantation was unusually clear-cut and courageous, but any
such recantation—as can be seen from a study of ex-Fellow
Travellers in England—makes it very difficult to pick up where
you left off. Bates is picking up in a country which his own
past—his past in England—does not obscure from him; at the
same time he is making a sympathetic and intelligent study
of another country, Mexico, for which his past—his past in
Spain—has equipped him.

Lastly Auden, whom people over here are never tired of
backbiting. London is full of silly rumours—Auden has gone
yogi, neo-Brahmin, Roman Catholic; it is even alleged that he
supported Willkie.[13] The accusations can be summarized
under two heads: (1) Auden has got religion; (2) Auden is now
just a faddist. (1) This is meant to be damning; it is not recognized, firstly, that the religious sense is something extremely
valuable; secondly, that it is something which Auden has
always had. What he has done recently is to concentrate and
control this sense, to divorce it from what is merely private or
ephemeral. (2) Auden, in a sense, has always been a faddist,
and seems less of one now than formerly; in any case his fads
are not the result of America. While in America he has written
two books of poetry—*Another Time* and *The Double Man*.[14] These
books have their faults and lack some of the attractions of some
of his earlier poems, but they are *not*, even if critics can be
found to say so, reactionary or escapist or stagnating. They
might be described as transitional; Auden has purged his
world-view of certain ready-made, second-hand over-simpli-
fications and is now attempting a new synthesis of his material.
Considering the range of his material and considering how
many writers have dropped all suggestion of synthesis, this is
an attempt for which we should all be grateful.

For the expatriate there is no Categorical Imperative bidding
him return—or stay. Auden, for example, working eight hours

13 The American Republican candidate Wendell L. Willkie (1892–1944) was a
popular campaigner for the presidency against Franklin D. Roosevelt (1882–1945)
and his New Deal 'extravagance', in the summer and autumn 1940.

14 *Another Time* (7 Feb. 1940); *The Double Man* (21 March 1941), called *New Year
Letter* in Britain (29 May 1941). See MacNeice's review of the former (April 1940) in
his *Selected Literary Criticism*, 114–16.

a day in New York, is getting somewhere;[15] it might well be 'wrong' for him to return. For another artist who felt he was getting nowhere it might be 'right' to return. In my own case, if I had stayed in America I do not suppose I should have felt morally guilty, though I might have felt *instinctively* so; not being on the track of a synthesis and being more attached to things than to ideas I might have felt I was only marking time in America (whereas artists of the opposite kind might be only marking time in England; war, after all, is monotonous, hostile to thought). Actually both my pleasure at being back and my regret, if I had not come, are equally unethical. Those who think it would have been selfish and irresponsible of me to stay in America might be interested to know that their opposite numbers in America thought it selfish and irresponsible of me to return to Europe. And they and their opposite numbers are both fools. The expatriates do not need anybody else to act as their *ersatz* conscience: they have consciences of their own and the last word must be said by their own instinct as artists.

[15] Auden's daily working routine was strict: Humphrey Carpenter, *W. H. Auden: A Biography* (1981), 279.

Touching America[1]

Last year—1940—I was in the USA from the end of January till the end of November. Inevitably I am now asked on all sides to tell people something about America. The first thing always to be said is that for a European to generalize about the USA on such short acquaintance is a sheer impertinence.

America, however, is always being generalized about, even by people who have never been there. There are, perhaps, two attitudes towards her which ought especially to be stigmatized: the *superior* attitude and the *adulatory*. (1) Just as Americans, generalizing from a tiny minority of British (their visitors) and from the pages of *Punch* and *The Times*, and certain English novels and plays and films, tend to think of Britain as an unspeakably caste-ridden nation consisting entirely of stuffed shirts and resigned drudges, so English people, generalizing from the Hollywood films and from a caricatural conception of the older type of American globe-trotter, tend to think of America in terms either of fantasy or farce—as a polylogue[2] of cigars and bad grammar or as one big pumpkin pie fairy story. (2) Latterly, owing to this war, which has turned the USA into the white hope of civilization, we find in some quarters that all the contours and jags of that very irregular country have been lost in an ocean of democratic whitewash. I will expand on these two points.

(1) Thanks to Hollywood, we think of the USA as a whirl of millionaires, hard-boiled business men, simple-minded toughs and free-living blondes—all of them housed in chromium. Thanks to such American literature as comes our way (lots of it fails to), we think of the typical American as a double-dyed materialist (in the popular sense of the word), very smart in practical affairs and very dumb in everything else, giving and taking hard knocks but quite insensitive. Streamlined extroverts. When you arrive in that country, however, you meet

---

[1] *Horizon*, 3: 15 (March 1941), 207–12.

[2] 'A discussion between more than two persons': *OED2*, citing this instance as the earliest traced in print.

innumerable Americans as neurotic as yourself, even more thin-skinned, and certainly no less concerned with spiritual values. There *are* Americans, as there are Englishmen, who are brassily self-assured, but, as a national characteristic, this brassy self-assurance is as much a myth as American efficiency or American sex-life. Many Americans can spare enough time from go-getting to have healthy doubts about themselves and their world. As for efficiency, alongside certain marvels of the machine age (the Hudson Parkway, for instance), there is a great deal of shoddiness and vagueness, of waste of time and energy (e.g. the postal system, some of the smaller railways, many of the small towns—let alone the South, which I have not visited). As for sex, their bark is much more than their bite. While New York intellectuals will tell the most risqué stories before strangers and use all the four-letter words, most of them would be appalled by bedtime Bloomsbury. Similarly, in many of their co-educational universities, though the boys and girls spend a deal of time necking in cars, etc., nearly all the girls are virgins. A decade ago it may have been different: many things have passed with the speakeasy era.

(2) On my return in April 1939 from my first visit to the USA[3] I was asked by a *British* citizen organizing a television programme about America to say a few big words at the end.[4] On asking what these big words should be I found that I was expected to say approximately this—that Europe to-day, including Britain, is all washed up, that our one last hope is in the USA, which is the only true democracy. (Eyes West, all of you.) I answered that I did not think it true (*a*) that British democracy, very imperfect though it was, was hopelessly moribund; and (*b*) that the USA was a perfect, or even near perfect, democracy; didn't they know the way Americans dealt with strikes, didn't they know that over there there were very strong elements of Fascism and, in particular, of anti-Semitism? Oh, yes, they knew all that, but maybe they had better get someone else to say the few big words. Maybe they had. It is bad enough to see people in misfortune and danger exonerating themselves by finding a scapegoat. It is, perhaps, nearly as bad to see them gleefully flagellating themselves and turning in idolatrous hope

3 Visit of Easter 1939: see *Strings*, chap. 37, 199–206.
4 Cf. ibid. 207–8.

to somebody else who is billed for their *deus ex machina*. The
USA has for many people to-day become such a scape-sheep.
Certainly we ought to be grateful that she exists, but this
unrealistic adulation is not—in the long run—either flattering
or expedient. Thus I was depressed in New York by the out-
and-out Roosevelt-worship of many of the Central European
refugees.[5] Understandable, but unpractical. It is very possible
that Roosevelt may turn out to have been the saviour of the
'western democracies'; that will not mean that he is either a
superman or a perfect democrat. Americans themselves, since
their war-scare, have tended to fall into a political Narcissism:
wherever you go you hear Irving Berlin's song, 'God Bless
America'. It must be remembered both by them and by us that
'Americanism' is not equivalent to Progress.

Having thus made clear that I suspect all gush about Americanism, I can say how much I like the country and most of the
people. The visitor from these islands is continually being
shocked—by the sponsored radio programmes, by the patent
sadism of the police, by the American Business Man (monstrous
hybrid of crook and baby), by the American Committee
Women and patronesses, by the New York intelligentsia (even
more self-conscious, more cliquey than the English), by the
cellophaned drug store food, by the worship of the gadget, etc.,
etc.—but he is also continually being inspired and even en-
lightened. You meet so many people in all spheres who are
curious about the world and whose wish to live has—for us—a
novel intensity. Take American undergraduates: while they
are naïve where their English (or, at least their Oxford and
Cambridge) counterparts are sophisticated, they can cope with
situations which would leave the English undergraduate child-
ishly gaping. Again, though their educational standard is
lower, their intellectual appetites are wider and healthier: you
rarely meet an American student who is *blasé*. Perhaps the open

[5] In the early years of the war Democratic President Franklin D. Roosevelt
(1882–1945), who had brought in the 'New Deal' of social welfare, set the USA on a
neutral, isolationist course, although he boosted arms production and a 'lend-lease'
policy for foes of the Axis powers; both he and his Republican rival Wendell L. Willkie
(1892–1944), while campaigning in 1940, promised to avoid direct American military
intervention in 'any foreign wars': Frank Freidel, in *Dictionary of American Biography*,
suppl. iii, *1941–1945* (1973), 658–9. (Roosevelt was elected for a third term in
Nov. 1940.)

air has something to do with it: there is such a lot of it there. (Skiing, for example, in America is a sport for clerks and workers.)

Now some extracts from my ten months' visit:[6]

Spring: I spent the spring in Ithaca, in upper New York State, where I was lecturing at Cornell University. *There was snow on the ground for two months.* I lived—board and lodging free—in an institution founded by a millionaire engineer (rough diamond), who had made his money in gold mines and wished to enable future engineers to get themselves polished.[7] So there were twenty-odd students (most of them no longer engineers) living for nothing in this very luxurious house while they took their courses at Cornell. Two or three members of the faculty, myself included, lived there too to contribute culture and uplift. Uplift was very important, for the Founder had specified: 'The purpose of this Association is to further the moral order of the Universe.' When these students had their weekly meetings to decide how to spend the (very considerable) community funds, someone every so often would drag in this question of the Universe. But nobody knew the answer. Nearly all these students, who were unusually intelligent, were at that time Isolationist. In arguments about the War they always had one ace—India.

The Fall of France: In our house at Cornell lived a Frenchman[8] who had spent the spring sun-bathing on a balcony and making newspaper cuttings and learning by heart little facts from the American *Who's Who* (for he was a careerist; some day he

---

[6] The second half of this article (last 4 paras.) includes details and persons omitted when the material was expanded for chaps. 2, 3 of *Strings*.

[7] 'Mr. Lucien L. Nunn [1853–1925], who made his first fortune in the Telluride mine in Colorado, brought to us [Cornell University] the Telluride Association. . . . The sumptuous building [Telluride House, 217 West Ave., Ithaca, NY] was opened in 1910, to demonstrate Mr Nunn's educational doctrines, then surely unique in America. The association would select a group of young men of exceptional promise and give them release from all material concern, a background of culture, the responsibility for managing their own household, and the stimulation of dwelling with resident faculty members and eminent visitors': Morris Bishop, *A History of Cornell* (1962), 410. See Telluride Association, *Constitution* (Ithaca, NY, 1912). Nunn was 'a pioneer in the high-voltage transmission of alternating current, with extensive mining and real estate interests in and around Telluride': *Encyclopedia of Associations*, 21st edn, 4 vols. (1987), i. 663.

[8] Called André in *Strings*, 25–7.

might meet some of the Who's Whos, then he could make con-versation). The week in which Paris fell was the week of Class Reunion;[9] the campus was flooded with comic old business men dressed up as pierrots or God-knows-what, according to the dictates of their class committee, each of them wore a baby hat bearing the number of his class year—1925 or 1911, or 1899 or 1066. All were trying so hard to be boys again together. The Frenchman, having breakfast on a terrace outside the caféteria, was repelled by this inopportune *bonhomie*. 'What is this?' he kept saying (his English was incorrect and florid). 'In this darkest hour of France's history. . . . What is this? They are *children*.' Then he would order himself a hot cereal and gaze into it with horror—'What is this? It is dog-soup.' And by his side, only too aptly, appeared a large dog of no known breed, with long white hair, pink eyes and a snipy imbecile face. 'Yes, it is dog-soup. For degenerate dogs. Like this one.' We had several such breakfasts together on this terrace, in a time of cantaloups and peonies, looking across the lake-valley to low hills which, on a misty day, resembled an Irish landscape. 'Poète, prends ton luth,' he would say suddenly—for he never kept step in conversation—or, with a histrionic gesture so that we took it for wit, 'La fin du monde. Merde!' A few days after I left I heard they had put him away in the State Asylum. Shortly before his removal he had explained to a friend of mine that he knew now he was not one of those whom God had chosen, it was not allowed to him ever to have initiative; from now on all he could do was obey—'Tell me something and I will do it. I want to *obey*. Set me a task—a hard one.'

The Fall: After six weeks in hospital[10] I spent the autumn (the Fall is a better name when the maples go pimento and coral) convalescing, first in New England and then in New York. In my hospital a nurse had said to me: 'Of course it won't be so bad for England as for France. They've got some kind of a gulf over there, haven't they?'—meaning the English Channel. But now Europe had come closer and, what with the presidential election, America was bubbling with hysteria. In

---

[9] The Germans entered Paris on Fri., 14 June 1940.

[10] Hospitalization for an operation in Portsmouth, New Hampshire, for 'a ruptured appendix and peritonitis', with 'streptococcal infection—they thought I would die': ibid. 27.

academic and intellectual circles this hysteria disguised itself as common sense or high-mindedness. Mr Archibald MacLeish, having spent two decades on a series of band-wagons, had published a pamphlet entitled *The Irresponsibles*, in which he attributed the present world chaos to certain writers of the 'twenties, such as Hemingway, and suggested that, even if Hemingway and Co. had written the truth, they had no right to utter such truths because they led to defeatism.[11] This piece of artistic treason (and nonsense) was properly answered by Mr Edmund Wilson in *The New Republic*.[12] Next, Dr Nicholas Murray Butler, president of Columbia University, called a mass meeting of his faculty and warned them that, if the USA went to war, there was to be no criticism of the Government line from anyone teaching at Columbia—they must either keep silence or resign.[13] Again, there was a proper answer: the New York press raised such a stink that Dr Butler had to recant.[14] More insidiously, however, a number of old Liberals, ex Fellow Travellers, etc., were issuing articles and books (and no doubt still are) abjuring the folly of rationalism and/or 'materialism', and offering as a panacea for world politics various brands of mushy but bad-tempered religion—or perhaps religiosity.[15] At the same time Mr Carl Sandburg explained that wisdom was to be found with the truck-drivers and not with the intellectuals.[16]

11 Archibald MacLeish's (1882–1982) *The Irresponsibles* (34 pp., 1940)—an attack on American writers for allegedly failing to take an active stand for democracy—was first published in slightly different form in *Nation* 150: 20 (18 May 1940), 618–23.

12 Edmund Wilson (1895–1972), 'Archibald MacLeish and "the Word"', *New Republic* 103: 1 (1 July 1940), 30–2, reprinted in *Classics and Commercials: A Literary Chronicle of the Forties* (1950), 3–9.

13 On 3 Oct. 1940 Dr N. M. Butler (1862–1947), long-time President of Columbia (1901–45), warned 'his faculty not to abuse academic freedom': 'Saying Columbia has enlisted in war, he urges those whose conduct hampers her "lofty aim" to resign': *New York Times*, 4 Oct. 1940, 1b–c; text of address on 14c–f. Dr Butler denied students the right to academic freedom.

14 For the controversy, see *New York Times Index 1940*, 411. After a week of uproar, on 10 Oct. Dr Butler retracted, reassuring 'faculty on rights: academic freedom, "firmly established" at Columbia, will remain': *New York Times*, 11 Oct., 23d, 26d–f.

15 The leading American periodical supporting socialism against both easy sentimentality and dogmatic religious solutions in the war crisis was *Partisan Review*: vol. 7 (1940)—in which T. S. Eliot published 'East Coker', MacNeice his poem 'The Preacher' (*Collected Poems*, 175–6) and an excerpt from *Strings*—for arguments like MacNeice's by Dwight Macdonald, Philip Rahv, and many others; MacNeice must have read *Partisan Review* in 1940.

16 Carl Sandburg (1878–1967) made this statement at a *Herald-Tribune* Forum in New York, 23 Oct. 1940: 'If you wish to pray or if you wish to sit in silent meditation

All this, in my opinion, is deplorable. Because it is both sentimental and cowardly. It may be good for an intelligentsia every so often to confess that 'there is no truth in us' but, after the catharsis of such humility, they should remember that there is damn little truth around anywhere, that truth—in the social and political, as in the artistic, sphere—is something which is made, or at least discovered, and that the intellectual has no right to abdicate his post of discoverer or to scrap the necessary instrument of Reason.

This dangerous tendency is not, of course, peculiar to America, and I have a hope that the intellects of America can stand up against it. As I said before, one thing about Americans—they are not *blasé*, they are not predisposed to the role of lost souls. And the re-election of President Roosevelt, in spite of the Third Term bogy, the superstitious oracles of Wall Street, the unnerving propaganda of the Press and all the appeals made by some of his opponents to the instincts of greed and panic, was—up to a point—a defeat for the forces of Unreason.

in a corner . . . you will get it from this poet [T. S. Eliot]. But if you want clarity on human issues he's out—he's zero. *A year ago I would have kept silent about him. . . .* Now I have to say that T. S. Eliot is anti-democratic and that he is mediaevalist, and that he is royalist and that he's so close to fascists that I am off him, to use a truck-drivers' phrase; and we've got to consider the truck-drivers in the present hour rather than the intellectuals.'—Cited by Allen Tate in 'The State of Letters', *Sewanee Review* 52 (Oct.–Dec. 1944), 610–11, with Tate's comments, 'Why could Mr Sandburg not have made his particular brand of violent choice a year earlier? Why can't we have both the truck-driver and the intellectual?'

London Letter [1]: Blackouts, Bureaucracy & Courage[1]

London, 1 January

My first day back in England I found myself in a train going to Birmingham, which in the last few weeks had been so severely raided.[2] In my carriage sitting under two little cones of light thrown on the indoor fog from shaded lamps were two private soldiers and a middle-aged man and wife from the Midlands. The two soldiers were taking forty-eight hours' leave, which includes travelling time. One of them was depressed and tired, had seen all of the world he wanted to, he said, kept falling asleep. The other was cheery and talkative, described with enthusiasm how a Highland regiment just before Dunkirk had put on kilts over their battle-dress before making a bayonet charge; it was a *beautiful* sight; but what a lot of *lovely* stuff we had had to leave behind there. He looked at his companion who was groaning, half asleep. 'Cheer up, lad,' he said, 'you'll be in the Roll of Honour some day.' The little Midland clerk and his wife, who were haggard from lack of sleep, were re-counting deaths from bombs—twenty-one in a household of twenty-three and the wire that announced it had taken two days to come.

The station at Birmingham, which I knew very well, was an unfamiliar crypt. As I groped along the platform through wheezing darkness rain fell on me where no rain ought to have occurred; I realized that most of the glass was out of the roof. I called up a friend, found he had discreetly moved out into the country and went out there in the night to find him. The village where I got off my bus was quiet in the misty night, a little church spire—very English—its only form of assertiveness; the

[1] *Common Sense* 10: 2 (Feb. 1941), 46–7. *Common Sense* was a leftist periodical co-founded and co-edited by Alfred M. Bingham (1905–) and Selden Rodman (1909–) in New York City.

[2] The air raids on Birmingham took place 28 Oct. and 12 Nov. 1940: see *The Times*, 30 Oct. 1940, 2e; 14 Nov., 2a.

air was dense with the smell of fried fish and chips and I knew I was back in England.

The next day I walked around Birmingham, feeling something of an intruder. The poorer streets seemed to have suffered most—rows and rows of toothless, eyeless houses, gutters of powdered glass—but the raiders had also got a big luxury shop [three words censored—Ed. < of *Common Sense* >] where my wife used to buy satin and swansdown; it was now a tangle of iron, a mess of rubble. From four o'clock on, the curbs were lined with workers, patiently standing in the drizzle waiting for buses as an angler waits for a fish that may never come. I spent that night in a room in the University where several of the faculty were on ARP duty,[3] including the Vice-Chancellor, an Australian, who entertained us by singing 'Waltzing Matilda', said to be Australia's only folk-song.[4]

Next, Oxford; which was much the same as ever, only more crowded. It has so far had no air raids and is full of evacuées; up to a thousand people are sleeping in an outlying moviehouse. During the summer East Enders from London were billeted in some of the colleges and waited on tenderly by the college servants who rose for the occasion above their traditional snobbery; rows of East End washing were hung across the Jacobean quadrangles. I had a conversation with a prominent economist and Labourite who was just back from London, from a committee of Civil Servants, and was deploring the unsurmountable timidity of that well-meaning but astigmatic tribe; no one (in these days when departmental activities interlock) will touch anything that could possibly be construed as outside his own Department; no one will act on his own initiative, he has to refer to a superior—you refer back and back till you get to the Minister. Pending further instructions; pending and pending. It is this bureaucratic aspect of England which is far the most depressing; the Committee Rooms appear to be blacker than the black-out, more dreary than the shattered

---

[3] Air raid precautions.

[4] Sir Raymond (Edward) Priestley (1886–1974), the Principal and Vice-Chancellor of Birmingham University 1938–52—who had been a geologist with both the Shackleton and Scott Antarctic Expeditions (1907–9, 1910–13) and had a distinguished World War I record—had been the Vice-Chancellor of Melbourne University, Australia, 1935–8. The popular 'Waltzing Matilda' has, of course, become the national anthem of Australia.

slums, more distasteful—oh ever so much so—than margarine. And then London. 'Oh what a shabby city!' is one's first impression—so many broken windows, so many windows boarded up, the same old grime and mist but less colour, less traffic, fewer people; gutted theatres still placarded with announcements of forgotten shows; huge and vulgar patriotic posters; cotton and woollen stockings and those tin hats which make their wearers look like old-time headmistresses. London for a month had been enjoying a lull; faces look less strained than in Birmingham though people on the whole are dour. The chief subject of conversation is food—'I have an onion; I can't decide when to use it.' About the War one can only say the obvious or swap rumours. But there are some funny stories circulating at the expense of the Foreign Office, the War Office, the BBC, the Ministry of Information, *et al ad infinitum ad nauseam*, and God helps those who can laugh at themselves.

If you want a Hogarthian contrast go down—any time after 7 p.m.—into one of the Tube stations (the subways) and follow it up by a visit to the Ritz bar. Night after night the same people sleep in the Tubes (the number of them is now put at about 35,000) lying on the platform where the trains come in, their heads to the curving wall and their feet to the trains; between their feet and the trains there is not more than a yard, so you have to be careful where you step. The sleepers lie packed together making a continuous layer of bodies from one end of the platform to the other. They sleep in a blaze of lights and their coloured blankets and patchwork quilts, their sandwiches and mouth-organs, give almost a Bank Holiday atmosphere, very different from that of the subways in Barcelona where the starving homeless lay in a charnel gloom. The smell these days, I am told, is nothing to what it was. Someone remarked to me that this was really Back to the Village, a revival of the archaic communal life in which the Tube station takes the place of the Village Hall. Now, for your contrast, go into the Ritz; the bar is noisy and crowded with officers in uniform but all of a peculiar kind, shimmying their hips and speaking in shrill or velvety voices—'My dear! My *dear!* My DEAR!' The Ritz however represents a minute minority. The vast majority of Londoners lead a life these days of very hard work, immeasurable patience, and next to no frills.

Every district in London has been damaged by bombs, the damage has been wonderfully indiscriminate, but it is far out-balanced (this ought to be underlined) by what has not been seriously damaged or what has already been repaired. Blooms-bury has suffered heavily and it is sad to see those grey brick Georgian houses in ruins but it cannot be much help to the Germans. When Virginia Woolf's apartment was disem-bowelled, left open to the air, I am told that for several days paintings by Duncan Grant (the rising star of the twenties) remained hanging on the remaining walls through the London drizzle and the blitzes that followed.[5]

Going to see the ruins soon becomes boring; one shattered building looks much like another—and much like any building being demolished by contractors in peacetime—and they smell surprisingly bad. But some of the more pretentious commercial architecture is aesthetically improved by bombing. A block of shops which has been gutted and its pediments broken and its plate glass gone and its arches left open to the wind takes on a new dignity or patina it lacked in its ancient but so recent days of Nineteen-and-Elevenpence the Yard. And sometimes, when a house has been cut in half, you get the pleasant effect of a doll's house—a bath in the bathroom and a dresser in the kitchen and wallpapers with roses and forget-me-nots and a mirror for the dolls to look into, not even cracked, but the dolls themselves have gone. The church of St Clement Danes in the Strand, one of Wren's elegances in Portland stone, looks none the worse for having had its windows blown out; outside it in the churchyard, just beyond the apse, a statue of Dr Johnson still stands among the debris,[6] unconcerned and pawky, with an open book in his left hand, looking up Fleet Street.

[5] After her London home at 37 Mecklenburgh Square was bombed Sept. 1940, the novelist Virginia Woolf (1882–1941) lived at Monks House, Rodmell, Sussex until her death: Lyndall Gordon, *Virginia Woolf: A Writer's Life* (1984), 263. The painter and decorator Duncan J. C. Grant (1885–1978), a member of the Bloomsbury Circle of the Woolfs and Bells, 'was one of the first English artists to be influenced by the Fauves and Cézanne, and contributed to the second Post-Impressionist Exhibition in 1912': *The Oxford Companion to Art*, ed. Harold Osborne (1970), 500.

[6] Percy Fitzgerald's statue of Dr Samuel Johnson (1709–84) was erected in 1910 in St Clement Danes's churchyard: *Boswell's Life of Johnson*, ed. G. B. Hall, rev. L. F. Powell, 6 vols. (1934, 1964), iv. 472. This church in the Strand was battered to a shell of walls in subsequent air raids 1941: *The Times*, 16 May 1941, 7d. It was rebuilt 1954–8, restored 'as a perpetual shrine of RAF remembrance', and reconsecrated 19 Oct. 1958: *The Times*, 7 Oct. 1958, 12e; 20 Oct., 5a.

Last night they dropped a great number of incendiary bombs, stage-lighting London; you could have read a book in the streets a mile away. The one fire which I saw close at hand was very beautiful—a large shop-building that seemed to be merely a façade of windows and these windows were filled to the brim with continuous yellow flame, uniform as a liquid but bubbling a little at the top of the windows like aerated tanks in an aquarium. There were no wild tongues of flame, no reds or blues or flame-colour proper, but above the building the smoke rolled up and outwards in great soft tawny clouds. Several AFS trucks (the Auxiliary Fire Service) drove up packed with fire-fighters all in tin hats and all with stubs of cigarettes in their mouths—their last cigarette before they got down to a job that would last them the night.

You will want to know about the Intellectual Front (I use this Stalinesque phrase deliberately). Well, there is no Front. The Left intelligentsia broke up in August and September 1939 and all the King's Spitfires and all the King's men have failed to reassemble it. I was asked by a well-known woman writer[7] to support a 'People's Convention' which will take place shortly in Manchester. [It took place January 11th—Ed. <of *Common Sense.* >][8] This Convention apparently is an attempt to revive the Popular Front with the Communist Party predominating. I asked why I should support this. She said because a revolution was needed immediately. I said I very much doubted (*a*) whether the British Communist Party could swing a revolution, (*b*) whether it would be the right kind of revolution. Apart from which, if we had a revolution—however successful—to-day, Hitler would invade England—and probably successfully—to-morrow. So powerful however is wishful thinking among the small minority of intellectuals who support such crackpot Conventions that they think the moment they

[7] Probably Sylvia Townsend Warner (1893–1978), the English novelist and poet, who had joined the Communist Party 1935 and served as a Red Cross volunteer in Barcelona, Spain. See *Strings*, 166.
[8] No report was published of a 'People's Convention' in Manchester on Saturday, 11 Jan. 1941, in *The Times, Manchester Guardian,* or *Daily Worker.* However, a 'People's Convention'—organized by the Communist Party and declaring as objectives 'A People's Government and a People's Peace'—met in London, Sun. 12 Jan. 1941: *The Times,* 13 Jan. 1941, 2e; it was repudiated by the Labour movement: ibid., 6 March 1941, 2e.

overthrow the present British Government the German people, sick of German victories and stolen foodstuffs, will rise and overthrow Hitler. There are other intellectuals, ex-Fellow Travellers, who no longer aspire to a revolution (there has lately been a slump in Barricades) but would like an immediate negotiated peace, assuming that everyone, including the Germans, would be so overjoyed by a few days' peace they would scrap all their armaments at once.

The majority of intellectuals however rest their hopes upon Hitler's ultimate defeat. They accordingly align themselves, *faute de mieux*, with the Labour Party, which is really more committed to winning the war than the Conservatives. It is a mistake however to hold the opinion, which I heard expressed in America, that the Labour Party now has the whip-hand in Britain. The Labour Party is still the prisoner of the Conservatives and has to soft-pedal its own aims for fear of frightening more Conservatives into the furtive camp of Appeasement. If a general election were held to-day the Conservatives would almost certainly retain a majority in the House of Commons. Thanks to the prestige of Churchill. It is a paradoxical situation. The Conservative Party, which contains the chief elements of appeasement, remains in power and so, to a certain extent, sabotages the practical effectiveness of the real War Party, the Labour Party, and it remains in power chiefly because it happens to be led by a man who is as zealous for victory as any of the Labourites although his peace aims will be radically different from theirs. It looks as if we must hope for a compromise, a pantomime transformation act—Churchill to win the war and Labour to win the peace. It is a lot to hope for but it is at least a better gamble than the other camps offer.

People have complained to me about their letters from friends in America. They say that these friends always take one or other of two lines, both of which are absurd; they either write 'I cannot bear to think of you in that Hell; how can you stand it?' or 'It must be so *thrilling* to be in England at this moment; I only wish I could be with you.' It is neither thrilling nor hell though it may have its moments of either. It is more of a Purgatory—routine, routine, routine, plenty to grumble at and plenty to admire, some moments of intense fear and hours and days, weeks and months, of waiting and working one's way not even to Heaven but a bit further up the spiral. You may doubt whether we are going up, but here we are in no position to doubt and we have no time to achieve levitations by Yoga. Better be hanged for a sheep than like one. I have just come across a letter from an American friend written last June saying that Britain to-day seems 'downhill and hopeless'. Having just returned to this country I wish to say honestly and as someone who has never been patriotic and who loathes propaganda, that Britain at the end of 1940 seems a good deal less downhill than I have ever known it before. In fact not downhill at all.

London Letter [2]: Anti-Defeatism of the Man in the Street[1]

London, 1 March

Having now been back in England almost three months I already find myself assimilated to this queer dream-world where the telephones don't work properly and the pies don't taste like pie and half the people are in uniform and the wind hums shrilly at night through the cables of the balloons and even the prostitutes wear slacks and being bombed out of your home is no longer a topic of interest and everyone just goes on—a fact is a fact and a job is a job and as for the general principles they can look after themselves. It is only too easy to do this, to kiss your hand in farewell to the general principles. There are so many people being magnificently practical that you almost feel ashamed of *thinking*. But there must be people to go on thinking—all the more so because certain elements in the ruling classes regard this as their chance to muzzle the intellectuals.

It is encouraging to find Stephen Spender organizing a series of a dozen articles for *Horizon* on the theme of 'War and the Future'; Julian Huxley, for example, has promised an article on Colonies and E. M. Forster one on Civil Liberties.[2]

The suppression of the *Daily Worker* last month caused little surprise.[3] It had ceased to have much to do with the British

---

[1] *Common Sense*, 10: 4 (April 1941), 110–11, with a woodcut caricature of 'No. 2 Briton: Ernest Bevin' by Bruce Gregory. The Rt. Hon. Ernest Bevin (1881–1951), the trade-union leader and statesman, was wartime Minister of Labour and National Service 1940–5; he entered the War Cabinet in Oct. 1940.

[2] The writer-editor Cyril Connolly announced a 'War Symposium' in his periodical *Horizon* 3: 14 (Feb. 1941), 90: 'This number introduces a series of contributions dealing directly with the war, which will consist of stories, essays, letters, or *reportage*.' There is no trace of the series 'War and the Future', or of the articles MacNeice mentions by Huxley and Forster, in *Horizon*. Sir Stephen Spender has written to me that he has no recall of this matter.

[3] On 21 Jan. 1941 the Home Office suppressed the *Daily Worker* and the *Week* because of 'systematic publication of matter calculated to foment opposition to the

workers; on my first evening back in London I heard in the dark street an emasculated Oxford voice intoning oh so wearily: '*Daily Worker!* All the latest news. Buy the *Daily Worker.*' The paper, like the voice of its salesman, was very much alone in the night. I shed no tears over its suppression but, like many other people, I disapprove of its suppression on two grounds—ethical and practical:

(1) A vocal opposition is even more desirable in wartime than in peacetime and the suppression of any organ of opinion, however wrongheaded, is a very bad precedent.

(2) By suppressing the *Daily Worker* the Government has encouraged people to think that it really had something in it. The only intellectual I have talked to who wholeheartedly approved of its suppression was, paradoxically, Mr John Strachey[4] who argued that the Communist Party in Britain is actively promoting sabotage and that therefore to deprive the saboteur of his press-organ is merely equivalent to depriving the burglar of his jimmy and is not an infringement of democratic rights. Not that Mr Strachey, speaking as an ex-Fellow Traveller, thinks the Communist Party will get very far in Britain either in the open or underground. In his opinion they are all washed up and for this reason—that, while in cold blood and under a quiet sky an ordinary person can accept the Party line, once the sky gets noisy his basic instincts, immune from dogma, reassert themselves. Example given by Mr Strachey himself: while distributing stirrup pumps in a working class district he came across a Communist family who at first flatly refused to have such a thing in the house (to put out a fire in their own roof would be helping the Imperialist War). Mr Strachey however left the pump inside the door telling them they needn't use it if they didn't want to. A few nights later the district was sprinkled with incendiaries and the Communist family, forgetting their

prosecution of the war to a successful issue'; its offices in Cayton Street, Clerkenwell, were raided by Scotland Yard: *The Times*, 22 Jan. 1941, 4f.

4 The Rt. Hon. (Evelyn) John (St Loe) Strachey (1901–63), the politician and writer, stated in a letter to the *New Statesman* 19: 479 (27 April 1940), 559, his reasons for breaking with the Communist Party, especially the *Daily Worker*'s attitude to the German invasion of Scandinavia, for that paper is 'prepared, for what they consider to be the interests of the Soviet Union, to give way to Hitler to any extent, and . . . are utterly irresponsible as to the consequences to the British people of such unlimited giving way'.

principles, ran hither and thither through the streets putting out fires with enormous gusto and efficiency. The same rebellion of instinct against ideology was shown by the Glasgow Transport workers who had passed a measure refusing to work during air raids; when the next raid occurred all the buses ran as usual.

The Old School Tie theme reappeared about the same time when one Colonel Bingham, in command of a cadet training centre, wrote a letter to *The Times* asserting that the old landowning and, in his own words, '(almost) feudal' aristocracy was the only proper source of army officers, and alleging that officers of more plebeian origin fell down on the job. The matter was brought up in the House of Commons and the Colonel was very rightly dismissed from his post.[5] There still is an England which does not know it is dead but it is finding its coffin less and less comfortable. I cannot see that the old caste system can survive this war. A week ago the papers were full of a libel action brought by the three Sitwells, Edith, Osbert, and Sacheverell, against someone who had alleged that as authors they had fallen into oblivion. Each of the Sitwells was awarded £350 damages—an award which in a few years should have a museum interest.[6]

Every so often one's friends reappear out of nowhere metamorphosized in uniform; they usually look younger, healthier, and sometimes cleaner than themselves as civilians. Most of those who are in the ranks find it extremely boring—'just like being back at school'—especially if they are herded with people ten years younger than themselves. But some are pleased to find themselves where they have no more need to make decisions. Those with commissions say they get excellent food; those whose military jobs are technical enjoy the technique; those whose jobs are labelled 'Intelligence' lament—in some cases— the misnomer. I lately had a letter from a friend who went into the Navy last summer, explaining—as follows—why he volun-

---

[5] For Lt.-Col. R. C. Bingham's letter, 'Man Management', and its consequences, see *The Times*, 15 Jan. 1941, 5f; 22 Jan., 2a; 24 Jan., 2e, 5c.

[6] The three Sitwells as plaintiffs claimed damages for libel in a review in *Reynolds News* of 18 Feb. 1940; the defendants were Co-operative Press Ltd. and Mr Sydney R. Elliott, editor of *Reynolds News*: see *The Times*, 7 Feb. 1941, 5e, 9f; 8 Feb., 2d; 11 Feb., 2f, 5d.

teered (he was in a reserved occupation)[7]: 'It seems a long time ago but when they got rid of Chamberlain and got the Labour chaps into the government there didn't seem any excuse for anyone who wasn't a doctrinaire communist not fighting and Chamberlain and Co. had got us into the position where we should all obviously have to fight either in our own back garden or elsewhere. The other thing which let me out was I had always felt I could honestly fight for America, and obviously Neville and his boys had got us into a position where America was in very real danger and would ultimately have to start fighting herself in one way or another, as is happening now.' The rest of his letter is a vivid presentation of the extraordinary blend of muddle and efficiency, comedy and courage, which composes His Majesty's Services. Owing to the censorship I cannot quote his more specific comments but I like the following description of the motion of a corvette: 'Being in —— on the Atlantic is like being in one of those super-modern roundabouts that go round and round very fast and also up and down and also swing violently from side to side, if you can imagine such a roundabout mounted on the back of an enormous tank careening across very broken country, the country being shaken with seismic convulsions.' This from a man who had spent ten years in an office and has a weak stomach. A great many people now are experiencing the same kind of hyperbole of novelty.

Another recent letter, from a visitor to Birmingham, has a postscript entitled 'Grim Tales from the Midlands' which concerns two young brothers in a working class family (the father had been out of work for years): 'A—— M—— (first-aid post warden): Don't run about like that you silly ass watching the bombs. If you'd seen what I've seen you'd have more sense. R—— M—— (crematorium man): If *I'd* seen what you've seen! If you'd seen what I've seen!'

This little bit of dialogue is very typical. So many people in the bombed areas have *seen* things—a hand sprouting out of a jumble of masonry or a great cloud of dust from a bomb rising

[7] Graham H. Shepard (1907–43), son of the illustrator E. H. Shepard (1879–1976), was an old school friend of MacNeice. He served in the Royal Navy on Atlantic convoys and was drowned at sea, autumn 1943; see MacNeice's poem 'The Casualty', *Collected Poems*, 245–8.

like a genie and inside the genie is a man with his legs cut off or a crying child whose mother has suddenly vanished. Not that the casualties up to date have been at all high in proportion to the enemy attacks; a soldier who had been stationed in a continually harassed port remarked to me that the bomb is 'a very un-lethal weapon'. But if anyone thinks that acquaintance with war makes the ordinary person condone it, he is mistaken. The British people in a sense are inured to enemy action but they *know* that war is foul; you must not be misled by their humour into thinking they have no feelings.

An incident last night proved to me—rather embarrassingly —the anti-defeatism of the Man in the Street. I was standing at a coffee stall at midnight with a friend who was talking rather wildly to the world (I was hardly listening) when he was suddenly swept away in a scurry of angry people and I found myself being struck at by vehement youths. Two policemen came up at once and asked what was going on; I said I had no idea. 'That's im!' one of the youths said (expressing a sheer hatred), ''e said Germany's going to win this war.' I had said nothing of the sort but the policemen, to prevent further trouble, asked me to go away. As for my friend, he had vanished; I am still hoping that he was not knocked out.

I spent most of a night lately down in the biggest subway station. There were 2,715 people sleeping there but only about 130 of these were children. One of the marshals told me that he was organizing a cribbage tournament between the platforms. We were in a short blind-alley tunnel lined with glazed tiles (the lights stay on all night) and while I was talking to the marshall, three of the railway conductresses arrived to go to bed. 'Had any trouble on your platform tonight, Madge?' 'Yes, woman carrying on about the old gent next to her. "I won't have it," she says, "I won't have this old bloke laying next to me. He's got *sweaty feet*." "Sweaty feet!" he says, "What if I have? You needn't turn your nose that way".'

A great many people at the moment are expecting an invasion in the near future and, in particular, a widespread use of gas. Hardly anyone expects the invasion to come off though I know of someone who carries laudanum on him in case it does. Many people would prefer the invasion to be attempted soon as they think it is our one chance of finishing the war quickly. In the meantime we are all encouraged to eat more potatoes and carrots, have our gas-masks in order, learn first aid, and how to use a stirrup-pump. Since the great Fire Raid on December 29th (when lawyers' safes became red hot and the great parchment deeds inside them shrivelled to next to nothing) fire precautions have been vastly improved and even small children in the last few weeks have put out incendiary bombs.[8] When Mr Herbert Morrison's fire-watching scheme has been fully put into practice, a purely incendiary raid will be probably less dangerous than going down a coal mine.[9]

I myself am now writing feature-scripts for the Overseas Department of the British Broadcasting Company and can tell you that their short-wave programmes for North America are being greatly developed. Apart from news commentaries and political talks the BBC are now properly conscious of the value of presenting Britain *as it is* to Americans. It is high time that ordinary individuals on both sides of the Atlantic should realize what their counterparts on the other side are like. From my own experience I think that there is little to choose—for unreality—between the popular British conception of Americans and the popular American conception of the British. I am not saying that these conceptions are uncomplimentary; the point is that they are quite fantastic. Neither the USA nor Great Britain is either a zoo or a museum or a midsummer night's dream; they are both just countries with a good deal in common and composed of individual human beings.

[8] The fiercest fire-raiding attempt of the war to date destroyed Guildhall, eight Wren churches, and many other buildings: *The Times*, 30 Dec. 1940, 4f; 3 Dec., 2c, 4a.

[9] Herbert Stanley Morrison, Baron Morrison of Lambeth (1888–1965), the Labour politician, Home Secretary, and Minister of Home Security, set up the National Fire Service and instituted a Fire Guard with regular fire-watching duties: *DNB*. He made the scheme compulsory: *The Times*, 20 Jan. 1941, 2f.

London Letter [3]: War Aims;
the New Political Alignment[1]

London, 1 April

If this letter appears predominantly critical and unexalted, it is because for the last month we have suffered comparatively little from enemy action. In a blitz you notice people's virtues; in a lull you notice their failings. The virtues are still there—one must not forget it—the morale is still excellent; the unforgiving minute—in a great many quarters though not in all—is duly deprived of its chance of sneers and vengeance. But not in all. A nation of amateurs, the British, in trying their hand at total war, are liable to become less democratic without a corresponding increase in efficiency. Yet there *is* another alternative and some people—*pace* such hearty obscurantists as Commander Southby (who in a recent broadcast deprecated the public discussion of war aims and also of social reconstruction)[2]—are trying to catch it as it flies: i.e., it is possible to become more efficient at the same time as, *and by reason of*, becoming more democratic.

A prevalent fallacy in the clubs (and in the Commons?) is that this war can be won by hand-to-mouth methods—take care of the means and the ends will take care of themselves. It has dawned on some people, however, that a clearer consciousness of aims and ends will promote the solution of some practical problems which have been falsely divorced from ideology. Aims and ends are not just a hobby of the intelligentsia; the man-in-the-street is not content merely to add unit to unit, and, while he has a genuine conviction that this war must be gone through with, he wants to know where he is going through with it *to*. A clear statement of intended social changes—*if* they

---

[1] *Common Sense* 10: 5 (May 1941), 142-3.

[2] Radio talk 'Unity of Purpose' on the BBC Home Service, 15 Feb. 1941, by Commander Sir Archibald (R. J.) Southby, RN (1886-1969), Conservative MP for Epsom Division of Surrey 1928-47, and the characteristic rejoinder the anon. article ' "Jollied Along" ', in the *New Statesman and Nation*, 20: 522 (22 Feb. 1941), 176.

were the right changes (i.e. in the direction of an intelligently planned economy and the levelling out of the social castes)— would enhance the national war effort and heighten, high though it is, the popular morale. It would also give an edge, at present sadly lacking, to British propaganda, which, as Hitler and Mussolini are happily aware, will never cut much ice in Europe until it can offer, in opposition to their own systems, something which is equally a system and is not just wishful thinking—putting the clock back, boys again together, making hay that never grew in a sun that could not shine.

'Utopianism'; that word is still a handy gag for the critic, is still a useful stick to throw into the works. Britain, however, still remains critical in parts; some of its criticism (that offered by the People's Convention, for instance)[3] may be 'Utopian' but much that is so labelled is merely realistic. We want, not less criticism, but more. Take the present Government which is conscientious and—certainly in comparison with its predecessors—both energetic and sensible. But it has been given since last summer almost a completely free hand and that is something with which no government on earth can be trusted. Being a coalition government and so having no official Opposition in Parliament, it has been allowed in the name of efficiency to go uncriticized. The Labour Party, the old Opposition, has thereby—taken as a body—degenerated into a gang of yes-men. It is now being realized that parliamentary criticism, far from hampering efficiency, tends to increase it and a new Opposition, probably to be led by Mr Shinwell, is crystallizing in the House of Commons.[4] I hope to write more of this movement in my next letter.

In the country as a whole, as in Parliament, there is a regrouping of interests going on which will cut right across the old distinctions. The Trade Unions, for example, can now— alas—be plausibly considered as pillars of reaction and it is no longer convincing to speak of Capital and Labour as if they

[3] See MacNeice's 'London Letter [1]' above with n. 8; also n. 6 below.

[4] During World War II, Emanuel ('Manny') Shinwell, Lord Shinwell (1884–1986), 'took upon himself the role of constructive critic believing the country needed a "win the war" Government': obit. *The Times*, 9 May 1986, 18e. For his wartime criticism, see his book *The Britain I Want* (1943). In the first Labour government of 1945, Shinwell became Minister of Fuel, under whom the mines were nationalized.

were two forces in chronic conflict with each other. Labour—taken to mean skilled and organized labour (which of course excludes a vast section of the population)—seems quite prepared to do a deal with the employers, to keep up prices in return for higher wages without regard to the general output of the nation, the proper development of man-power or the interests of the general consumer. The Trade Unions, that is, have become Torified, representing—nearly as much as the old Conservative party did—forces of privilege.

Roughly speaking one can say that the new division, the vital division, in this country will be between Planners and Non-Planners (or Anti-Planners). Muddling Through and *Laissez Faire* are dying hard—very hard indeed—and some of the 'planning' done so far seems to be merely a façade of 'state control' behind which the old monopolies scramble along as ever but now with a new sanction. Why, for example, has the Government only now brought in measures concentrating industrial production, measures which a High School boy could have seen to be necessary and which were mooted by the Shinwell group in Parliament over half a year ago? And what about the muddle over food, a muddle which anyone anywhere can see for himself without having resort to the expert's microscope or spectroscope? It is to be expected—and hoped—that a far more comprehensive system of rationing will soon be brought in which will preclude e.g. both the army habit of throwing surplus bread and meat into the dustbin and the rich man's continuance of pre-war gluttony in his cosy country hotel. (Lord Woolton *has* recently made it a very serious offence for anyone buying a meal in a hotel or restaurant to have more than one course of fish, meat, game, etc., eggs, or cheese.)[5] As for the home production of food I am told that the scientific experts are still disgracefully ignored.

Another subject which we must all the more concern ourselves with on the eve (if it is the eve) of Hitler's all-in Juggernaut is Civil Liberties. The BBC has just offended very badly (though not for the first time) in giving an ultimatum to a number of its artists—including Michael Redgrave and Beatrix

[5] Frederick James Marquis, the Lord Woolton and first Earl of Woolton (1883–1964), the Minister of Food: see *The Times*, 1 Feb. 1941, 5f–g.

Lehmann—banning them from its studios unless they withdraw their support from the People's Convention.[6] Many papers—notably the *News Chronicle*, the *Manchester Guardian*, and the *New Statesman* (none of which holds any brief for the People's Convention)—have raised a proper stink about this; the National Council of Civil Liberties is calling a meeting of protest and it looks as if there may be a motion proposed in the House of Commons condemning such discrimination. Seeing that Mr Attlee admitted recently in the House that the Government is opposed to such discrimination, it seems likely that the BBC may have to climb down from its tyrannical judgement-seat, the same kind of seat from which Sir Robert Vansittart passed judgement on Germany when he wrote his *Black Record*.[7]

I was at a tea-party the other day where people were discussing the position of J. B. Priestley: Is he now the second or the third most powerful man in the country?[8] This tribute to Priestley's eminence may surprise you; it only proves once again what the totalitarian countries have been demonstrating for years, that the radio has brought us back to the conditions of the Greek City State where the man who can hold the people's ear—or most of their ears most of the time—will acquire the most astonishing influence. Luckily Priestley is not a born demagogue or power-addict. On the other hand he is primarily a voice; what he says will depend on his affiliations and we must hope that the man who thus influences millions with his Yorkshire cooing, will go for his ideas to the right little batch of people. So far he has at least kept it before people's minds that Britain is changing and that it is necessary to direct

[6] See parliamentary reports in *The Times*, 12 March 1941, 2a–b; 13 March, 2e. The BBC ban was lifted a week later: ibid., 21 March, 2a. Sir Michael Redgrave (1908–85) and Beatrix Lehmann (1903–79) were outstanding actors.

[7] Sir Robert (Gilbert) Vansittart (1881–1957), created the Baron Vansittart 1941, was 'chief diplomatic adviser to His Majesty's Government', 1938–41. *Black Record: Germans Past and Present* (Jan. 1941)—the text of his seven broadcasts on the German people delivered on the BBC Overseas Service—was a sweeping indictment of Germany's historical record of militarism.

[8] John Boynton Priestley (1894–1984), the prolific English essayist, novelist, and playwright, gave widely praised weekly broadcasts as 'Postscripts' after the 9 O'Clock News on Sundays 1940–1. But the Government regarded him as a dangerous 'socialist', so the Minister of Information—Alfred Duff Cooper (1890–1954), later first Viscount Norwich—took him off the Home Service, though allowing him to continue to broadcast overseas 3 or 4 times a week. See John Braine, *J. B. Priestley* (1979), 108–10.

and control this change and not let it happen on its own as the act of an Unknown God.

I have just returned from three weeks in Ireland. I have no wish now to bring up the undying (though chameleonic) Irish Question but I would ask you to remember that the feeling in Eire is now predominantly pro-British (though still opposed to participation in the War), that the pro-German minority is extremely small and that De Valera's position is agonizingly difficult. Those who propose the application of the strong hand to Eire are forgetting their history but the other kind of extremist can be equally silly; an example is a recent little book by the Irish Republican, Jim Phelan, called *Churchill Can Unite Ireland*.[9] Mr Phelan's thesis is: End Partition in Ireland by a fiat and the whole country will automatically throw all its energies into the crusade against Hitler. Whereas what would really happen (remember Carson's gun-running in 1914)[10] would be civil war. Mr Phelan's validity as a spokesman for the whole of Ireland can be weighed by the fact that he relegates into the limbo of bad Irishmen—of mere British agents—both Parnell and Michael Collins.[11]

[9] One of Victor Gollancz's Victory Books, by James Leo Phelan (1895-*c*.1968), the Irish writer who wrote fictional and factual studies of criminals, gypsies, and tramps; in his youth he had been a member of the IRA.

[10] For gun-running by the Ulster leader Sir Edward Carson—threatening civil war when Britain was on the brink of war with Germany; see Ian Colvin's *The Life of Lord Carson* (1934, 1936), ii. 359-71.

[11] Both great Irish patriots who died in service to the country: Charles Stewart Parnell (1849-91), a Protestant, and Michael Collins (1890-1922), a Catholic. Condemnation of both sides highlights Phelan's radical position.

The Morning after the Blitz[1]

Summer came to London on a Wednesday and the Luftwaffe came on Wednesday night. They made a night of it; many people, both British and German, have called it the Biggest Raid Ever.[2] It certainly sounded so—like the banging of all the tea-trays and the loosing of all the fireworks and the rumbling of all the tumbrils and the breaking of all the oceans in the world. Just one long drawn-out lunatic symphony.[3]

I was in a restaurant when the guns started going heavily—a deep thudding and vibration that, as often happens, made me feel as if I were at sea. I went out into the streets during a lull; there was a strange flare apparently pinned on the sky, quite static like a great gilt ornament from a fantastic altar. I got home a little before midnight when the gunfire came surging back like a pack of hounds on the scent; and after that there seemed to be no more lulls. Feeling hungry all over again, I found a plate of cold herrings which I ate under the table like a cat. The floor of the basement shimmied underneath me and the whole house shook like a Chinese lantern in a breeze.

The droning of the German 'planes never gave over; it was like being inside a mad beehive. All the same, I didn't realize it was the 'biggest raid ever'. About 4 a.m. I went into the kitchen and found the door into the area blown wide open; the sky outside was an imitation of Sodom and Gomorrah. My neighbour was standing on his doorstep, smoking his pipe and looking down the hill with a connoisseur's detachment; there was a fire down there, blowing like washing in the wind with a drunken flamboyance. I went out into the street where two or

---

[1] *Picture Post* 2: 5 (3 May 1941), 9–12, 14, with photographs of bomb damage. From May to Nov. 1941 MacNeice wrote 9 scripts for the BBC World Service series *The Stones Cry Out*; No. 1, 'Dr Johnson Takes It', was broadcast 5 May 1941.

[2] The night of Wed.–Thurs., 16–17 April 1941: see MacNeice's penult. para. below, and *The Times*, 18 April 1941, 4f: 'Eight hospitals, several churches, and many other buildings and houses were hit, and there were heavy casualties in the raid, which was the heaviest yet experienced in London.' The raid lasted 'about 7 hours': ibid. 5c.

[3] Cf. MacNeice's 'The Trolls (written after an air-raid, April 1941)': *Collected Poems*, 196–8.

three men were discussing these strange occurrences—or not so strange at that, it was merely a question of degree. 'That's the worst night *we've* ever had round here,' they said with a regional pride. 'Hitler won't lick us now, not this way,' they said, as wisps of burnt paper sidled down on to their heads.

There was a violent crackling and hissing from the fire downhill, and a rich autumn smell of burning wood. And beyond my house the sky was a backcloth for opera or ballet, a sumptuous Oriental orange-print mottled with bursts of black and rolling like water so as sometimes to bury the moon—a half-moon that looked very clean and metallic in this welter of colour.

When the All Clear went I began a tour of London, half appalled and half enlivened by this fantasy of destruction. For it was—if I am to be candid—enlivening.[4] People's deaths were another matter—I assumed they must have been many—but as for the damage to buildings, I could not help—at moments—regarding it as a spectacle, something on a scale which I had never come across.

All these shattered shops and blazing stores, this cataract of broken glass, this holocaust of hall-marked and dog's-eared property—there was a voice inside me which (ignoring all the suffering and wastage involved) kept saying, as I watched a building burning or demolished: 'Let her go up!' or 'Let her come down. Let them all go. Write them all off. Stone walls do not a city make.[5] Tear all the blotted old pages out of the book; there are more books in the mind than ever have got upon paper.'

In a street with all the windows blown in, where every footstep meant a crunching of glass, a haggard man came trudging along with a suitcase through a scene that was half the dregs of night and half the reflection of fire. He took out his latchkey in front of a blasted shop. 'I've been bombed out at home,' he said, 'and now I come here, and look at this!' He vanished with his silent anger into his shop that was. Then women came plodding by with bundles; how many people, I wondered, are newly homeless? Ten minutes later I met two friends of mine

[4] Cf. MacNeice's 'Brother Fire', Nov. 1942: ibid. 196.
[5] Cf. 'Stone walls do not a prison make': Richard Lovelace (1618–58), 'To Althea, from Prison', st. 4. 1.

walking arm-in-arm in pyjamas and dressing-gowns; their flat had caught on fire. It was not yet 6 o'clock, but I suggested going to a restaurant for breakfast.

'In the old days,' one of them said contemplatively, 'you'd have gone anywhere to watch a good fire.' There were half a dozen fires to be seen in the course of our walk. Every variety of fire; one building would throw up a staggering column of ruddy smoke, tall as a tall tree; one would bulge in a mushroom of blackness; one would have flames that wavered from the window-edge like seaweed; the smoke clouds here would be harsh and sombre, while there they would be spun out soft in delicate dove-grey filaments. The hoses were playing on a big store from the street and from buildings opposite; the shifting pattern of water and smoke and flame was as subtle as the subtlest of Impressionist paintings; the jets from the hoses, I noticed with surprise, were a deep mauve, but this richness of colouring faded as the day grew brighter.

We tried three restaurants before we could get real food; the first could only offer us ice-cream sodas. Here and there we walked through a mess. Grandiose phrases or metaphors cannot cover it; it was just a —— mess. Shop-window dummies lolling amid wreckage; houses without eyes, without teeth, without bowels; snapped or buckled lamp-posts; hunks of masonry scattered like crumbs for sparrows. I was gazing into a shop of fancy goods that were open to the air and coated with powdered plaster. 'You can take one now,' a man shouted to me, 'price has gone down.' Wisecracks among the ruins; wisecracks and greetings and stories of the night—stories that in peacetime you'd think a bit tall, but which now are a matter of course and often an understatement.

About 7.30 I passed over a crossing where a bomb had left a crater and knocked the flagstones haywire, and walked along a shopping street where the pavement in places was as muddy and rough under foot as a crazy country lane. There was a continuous crash and tinkle as shopwalkers stood in the windows of luxury shops and swept out the glass into the street. A pneumatic pump was already busy opposite a church. Farther on, a small car had parked itself neatly in a crater.

And so on and so on; the kind of a Morning After you can't entirely believe in. An acrid morning; the streets shining in the sun with glass and water; a vomit of bricks and laths; the air compact of wood-smoke and brick-dust. A man in a half-existent shop was trying to telephone, saw me watching, and grinned: 'Taking the air,' he said.

Taking the air! The Blitz had certainly let some air in. A block of working-class flats had been ripped open to the world—the now familiar spectacle of the broken doll's house, the sort of doll's house you might have seen at the Caledonian Market,[6] with the walls askew and the wallpapers stained and no floors left in it at all. All the stuff that yesterday meant something, things you could use or enjoy, things that had a place in someone's life, were now just junk. And as for someone's life . . .?

By now it was a beautiful April morning—the daffodils in the squares outrageously yellow. There was one narrow street that in the sun had the air of a bazaar—bales of coloured cloth piled high on the pavements. But when you got near you saw it was not a bazaar at all; no, it was just salvage. And you felt that you mustn't stare: these things weren't meant to be seen in this way, any more than the pictures still hanging in the disembowelled parlour or the shining white bath that stands on the edge of an abyss.

At first sight, wandering round London, I thought the damage overwhelming. Hospitals and clubs and churches and luxury restaurants, tiny shops and department stores, flats and tenements and homes of all kinds, were shattered or scattered, spread-eagled or gutted. 'The whole place,' I said to myself, 'has fallen to bits overnight.'

But then I stopped to talk to a bookseller who was picking up his scattered stock in a shop that had suffered from blast; it looked as if it had struck a typhoon, but the damage, he explained to me, was 'only superficial' (of course, they would have to put the glass back; you can't have a bookshop without

---

[6] The Caledonian Market, Islington (North London)—opened in 1854 as a cattle market and discontinued at the beginning of World War II (*The Times*, 5 Sept. 1939, 5b)—had included a huge, disorderly, open-air pedlars' market every Friday, which attracted thousands of visitors from London and tourists from all over the world. 'During the war all the market square was used by the War Office and by various Government Departments': Robert Colville, *London: The Northern Reaches* (1951), 141. For a description of 'the Friday junk fair', see H. V. Morton, *In Search of London* (1951), 373-7.

glass). On thinking it over I realized that this kind of 'superficial' damage was greatly in excess of structural damage.

And this was made clearer by nightfall on Thursday; the clearing-up achieved during that day was astonishing: the rubble and broken glass had been swept into heaps, windows had been boarded up, buses were passing through streets impassable twelve hours earlier. It was all the difference between a raw wound and a wound that has been dressed.

One of the odd things about a blitz like this is the paradox of *distance*; you get two simultaneous but opposite impressions. The whole of London comes very near to you—the droning of the enemy 'planes puts you all on the spot at once, and the damage next morning, wherever it is, seems to affect you personally—but at the same time, in this bedlam of noise, you may be as ignorant of what's happening round the corner as of what's happening in Wales—and, if a bomb misses you, well, a Welsh bomb couldn't have missed you more successfully. Thus it was three days before I discovered that on Wednesday night HE[7] bombs fell in the next street that is parallel to mine, destroying several houses.

That London can take it may no longer be news,[8] but it remains—and will remain—a national asset. Thursday, April 17, 1941, was a day with a very strange feeling in the air—partly hysterical, partly fatalistic, but partly—I should like to say—*epic*. By Friday, to a casual observer, the town had returned to normal.

The Incident Officers were still collecting 'incidents' (the bureaucratic equivalent of tragedies), the Civil Defence services were still giving an astonishing exhibition of energy and devotion, a number of unexploded bombs were still roped off unexploded. But the population, having got some sleep, was very much back on its feet, the burnt buildings, charred and sodden, gave off no more smoke, but only dust or a smell, and the ruins of the day before yesterday had already—in the way

[7] High explosive.
[8] Proverbial. *London Can Take It*, a short GPO documentary film (released Oct. 1940) by Humphrey Jennings (1917–50) and Harry Watt (1906–), based on a dispatch by Quentin Reynolds (1902–65), had been widely screened; it 'shows how London and its citizens are successfully meeting and defying the ordeal of intensive attack': *The Times*, 18 Oct. 1940, 6c.

that ruins do—settled themselves into the landscape, some with the inconsequence of rubbish heaps and some with the dignity of very ancient monuments.

London Letter [4]: Democracy Versus Reaction & Luftwaffe[1]

London, 1 May

Writing this in the train while returning from a week-end in Plymouth (a peaceful countryside: sleek red cows in primrose fields and great slabs of gingerbread plough-land flow past the windows) an old lady of 78 beside me is having a spirited conversation with a man whose job is to pick up the dead: 'I don't mind picking anything up,' he says. 'I don't mind dumping it, but when I get home to me food . . .' Plymouth to London. Blitz to Blitz. Plymouth is one of the most recent examples of 'Coventration'.[2]

It was violently raided on two successive nights recently.[3] Unusually spectacular raids; the stock description is 'just like Fairyland'. The raiders had first put down a huge number of incendiaries (reckoned at 35,000 but many of them fell in the Sound) and had then plastered the flames with High Explosive. A retired Naval stoker said to me, 'I'd rather have ten Battles of Jutland[4] than two nights like that.'

The whole shopping centre of the town, with many wholesalers' establishments, the chief banks, several schools and churches, and nearly all the administrative offices, was neatly wiped out; half a square mile of the most thorough ruination I have seen. But deaths were surprisingly few (the official

---

[1] *Common Sense* 10: 6 (June 1941), 174–5.

[2] 'Coventration' (term varied from the verb 'to Coventry' as invented by German pilots): intensive bombing and devastation, involving indiscriminate mass murder of civilians, as inflicted on Coventry, Warwickshire, Nov. 1940: see *OED2*.

[3] In fact there were 5 nights (21–3 and 28–9 April 1941) in 9 that Plymouth had been the main objective of the German Air Force; MacNeice is here referring to the last two intensive raids. See *The Times*, 25 April 1941, 2c; 1 May, 2e.

[4] The Battle of Jutland (North Sea), 31 May 1916, fought between the Germans and the British—in which Royal Navy losses were roughly double, both in men and in tonnage, those of the German fleet—was 'the last great naval enagagement fought solely with surface ships'—Brigadier Peter Young, *A Dictionary of Battles 1816–1976* (1977), 367–9.

figure for civilians is less than 300) in proportion to damage to property. There were the usual hair's-breadth escapes by the hundred; forty-two people were buried alive for more than four hours in one shelter—and came out alive when another bomb fell and re-opened it.

Arrangements for the homeless were better than in many places, partly because the local authorities had learned foresight from the lesson of Coventry and partly because of the proximity of the Army and Navy, who immediately provided large quantities of food and took a leading part in rescue work and afterwards in demolition. After a night or two in Rest Centres nearly all the bombed-out families were removed to billets booked for them previously in case what had happened should happen. The surrounding villages made very generous offers of hospitality. And all the children remaining in Plymouth have returned to school though many of the schools are running in two shifts. Some of the school buildings have been taken over for communal restaurants; Plymouth hopes later to be feeding more than 20,000 in this way. I had a very solid meal in one such restaurant—a great hunk of meat-pie, cabbage, and potatoes; sago pudding and rhubarb and tea—for ninepence. Or about twenty cents. Later, it is to be expected that in most British cities communal feeding will become the rule rather than the exception. But this necessary innovation may be delayed; in this country Tom, Dick, and Harry can improvise brilliantly—and bravely—in emergencies, whereas the Ministries and Departments too often can't.

Since my last letter, the BBC, which had been banning artists on the ground of their political opinions, has been properly snubbed by Mr Churchill, and the subsequent appointment of four new Governors to the BBC should make its policy more liberal.[5] A defeat for Crypto-Fascism.

And the House of Commons about the same time saw a defeat

---

[5] As announced in *The Times*, 3 April 1941, 4f, the new Governors of the BBC were: Sir Ian Fraser (1897–1974), Ulster Unionist MP (later the Baron Fraser of Lonsdale); James Joseph Mallon (1875–1961); Arthur Mann (1876–1972), and Lady Violet Bonham Carter (1887–1969, later the Baroness Asquith of Yarnbury); these 4 joined the 2 continuing members, Sir Allan Powell (1879–1948, Chairman 1939–46), and Charles H. G. Millis (1894–1984).

for capitalist reaction.[6] Mr O. E. Simmonds,[7] a Birmingham industrialist, moved a motion directed against the Minister of Labour, Mr Bevin, on the ground that Mr Bevin's man-power policy was indulgent to the workers—in Mr Simmonds' words, 'a slacker's charter'. The Minister of Labour has legal powers which could easily make him dictator of industry; Mr Simmonds evidently wished to see these powers realized—but only one-sidedly, for, while the workers are no longer permitted to leave their jobs, Mr Simmonds wanted a restoration to the employer of the right to dismiss. Mr Bevin, replying, argued that present defects in production were more the fault of employers than employees. Mr Simmonds withdrew his motion.

I had a talk the other day with an industrialist employed on the Ministry of Supply (one of the patent drawbacks of these Ministries is that, in order to control and organize certain activities, they employ so many people who are themselves engaged in those activities for their own profit; or, putting it vulgarly, *Set a thief to catch a thief*). He told me—what to him was very surprising—that far and away the most efficient people with whom he now had to work were not industrialists at all but two professors of Philosophy. Which proves that the thieves are not the best qualified detectives. This discovery, we may hope, will later lead to the realization that *political* problems cannot be solved by 'politics' alone.

But the forces of reaction are still strong, as can be seen from the occasional volcanic outbursts of anti-intellectualism—in Parliament, in the press, and in pamphlets and books by such *simpliste* thinkers as Lord Elton.[8] Thus *The Times* the other day had a leading article, vague and inaccurate but virulent, entitled 'The Eclipse of the Highbrow'.[9] The attitude of *The Times* (the

[6] For this debate on war production in the House of Commons, see *The Times*, loc. cit.

[7] Oliver Edwin Simmonds (1897–1985), Ulster Unionist MP 1931–45, later Sir Oliver, had been responsible in the 1920s for the designs from which the Spitfire was developed in the 1930s.

[8] Godfrey Elton, the first Baron Elton (1892–1973), a former Labour supporter, Independent in politics, well known for his broadcast talks *It Occurs to Me* (1939).

[9] This article in *The Times*, 25 March 1941, 5d, referred to Lord Elton's anti-intellectual *Notebook in Wartime* (1941) as 'a sane and lively little book of reflections' and attacked the intellectuals of the 1920s and 1930s for preferring 'hasty brilliance' to the virtues of the common man as extolled by Lord Elton, so bringing the arts 'down to the level of esoteric parlour games' whereby 'to be a poet needed much the same

late advocate of appeasement) to 'highbrows' seems to resemble the attitude of Goebbels to the Jews. But *The Times* and those it represents will not get away with it.

In the USA there is naturally a clamour for an elucidation of British war aims. Over here little can obviously be said about the planning of a new Europe, though there *are* on the one hand people who seriously contemplate a restoration (passim) of the monarchies, and on the other hand idealists who feel they could set up a stream-lined federation of democracies overnight. The planning of a new Britain, however, is another story. More and more people—intelligent people—are voicing what will have to be done, and there is a surprising basic agreement among them.

I have heard Americans speak disparagingly of 'British empiricism'. It is true that the British have always fought shy of having what is called a world-view, but this shyness, while often hampering them, has also saved them from subordinating concrete reality to abstract ideology, from sacrificing life to logic. It is not, therefore, surprising that the most compelling proposals for reconstruction being made at the moment are those which are concerned with immediately practical problems and are made by people of immediate practical experience. See, for example, two recent long pamphlets by Mr Ritchie Calder (who during this war has made constant personal investigation of the bombed areas) entitled *The Lesson of London* and *Start Planning Britain Now*.[10] The latter begins with an arresting, but perfectly true, statement: 'Putting it brutally and

qualities as to be a maker of acrostics, and an admired stanza was scarcely distinguishable from an ingenious clue in a crossword puzzle'. For objections to this leader, see letters to *The Times*, 27 March, 5e, by Sir Kenneth Clark of the National Gallery and Sir Stephen Spender of *Horizon*; also 28 March, 5e, by Geoffrey Faber of Faber & Faber, and by Michael Roberts. Letters in support of the leader followed 29 March, 5e; 31 March, 5e; 1 April, 5e, and Sir Kenneth replied 7 April, 5d. For further comment on the controversial article, see Raymond Mortimer (1895–1980), 'The Eclipse of the Highbrow', *New Statesman and Nation* 21: 528 (5 April 1941), 360–1.

[10] Peter Ritchie Ritchie-Calder, Baron Ritchie-Calder (1906–82), the scientist, journalist, and broadcaster, reported in news dispatches on the blitz 1940–1 collected in *Carry On, London* (1941) that 'the Front Line was no longer in Europe but in London's East End' (obit. tribute by Paul Rotha in *The Times*, 6 Feb. 1982, 8g). Lord Ritchie-Calder's two books cited here by MacNeice were published in 1941. Lord Ritchie-Calder was Director of Plans in the Political Warfare Executive of the Foreign Office 1941–5, CBE 1946, later a leader of the Campaign for Nuclear Disarmament.

callously—the biggest slum-clearance scheme in British history is in progress. The writs are being served by bombers.'

Another writer who recognizes the bombs of the Luftwaffe as heralds of a social revolution is Mr George Orwell. His recently published booklet, *The Lion and the Unicorn*, (sub-title: *Socialism and the English Genius*) is the most brilliant piece of pamphleteering I have seen since this war began.[11] He has the defects of the pamphleteer—overstatement, flashy generalization, misdirected truculence—but his analysis of the English character and the social evolution of Britain, and his insistence on *local* factors are a relief after the dogma of the pedants and the jargon of arm-chair reformists. He is almost certainly right in his thesis that 'Progress and reaction are ceasing to have anything to do with party labels.'[12] 'Labour Party politics,' he says, 'had become a variant of Conservatism,'[13] but, since the war, or at any rate since the Blitz, the would-be socialist no longer has to choose between the somnolent and double-faced Labour Party and the also double-faced, unrealistic, and hopelessly alien Communist Party. Since the Blitz—in Mr Orwell's words, 'Being a Socialist no longer means kicking theoretically against a system which in practice you are fairly well satisfied with.'[14]

Now for my monthly complaint. On the whole things here are moving in the right directions but these movements are not either as rapid or as thorough or as co-ordinated as they should be. Thus I lately had some illuminating (or—equally—some mystifying) conversations with an official of the Ministry of Food. From these conversations and from some recent articles in the press (in particular, an article by a truck-driver in the *New Statesman* and another by a dietetic professor in the *Spectator*)[15] I have reached the conclusion which most housewives

[11] George Orwell (pseud. of Eric Arthur Blair, 1903–50), *The Lion and the Unicorn* (1941); pt. 1, 'England Your England', sects. 1–2, had appeared under the title 'The Ruling Class' in *Horizon* 2: 12 (Dec. 1940), 318–23.

[12] *The Lion and the Unicorn*, pt. 3, 'The English Revolution', sect. 1, para. 2, in *The Collected Essays, Journalism, and Letters of George Orwell*, ed. Sonia Orwell and Ian Angus, 4 vols. (1968), ii. 90.

[13] Ibid. ii. 94, penult. para.

[14] Loc. cit., last para.

[15] 'Rations and Racketeers', by W.J.N., a lorry driver, in the *New Statesman and Nation* 21: 527 (29 March 1941), 318–19; and 'Food Education', by Vernon Henry Mottram (1882–1976), in the *Spectator* 5884 (4 April 1941), 368–9. Mottram was

would endorse, that our production and distribution of food are still deplorably inefficient. Moreover, the scientific experts are still largely ignored and, in respect of nutrition, the public is still uneducated.

Here, as in other spheres, while the Government itself is not corrupt, it is, thanks to its residue of *Laissez-Faire* policy, the unconscious occasion of corruption in others; it gives much too free a hand to the Food Rings. We must not, says the Ministry of Food, interfere with 'the Trade'. All right: the Trade goes happily ahead—happily astern—concerning itself as ever mainly with profits, and the public finds that articles controlled in price just disappear from the markets. Take onions: the onion (controlled in price) has become a fabulous rarity, but it is stated by those who should know that certain of our lords of commerce have got onions cornered by the ton; if these onions were released, housewives might stop buying leeks which are uncontrolled and are now selling at six times their pre-war price.

In such ways not only the consumer but the small shopkeeper is victimized. Many of these little shopkeepers are on the verge of bankruptcy and have to scramble for their profits where they can, e.g. among the leeks. The sensible thing would be for the Government to take them all over as salaried State employees. But the Government of course would consider this an interference with individual liberty (the liberty to starve your own way). So the thousands of little shops (confectioners' and tobacconists' are especially noticeable) remain open but more or less empty, and behind their barren counters thousands of elderly bodies sit waiting like hungry spiders who have somehow by accident spun their webs in the Arctic. The large retailers, on the other hand, are not doing so badly and the chain-stores seem—where there are profits to be made—a good deal more adept at distribution than the Government.

No, the Ministry of Food is still too timid to organize (it hardly even co-operates with the Ministry of Agriculture). Sooner or later they will have to do something very drastic— and very complicated—but they wish to put it off as long as

Professor of Physiology in the University of London and the author of many books on nutrition, including *Healthy Eating* (1940).

possible. For example, they might introduce a maximum expenditure scheme limiting each individual's expenditure on food to say twenty-five shillings per week. Or they might bring in some kind of Food Tax apportioned to income by which the rich man would pay a half-a-crown for the same commodity for which the poor man would pay sixpence. But, being frightened of the inevitable difficulties in making any such scheme workable, they rationalize their fright by professions of liberalism: we are a nation of shopkeepers[16] and the Englishman's till and the Englishwoman's kitchen are inviolate. The till may be empty and the larder may be empty and the gas may be cut off in the kitchen but still they are all inviolate—we haven't copied our totalitarian enemies, we haven't interfered with 'individual rights'.

This economic non-interference, like political Non-Intervention, falls on people very unequally. It hits the small shopkeepers while indulging the large retailers and wholesalers. It gives poorer people in general the very just grievance that, while they are forced to wait for such bits and pieces as rationing combined with bad distribution allows them, the rich man can sidle from restaurant to restaurant and eat at least more than is good for him. Our answer is that in this war, unless a Ministry is conscious of the need for social equality, it won't be too successful in providing for the people either food or anything else.

I hope the Censor will have passed these strictures.[17] We cannot give you a just idea of the internal progress of this country if we pretend away the mess and muddle that impede it. There *is* mess and there *is* muddle. But there also is progress. Today's papers forecast a new law to prevent speculation in bombed sites.[18] The speculator in anything has a rough time ahead of

[16] Saying (*l'Angleterre est une nation de bouquitiers*) attributed to Napoleon by his surgeon Barry E. O'Meara, *Napoleon in Exile: or, A Voice from St Helena*, 4th edn, 2 vols. (1822), ii. 81.
[17] Three identifying words in MacNeice's first 'London Letter' of 1 Jan. (Feb. 1941), para. 3, had been censored. (The Director-General of the Postal and Telegraph Censorship Department 1940–5 was the international and commercial lawyer (Sir) Edwin Herbert (1899–1973), later the Baron Tangley.) During the war, censorship was a delicate and secret security matter, about which there was little news.
[18] The Ministry of Works and Buildings had announced in Feb. its determination to prevent such land speculation: 'Land and Reconstruction', *The Times*, 3 Feb. 1941, 5c; however, it was only in June that the Land Agents' Society suggested temporary legislation, under the Town and Country Planning Act (1932)—not, surprisingly, the

him. And—from the point of view of most of us—the rougher the better. Only very few people now think the word 'national' is the opposite of 'rational'. Our old nineteenth-century irrational 'democracy' is due to give place to democracy.

War Damage Act (1941)—'to check speculation in bombed sites': 'Sale of Bombed Sites', ibid. 7 June 1941, 2c.

London Letter [5]: Reflections from the Dome of St Paul's[1]

London, 2 June

Since for various reasons I may be unable to continue this series of Letters,[2] this is perhaps a good moment to attempt, not an objective summary of the situation in Britain, but some tentative generalizations on the atmosphere and the mentality of wartime London as I have encountered it. In war, as in peace but not perhaps so much as in peace, people tend to forget that London is two cities, divided by the historic square mile known as the 'City' itself; of these two cities the western one is the London known to tourists, the eastern one is unknown not only to the great majority of tourists but to the great majority of Londoners outside the working classes. Emendation: there is also the third city (South London) which stretches for miles on the other side of the Thames—a river which few Londoners of my acquaintance cross even once in a year unless on their way to the country. Of these three cities most people who describe London under air-attacks are talking about the western one (plus the 'City of London'), this area containing nearly all the famous names and the most spectacular damage. But you should remember that the effects of a blitz on the West End, horrible though they may be, are far less sinister than the effects of a blitz on one of the great drab tracts which consist of the homes of the poor. I have noticed myself that to walk along a great shopping street (imagine something like Madison Avenue) on the morning after a blitz, far from being depressing, is almost exhilarating (this may shock you but many people share my experience); every step that you take crunches on glass and the

---

[1] *Common Sense* 10: 7 (July 1941), 206–7.

[2] Because of his appointment to BBC Features, May 1941, MacNeice was busy as a radio scriptwriter and features producer; but see n. 7 below. The London Letter series was continued in *Common Sense* 10: 8 (Aug. 1941) to 12: 9 (Sept. 1943) by Stephen Spender.

whole street is tinkling as the shop-walkers stand in their windows and sweep the glass on to the pavement where luxury
objects lie scattered among torn-up flagstones and drunken
lamp-posts; maybe there is a crater in the middle of the street
containing a private car with water to the top of the wheels.
This is havoc, but it is not heart-breaking; you watch the great
emporiums burning and you feel like saying: 'What of it?
Maybe it was coming to them anyway. Man does not live by
paté de foie gras alone.'

What *is* heart-breaking is to see a poor street of dwelling-
houses which have just been disembowelled, a great cloud of
dust still hanging over the ruins and a smell of corruption seep-
ing through everything. And it is heart-breaking, too, to walk
through parts of the East End which may not lately have been
bombed but which were more or less evacuated under an earlier
terror and left to the rats and the damp—the petrifaction of the
memory of poverty. Street after street of empty stinking homes
which will never—or so we hope—be anybody's homes any
more.

London has had three extremely bad nights in the last six
weeks—April 16th and 19th, and May 10th.[3] The first of these,
still spoken of as 'The Wednesday', was billed by the Nazis as
the Biggest Raid Ever,[4] a description which many Londoners
would endorse. The raid continued till dawn and for many
hours the noise of the planes never let up. I walked round
London in the early morning; there was devastation every-
where and I got the impression 'They've made a job of it this
time.' But London recovers with astonishing quickness; by that
evening many signs of superficial damage (and much of the
damage always *is* superficial) had been removed; buses were
running, though some of them on altered routes; people had
returned to normal. The raid on the following Saturday caused
heavy casualties but in comparison with the Wednesday, people
—at least in the West End—dismissed it as just another raid.

For the raid of May 10th (now spoken of as 'The Saturday'),
I had a seat in the stalls, having arranged to spend that night on

[3] For the indiscriminate air attacks of these three nights, see *The Times*, 18 April
1941, 4f–g; 21 April, 2a; 12 May, 4a–b.
[4] See ibid., 18 April 1941, 4f–g, as well as MacNeice's article 'The Morning after
the Blitz' (May 1941), above.

St Paul's Cathedral. St Paul's has already had two direct hits,[5] but Wren's structure is standing up to it amazingly well (if you go back-stage in the cathedral you notice with what extraordinary ingenuity and thoroughness—and solidity—the whole thing is put together). St Paul's has a very efficient fire-watching organization; there were about 16 men on duty that night, who take it in turns to occupy advanced posts (e.g. up the dome) and to walk around from point to point looking for incendiaries while communicating with each other by telephone; all over the roofs and in the hidden galleries there are hydrants, water-tanks, stirrup pumps, and sandbags.

It was a night of a full moon which half the time was lost in fire-clouds, and from midnight till dawn HE bombs and incendiaries fell all over the City. The first big fires occurred south of the river and were reflected in it. A little later there were fires all around us, stretching to the East End on one side and to Westminster and further, on the other (it was about 2 a.m. that Westminster got it, but you will know all about that). I had not realized there was so much left to burn in our immediate neighbourhood but there was; a building next door sent up an enormous fountain of sparks like a genie, sparks which circled and sidled with the gentle inconsequence of snowflakes and fell down on to our heads. In a little time great tawny clouds of smoke, rolling in a sumptuous Baroque exuberance, had hidden the river completely and there we were on the dome, a classical island in a more than Romantic Inferno. It was far and away the most astonishing spectacle I have ever seen but I cannot describe it; all the old clichés pop up into my mouth but they are utterly and insultingly inadequate. When the HE bombs came near us, the whole cathedral would shudder and dust would come choking down the staircases. We inhaled the smell of burning.

When the day came up and the planes had gone, London was burning still; you could stand on the top of the dome and

---

[5] Although St Paul's was spared during the great fire of 29 Dec. 1940 which devastated a large area around it (*The Times*, 1 Jan. 1941, 6b), it suffered two direct hits from high-explosive bombs: in early Oct. 1940 the high altar was destroyed; on 16 April 1941 the floor of the N transept collapsed into the crypt, and all the stained-glass windows were lost: ibid. 11 Oct. 1940, 2a–b; 19 April 1941, 4f. See F. R. Banks, *London* (1958), 370–1.

warm your hands at it. I had never before realized the infinite variety of fire—subtleties never attained by any Impressionist painter. These fires were a wedding of power with a feminine sensuous beauty. A glowering crimson power mottled with black; a yellow liquid power—a kind of Virgin Birth—which is sheer destruction; a cracking, a hissing, and an underground growling. But up above were the softest clouds of smoke—soft as marabou—purple and umber and pink and orange which spread out and shaded off to blue. Looking at these fires from above I got them in perspective. When the fire takes over a new building, first of all it is the building that is on fire, but later it is the fire that is the solid object, the building is just a gimcrack screen that the fire has folded around itself.

I walked back to breakfast through burning and tumbling streets, stepping over hoses and dodging falling glass and falling water. I was in a rather childish mood of elation; being in St Paul's in a raid is much more glamorous—and in fact less frightening—than being in your own house. But when I turned into the street where I live,[6] it looked like a rubbish heap; none of the houses were down but most of the doors and windows were blown in and the pavements were thick with litter. I found my household on their hands and knees shovelling up soot and plaster and I became very depressed—not because of the soot and the plaster but because something very heavy must have fallen somewhere near and so must have killed some people in that very important category—the people one half knows, through passing them every other day. We had only to go less than 100 yards to find what had happened—to a circle of houses surrounding a railed-in garden; a whole quadrant had gone and all the remaining houses looked like skeletons. I at once remembered that during a raid on a dark night in December an unknown girl, whose face I could not see, had caught me up in the street and asked if I would walk home with her because she was frightened; and saying 'Good luck,' she had gone into one of those houses. It is quite true that raids tend to make people callous; statistics of casualties awake no response; but once in a

---

[6] Wharton Street, London WC1: on the evidence of his correspondence with the Dodds (now at the Bodleian Library, Oxford), MacNeice was staying with the Group Theatre choreographer Rupert Doone at 34 Wharton Street, Feb.–Sept. 1941.

way, as on this occasion, the tragedy—and the futility—of it all come, as they say, home to you.

Speaking of callousness, I have just read in your May issue a letter attacking an earlier Letter of mine and asserting that I 'label insensitivity as humour and mass behaviour as anti-defeatism'.[7] London war-time humour is, I admit, pretty crude, but it does not imply insensitivity (any more than did the equally characteristic humour of many Spaniards during the Spanish Civil War) and, as for mass behaviour, it may seem logical—at a distance of 3,000 miles—to predict mass behaviour in a blitzed community, but I should like to assure your correspondent that this prediction is wrong. Most individuals in and after an air-raid are not less individual but, if anything, more individual than they were in peace-time. This atmosphere of danger may coarsen you in some ways but it makes you more perceptive in other ways and it concentrates, rather than disperses, people's essential personality.

All the same I know we should ask ourselves every so often whether, living in these conditions, we are still seeing straight. I find that I vacillate as to the answer; sometimes I say to myself 'This is mere chaos, it makes no sense,' and at other times I think 'Before I saw wartime London I must have been spiritually colour-blind.' There is plenty of degradation—the cheapness inevitable in a world that involves so much short-term propaganda—and plenty of squalor, but there is also an exaltation and, when I say that, I do not mean anything in the nature of Rupert Brooke heroics[8] or last ditch bravado, I mean something much bleaker and, in one sense, humbler, something like the feeling you get on top of a mountain on a cold, grey day. T. S. Eliot in a poem spoke of 'the still point of the

7 Renée von Eulenburg-Weiner's letter 'Anti-MacNiece' [sic] in *Common Sense* 10: 5 (May 1941), 157; see also Chester A. Arthur's brief letter 'Pro MacNiece' [sic] loc. cit. The former objected to MacNeice's chauvinism over the suppression of the *Daily Worker* in the April issue, and found more promise in Stephen Spender. (Could this opinion have prompted the editors to exchange London correspondents—namely, Spender for MacNeice? However, MacNeice had signed his contract with the BBC, 26 May 1941, and was no longer as free as before.)

8 The 'canonization' of the English poet Rupert Brooke (1887–1915) as ideal patriot-soldier was based on his war sonnets of 1914 written before his departure for action in the Dardanelles—as well as on his good looks and 'romantic' early death in the Aegean—though he never lived to see combat.

turning world';[9] perhaps it is the still point of the *crashing* world that England has now become aware of. There is, in some quarters, an understandable swing-back to religion but the revival of religion (with its ordinary connotations) is something that I neither expect nor desire. What *is* being forced upon people is a revival of the religious sense.[10] And after the hand-to-mouth ethics of nineteenth-century liberalism and the inverted and blinkered quasi-religion of Marxism and the sentimentality of the cynical Lost Generation—after all that, we need all the senses we were born with; and one of those is the religious.

[9] Not only in *Burnt Norton* (1935) ii. 16, but also in 'Coriolan: 1. Triumphal March' (Oct. 1931), l. 34.

[10] A religious revival in the 1940s was one strong response to the war challenge. Such writers as T. S. Eliot (1888–1965), Dorothy L. Sayers (1893–1957), and J. Middleton Murry (1889–1957) participated in the Malvern Conference, 7–10 Jan. 1941, under Archbishop William Temple (1881–1944), which urged considerable reform on English society and on the Church of England; see *Malvern 1941* [Proceedings]. Eliot also contributed to and was occasional guest-editor for the *Christian News Letter*, ed. (during the war) Joseph H. Oldham (1874–1969). Other prominent Christian writers like Charles W. S. Williams (1886–1945) and C. S. Lewis (1898–1963) were active in lecturing during the war: e.g. Lewis's broadcast talks 1941, 3 series (collected in *Mere Christianity*, 1952). On rebirth, as of the Church in the war, along with establishment of the British Council of Churches 1942, see W. Cecil Northcott, 'The British Isles', in *Christianity To-day*, ed. Henry Smith Leiper (1948), 133–42.

Broken Windows or Thinking Aloud[1]

(i)

I am taking the liberty of thinking aloud—this is more for my own satisfaction than for yours. Being a reader, you want something crystal & perfect—lucidly self-consistent. Being a writer, I want to get rid of a burden.

You need not be afraid I am going in for self-flagellation, for washing my own dirty linen in public. Some of my colleagues have gone all humble; I consider that a mistake. There is a time for writers to be humble; this is *their time to be arrogant*.

A member of a giggling & twitching intelligentsia? Yes, no doubt I was one, perhaps am still. But it is better to giggle & twitch than to be a stock or a stone, & an intelligentsia—however decadent or 'bourgeois'—is something much finer than the TUC[2] or the Stock Exchange or London Society.

The Marxist obsession encouraged us to crawl, to pretend ourselves cogs in a machine or part of the pattern in the lino. This pretence of humility was morbid—it was like Colonel Lawrence effacing himself in the Tank Corps.[3] Now, with a war on, we need not be so anxious for self-effacement, we can leave that job to the bombs. This is our time to be arrogant.

Especially with people about like Lord Elton—writing off the intellect as fast as they can write.[4]

---

[1] A signed holograph manuscript, written *c.*1941-2, recently published in *Poetry Review* 78: 2 (summer 1988), 4–6. Ampersands appear throughout in the manuscript and have been retained.

[2] Trades Union Congress.

[3] T. E. Lawrence (1888-1935), 'Lawrence of Arabia', resigned from the Colonial Office 1922, rejecting his fame, 'enlisted in the RAF in 1922 as an aircraft hand under the name of John Hume Ross, and a year later joined the Tank Corps as T. E. Shaw, a name he adopted by deed poll in 1927. He later returned to the RAF, retiring from it shortly before he was killed in a motor-cycle accident near his home at Cloud Hall, Dorset': *OCEL*, 5th edn, 555.

[4] The Rt. Hon. Godfrey Elton, first Baron Elton (1892-1973), tutor in history at Oxford (Queen's College) when MacNeice was there, a devout Anglican, Imperialist, and Labour man, considered by some to be reactionary (*DNB 1971-1980*), had become General Secretary of the Rhodes Trust 1939 (-59); 'through most of his books

Not that my primary concern at the moment is writing. Whoso at the moment saveth his art shall lose it.

The War has thrown us back upon life—us & our writing too. But we were less alive[5] than our art because more negative. What we have done we need not recant; the trouble was what we were, but what we were has gone—or as good as.

In the first flush of this change the writer must beware of a lie—of denouncing his past work as well as his past self. There are saps like Archibald MacLeish who think that art can be negative, destructive.[6] Assuming that the present world-crisis has cancelled out Eliot & Hemingway. This is both nonsense & an insult.

The 'message' of a work of art may appear to be defeatist, negative, nihilist; the work of art itself is always *positive*. A poem in praise of suicide is an act of homage to life.

But different circumstances change the 'message'—the content—& so the method—the style. I notice myself that my two old methods—reportage & lyric—are ceasing to suit me. & I notice I have lost my nostalgia, am no longer worried by the passage of time.

Am ready to jettison the past—that is, my personal past. The general & historical Past remains printed in eternity; 'll[7] remain monumental even if all the monuments go—all its outward & visible signs.

Let them all go if they must. Take out your razor & shave away the houses; shave away the soil & the sub-soil. If the human animal remains, it remains—an animal & human; instincts, ideals, remain.

An asylum is not freedom & a man's best house is humanity.

---

runs a thread of anti-intellectualism': obit. tribute, *The Times*, 19 April 1973, 20g. He had just produced two rather superficial books—*It Occurs to Me: Broadcast Talks* (1939) and *Notebook in Wartime* (1941). Cf. n. 9 to 'London Letter [4]' above.

[5] 'less alive' is written above cancellation of 'dead'.

[6] The American poet Archibald MacLeish (1892–1982) who was Librarian of Congress 1939–44 'argued, in *The Irresponsibles* (1940), that the scholars and writers of his generation had abdicated their responsibility to fight fascism and thus had unwittingly helped to disarm and demoralize the Western democracies': R. H. Winnick, introduction to his edn of *The Letters of Archibald MacLeish 1907 to 1982* (1983), xv.

[7] 'll' is written to the left of the cancellation of 'Will'.

We had got this concept of freedom all wrong; comfort & security were blinkers.

Freedom must be reassessed. Because it is reappearing. & God must be reassessed whether he exists or not. For, whether he exists or not, God is reappearing too. And, as for the human race, it must be reassessed.

In case it is disappearing.

(ii)

> The best lack all conviction & the worst
> Are full of passionate intensity.[8]

These lines of Yeats remain the classic description of the last twenty years.

Oh, I know in the thirties the boys ran after conviction; they wrote high-minded poetry, they sat on high-minded committees. But High-Mindedness isn't conviction; it is like Self-Respect— a rather frowsy cul-de-sac.

Now the bombs have broken the end wall. Clearing the slums, cleaning the mind of fumes. So where do we go from here?

Some of us go jingo & some of us go religious—muzzily religious with a great deal of hand-washing. & some of us try to remain where we were—high minded nineteenth-century liberals (liberals in spite of a flirtation with Marx & Victorian in spite of—or because of?—our cult of the Future).

Some of us, that is, remain Static Progressives. The Gorgon's Head of Fascism has robbed us of initiative. Because to take initiative is to exercise power & all power—so we have been told & no doubt it is true—corrupts; & we do not want to become little Nazis.

That is another thing—Power—we shall have to reassess. Is there, do you think, an analogy with fire? All fire destroys but we use it on our hearths & in our furnaces.

Be that as it may, we Victorian liberals are frightened of getting ourselves corrupted. So we wash our hands of any shadow of power & trek for the Holy Mountain. If someone has

---

[8] Yeats, 'The Second Coming' 1919, ll. 7–8.

got to be corrupted it won't be us; let the politicians get on with the dirty work.

But supposing political problems cannot be resolved by politics alone? Much less by politicians alone—that sleep-walking race of careerists. Well, if *they* can't solve them, they needn't be solved; we're bound for the Holy Mountain.

This is a most understandable reaction. Hegel's apotheosis of the State[9] may have appealed to us once—until it was translated into concrete reality. This concrete reality has frightened us off political idealism.

So we've shrunk back into individualists with an airy fairy conception of freedom—a long flirtation with a will o' the wisp, a chronic parthenogenesis. You can see this in some of our younger poets whose slogan is 'Back to the Astral Plane'.

But isn't it a pity if you have to choose between the Astral Plane & High-Mindedness? Aren't there other choices?

'Empiricism?' You say that rather scornfully; it depends on what you mean by it. An 'empiricist' may be someone who lives from hand to mouth. Or he may be someone who follows an ideal that is always developing, implicit rather than explicit.

The Marxist ideal was proposed in this shape but the current went & froze. What good is a wheel if it turns in a vacuum? The Communist Party have become collectors of fossils. 'Yes', they say, 'we're Communists. It's the only logical thing to be.' But life cannot be solved by logic. Any more than Higher Mathematics can teach you to swim.

To live either happily or usefully, as to make works of art, requires a method which is in this sense empirical—that each case is unique. The number 2 may be always number 2 but no two men or no two pictures are identical. This does not preclude recognition of men as men or pictures as art, but it means that, to judge them, you need an open mind.

Yet the Open Mind is something a man gets bogged in. The Open Mind is good but encourages *Laissez-Faire*. & *Laissez-Faire* is bad.

A paradox often exemplified in psycho-analysis when it is mis-

[9] In G. W. F. Hegel's (1770–1831) philosophy, 'The state is . . . a totality above all individuals . . . an embodiment of the absolute idea . . . and since it is a unit, its highest development is rule by monarchy': *New Columbia Encyclopedia*, ed. William H. Harris and Judith S. Levey (1975), 1216.

taken for a religion. It opens you doors into a blank. The cured patient may be fighting fit but what is he going to fight for?

It is better to enter into heaven halt & neurotic than to have a sane mind in a sane body & not know what to do with them.

The analyst does not recognize Evil but neither does he give you a heaven—a Formal Cause. Just get yourself cured & everything will be dandy.

Mr Heard ditto: Save your own soul & then you can save the world.[10] I don't believe it.

Not that I believe Marx either when he leaves it to the spots to change the leopard.

Yet change in the human sphere *is* possible &, what is more, it is necessary, & such change has always two sides to it—it must be conditioned from without & it must be chosen from within. It is self-deception to ignore the conditions but to say you cannot choose is to make the Great Refusal.[11]

Today we are all being dragooned by outside conditions, we look like the shuttlecocks of War. It is therefore all the more necessary to think of ourselves as free agents. Freedom is our birthright. Perhaps you want to sell it for a mess of passive masochism?

If you refuse to be passive you've got to be active. But how interfering. Someone will object.

'Others must be regarded aesthetically & only oneself ethically.'[12] In saying this Auden sold out. Ethics presupposes not only judgement upon others but calculated interference with them.

Non-intervention in the ethical sphere must defeat even its own end—which is private salvation. One thing this war is doing in this country—it is stopping people tinkering with their souls. Lay off your soul & give the poor thing its head.

& why not shelve your private salvation & see what you can do with the world? Without bothering too much about life—

---

[10] In 1941 H. F. (Gerald) Heard (1889–1971) published *The Creed of Christ: An Interpretation of the Lord's Prayer* and *Training for the Life of the Spirit.*

[11] Dante, *Inferno,* iii. 60, *il gran. rifiuto*; cf. MacNeice's *Selected Literary Criticism,* 5 with n. 3.

[12] W. H. Auden, *New Year Letter* 1940 (first English edn, May 1941), 133, 4th note to l. 1244 under the heading *Judge not*: 'no-one can separate in another's suffering how much is tribulation and how much temptation. Therefore others must be regarded aesthetically and only oneself ethically. (Except ye become as little children . . .)'

your own—or Life with a capital L. & taking a special care not to think of death as cancellation, as the final reduction to nought.

Death in its own right—as War does incidentally—sets our lives in perspective. Every man's funeral is his own, just as people are lonely in their lives, but Death as a leveller also writes us in life. & Death not only levels but differentiates—it crystallizes our deeds.

We did not need a war to teach us this but war has taught us it. Before the war we wore[13] blinkers. Applied science, by increasing comfort & controlling disease, had—geared to a 'liberal' individualism—encouraged us to think of death as a pure negation, a nuisance. But applied science, by shattering a town overnight, by superimposing upon ordered decay a fantastic but palpable madness, has shown us the integral function of death. Death is the opposite of decay; a stimulus, a necessary horizon.

& this will affect our conception of Freedom . . .

(To be continued.)[14]

[13] 'wore' is written above the cancellation of 'had'.
[14] The article was left unfinished.

Northern Ireland and Her People[1]

Northern Ireland must be a puzzle to a foreigner; it is still a great puzzle to many Englishmen. This is true of both the whole unit and of its individual members. If you look at a map of Ireland you will find a small portion in the north-east (one-sixth of the island) cut off from the rest by an irregular border; this is 'Northern Ireland', otherwise known as the Six Counties or, sometimes, Ulster. It is to be noted however that this area excludes three of the counties of the old province of Ulster and, incidentally, the *most* northerly part of Ireland, which is in County Donegal. From a purely geographical point of view this partition looks odd. Those who visit the district however will find many things that at first sight seem still odder.

The visitor will probably land at the capital city, Belfast, an ugly city in a very beautiful setting. Belfast in peacetime had, it is said, more motor cars in proportion to its population than any other city in the British Isles; you may still however find yourself driving from the dockside to your hotel in a primitive horse-drawn vehicle known as an outside car (it has no roof and the passengers sit facing the sides of the street). Belfast, similarly, is an industrial city—with her magnificent ship yards, her world-famous linen industry, and the biggest rope factory in the world—but many of her citizens live in cottages of a country type (strung together into streets) and still more of them possess a countryman's outlook, while her streets themselves very often are filled with the mooing of cows. Northern Ireland, known to Southerners as 'The Black North', is generally assumed to be an industrial region. This is misleading. There is no 'Black Country' in the Six Counties and the majority of their inhabitants live by agriculture.

Let us consider these people themselves. If you met one of them in London you might take him from his accent for a Lowland Scot; the Belfast accent in particular is very like that of

[1] A typescript, dating from *c.*1941–4, now in the Bodleian Library; publication untraced; copy kindly sent by Edna Longley of Queen's University, Belfast. This article might have been prepared as a British Council lecture or pamphlet.

dialect (e.g. the word 'wee' is universal as a substitute for 'small'). The visitor will find this speech very hard to understand while the speaker himself, unlike the Dubliner, may very well give the impression that he has little wish to be understood. Any conception of the Irish character founded on evidence from the South must be discarded up here. Where the men of Dublin love talking, the men of Belfast consider it a waste of time (this is really only true of talking *to strangers* but I am still thinking of my visitor's first impressions). With a Dubliner you feel you know him after a first meeting but you probably will know him no better after a year; the Belfastman on the other hand has practically no window-dressing, he presents you at first with a blank wall, after some time you discover a door, later still—that is, if he trusts you—the door may be opened, in the end you may find you have got inside his character. And that is, on the whole, an assuring experience.

It will be seen from the above that the Northern Irish are, in some respects at least, very different from the Southern. Are they then not Irish? Are they, for example, more like Englishmen? The answer to this is definitely No. In spite of the fact that the Union Jack is more prominent in most small Ulster towns on any day in the year than it is in London except on special occasions, the ordinary Ulsterman would hate to be thought like an Englishman. For in Ulster eyes the English are affected and humourless and (this may be surprising to Continentals) shockingly lacking in reserve. In some quarters the English are also considered both hypocritical and godless. Hence arises a paradox: the majority of the Northern Irish (i.e. the Unionists, of whom more later) are politically the most fervent devotees of Crown and Empire you could find and correspondingly the most vehement critics of separatist Eire; as individuals, however, Northern and Southern Irish, Protestant and Catholic, will in most cases club together in the presence of an Englishman; however much they differ from each other, they both think of the Englishman as a foreigner. This is even true of those (usually more prosperous) families which are of recent English extraction.

If the Ulsterman is suspicious of the English, how does the Englishman react to the Ulsterman? There is one word that at once jumps to the Englishman's lips: the word 'dour'. This is certainly appropriate to the typical Belfastman; nothing could look much dourer than these tough figures in cloth caps whose first glance at you seems to imply antipathy and whose mouths are shut tight like a money-box (except when they open to spit, a habit which is merely a habit but which looks to the stranger very like a gesture of contempt); even when they know you well, their salutation is merely a quick sideways jerk of the head which also suggests contempt, but is really due to that instinctive economy which governs the Ulsterman's behaviour. These generalizations are not so true of the country folk, many of whom retain a natural grace and ease of manner and occasionally a rich and imaginative flow of speech. But in general the Northern character (and this is true of the Catholic-Nationalist minority as well as the Protestant-Unionist majority) can correctly be described as dour. Having admitted this, we should at once qualify it by pointing out that in nine cases out of ten this dourness is very deceptive. Nine out of ten of these people, who appear so craggy, offhand, sullen, and silent, will go out of their way to help you and refuse to take any reward for it. Thus hospitality is one of their most noticeable characteristics and—note this well—it is the hospitality not of men who are spendthrift but who are, if anything—when it is a question of spending on themselves—rather too careful about money.

What, however, disturbs the Englishman more than the Ulsterman's dourness is what is often called his bigotry. Party feeling takes a more savage form here than in any other part of the British Isles particularly at the time of a presidential election. Some of this political vehemence can be taken with a grain of salt; it is a standing joke that the Irish, whether of South or North, love an argument—or a fight—for its own sake. The root of the matter, however, lies in history—and very tangled history it is. In a short space it is impossible even to adumbrate the multiplicity of factors which have made Northern Ireland, politically, a problem country. To start however in recent times, and on an everyday plane, the Northern Irish are the only people in the United Kingdom who in our own time have been accustomed to hear gunfire in their streets. As recently as 1935 there were serious shootings and burnings in Belfast between Protestants and Catholics (NB the political alignment in this country is all but identical with the religious alignment).

It should be noted however, as a tribute to the common sense of the individual citizen, that the 1935 burnings were reduced in number by a typically Irish compromise; in many cases Catholics who lived in 'Protestant streets' and Protestants who lived in 'Catholic streets' made a quick exchange of houses and so preserved their property. The fact remains that Northern Ireland has in our time had more experience of political violence than England, Scotland, or Wales. This is why her policemen, unlike those in the other three territories, always carry arms when on duty.

To explain this situation, as has been said, we should properly look back to history. As, however, any historical analysis would have to go back to James the First's Plantation of Ulster (1609), if not to the Norman conquest (twelfth century), lack of space makes it preferable here to concentrate on the present day picture and then—very sketchily, alas—to suggest some of the causes of this effect. Without passing judgement, then, let us look at this picture. Here is a small area consisting of six counties—Antrim, Down, Londonderry, Armagh, Tyrone, and Fermanagh—which has a parliament of its own to manage its internal affairs though subordinate in other respects to the Parliament at Westminster. This is the only example within the United Kingdom of 'devolution', i.e. the only case where the British Government has delegated political powers to a separate legislature. This was brought about by the Government of Ireland Act of 1920; the Northern Irish (and perhaps this is unique in history) received this gift of comparative independence not with triumph but overtly under protest. Thus their first Prime Minister, writing to Mr Lloyd George, spoke of 'the sacrifices we have so recently made in agreeing to self-government'. To understand this apparent paradox you must know what is meant by 'Unionism'.

Political divisions in Ireland are not the same as political divisions in Great Britain. Last century's conflict between Liberals and Conservatives, the present day conflict between Capital and Labour, have made little mark upon Irish institutions or the Irish mind; there *is* a Labour Party in the Six Counties today but it is small and without much influence. What still matters in Northern Ireland is the ancient struggle between Unionist and Nationalist. The Unionists regard themselves as British and want to see their own territory an integral part of the United Kingdom (hence their original objection to self-government, which they only accepted as the lesser of two evils, the alternative being government from Dublin); the Nationalists regard Ireland as a separate *nation* and want the partition of Ireland ended and the whole island to have the same status as Eire (or rather, in most cases, an even more independent status—even if the difference is nominal—than Eire has yet achieved).

This political conflict, as already pointed out, is closely related to a difference in religion. In Northern Ireland the vast majority of Unionists are Protestants (i.e. Protestant Episcopalians or Presbyterians) and the vast majority of Nationalists are Roman Catholics. As one person out of three in Northern Ireland is a Catholic it will be understood why this minority, which can never either be submerged or come to power, is a frequent occasion of dissension. As well as the sectarian difference there is also, to some extent, a difference of race. Many of the Catholics are descendants of that Catholic population which dominated this district before the plantations of English and Scottish settlers. It is from these settlers that most of the Protestant Ulstermen are descended, as can be seen from their names; among Northern Unionists you will find comparatively few typically 'Irish' names, like Flaherty or Byrne or the names which begin with O'. You will on the other hand find many names beginning with Mc and derived from Scotland. The first Northern Ireland government (1921) consisted of ministers with the following names: Craig, Pollock, Bates, Andrews, Vane-Tempest-Stewart (the Marquis of Londonderry), Archdale. The telephone directory will prove to you at once the preponderance here of a non-Gaelic stock.

Lastly, though to a less degree, the political difference is reinforced by a class difference. There are rich Catholics and there are pauper Protestants but on the average the income per head and the standard of living, in Northern Ireland, are considerably lower among the Catholics. While this fact, on a balance, increases the discontent of the minority, in country districts it sometimes leads to a rearrangment of sympathies, i.e. you will find the Catholic small farmer and the *Presbyterian* small farmer drawing together in mutual suspicion of the Protestant Episcopalians (the latter being associated with the old landlord class). This may remind us that, though the Presbyterians today are almost solidly Unionist, they were still on the other side at the end of the eighteenth century, having shown then much the same feelings towards England that were to be found across the Atlantic among the New England farmers who supported the American Revolution. It should be remembered that, while the Protestant Episcopalians are mainly descended from English settlers who had been 'top dogs' in their own country, the Presbyterians are mainly descended from *Scottish* settlers who in those days were still known as Dissenters and were viewed with nearly as much suspicion as the Catholics by the ruling caste of England.

The foregoing paragraphs may have suggested that Northern Ireland is an unhappy country. This suggestion must now be modified. Politics are a conspicuous element in the Ulsterman's life and often colour his conversation but as people do not live by politics alone, you will not normally find the Northern Irish practising in private life the more narrow tenets they may hold as party members. This is proved *a fortiori* by the case of the Orangemen. The Orange Order is the spearhead of the Unionist party. It is a very powerful—and very emotional—organization, pledged to oppose the spread of 'Popery' and to maintain at all costs a place for Ulster in the British Empire. The Orangemen have an astonishingly flamboyant style of polemical oratory and yearly on the Twelfth of July (when they celebrate the Battle of the Boyne where William of Orange defeated the forces of 'Popery') they put on one of the most surprising spectacles in the British Isles. The Orange procession in Belfast on 'The Glorious Twelfth' takes over three hours to pass any given point and is a riot of colour and noise, pipes and drums (outsize drums at that), and innumerable huge silken banners on which are painted battle-scenes from Ulster or Empire history, portraits of local worthies or Disraeli or Queen Victoria, and—most common of all—William of Orange himself on a prancing white horse at the Boyne. To an English spectator these processions, and the speech-makings which follow them, appear not only primitive but sinister, smacking even of fascism. In fact, however, they probably serve for most Orangemen, who in private life are quiet and unemotional, as an emotional safety-valve—a case of what the Greeks called 'catharsis'. It is not to be denied that in moments of political crisis the Orange Order can become a storm-centre but normally its bark is far worse than its bite. A famous Orange leader expressed a belief that any good man must be a 'good hater' but for the great majority of Orangemen their idea of goodness is summed up in the common phrase: 'a decent wee man'. The Decent Wee Man is unostentatious, sober, industrious, scrupulously honest, and genuinely charitable. It is thanks to his predominance in Ulster that foreign visitors—such as Czechs and Hungarians—have been known to declare the Ulsterman far more 'human' and easy to get on with than the Englishman. For to anyone like a Czech or a Hungarian the Decent Wee Man feels bound to 'do the honours' of his country.

Let us now suppose that you are such a visitor. You have been warned that the Ulsterman is a strange fellow who does not wear his heart on his sleeve; you will not however need much intuition to find out that he has his own sense of humour —like the English in that it relies largely on understatement, like the Southern Irish in that it throws up rich and coloured phrases from a poetic imagination, like, perhaps, the Lowland Scots in that it plays very often upon sombre or macabre themes of death, disease, or disaster; the most notable point however is that the Ulsterman, far more than the Irish of the South, is able to laugh at himself. If you realize this and play up to it, you should soon find that Ulster 'dourness' melting away; he laughs at himself, you laugh at yourself, you both laugh at each other —you both know where you stand.

So much for the general character of the Ulsterman; let us turn, first, to his habits and, then, to the country itself which he lives in and which he is so proud of. Suppose you stay anywhere in the Six Counties with a typical middle class family. Such a family, unlike many of its opposite numbers in England—at any rate in southern England—will not be pretending to be an *upper* class family. The Decent Wee Man is too proud to be a social climber; he scorns fashionable luxuries; he lives within his income happily. You will find his house comfortable and clean but you will not, most probably, have much to say for his taste in furniture or decoration (his aesthetic standards are derived from commercial Belfast). His sittingroom will be rather overcrowded with out-of-date trappings and his mantel-piece will present a formidable array of portentously framed photographs—portraits of his relations for two generations back, especially of any who have gone into Holy Orders. Bibles and prayerbooks will also be conspicuous, this being a land where the Scriptures have by no means become a dead letter. His tablecloths and the sheets on the beds will probably be of the finest linen.

In this house you will be given plenty to eat, though by Continental standards the food will be monotonous and by southern English standards it will be served at the wrong times of day. In Northern Ireland, as in Eire, the vast majority of people (all except a few members of the old landlord or 'Ascendancy' class whose habits are stigmatized as 'English') will make their main evening meal Tea (i.e. 'high tea'), which can be served any time from 5 p.m. till 10 p.m. (this is true also of most of the smaller hotels) and consists usually of bacon and eggs or cold meat with strong tea and a large assortment of cakes, jams, blancmange and home-made bread. This last is very good indeed and the recipes for baking have been handed down within families for generations. The local beef is also very good but is usually overcooked. And the Ulstermen, like all other inhabitants of Ireland, are connoisseurs of potatoes; they like the mealy kind which flake, not the soapy kind which skid. About other vegetables they unfortunately care very little. Fish, when you get it, will be freshly caught—whether from the rivers and inland loughs or from the sea. There being a large herring fishery here, you should often get fresh herring and—again unlike England—you can eat and enjoy herrings without thereby incurring a social stigma.

After food, drink. Everyone will offer you tea at all times of day but, when it comes to alcohol, you will either be offered a great deal or absolutely none. In the Six Counties the split on the drink or temperance question is less bitter only than the split on religion or politics. Northern Ireland—it is hardly an exaggeration to say—is inhabited by hard-drinkers and tee-totallers. But those who drink carry their drink well and those who do not drink, though also opposed to card-playing, Sunday recreation and—very often—smoking, will still be by no means dull; over their strong tea they can display a considerable *bonhomie* and an unquenchable curiosity about what goes on in the world.

It is time to say something of the landscape in which these people live. I have heard a Hungarian who had just landed at Larne and driven up the Antrim coast describe this country as 'ein Zauberland'; and many parts of it—if the weather is right —*can* appear like a fairy-land. In the Six Counties there are highly picturesque stretches of coast and mountain; there are also very dull flats. In both cases, however, the important element is light. Owing to the moisture in the air sunlight in Ireland has the effect of a prism; nowhere else in the British Isles can you find this liquid rainbow quality which at once diffuses and clarifies. When the sun is not shining, however, (and this is often the case) the landscape relapses to a sodden grey monotony. It should be noted here that the average rainfall for the Six Counties is about thirty-five inches per year, while in some districts it approaches sixty inches. In Belfast (one of the drier places) the rainfall is eleven inches more than in London and it rains on seventy more days in the year. Those who find London quite wet enough might ponder on Bernard Shaw's thesis (in his preface to *John Bull's Other Island*) that it is the Irish climate that has made the Irish character. The climate is certainly one unifying factor between North and South in the island; both Northerners and Southerners feel at home in it and prefer it to the climate of England (which they find too extreme!) and they both have the same weather-standards. Anywhere in Ireland people will say to you 'It's a fine day,' when the sun is invisible and the sky slightly drizzling.

In most parts of Northern Ireland, with the exception of intractable sections of moor and mountain, the landscape is largely manmade. Even the mountains look different from, say, Scottish mountains because their lower slopes are chequered with tiny fields and dotted with white-washed cottages; these small farmers cultivate what they can. This brings us back to the basic fact in Ulster's social and economic life. There are about ninety thousand small holdings in the Six Counties; most of these are of between fifteen and thirty acres. Compare this with England and Wales where the holdings of over a hundred acres make over 20% of the whole; in Northern Ireland they make 4.4%. In Northern Ireland, consequently, everything is on a smaller scale—the farm buildings and the fields themselves; the hay instead of being built into great stacks is dumped in the fields in small 'cocks' which are about the height of a man. These quantitative differences lead to qualitative differences. Northern Irish farmers and farm-labourers use farm-tools—and kitchen utensils—and methods of agriculture which in England would be considered primitive but which still perhaps are the handiest in the circumstances. For example, a custom which has practically disappeared in England since the Middle Ages, here is still usual; the byre is built on to the dwelling-house so that both lie in one line and under one roof. Socially, the important thing is that most of these farmers are peasant owners and have the conservative instincts but also the independent spirit proper to their species.

It is impossible here to give in detail the varieties of the Six Counties. Look at the map and you should find a stimulus in the place-names themselves; most of them are Gaelic, dating back to early Irish history. Of the more common Gaelic prefixes, Bally- means 'town', Dun- 'fort', and Kil- 'church'. The component names, you will notice—names like Ballymena, Ballynahinch, Ballygawley, Dromore, Drumquin, Cushendall, Cushendun, Donaghadee, Tanderagee, Carrickfergus, Aughnacloy, Dungannon, Limavady—are quite unlike place-names in England. They should remind you at once that their historical background is also unlike. Downpatrick for example commemorates St Patrick; this is the part of Ireland from which Christian missionaries in the Dark Ages sailed *eastwards*. (It is also perhaps the part of Ireland which has most contributed to folksong.) Since then linen-mills have shot up their chimneys and spread out their smoke, gantries have arisen at the head of Belfast Lough, workers have congregated into drab streets of cement-covered houses, but the peat-bogs are still brown and the mountains are still blue and the present is inter-shot with the past. And for most of the population life is still full of colour; the cottagers coat their houses with a dazzling white-wash and against this white you may see a blaze of gorse (a plant known here as 'whin') or fuchsias planted in a hedge.

To leave the past and come to the immediate present. This district in its time has contributed many generals to the British Army—as well as thirteen presidents (that is, of Ulster stock) to the USA. Most of these have been noted for their energy and downrightness. The same qualities have been shown at home here today in the war effort. Belfast is busy building ships and turning out textiles for military purposes; also two thirds of all the shirts used in the United Kingdom. The linen mills, noted in peacetime for their exquisite lawns and cambrics, are now working on aeroplane wings, parachute harness, etc. In agriculture, whereas in peacetime much of the farming was subsistency farming, exports of foodstuffs have been greatly increased to Great Britain; e.g. 250 million eggs are shipped across per year. And the wartime increase in the area under tillage is nearly 15% more than the increase in England and Wales. Farming is also becoming mechanized; there are ten times as many tractors in the country as there were in 1939. More interesting perhaps —from a human point of view—is what has been happening within the armed Forces. In one famous North of Ireland regiment the recruits come about equally from north and south of the border and, of course, among the Northerners are many from the Catholic minority. It is a fact that these men, brought up in opposing camps, drop their mutual suspicion and latent hostility almost as soon as they get in the same unit; all that remain is badinage—'Sing us one of your blank rebel songs,' or 'Sing us one of your blank Orange ballads.' May we hope that the Good Haters are ripe to disappear and that the Decent Wee Men, from all quarters, are ready at last to sink their differences.

Indian Art[1]

Indian Art. (Faber and Faber. 7s. 6d.)
The Vertical Man. By W. G. Archer. (Allen and
Unwin. 15s.)

Indian Art, consisting of four essays by experts (H. G. Rawlinson, K. de B. Codrington, J. V. S. Wilkinson, and John Irwin), was published to synchronize with the current Indian Exhibition at Burlington House.[2] Like that exhibition itself this book, though highly instructive, has its obvious gaps. The Burlington House collection could not, owing to brute circumstance, include the grander specimens of Indian sculpture such as are found embedded for ever in enormous rocks or temples and does not include (owing to what presumption about British prudery?) those erotic imaginings which are not only characteristic of India but which at their best are beyond decent and indecent.[3] In spite of these deficiencies the Exhibition has, one may hope, proved to the British public, if not to some of our

[1] *New Statesman and Nation* 35: 888 (13 March 1948), 218. *Indian Art: Essays* by Hugh G. Rawlinson, Kenneth de B. Codrington, James V. S. Wilkinson, and John C. Irwin, ed. Sir Richard Winstedt (1947, soft cover 1966); William George Archer (1907–77), *The Vertical Man: A Study in Primitive Indian Sculpture* (1947). Archer had been in the Indian Civil Service 1930–48, and was soon to become Keeper of the Indian Section, Victoria and Albert Museum 1949–59. All these men were authorities on Indian art. On the occasion of the independence of India and Pakistan, MacNeice visited the Indian sub-continent, Aug.–Nov. 1947, collecting material for BBC radio programmes (broadcast March and May 1948).

[2] Over 1,000 treasures selected from museums and private collections in India were exhibited in the Royal Academy Winter Exhibition at Burlington House, Nov. 1947–March 1948, under the direction of Leigh Ashton (1897–1983), later Sir Leigh, then Director of the Victoria and Albert Museum: Alfred Munnings, letter in *The Times*, 15 July 1947, 5f. (In May 1948, prompted by this exhibition, the Victoria and Albert Museum published a booklet of 28 photographs, also entitled *Indian Art*, illustrating works of art selected from their Indian Section.)

[3] In India the 'sexual mysticism' of Tantrism, both Hindu and Buddhist, gave rise to characteristic representations of male and female genitalia (*lingam* and *yoni*) as 'symbols of the divine creative force', as well as to representations of couples in amorous embraces (*mithunas*) on ancient temples and other monuments—such as the remarkable erotic sculpture at Khajuraho (10th–11th c.) and Konarak (13th c.): Robert H. van Gulik, 'Sex and Erotica', in *Encyclopedia of World Art*, 16 vols. (1954–68), xi. 911–13.

professional critics, that Indian art need be neither incomprehensible nor repulsive. To be sure, one hears naïve objections to gods having more than two arms—this from people who have always accepted archangels with two or more wings. It is a pity that the Royal Academy did not devote one room to photographs of immovable masterpieces such as the sculptures of Ellora and Mahabalipuram and some of the great temples;[4] if Hindu architecture exists, as has often been stated, mainly as a ground for sculpture, that sculpture correspondingly cannot be fully appreciated without some idea of its architectural setting. It is also a pity that the catalogue on sale at Burlington House should have made no concessions to the public's ignorance. Why for example describe No. 463 merely as Nataraja? Why not add that this means the cosmic dance of Siva? This constipated erudition of the catalogue, excusable perhaps by lack of space, is repeated to some extent—where the excuse is not so obvious—in the book under review. Many of its readers, I feel, will hardly sense the values for the facts.

Facts about the background of art are normally preferable to gush about its essence but Indian works do perhaps call for some so-called 'interpretative' criticism. Not that these works are particularly 'difficult' for anyone who responds directly to mass and line in themselves; to such people the better Indian sculptures must come as naturally as drinking—but how many such people are there? If, as I think, the average intelligent person likes to have some 'literary' clues to the visual arts, then he needs more clues than our four experts here will grant him. When so very foreign a people is expressing itself, a generalization, even though unsound about what it is they are expressing, will be more stimulating to the uninformed reader than a pile of mere information. In contrast to *Indian Art* a recent number of *L'Amour de l'Art* does provide—and repeatedly—such a stimulus. Thus we find M. René Grousset of the Académie Française at once making a vivid, if (and because) arguable, point: 'L'esthétique indienne réalise ce miracle . . . d'être à

---

[4] For the Buddhist and Brahmanic caves at Ellora near Aurangabad (6th–8th c.), see James Burgess, *Report on the Elurâ Cave Temples* (1883; 1970); for the Pallava caverns and temples at Mamallapuram (Mahabalipuram) south of Madras (7th–8th c.), see Calambur Siva-rama-murti, *Mahabalipuram*, 2nd edn (1955). MacNeice wrote a fine poem 'Mahabalipuram' (1948): *Collected Poems*, 273–5.

la fois toute volupté tropicale . . . et toute spiritualité.'[5] And we find M. Philippe Stern making an equally door-opening comparison (risky though such comparisons are) between the Ajanta wall-paintings, Sanskrit sentence-structure and the Gupta theatre.[6]

Even so far as facts go, this book seems a little timid and narrow. The first essay for example, entitled 'The Historical Background', gives too much history—too many names and dates—and not enough *human* background. Without going the length of M. Stern, Professor Rawlinson could perhaps have thrown more light on Indian art if he had paid less attention to the chronicling of dynasties and more to that present or timeless India which shows itself in the luxuriance of grace-notes in music, in the intricacies of Hindu metaphysics, in the legends so fantastic yet so direct of the popular memory, and above all in the dance where a rigid tradition defines every gesture, yet in no way dams that supremely lyrical flow, a total impression which is nature based upon artifice. But within its limits Professor Rawlinson's essay is a useful anatomy of the bones behind the changing contours and colours. It is inevitably bitty; the epithet 'justly famous' tells us nothing about that staggering annunciation, the wall-paintings of Ajanta,[7] while in two short paragraphs on the Pallavas he obviously could not even start to assess the special qualities of their sculpture—an idyllic blend of strength and delicacy to be paralleled in the pastoral legends of Krishna.[8] It rested with the succeeding essayists to fill out this sketchy picture.

Up to a point they have done this; Mr Codrington particularly in writing of 'The Minor Arts of India' does put some flesh upon the bones. He allows the traveller Bernier and the emperor Jahangir to speak for themselves[9] and he properly

[5] 'Définition de l'Inde', *L'Amour de l'Art*, nos. 6–7 (1947), 236.

[6] 'De l'amour humain à l'amour mystique dans les fresques d'Ajanta', ibid. 293–4.

[7] For the inimitable, large frescos in the Buddhist caves of Ajanta (*c*.2nd–5th c.), see Ghulam Yazdani, *Ajanta*, 8 vols. (1930–55).

[8] In the *Mahabharata*, *Harivamshi*, and *Puranas*, Krishna, the last (human) incarnation or avatar of Vishnu, was glorified as the supreme god although described as a crafty Rajput chief: Hermann G. Jacobi, 'Incarnation (Indian)', in James Hastings's *Encyclopaedia of Religion and Ethics*, 13 vols. (1908–26), vii. 195–6.

[9] Mughal economic conditions reported in François Bernier's 'Letter to Monseigneur Colbert concerning Hindoustan', *Travels in the Mogul Empire AD 1656–1668*, trans. Irving Brock, rev. Archibald Constable, 2nd edn rev. Vincent A.

stresses India's cultural unity and continuity—at least in her villages. He also mentions such little but significant practices as 'the drawing of lucky designs before the thresholds'[10]—an art new every morning but at times at least an art. Mr John Irwin on 'Indian Sculpture' struggles lucidly with an enormous subject but he too suffers from having too much to cover. Incidentally—and this is to his credit and healthy for the layman—he expresses some preferences with which the layman may differ. Thus he admires the lion-capital at Sarnath which to some people's taste is just a very ancient prop for a Corner House.[11] And of the Mathura school of sculpture he remarks: 'What does distinguish all the work is the very poor quality of its mottled red sandstone . . .'[12] Yet several visitors to Burlington House have found that it is just the quality of this stone which makes these works, unlike Amaravati limestones in the same room, immediately acceptable.[13] Mr Irwin refreshingly manages to see things both with an eye on the social factors behind them and with an eye on the things. He is very sound on the Kailasa temple at Ellora:

> There is no contradiction in the fact that this sculpture is at the same time an art conspicuous both for its conventional iconography and for its astonishing life-quality. . . . In such art, iconographical conventions are not to be confused with the *conception* of a work of art; they are no more than the *matter* of the conception.[14]

Indian Painting, as Mr Wilkinson says in his essay (with a fitting aspersion on Ruskin), 'is a comparatively new discovery in Europe.'[15] He is confronted here with the enormous histor-

Smith (1914), quoted by Codrington in *Indian Art*, ed. Winstedt, 163–5; keen observations of flowers and birds in *The Tuzuk-i-Jahangiri, or, Memoirs of Jahangir*, trans. Alexander Rogers, ed. Henry Beveridge, 2 vols. (1909–14), quoted ibid. 187–8.

10 *Indian Art*, ed. Winstedt, 172: corr. 'before the threshold'.

11 Irwin, ibid. 65: 'In the best of the carvings such as the well-known lion capital from Sarnath (originally marking the spot where the Buddha preached his first sermon), realistic modelling is brilliantly combined with a stylistic finish to produce a unified, organic effect, and the whole admirably fulfils its architectural purpose.'

12 Irwin, ibid. 79–80, on the use of local stone from the Sikri quarries.

13 Amaravati carvings and sculpture (2nd–3rd c. AD) are described ibid. 86–7.

14 Ibid. 96.

15 Wilkinson, ibid. 105; and 106: 'Ruskin and the other high priests of criticism misled people by condemning all Indian art comprehensively, without examining the evidence.' See also 106 n. 2: 'Ruskin admired the delicacy of Indian art, but thought it distorted nature.'

ical gap between the great sweeping murals of Ajanta and the just-so miniatures of comparatively recent times (neither group much resembling what we are used to in the West). Having conjectured his way across this gap and assuming 'a real continuity', he properly avoids postulating another gap between the paintings of Hindus and Muslims. To represent life at all was an un-Muslim activity, and, as he points out, the Moghuls employed many Hindu artists; he is probably right when he maintains 'that the Mughal painters, though they learned from Persia and the West, did not paint like Persians or Europeans, but like Indians.'[16] A political moral could be drawn here but Mr Wilkinson, perhaps wisely, does not draw it. His essay is down-to-earth and includes not only pleasing information about Moghul pigments and brushes but also the striking remarks about painting made by the Emperor Akbar who felt that 'a painter had quite peculiar means of recognizing God'.[17]

Indian Art would have been the better for more plates; in *The Vertical Man*, which admittedly is twice the price, the plates are half the battle.[18] This is a fascinating study of a particular species of *primitive* Indian art. It is a book not only for art-lovers (some of these photographed stone or wooden idols have the impact of a strong dream) but also for anthropologists. Mr Archer, who argues that sophisticated Indian art is 'as little indicative of Indian sensibility as a whole as the cathedral styles are summaries of English sculpture',[19] discusses in one chapter 'the will to vital geometry' of the Indian villagers[20] and then develops a careful analysis of a particular village ritual and the myth behind it. It is a good myth—the story of 'the strong man who dies for love of the buffaloes'.[21] A little-known field to us where the buffaloes are so important; but look for it next time you step out of Burlington House.

---

[16] Ibid. 142.

[17] Ibid. 126.

[18] There are 48 illustrative photographs in Archer's brief book.

[19] Archer, 10.

[20] Ibid., chap. 1, 18; term adapted from Herbert Read's phrase 'vitalized geometry' according to 18 n.

[21] Ibid. 91.

An Indian Ride[1]

At Freedom's Door. By Malcolm Lyall Darling. (Oxford
University Press. 21*s*.)

Even the most casual visitor to India must be struck by the
complexity of almost every Indian issue and must feel at times
that there is no way out from these endless vicious circles and
dilemmas; the answers so readily offered by politicians will
only make the questions still more unanswerable. The country
is full of Utopians, and the more sweeping their generalizations
the weaker the evidence submitted. The European visitor who
spends most of his time in the cities and can converse with the
citizens only in English, should always remember that the
greater part of India is closed to him; the salon Communists
of Calcutta may talk fluently to him about the Village, but few
of them have spent much time in any of the sub-continent's ·
650,000 villages. The visitor who drives through the country
during the day may often wonder indeed where the villages and
villagers exist, for many of the former are built away from the
roads, while the latter get astonishingly lost in the landscape; it
is at dusk when the streams of home-going peasants converge
from every quarter that one is forcibly reminded that this land
is populated. Populated! But these millions we have heard so
much about and whom we now glimpse in the gloaming, remain
for us figures in a frieze, as beautiful perhaps as the Elgin
marbles but just as difficult to talk to. Yet there are Englishmen
who can talk to them and—what is more important—make
them talk. Most of the Englishmen who have the experience to
do this and to sift out fact from fantasy or flattery come from
the ICS;[2] sympathy with Indian nationalism should not make
us forget that many members of this remarkable service have

---

[1] *New Statesman and Nation* 37: 943 (2 April 1949), 334. The title of Sir Malcolm
Darling's (1880-1969) book is taken from the comment of an aged Muslim, a
Congress Pathan, 'We are still slaves; we have only got to freedom's door', quoted in
Sir Malcolm's book, 15, 300.

[2] Indian Civil Service.

been human as well as efficient, and have achieved, what is difficult in any country, an understanding of the peasantry. Such an Englishman is Sir Malcolm Daring, who at the age of sixty-six, and having spent forty-two years in India, rode on horseback from Peshawar on the North-West Frontier to Jubbulpore in the Central Provinces in no official capacity, but purely to learn how things were going.[3]

This fact-collecting crusade took place from November, 1946, till March, 1947, during that uneasy interim period which ended so much sooner than most people expected.[4] That Sir Malcolm travelled by horse was not romantic archaism, though he obviously relished the romantic aspect of it; the motor car, as he points out, can reach only a minority of villages, and these it will pass through too quickly. He even attributes the decline in administration partly to the new methods of transport:

Again and again we were waylaid . . . by groups of peasants in manifest distress and with little chance, it seemed, of gaining the ear of authority. Not so had it been when officials perforce rode their daily marches and pitched their tents in the remotest villages. Change came with the advent of motor and lorry and was accelerated by the political developments which followed the first war . . . Throughout the tour one had the feeling of an administration in only the loosest touch with the people and served by officials, many of whom, but not all [a qualification typical of this ex-official's fair-mindedness], paid far more attention to the demands of Government than to the needs of the people.[5]

Sir Malcolm, being primarily interested in how the peasants live, how much money they make and what they get to eat, is too much concerned with detail to speak with a journalist's

---

[3] Sir Malcolm Darling's route of 25 Nov. 1946 to 15 March 1947 is traced on a map on the end-papers of his book. Sir Malcolm—a friend of the writer E. M. Forster (1879–1970)—was in the ICS 1904–40. In 1907–8 he had been the tutor and guardian of the Raja of Dewas Senior (whose secretary Forster became in 1921), later was Vice-Chancellor of the University of the Punjab, 1931 and 1937–8, and Indian Editor for the BBC 1940-4, in which capacity he became known to MacNeice.

[4] The 5-month interim 1946–7 was that of the then Viceroy the Field Marshal Lord Wavell's (1883–1950) interim government of *Indian* politicians, which ended with the arrival of the new viceroy the Admiral LordLouis Mountbatten (1900–79), to oversee the immediate transfer of power from Britain to India and Pakistan, while riots and killing continued from rivalries and hatreds among Hindus, Muslims, and Sikhs.

[5] *At Freedom's Door* (1949), 309–10.

facile assurance—the details are far too prickly—but he is no defeatist. He welcomes Pandit Nehru's pronouncement that 'we are more interested in the peasant than in any other group of human beings', and considers that this attitude of Government 'might be the beginning of a new era for the Indian peasant. *But* [italics mine] . . . *the object must not be quick results. That way lies disappointment . . .*'[6] The statistics of India's agricultural output *and* of India's birthrate make this judgement unassailable,[7] the great value of a book like Sir Malcom's is that it translates such statistics into terms of human groups and individuals.

Sir Malcolm's literary style is undistinguished. He is incapable of describing sunrise or sunset, though he clearly was impressed time and again by these two regular transformation scenes which in some parts of the country give one one's only chance of really seeing the landscape. He has the vocabulary and innocent tricks of an old-fashioned aunt—his horse is 'fresh as a rose', and his truck is rescued from 'a watery grave' —but he does get down on paper what he went into the wilderness to see. His book is a parade of living persons: the Muslim Leaguer who says 'I am only a follower; whatever the League does is right'; the soldier returned from a German prison camp whose chief demand is for a ration system like those of France and Germany; the modernizing Muslims who, nevertheless, argue for purdah; the sweepers whose landlord precludes them from the lowest step of his verandah while their fellow untouchables, the tanners, may go up the steps but not on the verandah itself.[8] It is a cavalcade of poverty, ignorance, fatalism—and endearingness. And Sir Malcolm is too old a hand to generalize rashly. He will not admit that Indian villages are uniformly squalid or that sadhus are uniformly phoney. And, while he has a specially soft spot for the Punjab, he is typical of the ICS at its best in his avoidance of prejudice; it is only too easy for an Englishman in India to accept one race or region or community and write off the rest as impossible. Sir Malcolm, though

---

6 The address of the first Prime Minister of independent India, Jawaharlal Nehru (1889–1964), to the Associated Chambers of Commerce, 15 Dec. 1947, quoted and commented upon, ibid. 348.

7 Agricultural figures are cited, ibid., *passim*, as well as problems of birth control, 'the addition of nearly 100 millions to the population' of India 1925–46 (ibid. 339).

8 Ibid. 36, 50, 343, 285.

recognizing Pakistan as an accomplished fact, has his doubts about the two-nation theory since many of his own observations conflict with it:

> We met Muslims who for generations had had their genealogies kept and horoscopes cast by Brahmins, and passed villages owned by Muslim and Sikh, or by Hindu and Muslim, sprung from a common ancestor, and we even came across one village where Hindu, Muslim, and Sikh were of the same tribe.[9]

His villainies and his virtues are all of them concrete, and it is really very refreshing, after reading so many slogan-mongers, to hear someone mention 'the humanizing influence of water'.[10] To sum up, he is a keen observer, and he thinks for himself, but he is no axe-grinder. Many writers have said that the heart of Indian politics (or of all politics) is economics; Sir Malcolm would probably agree but, instead of the word 'economics', he prefers to use the word 'peasant', and to him it is more than a word.

[9] Ibid. 302.   [10] Ibid. 342.

India at First Sight[1]

India is the most *foreign* country I have ever visited. If we use the word 'foreign' for Italy or Iceland, we should really find some other word for India. My first visit to India lasted from August to November 1947, when the BBC sent out a whole team of correspondents, writers, and engineers to be in at the birth of the two new dominions. So I got my first sight of an extraordinary country at an extraordinary time.

Our human contacts were on the whole vastly more pleasant than we expected; we all, I think, had been afraid that as Britishers in general and BBC men in particular we might often meet with hostility. But when we arrived in the country there was a brand-new feeling towards the British; residents told us it was only a few months old. Indians knew they were getting their independence, and some at least of them knew that Britain had had quite a hand in it. And as for our team in particular, more than a few Indians showed a respect for the radio which they do not feel for the Press. For their own Press is fantastically corrupt, and certain British papers, at any rate, they suspect of prejudice and malice.

Not that conversation was always easy. Educated Indians

---

[1] *BBC Features*, ed. Laurence Gilliam (1950), 60–4, with two photographs on 65, and the following editorial headnote on 60: 'Son of an Ulster bishop, educated at Marlborough College and Merton College, Oxford, Classical scholar and lyric poet, radio dramatist and lecturer, MacNeice has won an outstanding place among modern writers by his masterly and imaginative command of the microphone. An acknowledged leader of the rebel intellectual poets of the thirties, since 1940 [error for 1941] he has enriched BBC programmes with a profusion of fine work, notably "The Dark Tower" (1945) [error for 1946], for which [Sir] Benjamin Britten wrote the music. His adaptation in verse of Goethe's "Faust" (1949) is one of the outstanding achievements of sound broadcasting. In 1947 he visited India as a member of the joint Features and News team sent by the BBC to report and commemorate the transfer of power to the people of India and Pakistan. "India at First Sight" is a pendant to the series of programmes that resulted from this visit.' L. D. Gilliam (1907–64), head of the Features Section of the Drama Department of the BBC, then from 1946 head of a separate Features Department, sponsored the school of dramatic documentary (in which MacNeice flourished in the 1940s), although he was something of a rebel in the Establishment: obit. notices on Gilliam in *The Times*, 16 Nov. 1964, 15c; 23 Nov., 16d.

are as politics-ridden as the Irish (perhaps this is inevitable with subject or newly liberated peoples), and are always on the look-out for scapegoats. When we arrived on the eve of Independence,[2] everyone was all smiles, but a few days later, when the Boundary Award[3] was made public . . .! The British were the villains again and we of the BBC, with the British label so patently attached to us, we had to stand in the dock and answer for perfidious Albion.[4] It seems we had sold out the Muslims, we had sold out the Hindus, we had sold out the princes. It was necessary to be cool and cagy and above all to laugh when the moment was ripe for it. Then the Hindus or Muslims or who-ever they were laughed too. Luckily we had been trained for this sort of thing. A BBC employee, belonging as he does to what is thought of as a straitlaced and straightfaced monopoly, must know when to use the grain of salt.

When we arrived at Karachi airport on August 8th, 1947, the Customs man looked at our papers and said, 'Lots of funny people we get these days . . . Tea-tasters . . . BBC . . .' And often after that we were thought of as funny people—but also, I think, as quite nice people. Everyone, at any rate, talked to us—contrary to the warning I had been given by a very import-ant Indian in London. Nobody ever hinted we were either spies or sensation-mongers. They thought of us as people who looked and reported—and they seemed eager to be reported. So we reported them as best we could and we never stopped looking. Looking for the first time at the wild schemozzle of an Indian bazaar. Looking down on the Constituent Assembly in Delhi, through a white whirr of revolving fans on to the heads of a

---

[2] The Independence of India and Pakistan as two separate 'Dominions' was declared at midnight, 14–15 August 1947.

[3] 'The awards of the Boundary Commissions [for the partitions of Punjab and of Bengal] have, as was generally expected, been unpopular with both sides, but much more so with the Muslims than with the Hindus': *The Times*, 19 Aug. 1947, 4g, on 'New Frontiers in India'. Riots, reprisals, burnings, killings, followed: 'The Sikh Rising', ibid., 27 Aug., 5b; etc. See also 'Final Boundaries of New Dominions', ibid., 18 Aug., 3a. (The hasty signing-over of the Hindu princely state of Jammu and Kashmir—with a large Muslim population—to India in 1947, has resulted in military confrontations between India and Pakistan ever since.)

[4] A famous phrase widespread during the French Revolution, deriving from Augustin, Marquis de Ximénèz (1726–1817), 'L'Ere des Français' (Oct. 1793), *Poésies Révolutionnaires et contre-révolutionnaires* (1821), i. 160.

white-clad gathering soberly declaring their freedom. Looking at the military yet truly religious spectacle of Muslims at evening prayer. Looking at a Hindu village festival, with children in holiday mood dangling their legs from the great temple car. Looking at a Salvation Army service conducted by ex-untouchables. Yes—and looking at the troubles. I arrived in a town called Sheikhupura the morning after a' communal massacre.[5] The survivors of the minority community were crammed into a schoolhouse and overflowed into the street; flies swarmed on the stumps of their arms and legs, and their eyes were haunted or, what was worse, quite blank. Never again shall I believe those romanticists who maintain that war was clean when people used swords and spears.

We saw both sides of this communal tragedy, and tried to view it without partisanship. What is more difficult is to view it without superiority; seeing such outrages one tends to conclude that their authors must be inhuman. But in fact (and on a much smaller scale I have found the same thing in Ireland) men can be not only intelligent but kindly, not only charming but generous, in all respects but one, and in that can be demons. 'Tantum religio . . .' is a quotation[6] that occurs to one, but here, as in Ireland and elsewhere, it is not only religion that is the root of the evil; religion is complicated with other factors, especially the economic. And who were we to feel superior? Did we not come from twentieth-century Europe? And were we quite sure that the British themselves were not responsible for some of this? So in that inferno of the Punjab we looked and reported what we had to and tried to cast no stones.

Many people in England that autumn imagined that the

---

[5] Shekhupura or 'Shaikpura', an agricultural and commercial centre, a town of West Punjab, Pakistan, 20 miles WNW of Lahore, population about 20,000 (half Muslim, half Sikh and Hindu), suffered a reprisal massacre mostly by Muslims on 25 Aug. 1947: 'Within 24 hours at least 800 people, nearly all Sikhs and Hindus, had been shot, stabbed, speared, slashed, clubbed, or burned to death. . . . Whole areas, Muslim as well as Sikh and Hindu, had been reduced to ashes': 'Punjab Violence Growing', *The Times*, 29 Aug., 4g. Cf. MacNeice's poem 'Letter from India, for Hedli' (1947), st. 10, *Collected Poems*, 269: 'I have seen Sheikhupura High School | Fester with glaze-eyed refugees'.

[6] *Tantum religio potuit suadere malorum* ('So much of evil could religion prompt'): Lucretius (94?–55 BC), *De Rerum Natura*, i. 101, apropos Agamemnon's ritual sacrifice of Iphigenia. (See MacNeice's article on Lucretius, 'The Passionate Unbeliever' (May 1936).)

whole sub-continent was dissolving in fire and flood. This was a grotesque misconception. Most places and people we met were undisturbed, if not happy. And how fascinating many of those places and people were. I am left with a swarm of memories, delightful, touching, or humorous. Calcutta, for instance, that hideous city. Here I began by staying with a Government official who, though a Hindu by birth, had no use whatever for the Vedas and (what nowadays is yet more blasphemous) said he could see no difference between 'subject' and 'sovereign' peoples; what interested him was the fisheries in the Bay of Bengal. I then stayed with a Bengali poet who invited me to a picnic in the Botanical Gardens. His idea of a picnic was to buy a lot of wet foods in paper bags fresh from a Chinese restaurant. There was a monsoon downpour in the Gardens, so we ate these in a small car surrounded by gaping children. We laughed a lot (as usual), and that evening I had dinner with a Communist intellectual whose name was that of a great Hindu god; his daughter aged eight had just written a satirical poem on Mr Churchill. Finally, I visited Jamini Roy, the best-known living Indian painter,[7] a dear old man who spoke very broken English and had two top front teeth missing. For years, though himself sophisticated, he has been trying to recover the virtues of primitive painting. He explained to me the difficulties of conserving the proper 'mythology mentality'; it has two very serious rivals, the 'philosophy mentality' and the 'industry-and-science mentality'; if either of these latter should infect your work, you must look at your work and condemn it—'This is *not*! This is *not*! This is *not*!'

Or take Benares. Here I stayed in an eighteenth-century palace built on the Ganges and owned by two Hinduized Frenchmen. Next door was a holy man who seemed to spend an hour or so every evening beating dustbin lids together. My hosts had enormous charm and a profound contempt for

---

[7] (1887–1972), Bengali painter who renounced European methods of painting and adopted techniques (psychological perspective, colour palette, etc.) of Indian village painters to portray local folklore (and even Christian themes) in works that have sometimes been compared to those of Matisse and Picasso. After partition, when MacNeice saw him, he had left Lahore (where he was director of the School of Fine Arts, 1938–47) for Delhi (where he became interested in forming the 'Silpi Chakra' art society). See Bianca Maria Alfieri, 'Roy, Jamini', in *Encyclopedia of World Art*, 15 vols. (1968), xii. 587–90.

Europe; France in particular they thought very decadent. We would lie about on cushions while one of them played the Veena[8] and occasionally a huge pet crane would stalk from behind a screen. Benares has a very rich physical presence which I tried to suggest in my script.[9] It was here that I went to call on the famous Radhakrishnan,[10] Vice-Chancellor of the University (though more often than not he is in Oxford), and found the University gates picketed by students in protest against the raising of their fees.[11] Student strikes are a common occurrence in India, but, if this one was typical, they are quite merry affairs.

Madras? Here my colleague, Francis Dillon,[12] and I had two of the best but most dissimilar meals of our lives. One was with a Shell Mex official who owned the most beautiful Persian carpets and a King Grey parrot[13] that had perfect timing; I

[8] The *Vina*, a S. Indian long-necked plucked lute, is popular as both a household and a concert instrument: *New Grove Dictionary of Music and Musicians*, ed. Stanley Sadie, 20 vols. (1980), xix. 780.

[9] 'India at First Sight', broadcast 13 March 1948, a portion of which was published as 'The Crash Landing' in *Botteghe Oscure* 4 (1949), 378–85.

[10] Sir Sarvepalli Radhakrishnan (1888–1975) was a famous philosopher, statesman, and author of many books, Vice-Chancellor of Banaras (Varanasi) Hindu University 1939–48, Spalding Professor of Eastern Religions and Ethics at Oxford 1936–52, later Vice-President and then President of the Republic of India 1962–7. His photograph is included in *BBC Features* (1950), 65.

[11] In 1948–9 Dr Radhakrishnan was chairman of an Indian University Education Commission. Published by the Government of India, *Report of the University Education Commission* (Dec. 1948–Aug. 1949), 2 vols. (1950–1), included the following para. on student protests at Banaras Hindu University: 'In order to balance the budget the income of the University has to be increased. It may not be possible to increase the receipts from students' fees as already there are frequent protests against the recent increases. If our recommendations about scholarships, maintenance grants and fellowships are accepted the expenses of the University will be further increased. Therefore the University will have to look to the Governments, Central and Provincial, for increased grants': chap. 15, sect. 5, 461. (A University Grants Commission was established Nov. 1953.) See also Humayun Kabir, *Education in New India*, 2nd edn (1959), chaps. 5, 8 on Indian universities and on student indiscipline.

[12] Francis (Jack) Dillon (1899–1982) learned the pioneering craft of radio features from E. A. F. (Archie) Harding (1903–53) and D. Geoffrey Bridson (1910–80) at BBC Manchester in the 1930s, and after serving at BBC Bristol 1938–40 transferred to BBC London for the war effort. In the BBC Features Department 1946–61 he developed his own documentary programmes (e.g. 'Country Magazine'), wrote and produced a wide range of features (from documentary histories to folk-singing to satirical fairy tales) with gusto and wit. See obit. tribute in *The Times*, 11 Dec. 1982, 10g.

[13] *Psittacus erithacus princeps*, of the grey parrot family noted for talkativeness: see the 12th Duke of Bedford's (H. William S. Russell) *Parrots and Parrot-like Birds*, rev. (1954), 45–7.

remember crab soup, champagne, and a Madeira that took us back to Madras in the eighteenth century; on our way home we found a Sikh who had been stabbed in a brawl and took him to hospital. The next day we had our other dinner, with some Brahmin archaeologists and friends, in a vegetarian restaurant. Here we ate off banana leaves—chutney at the left top corner, tumeric at the right top corner, rice in the centre, etc., etc., and, of course, chappatis to eat with. At the end of it Dillon and I were garlanded with wet pink roses.

The Frontier? But of course, yes. Four of us (Wynford Vaughan Thomas,[14] Dillon, an engineer, and myself) arrived in Peshawar by recording van; this was then almost the only way of getting there, and luckily people on the roads always thought we were some sort of military. The first thing we needed was petrol, and we were sent to see the District Commissioner. We found a very handsome, very courteous, very busy, young man scoring out things with a blue pencil. 'Excuse me, gentlemen,' he said, 'I shall be at your service in a moment, but just at the present I am composing . . . a curfew.' He got us our petrol, of course, and we then found another benefactor, a Muslim professor, who looked rather like Groucho Marx and seemed to have his old pupils in all the key positions in the country, including the jaws of the Khyber. He had managed to keep in with everyone of every party, and on the same day took us to see the Khan brothers and their bitter enemy, the new Prime Minister.[15] Vaughan Thomas did most

---

[14] Wynford Vaughan-Thomas (1908–87), the Welsh author and journalist, joined the BBC in 1937, became a noted BBC war correspondent, was a well-known radio and TV commentator, later appointed Director of Programmes, Harlech Television Ltd. 1968–71, then Director, 1971. See his autobiography *Trust to Talk* (1980) and obit. in *The Times*, 5 Feb. 1987, 14f.

[15] Liaquat Ali Khan (1895–1951), the Oxonian lawyer, Punjabi socialist political leader, the first Prime Minister of Pakistan 1947–51—undisputed leader after the death of the Governor General, M. A. Jinnah (1876–1948), long-time President of the All-India Muslim League—was bitterly opposed to the non-violent 'Khan brothers', friends of Gandhi and long-standing rivals of the Muslim League, each at some time Chief Minister of the NW Frontier Province: Dr Khan Sahib (1882–1958), the elder brother who in old age relented and joined himself to Pakistan as a patriot; and his younger brother, Khan Abdul Ghaffar Khan (1890–1988), 'the frontier Gandhi', saintly leader of the Pathans and founder of their Red Shirt movement, who remained loyal to the principles (non-violent non-co-operation) of Mahatma Mohandas K. Gandhi (1869–1948)—and who, after repeated imprisonments (by the British and then by Pakistan), eventually (1984) moved to Afghanistan. For Dr Khan Sahib, see

of the talking to both parties and showed himself quite as deft
as the Professor. Abdul Gaffar Khan, 'the frontier Gandhi',
received us sitting on straw on a veranda and surrounded by
his henchmen bristling with bandoliers. But on the Prime
Minister's lawn we found some still more Homeric characters,
a dozen tribesmen from Waziristan[16] who had come to ask
permission to march on Delhi. That evening we dined with
some very orthodox Muslims who did not drink but had laid on
quantities of whisky for us.

Lucknow? This charming city, full of trees and decadent
Mogul architecture, seemed to me somewhat unreal. I had
dinner with one of the so-called 'Barons of Oudh'[17] (a set of
notorious land-owners) who looked like a great stage chef and
collected silver hookahs. He had never been to Europe, but
would, he said, like to visit Germany. But why Germany?
'Because there they have a very early copy of the Koran—*yes,
and they've learnt a lot from it.*' Still, there was one thing very real
in Lucknow, and that was Mrs Sarojini Naidu,[18] whose guest
I was at Government House. She was then acting Governor,
which she disliked ('I've seen enough police in my time, and

---

obit. notices in *The Times*, 10 May 1958, 8e; 13 May, 14d; 19 May, 15c. For Ghaffar
Khan, see his memoirs *My Life and Struggles*, trans. Helen H. Bouman (1969) and G. L.
Zutshi, *Frontier Ghandi* (1970).

[16] The Waziri people include the Darwish or Wazir in the north and the Mahsud in
the south, of a region in the NW Frontier Province, Pakistan—once the crux of the
colonial-British 'frontier problem'.

[17] Oudh (Awadh or Ayodhya), a tract including the Lucknow and Faydabad
districts of the Indian State of Uttar Pradesh (United Provinces), had been ruled by
nawabs and kings (1722–1856), and its annexation by the British became one of the
causes of the 1857 Mutiny. After the Mutiny, the great *talukdari* families (agricultural
landlords or landed gentry) ousted from their estates were reinstated, although—as a
result of the Uttar Pradesh Panchayat Act of 1947—a new rural hierarchy of officials
and village organizations sprang up. This 'Baron of Oudh' may have been one of the
old *talukdari* landowners. For Oudh, see C. Collin Davies, 'Awadh', in *Encyclopaedia of
Islam*, new edn, many vols. (1960–), i. 756–8.

[18] Mme Sarojini Naidu, *née* Chattopadhyay (1879–1949), 'the Nightingale of
India', was a political activist, feminist, and Bengali poet (3 vols. of poetry in English,
translated into all Indian dialects), who became first Indian woman president of the
Indian National Congress 1925 and first Indian woman to be a state governor (of
Uttar Pradesh 1947–8). She had attracted Indian intellectuals to her salon in Bombay.
See *New Encyclopaedia Britannica*, 15th edn, 30 vols. (1974, 1984), Micropaedia vii.
168–9. (This article—'India at First Sight' by MacNeice—was written between
March 1949, date of Mme Naidu's death, and Jan. 1950, date of his departure for
Greece.)

now I have to have them around me'), but the people revered and loved her and called her 'our mother'. She had no use for the 'communal nonsense', and forcibly mixed Hindu and Muslim at her parties. She told me that her provincial ministers never laughed, so she kept making jokes for the good of their souls. Mrs Naidu's sense of humour was rightly famous. But she also had real imagination and real heart. 'No one can accuse me of being pro-British'—she had been after all President of Congress and spent much time in our jails—'but I wept when they pulled down your flag on the Residency. I think we ought to have left it there. A holy place after all is a holy place.' A country that can produce a Mrs Naidu is one to visit. I am glad I had the chance.

About Ireland[1]

Dublin. By Maurice Craig. (Cresset Press. 42s.)
Ireland and the Irish. By Charles Duff. (Boardman. 15s.)
The Emerald Isle. By Geoffrey Taylor. (Evans. 12s. 6d.)
The Face of Ulster. By Denis O'D. Hanna. (Batsford. 15s.)
Connacht: Galway. By Richard Hayward. (Arthur Barker.
  21s.)

Ireland to-day being tourist-minded, more and more books
may be expected about her, all of which no doubt will sell,
especially to travel-restricted Britons. The danger is that in the
purveyance of easy and carefree reading an author may lapse
into easy and careless writing. For most books about Ireland
are mainly a rehash of old materials though there are a few, like
Dr E. E. Evans's *Irish Heritage*, which do fill a notable gap;[2] to
this specialist minority belongs Mr Craig's book on Dublin.[3]
The more general books therefore have to be treated like anthologies and judged by their range, sequences, contrasts and,
above all, by their omissions. Thus these new books are all
lavishly and attractively illustrated, but we could begin by
asking why they illustrate so much of one kind of thing and so
little of others. The Irish and Ulster Tourist Associations take
excellent photographs but they naturally are over-concerned
with the 'scenic'; thus Mr Duff and Mr Taylor produce identical photographs both of Clifden and Glendalough.[4] One needs
more pictures like Mr Taylor's Orange Celebrations, Mr
Duff's turf-cutters, Mr Hanna's very ordinary village streets.[5]

---

  [1] *New Statesman and Nation* 43: 1106 (17 May 1952), 590, 592.
  [2] E[myr] Estyn Evans's *Irish Heritage: The Landscape, the People and their Work*, with
  illustrations by the author (1942), filled a gap on Irish folk-ways and customs. Evans
  was Head of the Department of Geography, Queen's University, Belfast.
  [3] Maurice [James] Craig's *Dublin 1660–1860* (1952) supplied a need for a historical
  book on the long tradition—subdivided into 'Ormonde's Dublin', 'Swift's Dublin',
  'Grattan's Dublin', and 'Whose Dublin?'
  [4] Duff, facing 48 and 128; Taylor, facing 144 and 48.
  [5] Taylor, facing 145; Duff, facing 112–13; Hanna, facing 25.

In none of these books is there an illustration of a cottage interior or a pub interior, or even of the Belfast shipyards.

Again, when a man is saying something not very new, he ought to say it extra well. With touristic subjects there is a terrible temptation to be arch or corny. Thus Mr Hayward,[6] while very informative, is unduly addicted to superlatives and to words like 'lovely' and 'veritable' and allows his landscape to 'wax in splendour' on two pages running. And Mr Hanna, who does not overwrite in the same way, has one most irritating habit, presumably due to a straining after freshness. Freshness, I admit, is needed but why should foals seen from the train be 'a Chirico fantasy'[7] or the Ulster mountains (only two pages later) be 'like a Frank Dobson study of a female nude',[8] or the Giant's Causeway be 'a Max Ernst nightmare'?[9] And why should the boats on Lough Neagh remind one of Galilee? And why, oh why, is Errigal mountain 'a twin sister of Fujiyama'?[10] Of these four authors (I exclude Mr Craig, who writes with the dryness proper to a book of reference) Mr Taylor is the only one whose writing in itself is vivid. Perhaps his style is natural and fresh not only because he is a poet but because, unlike the other three, he is not at all frightened either of saying the wrong thing or of leaving out what bores him; in fact, he is not playing to the tourist. Still, all these books have their merits, i.e. (in popular jargon), actuality content, entertainment value, and glamour.

Mr Craig's *Dublin*, subtitled 'a social and architectural history' of the years 1660–1860, is a solid piece of scholarship for students of history and architecture but could also at moments entertain the general reader, as in its descriptions of eighteenth-century gamblers, 'pinkindindies',[11] and Fellows of Trinity. His account begins with the Restoration which in

---

[6] Richard Hayward's book in the 'This is Ireland' series is entitled *Connacht and the City of Galway* (1952).

[7] Hanna, 18.

[8] Ibid. 20.

[9] Ibid. 54.

[10] Ibid. 98.

[11] 'There flourished in Dublin at this time a class of nocturnal strollers known as the "pinkindindies", skilled in the art of "pinking" or slashing their victims with the points of their swords which protruded below the open end of the scabbard. They used this technique to recoup their gaming losses at the expense of unaccompanied pedestrians': Craig, 156.

Ireland was 'as much the Restoration of the house of Butler[12] as of the house of Stuart' and which also, as he points out, meant the end of the Irish Middle Ages. His account ends, thanks to the same Irish time-lag (which all these authors very properly mention), with 'Georgian' houses still going up in Dublin. Dublin, built largely by Englishmen for Englishmen, remains a Georgian Mecca the width and vistas of whose streets must be a revelation to Londoners. Luck came into it, of course. As Mr Craig says of Gandon,[13] who designed both the Custom House and the Four Courts:

He was, of course, very fortunate; no man can be a great architect who is not. Very few are given the chance to build two monumental buildings on riverside sites near enough to be interrelated but not near enough to interfere with one another, and so placed that they dominate an entire city.[14]

The book contains an invaluable appendix listing the worthwhile buildings in some seven or eight score streets.

Mr Hanna also, being an architect,[15] gives considerable space to architecture, and this is the more original part of his book, since very few people have bothered with Ulster buildings before him. The 'Ulster bawn or defended farmhouse' is certainly an attractive species,[16] while the Ulster church, if not to everyone's taste, is an interesting phenomenon (the time-lag again) from which Mr Hanna derives the thesis that 'This country carried on the Gothic idea for nearly a century after it had died in England, and the result was a strange mixture of Gothic and Renaissance, which I have called "Planters Gothic."' Mr Hanna—and who can blame him?—would like to see more colour in the Ulster town. Mr Hayward would like to see more taste throughout the country; he is angered—and who can blame him?—by the demolition of Coole. His book on

[12] For the Butlers who were earls (and dukes) of Ormonde in Ireland in the Renaissance, Restoration, and earlier, see the *DNB*. (William Butler Yeats had been proud of his Butler ancestry: Joseph Hone, *W. B. Yeats 1865–1939* (1962), 2, 274.)

[13] James Gandon (1743–1823), the architect, one of the original members of the Royal Irish Academy: see *DNB*.

[14] Craig, 249.

[15] Hanna, 'Preface', *The Face of Ulster: Antrim, Londonderry, Fermanagh, Tyrone, Armagh, Monaghan, Cavin, Donegal and Down* (1952), v.

[16] Ibid. 34, 59, 63, 70, 106; also illus. facing 64.

the City and County of Galway is packed with fascinating fact and illustrated with pencil drawings by Mr Raymond Piper.[17]

Ireland and the Irish is half history and half guide-book; as the latter it is useful for strangers who want 'convenient centres' for 'excursions'; as the former it is full of sound sense. Mr Duff is right, for instance, in stressing that the Irish are 'basically conservative and calculable' in spite of their habit, as he puts it, of shaking the kaleidoscope, especially when with strangers. He is right in insisting that the Irish, both Protestant and Catholic, are puritan. And in linking realism and dreaming as 'almost commonplace Irish characteristics'.[18] And in denying that the word 'Celtic' means anything racial. And in deploring what happened to Davy Byrne's.[19] My chief criticism is that he tends to admire too many things too much (as indeed do Mr Hanna and Mr Hayward). Ireland at certain times and places can be most uncouth, most depressing, most destructive.

Mr Taylor's book is short and personal. Deliberately eschewing politics he begins with the statement that 'Ireland is unique among European nations in having no history[20]—apart, that is, from natural and supernatural history. Almost at once he moves on to frogs and then to gardening and shortly to Firbolgs.[21] And various people are going to be shocked by him. He will shock non-Irish Philhibernians by asserting: 'As a philosophy in Church or State, Liberalism is alien to the Irish.'[22] He will shock antiquity-lovers by his attitude to ruins, Gaelic Leaguers by his irreverence for the Book of Kells[23] and his opposition to any neo-Celtic art movement, Americans by his dread of their 'contaminating' influence and his colleagues

---

[17] Raymond Piper later illustrated the hunting classic by Arthur Stringer, *The Experienced Huntsman*, 2nd edn, ed. James Fairley (1977), with his fine soft-pencil drawings.

[18] Duff, chaps. 4 and 5.

[19] Ibid. 164–5. The old Davy Byrne's pub was made famous in Joyce's *Ulysses* (1922).

[20] Taylor, 13.

[21] Ibid. 26 ff. Firbolgs: In Irish myth, early settlers of ancient Ireland.

[22] Ibid. 33.

[23] 'The scribe of the *Book of Kells* was a doodler': ibid. 34. An ancient (8th–9th c. AD) manuscript of the four Gospels, with magnificent, elaborate, illustrative patterns combining abstract and animal forms, probably written at Kells, Co. Meath; housed at Trinity College, Dublin, since the Restoration: *OCEL*, 4th edn, rev. Dorothy Eagle (1967), 444.

by the remark that Miles na gCopaleen is 'the most interesting and I think, most important of contemporary Irish writers.'[24] And he will very much shock Dubliners by declaring that 'in the art of polite conversation Belfast has now and easily taken first place from Dublin.'[25] An enjoyable book—and good for one.

[24] Brian O'Nolan's pseud. as satirical columnist in *The Irish Times*; also known as Flann O'Brien. See Taylor, 149–50.

[25] Taylor, 113.

Notes on the Way [1][1]

The often-met paradox of nostalgia for the unknown (how can
we be homesick for homes we never had?) is confirmed by the
shock of familiarity with which the unknown sometimes greets
us. Such familiarity of course can be illusory and is never
comprehensive. Thus in India, the most 'foreign' country that
I have visited, while constantly surprised by its novelty, at the
same time I often had the feeling that 'this is where I came in';
the Indian bazaar, for instance, surpassing in its noises,
colours, and smells all the descriptions one has read of it, yet
shows a family resemblance to . . . to what? we ask ourselves,
and find it is our own Middle Ages. And a feast day in an
Indian village—temple car, marigolds and all—while somewhat like an English Sunday school outing, seemed to me still
more like an English medieval Church Ale.[2]

It is this factor of familiarity in the foreign or rather of the
restoration of our own lost past or of our missing relations that
must greatly influence most of us in our reactions to art. It is
fashionable and now almost a moral duty to consider works of
art 'on their merit'—but how many of us can do this? In Paris
this May I went from an exhibition of Twentieth-Century Art
(Picasso, Juan Gris, Mondrian, etc.) back to the permanent
collection of the French Impressionists in the Jeu de Paume.[3]
And what a relief I found it; here I was again 'at home'. This
no doubt sentimental and 'literary' reaction was due not only
to my preference for the way in which the Impressionists used

[1] *Time & Tide* 33: 26 (28 June 1952), 709–10. 'Notes on the Way' was a series
written over the years by many writers including T. S. Eliot and MacNeice. The
editor allowed 'an entirely free pen' to contributors, but did not necessarily agree
'with the opinions expressed' (headnote).

[2] 'A periodical festive gathering' associated with a church: *OED 2*.

[3] In May 1952 there was a Festival of Arts in Paris, mainly musical, under the title
'Masterpieces of the Twentieth Century': *The Times*, 19 Jan. 1952, 2f. 'An exhibition
of twentieth-century painting, selected by Mr J. J. Sweeney and Mr René Huyghe,
was held at the Musée d'Art Moderne': ibid., 10 June 1952, 2d. The Jeu de paume,
the Louvre museum annex, had received the works of the Impressionists (and of their
associates) 5 years before, in 1947: *Grand Dictionnaire Encyclopédique Larousse*, 10 vols.
(1984), vi. 5857.

paint but also to a preference for the period which produced and is reflected in that painting.

Escapism? I suppose so—if that tiresome word can be specific enough to cover a quite specific liking for a pleasant kind of life which people really lived and for the lyrical paintings which remain among us to preserve it. Yet I would not be transported back into the café and theatre society of Manet and Degas;[4] against me are ranged all the clichés about 'putting the clock back' and 'making one's bed'—clichés which, like Kipling's 'Gods of the Copybook Headings',[5] are not only clichés but are solid and have bottle-glass on top of them. These thoughts occurred to me after visiting the New Burlington Galleries to see the astonishing replicas of some of the mosaics from Ravenna.[6]

Here I was, in a sense, not so much at home as in my Indian bazaar—or in the Caves of Ajanta—or even in the churches in Ravenna which contain the originals; the mosaics *belong* in those churches whose absurdly modest brick exteriors both act as a bridge to their mystery and rivet that mystery to earth. And since those churches, like all Christian churches, are part of any Englishman's or Irishman's background, the mosaics must be part of it, too. But take the smaller part out of the greater and plump it in pieces in a London gallery and then you must see how queer it is; queerer than Ajanta or early Greek sculpture or Chinese pots or Italian Primitives or Brueghel or Bosch or even Braque or Brancusi.[7] Also it is queerer than much Byzantine work, especially than the late

---

[4] Both prominent French painters standing apart from, yet associated with, the Impressionists: Edouard Manet (1832–83) and Edgar Degas (1834–1917).

[5] Rudyard Kipling's poem (1919) about certain commonplaces or clichés which yet remain sound and lasting through the ages. Cf. MacNeice's poem 'The Truisms' (1960).

[6] 'An exhibition of [58] mosaic replicas of parts of the mosaic decorations in various churches of Ravenna', some 'quite large portions of wall', was shown by the British Arts Council at the New Burlington Galleries, 17 May–22 June 1952: *The Times*, 23 April 1952, 8e.

[7] Out of context any original art of whatever country will look strange. Brueghel, a family of Flemish painters (mid-16th to early 17th c.); in this case, probably Pieter Brueghel the Elder (*c*.1525–69) known as 'Peasant Brueghel'. Hieronymus Bosch of Brabant (*c*.1450–1516), the greatest painter of obscure late-medieval fantasies and grotesques. Georges Braque (1882–1963), the French painter and co-founder with Pablo Picasso of Cubism (1907–14). Constantin Brancusi (1876–1957), the Romanian sculptor of simple, highly polished, later abstract, shapes.

flowering (or 'decadence') of the wall-paintings at Mistra in the Peloponnese.[8] At Mistra we can feel we know where we are, not only because of the immediate charm of colour and line and because of a gaiety and humanity not usually associated with Byzantium but also because they are *paintings*—not mosaics. For all that, just as one's great-great-grandfather might have more appeal than one's first cousin, the alien technique and the still more alien mentality of the Ravenna mosaics may excite in us a profounder nostalgia than more humanist works which easily 'click' with one's self but not with the whole self.

The homes that we have content few of us. In England today city-dwellers hanker for the country, countrymen either for a non-existent London (or America) or for the rural 'old days'; intellectuals for older days still—or maybe for newer days or days that never could be; the particular target may be wrong, but it usually symbolizes a greater spaciousness combined with a clearer order, a pattern of living that is more highly coloured but simpler, unfairer perhaps but easier to understand. Among intellectuals the fashions in nostalgia change. Once it was Periclean Athens, Augustan England, or other 'ages of reason'; now there is a marked swing back towards the Middle Ages— for reasons more akin to those of T. E. Hulme than to those of Chesterton.[9] The Renaissance (to which some would add the Reformation) seems, like the Industrial Revolution, to be crying for a counter-revolution; once they have grown out (not that all of them do) of a starry-eyed adolescent anarchism, most of our intellectuals begin to long for *system*, even for a ruthless system in which their intellect is sacrificed to 'ends' outside itself.

Hence the obvious cases of oblation to Moscow or Rome but for every one of such oblates there are thousands who, unable to dedicate themselves fully to the liberalism or humanism which they still, at least partly, believe in, sublimate their self-dedicatory urge into mere day-dreams of systems to which they can never belong and for which they need never do a hand's turn. For there is really no question of returning to the Middle

---

[8] Mistra in Southern Greece was the site of the third great 14th-c. Byzantine school, and contains famous religious frescos.

[9] The English writers T. E. Hulme (1883–1917) and G. K. Chesterton (1874–1936) stood for a return to conservative values (classical and Catholic, respectively).

Ages—or to D. H. Lawrence's Mexico.[10] And so our nostalgias nourish and are nourished by accidie—a medieval name for a vice which is only too modern, our moral or rather our spiritual paralysis.

'The best lack all conviction,' wrote Yeats,[11] a poet who tied himself in knots trying to acquire convictions. Environment and heredity helped him but few of us are so lucky. Rightly suspicious of 'the worst' and their 'passionate intensity' but with little to set up against them, we are only too ready to turn our faces to the wall. This accidie, of course, is not confined to intellectuals. The dying Mrs Gradgrind in *Hard Times*, when asked if she was in pain, replied: 'I think there's a pain somewhere in the room but I can't positively say that I have got it.'[12]

For everyone to-day there is a pain 'somewhere in the room', but any intellectual, unlike Mrs Gradgrind, is in duty bound to be rather more precise about it. He need not claim it—or all of it—as *his* pain (the arm-chair martyr and the arm-chair saviour are bores), still less need he offer a cure for it, but he must know that it is there and have some notion what it is. But once he knows it is there and has even glimpsed what it is, he will never again be quite easy in his mind. And, while an artist needs some uneasiness of mind, too much of it leads to accidie. What is the escape (as distinct from 'escapism')? The 'ordinary man',[13] who used to be saved by his faith, is now very often saved by just not thinking too much—which indeed he has little time for. But the intellectual, with the time and the duty to think, has to find something more positive.

---

[10] Lawrence's travel book *Mornings in Mexico* (1927) and his novel *The Plumed Serpent* (1926) presented a panorama of then exotic, vital folk life.

[11] W. B. Yeats's poem 'The Second Coming' 1919 (1920) on the sheer 'anarchy' following World War I: 'The blood-dimmed tide is loosed, and everywhere | The ceremony of innocence is drowned; | The best lack all conviction, while the worst | Are full of passionate intensity,' (ll. 5–8), and on the compensatory archetype of a bestial man, an anti-Christ, often taken as a prognosis of the rise of Fascism in Europe.

[12] Charles Dickens's *Hard Times* (1854), 2. 9, para. 40. Cf. *Selected Literary Criticism of Louis MacNeice*, 224 with n. 2.

[13] MacNeice's idea of the 'ordinary man' was central to his idea of the poet as 'not too esoteric': *Modern Poetry* (1938; 1968), 198.

Notes on the Way [2]¹

There is a pain 'somewhere in the room' (as the dying Mrs Gradgrind said in *Hard Times*)² and, as the room grows smaller and more crowded and we more 'globally minded', we cannot but be more aware of it. But what, we repeat, are we to do? The writers of the 'thirties had a ready answer: we were all to be 'socially conscious' and therefore politically active—and, if we were not, we were 'escapist'. But the writers of the 'thirties —and I say this as one of them and as one who was sometimes labelled a 'social consciousness poet'—were too often examples of that strange but not uncommon phenomenon, the hypocrite in good faith. Thus their 'social consciousness' too often meant a narrow and inhuman conception of society—a 'society' in which neither personal relationships (or at any rate the sense of family) nor regional loyalties nor religious ties should count— while their 'political activity' mainly meant *talking* politics. But to-day we have lost our faith in committees and have also lost that naïve sort of optimism which was oddly wedded to a sense of (other people's) doom, while we are on the other hand recovering that respect not only for individuals but also for groups which our social theories precluded and that respect for the world which is lost in almost any 'world-view'.

A world-view is a Teutonic thing, which is why, no doubt, people prefer to say *Weltanschauung*. The English for better or worse—I think for better—have generally tended to be empiricist. But the influence of German Idealism, which is still among us, if disguised, makes us sometimes admit this only with an air of apology; it is assumed that an empiricist is a less imaginative, less courageous, less spiritual person than the man with the *Weltanschauung* who knows all the answers. But in fact to 'know all the answers' is not only comparatively easy but means in the long run the death of the imagination. Both Hegel and Marx were highly imaginative in some respects, but theirs is a kind of

¹ *Time & Tide* 33: 28 (12 July 1952), 779–80.
² See the ending of 'Notes on the Way [1]' above.

imagination that is alien both to the ordinary man and to the artist, while their grasp of 'the world' or of 'history' was an ugly grasp which the world in the end will elude although first insulted and hurt by it. Christ was not so doctrinaire; whatever his followers did, he left us no rigid system, but he did leave that sense of wonder which makes for humility, elasticity, sympathy.

In our own Christian country (we may as well call it that, since our past is more important than what we may think our present) this elasticity and sympathy are shown in our law as in our poetry—and we may still be thankful that we lack a rigid Constitution. Now, as anything rigid saves thought and moral energy, so to be an empiricist in the English tradition demands not only toughness but a good deal of self-confidence. But with both the pain in the room and the crowd in the room increasing, it is harder for us to have either. Which brings us back to the growing danger of accidie.

I suggested in my former 'Notes on the Way' that the ordinary man used to avoid this by 'faith'—by that combination of a customary ethic with a mystical assumption of values (the *feeling* that we are members one of another) which permeates most of our history. But if such a faith disappears, we are left with an empty nostalgia and a living from hand to mouth. Which is how many people live, though not perhaps as many as one would think. The behaviour of the British civilian population during the Blitz did seem to imply not only that their empiricism is still an efficient and humane one, but that it still has its mystical sanction behind it. Otherwise why not give up? Why bother to help other people? Why bother to help oneself?

During the War there was a great deal of talk about the Common Man, much of it simultaneously sentimental and patronizing. The Common Man, most of us would now admit, is neither a pattern of virtue nor a potential world-saviour. But he has those virtues which, as Aristotle would say, are proper to him and he can, it seems, on occasions save himself. This is more than many intellectuals have or do. The virtues proper to *them* are more complicated and difficult and to save themselves they need more specialized weapons. Yet it *is* mainly a difference of specialization, of degree. Faith apart, the Common Man avoids accidie by doing things, making things, watching things, and, last but not least, by self-indulgence. The same escapes are open to the intellectual, but the things which he does and makes and watches are special. And he often compares pretty badly on his plane with the Common Man upon his. Most spectators at a cricket match understand the placing of the field; many quite sophisticated readers of poetry cannot even see a leg-trap and assume that the poet is always bowling at the stumps.

Worse than that, many artists themselves are much less handy in their art than the Common Man is at overhauling an engine or rigging up a hen house. This is partly of course to be expected, since a work of art by its nature cannot be so clearly blueprinted as hen houses or engines. But it is also due to a disproportionate stress upon 'art' as distinct from craftsmanship. Too much theorizing about essences and fundamentals has led some artists into an untraditional and quite unwarranted contempt for the surface. A work of mere craftsmanship may be *all* surface but a work of art, whatever its iceberg depths, cannot be *without* a surface and so cannot dispense with craftsmanship. The artists of an empiricist nation should never have fallen into *this* fallacy; it is sad to hear English writers (and both Marxists and 'neo-Romantics' have been guilty of it)[3] talking as if a work of art could be judged entirely by what it 'expresses'. For the artist is primarily a 'maker'—and this is what saves him from accidie.

The artist's paradox indeed is that, while *qua* artist he is up against profundities—the *lacrimae rerum*[4]—and therefore peculiarly susceptible to accidie, *qua* craftsman he must deal with surfaces which, if he treats them properly, are bound to throw back some light on him. And just as a poet must be both artist and craftsman, so a poem is not only a spiritual experience but also a physical organism. And the former should have looked after itself but the latter must be looked after. To 'cultivate

---

[3] Marxist and 'neo-Romantic' writers were equally guilty, in MacNeice's view, of extreme interpretations of experience—either totally 'objective' and materialistic or totally 'subjective' and 'spiritual'—both fallacious, to the neglect of art as 'making', constructive, craftsmanly.

[4] Virgil, *Aeneid* i. 462: 'tears [shed] for things'; cf. MacNeice's *Selected Literary Criticism*, 151 n. 8.

one's garden' is a cliché[5] that to-day sounds almost defeatist but it is not defeatist—or escapist—if one thinks of and treats one's garden as part of the landscape—and remembers that pain in the landscape which, however minutely, it may mitigate.

We cannot live, as persons, by personal relationships alone and we cannot live, as artists, by craftsmanship alone—but we certainly cannot live without them. In answer to all the panaceas, so deep or so broad, offered us to-day by politicians, psychoanalysts and others, I should sometimes like to use a slogan: 'By their faces ye shall know them.' A good face, whether of a person or of a poem, is something that has grown from the inside, yet remains a face, a surface. But any real face as distinct from a dial, has some connection with a soul.

---

[5] Voltaire, *Candide*, chap. 30: ' *"Cela est bien dit", répondit Candide, "mais il faut cultiver notre jardin"* ' ('That is well said', replied Candide, 'but we must cultivate our garden'—i.e. attend to our own affairs).

Wedding of Simon Karas[1]

Simon Karas was married on Boxing Day, 1950. This was a wedding unlike any other wedding, and to one who was fortunate enough to attend it the memory has already grown into myth, to rank with the keenest romances of one's childhood or with one's most revealing adventures in the spheres of art or literature. An ordinary Greek wedding, while colourful and charming, is a short ceremony and, to a Western eye, has something casual about it. Karas's wedding, which was not just Greek but *Byzantine*, was neither short nor casual; he himself, as Byzantinist and musician, had directed at least two full rehearsals of it.

This particular form of service had not been used, so I was told, for centuries, while the church in which it took place is a church where no one gets married. No one except Karas. For the church is the famous monastery church of Daphni, one of the masterpieces of Byzantine architecture.[2] And Karas is a man who eats and drinks and wakes and sleeps Byzantium. Perhaps the key word is 'wakes', for it is hard to imagine him asleep. He is a scholar and enthusiast, so it was only to be expected that his wedding would be special and thorough.

[1] *Radio Times* 116: 1504 (5 Sept. 1952), 13. MacNeice was seconded to the British Institute and the British Council in Athens, 1950-1. MacNeice 'was present at this extraordinary ceremony which the bridegroom had himself rehearsed and directed' (headnote). At the foot of the page is a photograph of the church. Karas (1905–   ), the 'Greek musicologist and folk music scholar, . . . founded the School for National Music in Athens, where he lectured in neo-Byzantine chant, traditional Greek folk music and dances, and national instruments . . . build[ing] up archives of traditional ballads and songs recorded in remote villages . . . to study in particular their possible relationship to Byzantine monophony'; 'from 1937 to 1970 he was director of the folk music division of the Greek radio': *New Grove Dictionary of Music and Musicians*, ed. Stanley Sadie, 20 vols. (1980), ix. 802. NB the name Karras in the published article has been corrected to Karas.

[2] Built 1082-1103 on the 'inscribed-octagon plan', a 'structure permitting erection of a large dome without the use of pillars obstructing the view of the presbytery': *Encyclopedia of World Art*, vi. 875. 'Contemporary with the building . . . are the finest mosaics of their period, characterized by such an elegance of design, richness of colour, and skill of composition that they command universal admiration': Ormonde Maddock Dalton, *Byzantine Art and Archaeology* (1911, 1961), 396.

And special and thorough it was—and also enchanted and enchanting.

Twice a week Karas's house in the middle of Athens is packed with his disciples who come to play or sing there under his ruthless direction; he gets very angry with them, his eyebrows explode, but they take it. These disciples, who mainly have poorly paid jobs as shop-girls, butchers, or housemaids, but who all subject themselves to their master's exalted standards, were naturally in the forefront of his wedding. Before the day they had sung the traditional song for the baking of the wedding cake; on the day itself they sang the appropriate songs for the bridegroom's rising, the bridegroom's shaving, the calling on the bride, etc. Then, having played and sung him out to Daphni, half a dozen miles by bus, it was they who under his eye sustained the arduous and intricate—and generally unknown—music of a service which lasted three hours. For most of this time the bridegroom and bride stood dead centre of the church under the dome in which is the great mosaic of Christos Pantocrator.[3] Bishops and priests in astonishing vestments emerged and disappeared and re-emerged from the sanctum; a crowd of Athenians—for this was an unprecedented occasion—stood and stood, facing in on the centre, but it was the central couple who dominated. One felt that for once someone had really put the clock back.

Not everyone accepts Karas's interpretation of Byzantine music, but this is a subject outside a Westerner's scope; all I can say is that this music in that setting seemed to me right and significant and moving. And there were extraordinary moments when it almost ceased to be music, almost became ultra-violet, a mere vibration in the floor and the walls. The church, which outside looks small and modest, inside seemed large—a familiar Byzantine paradox, while its famous mosaics were fulfilling another Byzantine paradox, carrying their conventionalism with the most natural air and blending austerity and happiness. The same was true of the service itself, which was austere but happy. When it was over the disciples

---

[3] For a photo of the Christ Pantokrator (Christ as Judge of All), a mosaic in the dome of the church, see Dalton, 397 with fig. 231: 'a colossal bust . . . round whom . . . stand sixteen prophets'.

played Karas and his bride home through a very radiant morning and in the evening there was a party in his house. The two white bridal crowns hung on the wall as the guests danced in at one door and out at another, with excitement and yet with dignity, round and round with Karas himself leading them.

Statement on Belief[1]

When faced with this question 'What do I believe?' I assume it is a question not so much of fact as of value. The answer therefore should not be such an answer as 'I believe *that* the cup is on the table,' or 'I believe *that* two and two make four'; it should be an answer such as 'I believe *in* cooking with garlic,' or 'I believe *in* splashing in my bath.' This latter kind of answer cannot, as I see it, be assessed purely in terms of fact. I know that there will always be some tiresome person to say: 'You believe in cooking with garlic because it stimulates the digestion, so what you really meant was, "I believe that cooking with garlic is good for me".' But this of course is not what I really meant at all. I would still do these things if they were not—in the utilitarian sense—'good for me'; I enjoy both the taste of garlic and a good splash, and when one enjoys anything it seems to me that that thing becomes an end in itself, even though at the same time it may be a means to something else. So this question 'What do I believe?' seems to me to be a question of ends—and also of starting-points.

It is not a mere question of fact or of utility. Lots of things

[1] Article headed 'Louis MacNeice' in *This I Believe: The personal philosophies of one hundred thoughtful men and women in all walks of life*, foreword Edward R. Murrow, ed. Edward P. Morgan (1953), 64–5, with brief *vita* of MacNeice on 65. 'Ed' (Edward) or Egbert Roscoe Murrow (1908–65) was a famous American journalist, broadcaster, and author, prominent during World War II as European correspondent for CBS, stationed in London and covering the war from start to finish. His radio broadcasts *This Is London 1939–41* (pub. 1941) were followed by 'Hear It Now', by *This I Believe* (three books, 1952–4), and by the TV *See It Now* (1955). In 1961–3 he served as director of the US Information Agency. See his *In Search of Light: The Broadcasts of Edward R. Murrow (1938–61)*, ed. Edward Bliss, Jun. (1967) and A. M. Sperber, *Murrow: His Life and Times* (1986). 'This I Believe', launched 1949 in the USA, was a daily 5-minute radio programme introduced by Murrow and a weekly 600-word newspaper article. Successful 'men and women of many races, colours and faiths, people known and unknown', were invited to participate: Ward Wheelock, 'The Power of an Idea', in *This I Believe* (1953), xvi. Among British contributors to *This I Believe* (1953) were: A. J. Ayer, Jacob Bronowski, Sir Hugh Casson, Dame Edith Evans, Aldous Huxley, C. Day-Lewis, Malcolm Muggeridge, Gilbert Murray, Sir Harold Nicolson, Arnold Toynbee, and Rebecca West; among American contributors: Pearl Buck, Martha Graham, Helen Keller, Thomas Mann, Margaret Mead, and Carl Sandburg.

are useful for the preservation of life and their comparative usefulness may be a question of fact. But life itself—what is the use of life? I defy any scientist or rationalist or collector of facts to answer that one. Either you assume life is worth while or you don't—and that is a question of value.

Well, I—like the vast majority of people—assume that life is worth while and that is my starting point. But as to the end— merely to live is inadequate; some kinds of life seem to me preferable to others. Someone at once of course will bring in the *de gustibus* argument[2] and say: 'That is all very well but your preferences are not the same as mine, so it's every man for himself, an extreme individualism which means, collectively, anarchism.' I do not, however, accept the *de gustibus* argument. Apart from the fact that, whether we want to or not, we have to live in communities, I think that human individuals are much more like each other than they are unlike each other. One may live on bread and another may live on meat but they all feel hunger when they're hungry. And on a much higher plane than that of hunger I think that all human beings have a hankering for pattern and order; look at any child with a box of chalks. There are of course evil patterns or orders—which perhaps is the great problem of our time. What I do believe is that as a human being, it is my duty to make patterns and to contribute to order—good patterns and a good order. And when I say duty I mean duty; I think it is the turn of enjoyment, I believe that life is worth while *and* I believe that I have to do something *for* life.

---

[2] Latin proverb and cliché: *de gustibus non est disputandem* ('there is no disputing of tastes'—i.e. arguing on the basis of mere likes and dislikes).

The Other Island[1]

Mind You, I've Said Nothing! By Honor Tracy. (Methuen.
12s. 6d.)
The Silent Traveller in Dublin. By Chiang Yee. (Methuen.
21s.)

No two books about Ireland could be more unlike than these.
Mr Chiang Yee is too gentle, Miss Tracy too savage, by half.
Mr Chiang Yee, well-known as a patron of giant pandas, finds
one, sure enough, in Dublin—only (and this is significant) it is
a stuffed one. Lovers of the whimsy and the woolly, who would
pat your Kerry Blue if only it hadn't got teeth, should enjoy
both the text and illustrations of this Silent Traveller; still, it is
much to be doubted whether a *silent* traveller can really get to
know Ireland. Miss Tracy is anything but silent and could hold
her own in the Pearl Bar at its noisiest and, what is more, at
its moments of greatest malice. Speaking as an Irishman of
Southern blood and Northern upbringing, whose father was a
Protestant bishop and also a fervent Home Ruler, I salute with
delight this brilliant and unjust book, which I take it is bound
to be officially banned, universally denounced, and avidly read
in Dublin.

Miss Tracy says a great many things which few Irishmen
would have the guts and few Englishmen the wits to put down
in black and white. Her title is a winning gambit and her
subtitle, 'Forays in the Irish Republic', is fair—or unfair—

[1] *New Statesman and Nation* 46: 1183 (7 Nov. 1953), 570, 572. Honor L. W. Tracy
(1913–89), the English humorist 'known for her novels and sketches about contemporary Irish life'; 'her identification with Ireland began with' this book, 'an
hilarious collection of essays about the mores and manners of postwar Ireland':
Dictionary of Irish Literature, ed. Robert Hogan (1979), 663. Dr Chiang Yee (1903–77),
born in China, 'an author, poet, painter and professor . . . of Chinese at Columbia
University, . . . had a series of careers in China, England and the United States, . . .
teaching painting, sculpture, calligraphy and East Asian languages and cultures, . . .
and was best known for twelve art-travel books entitled "The Silent Traveller in . . .";
Dr Yee was a Phi Beta Kappa Orator at Harvard in 1956 and served there in 1958–9 as
Emerson Fellow in Poetry': *New York Times Biographical Service 1977*, 1477–8.

enough; the Republic, if it loses its sense of proportion (a sense which Miss Tracy would deny it), might well make her its Enemy Number One. But a sense of proportion should enable any reader to find her destructiveness instructive; Thomas Love Peacock, for a parallel, can teach us a lot about the Romantic Revival[2] but we cannot learn anything from him if we expect to learn everything. Miss Tracy has the virtues and the drawbacks of a truly ferocious common sense. Her book will infuriate the Irish (though, as she foresees, they may enjoy that) but will also distress some of the English whose interest in Ireland, as she knows, 'is often rooted in misconception.'[3] 'There'll always be an Ireland,' she concludes, 'if England has anything to say in the matter.'[4]

This is the most astringent book about Ireland since Shaw and the most amusing since Somerville and Ross.[5] Many Irishmen, of course, would say that the wit of *John Bull's Other Island*[6] and the humour of *The Irish RM* were quite off the Irish target. This is not so and I especially admire Miss Tracy for daring (what is perhaps the most daring thing in a daring book) to maintain that 'Stage Irishry' is not only a fact but a virtue; after all, this is only another way of saying that as a race we have a sense of theatre. 'Not only', says Miss Tracy, 'do "stage" Irishmen abound to this day but they are far pleasanter than the other kind.'[7] Anyone who knows the other kind—the dour, self-righteous, know-all, give-nothing-away, obtuse, and mealy-mouthed kind—must surely agree with this. Miss Tracy finds plenty of theatre without even going in search of it.

A woman stood arguing with the vendor of a statuette of Blessed Martin de Porres.

'He's not very black.'

---

[2] See the 7 little novels or tales of Peacock (1785–1866), 5 of which wittily satirize the excesses of certain Romantic poets such as Wordsworth, Coleridge, Southey, Byron, and Shelley.

[3] Tracy, 15.

[4] Ibid.

[5] Edith O. Somerville (1858–1949) and 'Martin Ross' (pseud. of Violet F. Martin, 1862–1915), 'second cousins of Irish families who separately and together wrote some 30 books, mainly set in Ireland', especially *The Irish RM* series (1899, 1908, 1915): *Oxford Companion to English Literature*, 5th edn, ed. Margaret Drabble (1985), 919.

[6] A satirical play about Ireland (1904) by G. Bernard Shaw (1856–1950).

[7] Tracy, 17.

'That's the blackest we do at three and six. There's a darker one for seven shillings.'[8]

What will be most resented in Ireland is Miss Tracy's attitude to the Roman Catholic Church. Irish Catholics would probably prefer even the polemics of Sean O'Casey to this not even angry analysis:

> Some Catholics are pleased to see in their moral ambiguities the proof of one more superiority over the Protestant . . . the Church herself sets no great store by virtue. Organization is her business and very capably she attends to it. When first I came to know Ireland I was dismayed by the conduct of many of the bishops and clergy because I had a mistaken idea of what their function was. Their arrogance, their pride, their vindictiveness, their greed, did not square with what I took to be the mission of a Christian priesthood. But after time had passed I began to see the error. . . . They were not following the Way and the Truth at all, they were running a country.[9]

Though such remarks will pain many truly religious people (and in spite of Miss Tracy there are many such in Ireland and of all denominations), it should be remembered that many good Catholics from Catholic countries on the Continent have been shocked and depressed by the narrowness and arrogance which their own Church shows in this 'most Catholic of countries.'[10] I only regret that Miss Tracy has not attended in equal detail to the Orangemen.

'Aren't the Irish sweet!' I heard this remark some years ago at a performance (God save all here!) of *The Playboy of the Western World*.[11] Anyone who still believes that we're all sugar and spice should be cured by reading Miss Tracy. But after the cure (a cure as good as a feast) we must scrupulously remind ourselves that she is after all a satirist; she may tell us nothing but the truth but she does not tell us the whole truth. There are other small countries which, having had more than their share of sentimental rhapsodies, could do with such a douche of cold water. Someone with Miss Tracy's gifts could have, for example, a high old time with modern Greece. Half a day in Athens

---

8 Ibid. 28.
9 Ibid. 129–30.
10 Proverbial.
11 Famous comedy of Irish life (1907) by John Millington Synge (1871–1909).

could throw up wonderfully comic examples of corruption, double-talk, pretentiousness, idleness, or fecklessness. Without telling a single lie the modern Peacock could suggest that the Greeks by and large are hopeless, though, of course, vastly amusing. Which would make their behaviour during the Italian invasion and the German occupation inexplicable. In the same way there is nothing in Miss Tracy's book that could possibly account for the heroism that not a few Irishmen have shown in our time both at home and abroad, or that could even (though she has a good word for two novelists)[12] account for the very large part played by Irish writers in modern literature.

[12] Seán O'Faoláin (1900–   ) and 'Frank O'Connor' (pseud. of Michael Francis Donovan, 1903–66), in Tracy, 56, 119.

Greece and the West[1]

Fair Greece, Sad Relic. By Terence Spencer.
(Weidenfeld & Nicolson. 25s.)

Anyone who goes to Greece and looks at the buildings must surely be struck by that great historical gap commented on by Mr Osbert Lancaster.[2] Greece's visible peculiarity is that she appears to have ceased to exist before Renaissance times and then, in the nineteenth century, to have made a sudden jump back into an existence which, if we were to judge by the 'Bavarian' houses of Athens, shows little connection either with the classical or with the Byzantine past. The reason for this, of course, is the long period of Turkish occupation, which from 1460 onwards precluded the further development of Greek culture as ruthlessly as the Greeks themselves, when they came back into their own, swept away those minarets which must have added such charm to their landscape.[3] But it is a mistake to assume that during those blacked-out centuries the Greeks had lost their identity; they retained after all both their language (which was blooming at least in folk song) and their religion (though that, like so many things in Greece even

[1] *New Statesman and Nation* 47: 1210 (15 May 1954), 636. The title of this, Spencer's first book, is taken from Lord Byron's *Childe Harold's Pilgrimage* 2. 73. 1; the subtitle reads: *Literary Philhellenism from Shakespeare to Byron* (1954). Terence J. B. Spencer (1915–78), the prominent Shakespeare scholar and author of many books, was a British Council lecturer at the British Institute, Rome, and the Institute of English Studies, Athens, 1939–41, served in the pioneer corps 1941–6 (mentioned in dispatches), and was appointed to many academic posts, his last as Professor of English Language and Literature, Birmingham University, 1958–78.

[2] (1908–86), the English cartoonist who served as First Secretary with the British Embassy, Athens, 1944–6, joined the *Architectural Review*, and recorded his impressions of modern Greece in a book which he also illustrated: *Classical Landscape with Figures* (1947), in which, 53–9, he remarks on the historical gap in architecture produced by the Turks and 'the Bavarian' influence of the first king in modern Greece, the autocratic King Otho (1815–67; ruled 1832–62).

[3] 'Few signs were allowed to remain in Greece [after 1830] to show that the country once contained a large Turkish minority. The minarets and mosques were destroyed': William St Clair, *That Greece Might Still be Free: The Philhellenes in the War of Independence* (1972), 351.

to-day, tended to work both ways. See Mr Spencer: 'The Patriarch became, in reality, an official of the Ottoman imperial system; and accordingly the respect of the religious Greeks for their Patriarch involved a kind of allegiance to the Sultan').[4] It is a mistake again to assume that during those same centuries Western Europe had lost all interest in Greece. Mr Spencer's very well documented book is largely devoted to refuting this second assumption. Philhellenism, we all know, burst into full Byronic bloom in 1821.[5] Mr Spencer proves that it had a long history before that, especially in England.

Fair Greece, Sad Relic may be what its author calls it, 'a laborious book which marches along on its footnotes'[6] but, if so, not only is the main line of march made clear and convincing but there is plenty of entertainment in passing. Since the march leads us not only to liberation but to Byron, a spotlight is turned upon Byron's many poetic predecessors, some big, most of them little, beginning with Ariosto, who complained of the Pope's disregard of Greece's enslavement.[7] Then we have Ronsard[8] and, later, one Richard Zouche, of New College, Oxford, who in 1613 wrote of

> Greece the dismal Sepulchre
> Of Learning, Virtue, Valour, Policy . . .[9]

But this was mere lament; 'the first of English Philhellenes', John Milton, wanted something done about it. In 1652 he wrote a Latin letter to a Greek in Athens insisting that, *if only* the Greeks will recover their ancient virtues, then they will be able to regain their liberty *and* other nations will help them: *neque*

---

[4] Spencer, 98.

[5] The Greek War of Independence was fought 1821-9, and the world-renowned Lord Byron, much of whose poetry was inspired by love of Greece, died in his tent at Missolonghi, 19 April 1824, during one of the campaigns, thus inspiring not only Britain but the world in the Greek cause and into the full flowering of Philhellenism.

[6] Spencer, ix-x.

[7] The Renaissance Italian poet Ludovico Ariosto in *Orlando Furioso* (1532) 'jeers at the papal disregard for the plight of hapless Greece': Spencer, 7.

[8] The Renaissance French poet Pierre Ronsard in *Le Bocage Royal* (1567) 'suggested to Charles IX (an unstable youth . . .)' to use his 'very Christian arm . . . in a Turkish war' for Greek liberation: Spencer, 112.

[9] The Renaissance English poet Richard Zouche in *The Dove* (1613), quoted here, 'Seems to mourn the calamities of Hellas': Spencer, 65.

ipsos sibi Graecos, neque ullam Gentem Graecis defuturam esse confido.[10] In 1683, after the Turks had been driven out of Vienna, Edmund Waller[11] makes a flattering appeal to Charles II to go one better and drive them out of Greece.[12] Later he repeats the appeal to James II:

> The *British* monarch shall the Glory have
> That famous *Greece* remains no longer slave . . .[13]

In the eighteenth century such sentiments are multiplied. Thus in Dr Johnson's forgotten tragedy *Irene* ('Fill all thy ardent breast with *Greece* and Virtue')[14] Mr Spencer remarks that

by anachronism he attributes to Greeks of the fifteenth century feelings of devotion to the Liberty of their country which were, in fact, coming into existence among the Greeks contemporary with Johnson; and which were to be given revolutionary expression before Johnson's death.[15]

In 1762 appeared 'the first elaborate treatment of modern Greece in English poetry', *The Shipwreck* by William Falconer, who had visited the country as a second mate.[16] And so on, through many minor or minimal poets, till in 1809 they are joined by a novelist, Miss Sydney Owenson whose *Woman, or Ida of Athens* was, it would seem, one long gush of Philhellenism.[17] But creative writers are only part of Mr Spencer's story,

---

10 'Then, I am confident, neither would the Greeks be wanting to themselves, nor any other nation wanting to the Greeks': conclusion to *Familiar Letters* 12, 'To the most distinguished LEONARD PHILARAS of Athens, Ambassador from the Duke of Parma to the King of France', London, June 1652, by John Milton (1608–74): Milton's *Works*, Columbia edn, 18 vols. (1931–8), xii. 58–9.

11 The Renaissance English poet Edmund Waller (1606–87) wrote poetry of polish and simplicity; he is remembered for such poems as 'Go, lovely rose': *OCEL*, 5th edn, 1040.

12 Waller's poem 'Of the late Invasion and Defeat of the Turks, in the year 1683', cited by Spencer, 120.

13 'A Presage of the Ruin of the Turkish Empire', ll. 37–8, cited at greater length by Spencer, 120–1.

14 *Irene* (1736, performed 1749), a blank verse tragedy, IV. i. 8, cited at greater length by Spencer, 254.

15 Spencer, 255.

16 '*The Shipwreck, a Poem in Three Cantos* . . . did much to familiarize the reading public with those sentiments which Byron was to express with far greater power half a century later': ibid. 259.

17 'Miss Sydney Owenson (later Lady Morgan) [1776–1859] followed her success

which starts with the 'disappearance' of Greece in the fifteenth
century and moves on to the establishment of trade between
her and the West in the sixteenth, a contact which did not, to
begin with, improve the reputation of the Greeks. Mr Spencer
points out—and, as usual, proves his point with many quotations—that the common noun 'greek' was used by the Eliza-
bethans to mean either a waster or a crook[18] and that 'it was
with the considerable disadvantage therefore, of a derogatory
name, that the Greek nation re-entered the consciousness of
Europe'.[19]

In the next two centuries, what with currants and coffee and
a growing interest in the Greek Church and in objects of art
and in topography, England and France became increasingly
conscious of Greece. As early as 1610 we find an English
traveller in Arcadia[20] who was inspired by his surroundings to
a prose worthy of Amanda Ros:[21] 'The remembrance of these
sweet seasoned Songs of Arcadian Shepherds which pregnant
Poets have so well penned, did recreate my fatigated corpse
with many sugared suppositions.'[22] A seventeenth-century
manuscript directs an agent that if he 'meet with any statues or
Colossus too great to be carried away whole, he must employ
men to saw it asunder with iron saws and sharp sand . . .'[23]
And about the same time we find a Patriarch of Constantinople,[24] a friend of the British Ambassador[25]—but not of the
French Ambassador[26]—who 'conceived the extraordinary plan
of reforming the Greek Church by bringing its doctrines into
harmony with Calvinism', and who finally was strangled and
thrown into the Bosphorus.[27] By the eighteenth century Lady

The Wild Irish Girl [1806] with a four-volume romance *Woman: or, Ida of Athens* in
1809': ibid. 286.

[18] Ibid. 35–40.
[19] Ibid. 40.
[20] William Lithgow (1582–1645?: *DNB*), quoted by Spencer, 62–3.
[21] 'Amanda McKittrick Ros, née Anna Margaret McKittrick (1860–1939), [the]
Irish writer, known as the "the World's Worst Novelist" ': *OCEL*, ed. cit. 845.
[22] Spencer, 63.
[23] Ibid. 79–80.
[24] Cyril Lucaris (*c.*1572–1638), elected Patriarch of Constantinople 1621,
published his famous *Confessions* in 1629: Spencer, 89–90.
[25] Sir Thomas Roe (1581?–1644), ambassador at Constantinople 1621–8: ibid.
[26] Untraced.
[27] Ibid. 89.

Mary Wortley Montagu[28] is showing an 'eye for the continuity of the life of the Greek peoples from ancient into modern times'[29] and, a little later, further sympathy is excited by the Society of Dilettanti.[30] Simultaneously, Russia is getting interested in pushing out the Turks but, what is much more important, the Greeks themselves are getting interested.[31] And, as Milton had foreseen, once the Greeks bestirred themselves,[32] they did receive help from the West and, in particular, from Britain.

[28] 'Lady Mary [née Pierrepont, 1689-1762] wrote her famous letters from Constantinople' ostensibly (recorded in the Levant 1716-18, not published until 1763, but 'a work of literary artifice'): ibid. 146.

[29] Ibid. 148.

[30] Ibid. 160-4. The Society of Dilettanti, founded 1732 as a gentleman's dining society: see Lionel Cust's history of that society (1898).

[31] Spencer, 179.

[32] Milton, 'the first of English Philhellenes' (ibid. 113), wrote an eloquent letter to Philaras on Greek liberation (cf. n. 10 above).

The People of the Sea, by David Thomson[1]

The People of the Sea by David Thomson. (Turnstile Press. 12*s.* 6*d.*)

When Yeats sent Synge to the Aran Islands in search of 'all that was salt in the mouth',[2] the Gaeltacht was still a *Terra Incognita*. Since then that impoverished fringe of Ireland (and to a lesser extent of Scotland) has become so fashionable among writers and readers—and romantic nationalists—that it has brought the inevitable reaction; I have no doubt that the recent evacuation of the Great Blasket[3] was greeted with cheers by the hard-drinking, hard-thinking patrons of the Pearl in Dublin. For various obvious reasons these minority cultures seem doomed, yet to take an interest in their story-telling and their song (which indeed are their only two art forms) should not be condemned as sentimental. For, after all, they *are* both interesting and beautiful. Mr David Thomson in this fascinating book about seal lore has had to collect some of his stories at second-hand through an interpeter but most of them he took direct from English speakers—though their English, of course, was dialect. These stories, whether from the Gaelic or from dialect,

[1] *London Magazine* 1: 9 (Oct. 1954), 94, 96. David Robert Alexander Thomson (1914–88), an English writer interested in traditional lore, tutored privately in Co. Roscommon, Ireland, 1932–43; then worked for the BBC 1943–69 as writer-producer in the Features Department (with MacNeice). (Cf. MacNeice's *Minch* (1938) for Gaelic lore.) *The People of the Sea* (1954), a legendary of seals, was later twice revised with the subtitle *A Journey in Search of the Seal Legend* (1965, 1980), with a foreword by Gavin Maxwell (1914–69), the English writer on travel, animals, and conservation. Thomson is best known for two evocative autobiographies, *Woodbrook* (1974) and *Nairn* (1987): obit., *The Times*, 1 March 1988, 14 f.

[2] Yeats, 'J. M. Synge and the Ireland of his Time' (1910), sect. 9, in *The Cutting of an Agate* (1912), *Essays and Introductions* (1961), 326: corr. 'all that is salt in the mouth'. Cf. MacNeice's *Selected Literary Criticism*, 186 n. 4.

[3] The Blasket Islands, a group of rocky islands in the Atlantic, just West of Slea Head, Co. Kerry, at the entrance to Dingle Bay. Great Blasket remained the only inhabited island of the group until 'the last inhabitants were taken off . . . in the steamer *Naomh Lorcan* in late November 1953': D. J. Hickey and J. E. Doherty, *A Dictionary of Irish History since 1800* (1980), 36.

he has managed to get on to the page with an almost uncanny skill, keeping the peaty flavour, yet avoiding Kiltartanese.[4] His writing is neither arty nor whimsy nor patronizing but runs clean and supple from beginning to end; which is not only a remarkable technical feat but a feat of understanding and heart.

The initial inspiration of this book (which is really a Quest in which the hero must find an animal to talk to) lies back in Mr Thomson's childhood. On the coast of Nairn he was drawn to the great grey seal (or selchie) before he had ever seen one— and the first one he met was being killed in a bothy, reluctantly killed by a man from the West Highlands who had more love and more fear of the seals than the Easterners. ' "She was gone astray, I'm thinking. She's a stranger this side. She's come out o' the West some way. She's like myself." He looked across the table at me and stopped chewing. "It's no' an easy thing to live wi' strangers." '[5] Long after this, an adult but still seal-struck, Mr Thomson visited South Uist, which is real selchie territory. And next he moved on, be-Virgilled by Séamus Delargy who has done so much research in Irish folklore,[6] to Ballinskelligs Bay in County Kerry. Here he has a most vivid digression on the long vanished 'hedge-schools'. 'The boys made their own ink from acorns,' Tadhg said. 'There were no seats in the school, only stones, and one of these masters that taught my father, he used to greet the boys in the morning with a shout: "Out for moss, boys!"—for he intended every day to put cushions on the stones. So they would all run out up the hill and stay the whole day long, and when they came back in the evenings he would try to punish them, but he could never reach them because he had only one leg.'[7]

The book is full of such digressions—and Mr Thomson is equally good at re-creating landscape and character—but they are all peripheral to his main theme, his myth. And a very

---

[4] Irish speech as represented by Lady (I. Augusta) Gregory, née Persse (1852-1932)—friend of Yeats, prominent in the Irish Literary Theatre and the Abbey Theatre—as an artificial language, associated with legends of her home ground (Coole Park, near Kiltartan and Yeats's Thoor Ballylee), in books of Irish lore (1902-20).

[5] Thomson (1954), 14.

[6] James H. Delargy, *The Gaelic Story-Teller, with some notes on Gaelic folk-tales* (The Sir John Rhys memorial lecture 1945; British Academy, 1947).

[7] Thomson, 41.

living myth it was for the people he talked to in Ireland and the Hebrides. Indeed, the first virtue of this book is that Mr Thomson was *able* to talk to them, or rather to get them to talk. Four out of five professional writers would have failed to elicit this material—let alone so to transpose it to the page that the oral quality survived. As for the myth itself, we are mostly so urbanized that our selchies have gone underwater—only to surface sometimes in our dreams. Even the mermaid still exists, on one plane, but the selchie has the advantage of still existing on two. He is 'out of this world'—when you meet him in the peasant mind; he is very palpably in it when you're lucky enough to see him in the flesh. In the fishermen's stories he can put on human shape, can seduce your wife, can carry you on his back to a fair and there drink rum with you. 'But what is in the mind of them, I don't know—the creatures.'[8] A beautiful and sympathetic animal, a beguiling and sometimes frightening fable. Mr Thomson blends the two for us; they were blended already in the world of his Michaels and Anguses.[9] It is good that he could capture *their* seal before it disappears with themselves.

[8] Ibid. 73.
[9] Characteristic Irish and Scottish names, respectively.

Indian Approaches[1]

Expedition Tortoise. By Pierre Rambach, Raoul Jahan, and
F. Hébert-Stevens. (Thames & Hudson. 30s.)
The Ride to Chandigarh. By Harold Elvin. (Macmillan. 25s.)
Goa, Rome of the Orient. By Rémy. (Arthur Barker. 21s.)

India is not only a land of paradoxes but the cause of paradoxical
behaviour in her visitors; 'it does something to you, you know'.
Each of these three new books is the outcome of a first visit to
that attractive–repulsive, exhausting–exhilarating, soporific–
effervescent, tragical–comical–historical–pastoral sub-continent.
Of the three books, *Expedition Tortoise* is far the most illuminating, being a composite account of the adventures and impressions of five highly intelligent young men, four of whom were
French students of architecture; they all started off in 1950 on a
spree into North Africa but only three reached India. Two of
these, Rambach and Vitold de Golish, have recently published
a most attractive book, *The Golden Age of Indian Art*, based on
their researches into some hitherto neglected temples, mostly
sixth to eighth century AD.[2] While on their travels, they often
paid their way by working in architects' offices and were later
employed or assisted both by the Musée Guimet and by a

[1] *New Statesman and Nation* 53: 1357 (16 March 1957), 346–7. *Expedition Tortoise*
trans. Elizabeth Cunningham from *Du Nil au Gange: à la découverte de l'Inde* (1955) by
Rambach, Jahan, and François Hébert-Stevens. Harold Elvin (1909–85), the English
novelist, poet, organist, essayist, artist, humorist, cyclist, and eccentric, was the
author of prize-winning Russian travelogues (such as *A Cockney in Moscow* (1941) and
The Incredible Mile (1970)), of memoirs, and of novels: obit. in *The Times*, 31 Jan. 1985,
12g. 'Colonel Rémy (the *nom de guerre* of Gilbert Renault-Roulier, 1904–84), one of the
best-known heroes of the French Resistance', gave up a banking and film career after
the German invasion of France to enlist in the Free French Forces 28 June 1940 in
London under Général Charles de Gaulle; moved secretly back to occupied France in
Aug. to head undercover intelligence services called 'La Confrérie de Notre Dame de
la Victoire' (later 'CND-Castille'); after the Germans discovered his identity by June
1942, he was recalled to London. Loyal to de Gaulle and a member of his cabinet, he
fell out with him over the rehabilitation of Pétain and differences over Algeria (see his
many books of memoirs): obit. in *The Times*, 31 July 1984, 14g; tribute, 4 Aug., 8g.
[2] Pierre Rambach and Vitold de Golish, *The Golden Age of Indian Art: 5th to 13th
century* (1955).

Danish ethnologist from the National Museum of Copenhagen. But their book is not simply intellectual or aesthetic; it is full of high spirits—and of humanity. Starting with comic picnics in the African desert it ends in a Hindu monastery where the architects-turned-acolytes were surprised to find their fellow-monks celebrating Christmas Eve, Christ being regarded as an incarnation of Vishnu.[3]

At Luxor the students met Schwaller de Lubicz, author of *Le Temple dans l'homme*[4] and *bête noire* of some more orthodox archaeologists, and were impressed by his theories which they seem to have tried to apply later to Indian temples—'the temple is a diagram of the cosmos'[5]—but, whatever the validity of such theories, they are certainly right in stressing the basic contrast between India and other countries which contain such ancient remains; in India, unlike Egypt, 'the villagers believe that they are the direct descendants of the men who built these temples 1,500 years ago'[6]—and they worship the same gods and practise a similar way of life. The Frenchmen were the more able to appreciate such continuity in that, like Mr Elvin, they travelled the hard way, sleeping in mud huts or in the open and eating the same food as the peasants. Thus M. Hébert-Stevens, riding a motor-cycle solo through the Middle East, is at one moment having funny encounters with brigands and at the next moralizing on Afghanistan, a country which 'used to be a cross-roads in the middle of Asia' but which now, though acting as a buffer state, has 'become the end of the world'.[7] Anyone who has gazed from the Khyber Pass towards the Hindu Kush will appreciate this fascinating peripeteia.

The most interesting part of *Expedition Tortoise* is the description of the vanishing hill tribes in Southern India, 'petrified' primitives such as the Toda in Mysore, who reminded the Frenchmen of Ancient Greek statues and whose 1,300 sins include 'To sit down on a verandah and force one's mother-in-law to leave it,' or such as the very different Kanis in Travancore, whom no Hindu ever wants to meet and who 'live in the

[3] *Expedition Tortoise* (1957), 317 ff.
[4] Renée A. Schwaller de Lubicz, *Le Temple dans l'homme* (1949). For the meeting, see *Expedition Tortoise*, 60 ff.
[5] Rambach and de Golish, *Golden Age*, 19.
[6] *Expedition Tortoise*, 201.
[7] Ibid. 151, 156 ff.

wood age', using neither metal nor stone.[8] All these the Frenchmen took to their hearts. Mr Elvin, their less sophisticated
English counterpart (where they call their vehicles Tortoise and
Sophie, he calls his ordinary push-bike Sir Walter) also found
India a revelation. *The Ride to Chandigarh*, which in fact means
the long, long road to Maxwell Fry,[9] is another book worth
reading. Lovers of India should not be deterred by the style,
which is a curious blend of whimsicalese and slap-on-the-
backery; a man is never a man but always a 'fellow'. Mr Elvin,
for all that, has a heart, an eye, and an ear. He is perhaps too
romantic about Mumtaz (whose tomb is the Taj Mahal) but he
genuinely loves the landscape, the architecture, and the people.
He is full of vivid touches—'the mountains all looked as if their
trousers had slipped' or 'Camels turning the wells with their
proud-prostitute walk',[10] and is good when he is quoting the
people he met. There is the garrulous German from Unesco:
'they beat us these Indians; see an American or a German face,
just skin pulled over nothing . . .' and the Gujerati student
(one of four who cycled with him for part of his huge journey
from Bombay to the Himalayas) whose reaction to the caves of
Ellora was: 'Ellora was built by the gods to the glory of the
human body.'[11]

Mr Elvin's own reaction to Ajanta is equally valid: 'These
paintings are masterpieces in a dozen ways, but first they are
masterpieces of *peace*.'[12] To turn from him to the third book, on
Goa, is to enter a more querulous and jangling atmosphere.
M. 'Rémy' on his first page describes Nehru as 'disconsolate
at not being born a European'; on his last he seems to bank on
Portugal as the God-ordained leader of the Western World.[13]
In between is a rather dull rehash of much very astonishing
history—Vasco de Gama, Albuquerque, St Francis Xavier.

[8] Ibid. 264-5 (the Toda), 288 (the Kanis).

[9] Edwin Maxwell Fry (1899–1987) was the senior architect with his wife Jane
Drew, who, in collaboration with Le Corbusier, designed and built the new capital
city of the Punjab at Chandigarh, 1951-4. Near the end of his book, Harold Elvin
meets up with Fry at Chandigarh.

[10] Elvin, *The Ride to Chandigarh* (1957), 140, 308.

[11] Ibid. 50, 165.

[12] Ibid. 191.

[13] Renault-Roulier (pseud. 'Rémy'), *Goa: Rome of the Orient*, trans. Lancelot C.
Sheppard (1957), 9-10, 238.

Rémy is probably right about the propagandist twists of the Bombay press, but he himself is patently propagandist, showing the flag in a museum—and is it not odd to talk of 'the mere empiricism of geography'?[14] As colonists the Portuguese have probably been in some ways—though certainly not in all—preferable to the British, but, when all that has been admitted, Camoens has been dead even longer than Kipling.[15]

[14] Ibid. 236.

[15] Luis de Camoens (1524?–1580), the greatest Portuguese poet, author of the patriotic epic *The Lusiads* (1572); Rudyard Kipling (1865–1936), the British patriot-poet. The Portuguese were the first European colonizers in India; their colonies remained in Portuguese hands until 1961 when India annexed them.

Irish Pack Quell the Uppercuts[1]

Ireland .... 9 pts. Australia 6

Dublin, 18 January

The match between Ireland and Australia at Lansdowne Road[2] to-day was a very odd one. No one seemed to expect either side to win, and before the game, on a morning of dreary drizzle, no one seemed even to be excited about it.

But the game—which provided Ireland's first victory over a touring side—proved extremely exciting, though uncommonly crude, not to say savage; one couldn't envy the referee.

When it began a watery sun was emerging over the Wicklow Mountains, and there was a strong and bitter wind, which in the first half was behind Ireland: so that when the scores were level at half-time, few spectators would have betted on an Irish victory.

It was a victory primarily due to the untried Irish pack, who stood up astonishingly well to their much heavier (and upper-cut-minded) opponents.

The new centre, 18-year-old Hewitt,[3] made a promising first appearance in spite of a few lapses in defence. Mulligan, brought in at the last moment for O'Meara, showed great intelligence and agility.[4] So did Kyle,[5] who was as cool as ever

---

[1] *Observer* 8690 (19 Jan. 1958), 24. W. J. Evans of the Welsh Rugby Union was referee for the game; touch judges were P. Lardner of the Irish Rugby Football Union and G. N. Vaughan of the Australian Rugby Union: information in these footnotes is taken from a copy of the corrected programme, plus *Oxford Companion to Sports & Games*, ed. John Arlott (1975), cited as OCSG.

[2] 'Football ground, Dublin, headquarters of the Irish RUGBY UNION': *OCSG*, 598.

[3] David Hewitt (1939–), left centre, then studying Law at Queen's, Belfast, and son of a famous Irish international, was a new (international) cap for Ireland.

[4] Andrew Armstrong Mulligan, scrum-half of the Cambridge University Wonders, replaced John Anthony O'Meara (1929–) from Cork, then a solicitor, whose first cap was against France in 1951. This international would have marked his 22nd cap. 'A quick, athletic player, and usually the dominant partner at half-back, he played in three successive University matches (1955–7), and won twenty-two Irish caps': *OCSG*, 705.

[5] John William Kyle (1926–), then a doctor in a Belfast hospital, was first capped for Ireland in 1947. This game, in which he played stand-off, marked his 44th cap. For

and brought off innumerable, and very welcome, relieving kicks.

Summons was the outstanding player for Australia,[6] and Curley was excellent at full-back.[7]

To begin with the tourists pressed, and the first score was a try by their left-wing, Phelps.[8] Ireland then got into the Australian 25, but frittered away their chances with a series of attempted drop goals, started by Kyle and continued by Tom, Dick, and Harry. Pedlow[9] just missed with a penalty kick, then equalized with another which glanced off an upright.

At half-time the saffron-kilted band played 'On Lough Neagh's Bank When the Fisherman Strays'.[10]

The second half opened with an uppercut at the expense of Murphy[11] (who went off for two minutes) and a storm of booing. Then Australia were all but over; but there were some fine relieving Irish rushes, and a typical mark by Kyle.

Next, to give Australia the lead, came a beautiful try by Summons, who changed direction and ran clean through the Irish side. Ireland's supporters wrote the game off: but how wrong they were!

Almost at once there was a magnificent Irish movement, which went across the field and back again and most of the way down it (everyone seemed to handle, and handle exquisitely),

a later international with Kyle, see MacNeice's article 'Nine New Caps' (Feb. 1962) below. Kyle was 'the dominant figure in Irish Rugby during its successful period after the Second World War': *OCSG*, 586.

[6] Arthur Summons (1936–), five-eighth of New South Wales, was then a school-teacher just recovered from a severe shoulder injury.

[7] Terence (G. P.) Curley (1938–), full back, of NSW, was then a chemical engineer trainee and a relatively young player (19).

[8] Rodney Phelps (1934–), left-wing, of NSW, was then a dentist declared to be 'probably the best utility man in the team, with ability to penetrate from any position. . . . Broke his right arm in June, still had it in plaster when selected.'

[9] Alexander Cecil Pedlow (1934–), left-wing, of CIYMS, was then a dentist in Belfast. This was his 17th cap.

[10] Thomas Moore's (1779–1852) 'Let Erin remember the days of old', st. 2. 1: corr. 'On Lough Neagh's bank as the fisherman strays'—*Irish Melodies* (1808–34).

[11] Noel Arthur Murphy (1938–), a forward and a new cap, was then an insurance official in Cork. 'A fast, strong and determined runner, Noel Murphy is the son of a famous Irish International': programme note. 'Although twice dropped by Ireland for a whole season, he was recalled in 1969, at the age of 30, to lead the pack and bring his total number of caps to 41, a national record for a forward': *OCSG*, 705.

and immediately after this the ball was kicked over the line and Wood fell on it to make the scores level.

Tension now increased, though that had seemed hardly possible (a spectator from Munster, in deploring the booing, said that these things should be fixed on the field and not in the stands).

Australia were still looking dangerous. But when they were on the attack, Hewitt intercepted and passed to the veteran Henderson,[12] who proceeded to run half the length of the field. He just got over the line as he was tackled.

In injury time Australia were pressing again, but Kyle made two marks running. It looks certain now that he will beat Ken Jones's record.[13]

Ireland.—P. J. Berkery (London Irish); A. J. F. O'Reilly (Old Belvedere); N. J. Henderson (North of Ireland) (captain); D. Hewitt (Queen's University, Belfast); A. C. Pedlow (CIYMS [Church of Ireland Young Men's Society]); J. W. Kyle (North of Ireland); A. A. Mulligan (Cambr. Univ.); B. G. M. Wood (Garryowen); R. Dawson (Wanderers); P. J. O'Donoghue (Bective Rangers); W. A. Mulcahy (University College, Dublin); J. B. Stevenson (Instonians); J. A. Donaldson (Collegians); J. R. Kavanagh (Wanderers); N. Murphy (Cork Constitution).

Australia.—T. G. P. Curley [N.S.W.]; R. Phelps [N.S.W.]; S. White [N.S.W.]; J. M. Potts [N.S.W.]; K. J. Donald [Queensland]; A. J. Summons [N.S.W.]; D. M. Connor [Queensland]; N. Shedhadie [N.S.W.]; J. V. Brown [N.S.W.]; R. A. L. Davidson [N.S.W.] (captain); A. S. Cameron [N.S.W.]; D. N. Emanuel [N.S.W.]; J. E. Thornett [N.S.W.]; N. M. Hughes [N.S.W.]; P. T. Fenwicke [N.S.W.].

[12] Noel Joseph Henderson (1928–), B.Sc., right-centre, 'an all-round sportsman', of the North of Ireland Football Club, was then a sales superintendent with a Belfast petroleum company. This game marked his 32nd cap (1st in 1949).

[13] Kenneth Jeffrey Jones (1921–), 'wing three-quarter for Newport, Wales, and British LIONS. . . . created a Welsh and, in its day, a British record by winning 44 caps, 43 of them in consecutive games. . . . In 1948 he won an Olympic silver medal in the 4 × 100 metres relay event': *OCSG*, 542. Kyle fulfilled MacNeice's prediction: he 'set a world record of 46 international caps', surpassed by [Colin Earl] MEADS (1935–) [of New Zealand]: 'retired 1972 after 55 Test appearances', and by [Thomas Joseph] KIERNAN [of Ireland] (1939–) who equalled Meads's world record: ibid. 542, 575–6, 586, 648–9.

A Light Touch under the Stars[1]

When I was invited this year to write a script for *Son et Lumière* at Cardiff Castle (to form part of the Festival of Wales)[2] I had never been present, either in Britain or France, at any performance in this peculiar new medium which the French had recently invented,[3] with their flair for capitalizing their own antiquities and beauty spots.

Nor did I have such an experience until, on July 17 this year, my own script had been translated into sound and light at Cardiff (a sea change if ever there was one). Though I say it myself, I enjoyed this performance; at the same time I am

[1] *Daily Telegraph*, 9 Aug. 1958, 6. Subnote: '*The Daily Telegraph is presenting Son et Lumière at Cardiff Castle nightly, except Sundays, at 9.45 p.m. until Aug. 30 and at 9 p.m. from Sept. 1 until Sept. 27.*' There is also a plain headnote. 'Cardiff Castle, an early Norman fortification . . . built on the site of a Roman fort, in the late eleventh century. The motte and bailey structure, rebuilt in stone in the twelfth century, became the centre of the feudal lordship of Glamorgan. . . . In 1766 the castle became the centre of the Bute estate and parts were rebuilt. . . . The castle and grounds were presented to the City of Cardiff by the Bute family in 1947': *Oxford Companion to the Literature of Wales*, ed. Meic Stephens (1986), 75, referred to below as *OCLW*. The scheme for this entertainment is now at HRC, Austin, Texas.

[2] The 1958 Festival of Wales (spring to autumn) was officially opened on 3 May by the Duke of Gloucester: *The Times*, 25 April 1958, 12e. Peaks and headlands were ablaze with beacons to mark the inauguration; under the leadership of Alderman Huw Edwards, the Welsh Tourist Board hoped for 200,000 visitors from abroad; the centrepiece to the festival was the British Empire and Commonwealth Games at Cardiff in July: ibid., 5 May, 7c. The 6th Empire Games were opened by the Duke of Edinburgh; the great Welsh Rugby athlete Kenneth Jeffrey Jones (1921–) [who had won an Olympic silver medal in the 4 × 100 metres relay event in 1948: *OCSG*, 542] carried the Queen's message: ibid., 19 July, 3f–g. HRH Prince Charles Philip Arthur George (1948–) was created 21st Prince of Wales at the concluding ceremony of the Games: 28 July, 8f–g.

[3] '*Son et lumière* was introduced in France in 1952 by Paul Robert-Houdin, curator of the Château of Chambord, one of the great Renaissance castles of the Loire Valley. He conceived the idea of sound and light spectacles after witnessing the dramatic effects of flashes of lightning upon Chambord during a thunderstorm in 1950. . . . During the next few years *son et lumière* programs spread rapidly in France and elsewhere, becoming major tourist attractions'; later at the Acropolis, Athens, 1959; at the pyramids of Giza near Cairo; at Independence Hall, Philadelphia.—*Encyclopedia Americana*, int. edn, 30 vols. (1985), xxv. 218. The Robert-Houdins were a family of French magicians, from whom [Harry] Houdini (pseud. of Erik Weisz, 1874–1926) took his name; for the Robert-Houdins, see *La Grande Encyclopedie*, 60 vols. (1975), xlvii. 9839.

pleased that I shall never have to work quite as much in the dark again.

Son et Lumière is in some ways brand new and in other ways almost old-fashioned. The old-fashioned side of it I knew about, having spent much of my time since 1941 in writing plays and feature programmes for sound radio. The sound part of *Son et Lumière* has much in common with a certain kind of radio programme, but with two important differences: the sound in this latest medium is stereophonic, and it is addressed to a crowd of people (say two thousand) gathered together— and after nightfall at that—in, of all places, the open air.

Open-air audiences are notoriously difficult to woo, especially if one's touch is on the light side. Since the floodlights and loud-speakers went up at Cardiff, several people have said to me in surprise: 'You know, you actually got laughs. Nobody ever gets laughs in the open air.' On the other hand I feel wiser after the event.

If I wrote for this medium again, I should take more care to avoid certain pitfalls and also to make doubly sure that both the main points and the transitions were made crystal-clear to any sort of audience in any sort of weather.

Hitherto *Son et Lumière* has taken the form of a historical pageant though, unlike the traditional pageant, it is divorced not only from costume but from flesh and blood. Human beings have to be suggested purely through lights and stereo-phonic sound—and it is astonishing how suggestive these two things can be when they are subtly and convincingly blended by a producer like Mr Peter Wood.[4]

The French, I understand, have so far used this pageant form mainly in the grand manner of Racine[5]—heroic, formal, unexceptionable. This, while all right for the Palace of Versailles and for a typically French audience and their gallophile visitors, did not seem quite right for Cardiff or indeed for anywhere in Wales. My Irish ancestry and background—plus, perhaps I should add, about an eighth of Welsh blood[6]—reminded me

---

[4] Peter (L.) Wood (1928–   ), English theatrical and TV director, has been Associate Director of the National Theatre since 1978.

[5] Jean Racine (1639–99), the great French dramatist of the neo-classical era.

[6] MacNeice's father, the Rt. Revd J. F. MacNeice, was one-quarter Welsh through his maternal grandfather John Howell: see William T. McKinnon, *Apollo's Blended Dream* (1971), 6.

that in the less Anglo-Saxon parts of these islands one should always, when cooking a new dish, throw in a grain or two of salt.

As a script-writer, therefore, I was faced with two problems: (1) how to unify two thousand years of history (the data for which had been supplied most admirably by Prof. William Rees);[7] and (2) how to humanize this almost unknown medium for an audience who, I knew, would be lacking neither in humanity nor humour.

The answer to both problems turned out to be the same. Invent a central character who is not a Great Man but a little man (though perhaps with moments of greatness),[8] who is not the Welsh at their most heroic but is present on heroic occasions and who also, whatever the occasion, remains indestructibly Welsh.[9] Then, having invented this man, have him reborn through the ages. Or, as his theme song puts it,

> But, when I'm dead, I keep my head—
> And here once more come I!

This character we devised between us on a cold, bleak day in Cardiff, after looking at the Roman walls, a Norman dungeon, and some very eccentric nineteenth-century décor, and we gave him the name of Dai Sidestep[10] (the earliest intention was

---

[7] William Rees (1887–1978), the prominent Welsh historian, published widely in historical geography, his masterwork a 'unique map' of *South Wales and the Border in the Fourteenth Century* (1933). He was appointed Professor of Welsh History at Cardiff in 1930, and continued as Head of the Department of History 1935–53. 'Abstemious, patient, tireless, he was the last survivor of the first generation of major Welsh historians.' He wrote *A History of Cardiff* (1962): *OCLW*, 510.

[8] MacNeice's doctrine of the ordinary man was a central idea in many of his poems and plays: see *Modern Poetry* (1938; 1968); 198, for this idea in reference to the poet.

[9] 'The word "nationalism" was first used in English in 1844 and in Welsh ('*cenedlaetholdeb*') in 1958. Patriotism, or a sense of nationhood, has a long history among the Welsh. The adoption of the name *Cymry* (from the Brythonic *Cambrogi*, "fellow countrymen"), probably in the late sixth century, indicates an early consciousness that the Welsh were to each other what they were not to anyone else.' Nationalism became 'a significant force' only in the later 19th c. A 'wave of Nationalist fervour . . . led to the founding of such institutions as the University of Wales, the National Library and the National Museum of Wales.' In 1925 *Plaid Cymru* [the party of Wales] was founded, so 'Welsh Nationalism was given overt political expression'; *OCLW*, 426.

[10] 'Dai' (abbreviation of Dafydd/David, Devi, Deio) is a very common Christian name in Wales, used by many writers, often as an archetypal 'ordinary man' or everyman—as by David Jones (*In Parenthesis* (1937), pt. 4: 'Dai's Boast'), Idris Davies

to end the programme with a Rugby football international); this chameleonic Dai found his ideal embodiment (if that is the word for a voice—but what a voice!) in the film star Stanley Baker.[11]

Mr Baker had to serve a dual purpose—as a narrator linking one period with another and as actor in a whole series of dramatic period vignettes. When he is narrating he speaks intimately from behind the audience's shoulder, dropping the words like honey into their ears; when he is in action he may be shouting defiance against Roman or Norman or any other kind of foreign intruder, or lamenting the death of a dancing bear, or cuddling a kitchen wench after the Battle of Agincourt, or grumbling during an air raid in World War II.

Mr Baker was supported by a largely Welsh cast who doubled with fervour all sorts of parts, ranging from medieval archers to hellfire preachers. It was gratifying to find what a range of voice can be used in this medium.

Apart from the human voice the other sound ingredients in *Son et Lumière* are, of course, just as in radio, music, and effects. The music on this occasion was most efficiently and ingeniously composed by Miss Elisabeth Lutyens,[12] who has had great experience in writing music for films. As for the effects which in this medium appear to need especially careful selection, they are of the greatest value in making the figures of the past three-dimensional rather than pasteboard.

While Prof. Rees had supplied us with rich and varied historical material, the history of Cardiff Castle is not as

(*The Angry Summer* (1943) with the unemployed miner Dai), Dylan Thomas (*Under Milk Wood* (1954) with the baker Dai Bread of two wives), etc. See H. M. Evans and W. O. Thomas, *Welsh–English/English–Welsh Dictionary* (1969), 459 ('Personal Names') and *OCLW*, 125 ('Dai').

[11] Sir Stanley (1927–76), the Welsh actor knighted 1976, who played 'a tough and intelligent HEAVY' in the film *The Cruel Sea* (1952) and in many thrillers, eventually formed his own film and TV production company: *The Oxford Companion to Film*, ed. Liz-Anne Bawden (1976), 49; this work is referred to below as *OCF*.

[12] A. Elisabeth Lutyens (1906–83), married to the conductor Edward Clarke 1942–62, was 'one of the first and most important English composers to adopt serial techniques (derived from Webern) and to adapt them flexibly to different media (concert, opera, radio play, and even horror film)'. Her works included 'over 200 radio scores in collaboration with, among others, Louis MacNeice and Dylan Thomas': *The Times*, 15 April 1983, 12g. For a fuller exposition, see *New Grove Dictionary of Music and Musicians*, ed. Stanley Sadie, 20 vols. (1980), xi. 376.

fraught with immediate associations as the history, say, of the Tower of London or Holyrood House. We had, therefore, to select our episodes both for their intrinsic dramatic value and on the two conflicting, yet reconcilable, principles of continuity and contrast.

Our original scheme included certain exciting or amusing bits of history—or legend—which we later had to scrap just because there was not time for them. I particularly regret an Arthurian episode (with some fine chivalrous music by Elisabeth Lutyens) which featured Rachel Roberts[13] as a Glamorgan witch interpreting the croaks of a raven. We also lost some nineteenth-century light relief when Dai got himself sacked three times running by the first three Marquises of Bute.[14]

Still, what remains includes not only such famous Welsh patriots as Ifor Bach[15] and Owen Glendower[16] but phenomena (not peculiar to Wales) such as the Black Death, the Civil War, and the Industrial Revolution. All through this pot-pourri the central character, Dai, acts as both conductor and chorus. As he says himself in his peroration:

I have paddled in the dew of the years and stepped into my own shoes time and again, and dodged my way through the rumours of wars.

---

[13] Rachel Roberts (1927–81), the British actress of stage and cinema, gave outstanding performances in the films *Saturday Night and Sunday Morning* (1960) and *This Sporting Life* (1963); for a time she was married to Rex Harrison (1908–   ): *OCF*, 597.

[14] 'The Bute family, "the creators of modern Cardiff", were descended from Robert II of Scotland and were established as landowners on the Isle of Bute in the fourteenth century. . . . The fifth Marquess (1907–56) presented the Castle and its park to the city of Cardiff in 1947': *OCLW*, 62.

[15] 'Ifor ap Cadifor (Ifor Bach, *fl.* 1158), Lord of Senghennydd, Glam[organ]. Among his exploits was an attack on Cardiff castle in 1158 during which he captured William, Earl of Gloucester, his wife and son, refusing to release them until the lands stolen from him by the Normans had been restored. The attack was a favourite subject in the competitions of the Eisteddfod during the nineteenth century, perhaps as a result of Taliesin Williams's long poem, *Cardiff Castle* (1827)': *OCLW*, 280–1.

[16] 'Owain Glyndŵr . . . (*c.*1354–*c.*1416), Prince of Wales and national hero, was the descendant through his father of the rulers of Powys and, on the distaff side, of the rulers of Deheubarth. . . . He made no attempt to assert any lineal claims to power in Wales until 1400, by which time he was in middle age.' He is well known in theatre by his portrait in Shakespeare's *I Henry IV*: 'At my birth | The front of heaven was full of fiery shapes . . . | I am not in the roll of common men.' 'Glyndŵr's meteoric rise, his strenuous attempts to establish Welsh statehood and the visionary nature of his policies have been a powerful inspiration to Welsh patriots, especially to the advocates of political Nationalism in modern times': *OCLW*, 444.

. . . I have eaten and drunk in the tight corners of history, have peddled and fiddled and jinked and jigged and drawn the long bow and sung in the choir.

Son et Lumière is almost certainly here to stay. It is capable of many variations and undoubtedly many of the ancient buildings in England, Scotland, Ireland, and Wales will afford opportunities to make of our history something that both sounds and shines. But, history apart, I can see yet other developments for it.

As in other media, its very limitations can be assets. One of its charms is that, though it concerns human beings, one never sees the human figure: the senses are gratified by sound and light, but the imagination is still given play just because everything is not filled in.

I think myself that it would be fascinating to take some large country house (picked for its appearance rather than its history) and make it the setting for a 45-minute play in *Son et Lumière*. This, so far as I know, has not yet been done (the hand of Racine still lying heavy on the medium), but I am sure that it could hold an audience.

From the formal garden come the whispers of lovers for whom later that second window from the left will suddenly light up in the western tower; or grooms laugh and swear in the stable from which shortly horses will burst in pursuit, both the lights and the sound of hoofs moving round the curve of the drive and dwindling into the distance. Or, if you want a ghost, with the greatest of ease it can fade itself in and out of both vision and hearing.

And so on and so on—with endless variations. You can hear the wedding ring thrown across the bedroom, or watch the bonfires burning for the heir's coming of age; you can be in at a death or a birth and always with the requisite suspension of disbelief.[17]

I hope such experiments will be made very soon. Our British summers could do with them.

---

[17] S. T. Coleridge's saying, 'that willing suspension of disbelief for the moment, which constitutes poetic faith': *Biographia Literaria*, 2 vols. (1817), chap. 14, para. 2.

Talking about Rugby[1]

Ireland begins at Euston Station, whether you are travelling to Dun Laoghaire, Dublin, Belfast, or Larne. For myself Euston was the first patch of English soil (if soil is the word) that I set foot on. But it does not seem to me now what it was in 1917. The Great Hall has long since lost its model trains and engines that did things at the drop of a penny; nor does it now look so great; I cannot agree with Auden that its staircase would fill out any modern 'dictator's dream'.[2] Still, platforms 12 to 15, grimy and malodorous as ever, retain at least the glamour of Irish voices alight with the thought of homegoing. And for me, who feels at home either side of the anomalous border, it makes no odds whether those voices are northern or southern. The 'dour' Ulsterman and the 'free-and-easy' Southerner (both epithets need qualification) have much more in common with each other, I realize now, than either has with the Englishman. I wonder if English visitors to Ulster are not sometimes embarrassed by the ubiquity of the Union Jack which, in symbolism if not in colour, has suffered such a sea-change in its passage up Belfast Lough.

The border, of course, is all very well for politicians (some of the Anti-Partitionists would be lost without it); but the ordinary Irishman on both sides, being a magnificent hypocrite and also basically practical, manages largely to ignore it. In two fields at least it is completely ignored—in the churches and in rugby. A 'good hater' of an Orangeman will serve most devotedly in an Irish XV under a 'papish' captain. And vice versa. A South African friend of mine told me that, the day after a 'British' touring XV had won their last test match in Cape Town, two of the Irishmen who had contributed to the victory took a taxi into the veldt, where, having started on politics, they got out and fought each other to a standstill. After which they had a

---

[1] *New Statesman* 57: 1459 (28 Feb. 1959), 286, 288.

[2] 'An artist you said, in the waiting room at Euston | Looking towards that dictator's dream of a staircase | An artist you said, is both perceiver and teller, the spy and the gossip'—W. H. Auden's 'Letter to William Coldstream, Esq.' [the painter], in Auden and MacNeice's *Letters from Iceland* (1937), 223.

very good lunch together. After which they returned to Ireland, ready to back each other up to the neck in the next match against 'the ould enemy'—England. Not that rugby is approved of by all the people in Ireland; Mr De Valera, once a keen player and still a great fan, may not attend any rugby match and has to content himself with radio commentaries. To the Gaelic League, of which he is president, 'Saxon' sports are supposed to be anathema. Yet any Gaelic Leaguer is sorry when the Irish XV is defeated. One reason for this is that four times out of five in this as in many other games (golf perhaps is an exception) Ireland is billed as the underdog.

All underdogs together then, the London Irish shake off the banana skins of Euston and start on the golden and liquid journey to Lansdowne Road.[3] As on Flecker's road to Samarkand women are hardly encouraged to accompany them[4] (though many more women do go to Lansdowne Road than to Cardiff Arms Park, perhaps because the Welsh, while much more sexy, are also by nature more restrictive). Anyhow both the playing and the watching of rugby are largely a matter of male ritual; it stands to some other sports as Mithraism stood to Christianity, and its emblem too might be the Bull. Both the physical violence involved and the endless chewing over of statistics, records, and anecdotes appeal, of course, to adolescents. All the same the adolescent, like the child, has a right to survive in the adult; we don't all want to grow up into Shaw's horrible old sages.[5]

If the Ancient Greeks had made our unnatural dichotomy between brain and brawn—or, as Oxford used to put it, between 'aesthetes' and 'hearties'—the fifth century BC would have been the poorer both in literature and sculpture. While many British intellectuals still look down on rugby (Association football seems to have more appeal, for instance, to logical

---

[3] See 'Irish Pack Quell the Uppercuts' above, n. 2.

[4] John Elroy Flecker (1884–1915), *The Golden Journey to Samarkand* (1913), epilogue, *Collected Poems*, ed. J. C. Squire (1916, corr. 1946), 148, chorus of merchants: 'We take the Golden Road to Samarkand', and 150, a woman: 'They [men] have their dreams, and do not think of us.'

[5] In G. Bernard Shaw's *Back to Methuselah: a metabiological pentateuch* (1921, rev. 1945), pt. 5, 'The Ancients lecture young people on the folly of such vanities as art. The Ancients have come to realize that their only true creative powers are over themselves. . . . The day will come, they prophesy, when there will be no people, only thought, and that will be life eternal': C[harlie] Lewis Broad and Violet M. Broad, *Dictionary to the Plays and Novels of Bernard Shaw* (1929), 29–30.

positivists), I am glad to have met at least one poet who had once played full back for Scotland—'when the other full back', he modestly explained, 'was crocked'. This highly sensitive young man held forth at length on the mystique of it all. But naturally our code, with its oval ball and consequent unpredictability, must appeal more to the poet than to the scientist. Another obvious reason why many poets like it is its sheer animality. An Irishman once said to me of a famous Irish forward: 'If he came in here now you'd think him a harmless big slob of a fellow—but put him on the field and he'll kick his grandmother to bits.' That is the language of Homer.

In the four home countries the game varies in status. In England, at least in the south, it still remains largely a snob game smelling of the public schools (remember *The Loom of Youth?*).[6] It is very different in Wales, where the goalposts are rooted in the coalface. In Ireland it is something in between; there are grounds in Munster where visiting sides have faced stoning. One notable fact about modern Irish international teams, as compared with ancient ones, can be proved by looking at the names on the programmes. The 'Ascendancy' names have gone out and 'native Irish' names come in. As for the international grounds, each has a very distinctive character. Lansdowne Road has the prehistoric charm of the Irish pipes, and the unique hazard of a level crossing just outside it. Still the whistle of the railway engines is just as much a part of its *persona* as the strains of 'Let Erin Remember'.[7]

As for this year's England match, Erin will only remember it with sorrow; she had all the chances and threw them away. But this did not affect the ritual of the Bull. For the rest of that day, in the Shelbourne and the Dolphin and Jammet's and innumerable bars and 'bonafides', the Bull stood chewing the cud, up to his withers in porter. 'If only the selectors had a titter of wit' . . . 'If only that drop-kick had gone one foot to the left' . . . 'If only they'd tried a Garryowen when' . . . 'If only Jackie Kyle had been playing!' And so, but very late, to bed to dream of Europa—which means to say, of the next match.

[6] Alec (Alexander R.) Waugh, *The Loom of Youth* (1917), a novel attacking the public school system; it caused a sensation. (Waugh had gone to Sherborne [MacNeice's old school] and thence to Sandhurst.)

[7] Thomas Moore's (1779–1852) 'Let Erin remember the days of old', *Irish Melodies* (1808–34).

Modern Greeks[1]

The Flight of Ikaros. By Kevin Andrews. (Weidenfeld and Nicolson. 21s.)

Many Europeans and Americans visiting Greece fall so in love with it that they gush into print and give a very one-sided picture. Thus *The Colossus of Maroussi*, by Henry Miller,[2] though some of its gush is good, suggests that Greece is a never-never land where Miller can become Peter Pan. Even that very attractive film, *The Immortal Land*, made recently by Basil Wright with a script by Rex Warner,[3] lays too much emphasis on the Glory that Was and too little on the Suffering that Is.

Now at last comes Kevin Andrews to redress the balance. He also is in love with the country—its landscape, its ruins and above all its people—but he sees the other side of that dazzling medal or moon and much of the time, fully conscious though he is of both comedy and idyll, he turns its dark side out. *The Flight of Ikaros* (the title is somewhat fancy for its content) recounts his experiences in Greece from 1947 to 1951, a peculiarly black period, when one of his chance acquaintances could remark—and this is typical: 'This old man has another son who swore long ago to kill his brother, but he was lazy and did nothing about it. Yesterday at last his mother said to him: "Go out and kill him now; the whole village despises you." '[4]

---

[1] *Observer* 8748 (1 March 1959), 19. See Kevin Andrews, 'Time and the Will Lie Sidestepped: Athens, the Interval', *Time was Away* (1974), 103–10. Andrews was a Harvard graduate student in Classics and American Literature, in Greece at the time of the Civil War 1946–9 and afterwards (from 1947 to the end of 1951); he met MacNeice in Athens 1950–1, and again in England in 1952 and 1957. In 1974 Andrews issued a long poem *First Will and Testament*, taking off from Auden and MacNeice's 'Last Will and Testament' in their *Letters from Iceland* (1937), 236–58.

[2] Miller's book (1941) had appeared as both a Penguin (1950) and a New Directions paperbook (1958).

[3] This travelogue of a few months before (Oct. 1958), narrated by Leo Genn, was intended to be 'a poetic meditation'—Basil Wright, as quoted by *The Times* film critic, 'Basil Wright's Film on Greece', 16 Oct. 1958, 4c.

[4] Andrews, *The Flight of Ikaros* (1959), 92.

Mr Andrews is probably the only American who ever got inside the skin of the Greek shepherd and managed to break through what he himself aptly describes as 'those barriers of hospitality or suspicion'.[5] Speaking demotic Greek like a native, he played his reed flute round Kalamata in company with a street-musician. He became *Koumbaros* (= godfather but a great deal more) in a shepherd's family at the Isthmus. He deliberately put himself into a third-class ward in a hospital where his fellow patients 'all behaved as if they were on holiday'.[6] And he repeatedly got himself into trouble, not to say danger, with the police, the military, and distrustful civilians. The Civil War had made everyone distrustful—from fear. Yet the Greeks in his book come to life as individuals; it contains three characters of full-blooded impact, one of whom eventually admitted that he had killed over 500 people—to avenge the death of his brother. It is typical of Mr Andrews that he still remembers this man fondly.

Mr Andrews's prose has the excellence not of the mandarin (he could not compete with that brilliant philhellene Mr Leigh Fermor)[7] but of someone who finds the right phrase because of an inner necessity. Anyone who has lived in Greece will know how true is the following:

I remained constantly aware of a sword-dance of bright eyebeams crossing, the hot wires of curiosity and evasion shifting and quickening round me.[8]

Or take his description of the master killer, before he knew what a master he was:

I recognized the chestnut-coloured eyes and the warmth and friendliness that seemed to flicker intermittently like a snake's tongue round the edge of something else deep inside him that was not gentle.[9]

He can also most vividly convey the physical atmosphere of a scene. But some of his best points are made through the mouths

---

[5] Ibid. 105.

[6] Ibid. 68.

[7] Patrick M. Leigh Fermor (1915–), the award-winning British travel writer, had just published *Mani: Travels in the Southern Peloponnese* (1958). He had been Deputy Director of the British Institute, Athens, 1946.

[8] Andrews, *Ikaros*, 27.

[9] Ibid. 148.

of his characters. As when someone says of Marshall Aid:
'Forgive us if it seems more to us like window-dressing.'[10] Or
of corruption: 'It goes without saying that a member of your
family need not be condemned. Your father has enough sheep
and goats to keep any judge content.'[11] Or of politics: '"You
heard old Plastiras . . . telling us to love our enemies? Those
words have done for him," said the young man with a look of
delight.'[12] If you want some truth about Greece, here it is.

[10] Ibid. 63.   [11] Ibid. 216.   [12] Ibid. 183.

Twin to Drink?[1]

Report on Rugby. By W. John Morgan and Geoffrey Nicholson. (Heinemann. 18s.)

Mr T. S. Eliot long ago expressed his contempt for the noisy people who travel in excursion trains to football matches,[2] and the same contemptuous attitude persists among younger intellectuals, although it seems to be on the decrease. Rugby football in particular is thought of in many quarters as a game that is only played by and watched by oafs. Yet I have had conversations about Dylan Thomas with a man who had played rugby for Wales and about Aeschylus with a man who had played rugby for Ireland. But then of course both Aeschylus and Thomas *could* be thought of as primitive writers (no soccer players they).

Mr John Morgan and Mr Geoffrey Nicholson in their fascinating book on this very strange sport treat it not only technically and historically but sociologically and, to some extent, psychologically. They quote an American judgement that 'Rugby, in the very home of the industrial revolution, seems pre-industrial';[3] they also quote a Mr Michael Craven who alleged in 1893 that football was the 'twin sister of the drinking system'.[4] One of their own main objects seems to be to answer the common accusation that a continued interest in rugby means 'a refusal to grow up'. Their answer seems to me on the whole satisfactory though I do not altogether relish their occasional

[1] *New Statesman* 59: 1505 (16 Jan. 1960), 80. For title see MacNeice's second para. with n. 4 below. W[illiam] John Morgan (1929–88), also author of the novel *Small World* (1956), and Welsh news and rugby correspondent for the *Observer* in the 1950s, recently retired from the directorship of Harlech (Welsh) Television. Geoffrey G[eorge] Nicholson (1929–), the free-lance English journalist and writer, edited *Touchdown* (RFU, 1971), was sports editor of the *Observer* 1976–8, and wrote (with Clem Thomas) *Welsh Rugby: The Crowning Years* (1980).

[2] 'The possessors of the inner voice ride ten in a compartment to a football match at Swansea,' etc.—T. S. Eliot, 'The Function of Criticism' (1923), sect. ii, end para. 2; in *Selected Essays*, 3rd edn (1951), 27.

[3] *Report on Rugby* (1959), 22.

[4] Title of chap. 2, ibid. 18.

lapses into the tones of the sporting parson-schoolmaster. The old public school stress on the moral aspect of games has probably put as many boys off games as have been put off Shakespeare by examinationitis.

This book pays particular attention to the varying social status of rugby in the different countries. 'In Edinburgh,' say the authors, speaking of the later nineteenth century, 'the new masses had no part of it, in Swansea they very much did; in the south-west of England gentry and labourers played together; in London it remained the game of old public school boys.'[5] These differences largely persist today and the authors plausibly maintain that they have caused differences in the national styles of play, e.g. that the Scottish emphasis on 'Feet' was due to the fact that 'the schools dominated Scottish football', that 'schoolboys are natural Puritans', and that, to such, 'close play which involves a high degree of physical contact and exertion is more desirable than solo performances'.[6] One could wish they had tried to pin down similar factors in South Africa and France. The lion's share in this book falls, not unexpectedly, to Wales,[7] but the authors are not doctrinaire and do not maintain that there is only one way in which the game should be played. Nor do they maintain, what we often hear to-day, that a game must be dull if play is kept close; they instance the England-Wales match of last season at what might have been called Cardiff Arms Porridge Bowl. They are good both on the 'robust' element and on the mystical element—which in fact can overlap. But I do not agree with them that 'in Rugby there's an almost mandatory abjuration of displays of triumph'.[8] What else is the meaning of those leaps in the air and those arms thrown above the head? Still, their book is probably the best on the subject and it contains some pretty illustrations, ancient and modern.

[5] Ibid. 45.   [6] Ibid. 48, 52, 54.   [7] Ibid. chap. 7 *et passim*.   [8] Ibid. 23.

When I Was Twenty-One: 1928[1]

On my twenty-first birthday I was depressed. Apart from a pair of gold cuff-links, bought for me in Belfast (that Northern anti-Athens), there was no celebration, and there was another month to go before I could escape from the puritanism and mud of my Ulster surroundings to the honey-coloured finials and gilded understatements of Oxford, where I was still *in statu pupillari*. The Long Vacation of 1928 had seemed a waste of time. I had been made to accompany my father, then a Church of Ireland archdeacon, on a Cook's Tour in and out of the fjords of Norway on a liner where one had to dress for dinner—and in a stiff shirt at that—and where people under 40 were a small minority. There was on board one American group of young men and women—the kind my family would have described as 'fast'—who spent their days playing 'Dance, Dance, Dance, Little Lady' on a portable gramophone, but I was much too throttled by my father's dog-collar to try to get to know them. So I pretended I had no wish to know them and sent one of my fellow Old Marlburians a postcard saying '*Qu'allais-je faire dans cette galère?*'

I had with me John Stuart Mill's *Logic*[2] and the *Oxford Book of Medieval Latin Verse*,[3] and when we arrived at Spitzbergen the remoteness of my reading material chimed very nicely with that almost abstract landscape, a series of bold steep pyramids slashed out in black, white, and khaki. As for the only human beings on Spitzbergen, the unfortunate coal-miners (and the coal was low grade too), whose summer was a monotony of light, whose winter a monotony of night, whose only vegetation

---

[1] *The Saturday Book 21*, ed. John Hadfield (1961), 230–9. Cf. the corresponding portions on Oxford in MacNeice's autobiography *Strings* (1965), chaps. 19–24, written 20–1 years earlier 1940–1. John C. H. Hadfield (1907–　), the English writer, editor, and publisher, edited *The Saturday Book*, 1952–73. For MacNeice's title, cf. Yeats, 'If I Were Four-and-Twenty' (essay of 1919), in *Explorations* (1962), 263–80.

[2] *A System of Logic, ratiocinative and inductive, being a connected view of the principles of evidence and the methods of scientific investigation* (1843; rev. and enl. through 9 edns to 1875; People's edn 1884).

[3] Chosen by [Sir] S[tephen] Gaselee (1928).

lichen, they struck me not as human beings but as walking, wild-eyed props. Perhaps most people then seemed props to me; I was still assimilating life to the theatre, and the sort of plays I liked were *From Morn to Midnight* and *The Adding Machine*, both of which I had seen at the Oxford Playhouse.[4]

My upbringing had made me very shy because so many human contacts in my father's Ulster parish were taboo. The Catholics were obviously taboo; most of the working classes were given to drink, bad language, and the throwing of rotten eggs; and many of the 'gentry' were ruled out because they were 'fast', which meant little more than that they kept a decanter of whiskey on the sideboard, gave bridge parties and dances, and went to race meetings. On the other hand the minority who were accepted by my family seemed to me on the whole, when they were not positively repellent, to be just plain boring. I was very snobbish about accents, and the Belfast accent struck me as not only the ugliest but the least aristocratic of the lot. All islands are insular but some seem more insular than others, and on my twenty-first birthday I was eaten up with envy of my friends who at that very moment were discovering Germany or Greece.[5]

In 1928 it was a commonplace among undergraduates that Germany was 'the most civilized country in the world'. I often wonder what difference it would have made to me if I had had a Berlin to say goodbye to.[6] But my knowledge of things German was, and has remained, second-hand. From the age of 13 I had been addicted to the myths of the Northmen; my Valkyries being always ready to ride again, it seems strange that I missed Wagner. But at Oxford I did discover Nietzsche, beginning

[4] Both are Expressionist plays about the empty lives of social victims in a commercial world, featuring characters as abstract types and cyphers: George Kaiser, *From Morn to Midnight* (1916), trans. Ashley Dukes; Elmer Rice, *The Adding Machine* (1923).

[5] Auden and Isherwood went to Berlin 1928: Humphrey Carpenter, *W. H. Auden* (1981), 84 ff; the Beazleys to Greece, according to John Hilton (in his letter to the editor, 9 Aug. 1987). (Prof. John Beazley was a classical archaeologist, married to Mary, widow of David Ezra; Mary's daughter Mary Ezra became MacNeice's first wife 1930–5. See Barbara Coulton, *Louis MacNeice in the BBC* (1980), 22.)

[6] Cf. Isherwood's *Goodbye to Berlin* (1939); this and *The Last of Mr Norris* (1935) were re-issued as *The Berlin Stories* (1946) and became the basis for John Van Druten's play *I Am a Camera* (1959) and the Broadway musical *Cabaret* (1966): *New Columbia Encyclopedia* (1975), 1370.

with *The Birth of Tragedy*,[7] which I found a welcome, if perverse, antidote to the current brand of Philhellenism that so over-emphasized the reason. Next and inevitably, beguiled by the title, I plunged into *Thus Spake Zarathustra*, from which of course, given the slightest romantic leanings, anyone can extract almost anything he wants.[8] At the same time I was flirting with Schopenhauer, being only too willing both to mimic his pessimism and to fumble through the dark night of the Will.[9]

My philosophy tutor, one of Oxford's last neo-Hegelians,[10] had encouraged me to look once—but only once—at the British empiricists and then to turn away to the German idealists, and, although I read these latter only in translation, their inter-voluted jargon fell upon my ears (repeat 'ears') like an Open Sesame; the cave—excuse me, the club—was very select; the thieves—excuse me, the clubmen—had cornered the Absolute. While these predilections of mine presuppose both affectation and make-believe, I think they were also governed by some-thing deeper. Having been brought up in a traditionally reli-gious family, and having, true to my period, reacted violently against the Christian dogma and, to some extent too, against the Christian ethic, I felt morally naked and spiritually hungry. So I was tempted to experiment simultaneously with two very different types of cure or defence—the Gallic grain of salt

[7] F. W. Nietzsche's *Die Geburt der Tragödie aus dem Geiste der Musik* (1872; *The Birth of Tragedy from the Spirit of Music*), 'in which in addition to underlining the Dionysiac element in Greek Civilization [an interest which MacNeice shared with his mentor E. R. Dodds] and its expression in tragedy, he praised the work of R[ichard] Wagner, whose friend he had been since 1868': Henry and Mary Garland, *Oxford Companion to German Literature*, 2nd edn M. Garland (1986), 669.

[8] Nietzsche's best known work, *Also sprach Zarathustra*, written 1883–5 (1883–92), a long prophetic rhapsody, mostly in prose, denouncing the civilization of his day and 'attacking those who look nostalgically to the past or believe in a future life, condemning asceticism, and glorifying war'; it 'develops no coherent argument': Garland, op. cit. 20.

[9] Arthur Schopenhauer (1788–1860), 'the radical philosopher of pessimism, who described himself as the only worthy successor to Kant, assimilated all the negative trends of a disillusioned age'; 'In defining the world (in analogy to Kant's thing-in-itself, Ding-an-sich) as Will ("als Wille"), he challenge[d] the concept of the individual free will as found in Schiller's adaptation of Kant, but [saw] it as blind will, which makes man slave to his nature, his emotions, and sexual drives': ibid. 812–13.

[10] Geoffrey R. G. Mure (1893–1969), the idealist philosopher and author of books on Aristotle and Hegel, MacNeice's Oxford tutor 1928–30 (*Strings*, 125). See Mure's article 'Oxford and Philosophy', *Philosophy* 12 (1937), 291–301.

(recently, for instance, I had lapped up *Candide*) and the hidden
magic of the Rheingold.[11] Let everything either be vanity or
One! It was to take me some time to close for a middle way.

When my undergraduate friends praised the 'civilization' of
Germany they were not so much swayed by the above considerations as by the glamour of intellectual gatherings in Berlin
and even more perhaps by the decadence of Berlin night-clubs.
In the former, it seemed, politics, which in Oxford were still
unfashionable, had blossomed out into a dashing form of Com-
munism much less fusty than anything to be found in Britain or
Russia—though I *had* been attracted by what I had heard of
Soviet experiments in non-naturalistic theatre and naturalistic
divorce. As for Decadence, any form of this was an assertion of
the rights of man. Oxford was then in transition, most of the
Ambrose Silks and other Evelyn Waugh veterans having gone
down.[12]

At the first Oxford party I was taken to as a freshman, in
October 1927, the only drink was champagne in tumblers, and
there was a beautiful young man who spent the whole evening
in the same armchair, talking to no one except a stuffed spotted
dog which he joggled up and down on its lead. But there were
few more parties of this sort, and, though one or two male
undergraduates still used powder and lipstick, and to get on in
the OUDS[13] it still helped if one were or pretended to be homo-
sexual (a fact which prevented me joining the OUDS), the
Oxford Decadence was all but over, and anyhow, I thought,
could not even at its peak or nadir have competed with these
mysterious goings-on in Berlin. We were nearly all of us
ashamed, at least as regards culture, of being British; almost
anything from the Continent, including its vice, was assumed
to be more 'significant' than its British counterpart. I was
therefore delighted when in 1928 I met my first German baron.[14]

This baron had a sallow complexion, long black fingernails,
and an insidious bonhomie. 'Soon,' he would say, 'we must

---

[11] Voltaire's *Candide* (1759); Wagner's *Das Rheingold* (1853–4).

[12] Ambrose Silk, a Jewish aesthete and outsider dedicated to ivory-tower art, in
Evelyn Waugh's *Put Out More Flags* (1942); disguised as a priest, Ambrose is spirited
away to exile in Ireland.

[13] Oxford University Dramatic Society.

[14] The Baron and Germany are not mentioned in the Oxford chapters of *Strings*.

have a jolly *Bierabend*.' I think he may have come to my rooms for the first time when I was giving tea to Walter de la Mare, who was visiting Oxford to lecture on poetry.[15] I took to de la Mare very much as a person, but had little interest in his forthcoming lecture because he was not *avant-garde*. The baron on the other hand was assumed to be very *avant-garde*. He let us know that he was surf-riding on the crest of a wonderful new movement, of which I had not heard, called Nazi; this apparently enabled him to offer us free trips to Germany by air. Soon after our first meeting he revealed that he was a journalist and showed me an article in a German newspaper in which my rooms in Merton were described as though I were the Rimbaud of my day, making original movements with my hands among candles stuck in bottles and original modern paintings (in reality Zwemmer prints).[16]

I asked the baron to lunch, carefully providing hock. Two of my other guests were Jewesses, whom I regarded as highly cosmopolitan;[17] I was much disappointed by their reaction to the baron. Next the baron went visiting Eton for his paper, and his enthusiasm for English poetry grew till he started reciting, in a guttural 'poetry voice' and with a lush over-emphasis, 'When the hounds of Spring are on Winter's traces'.[18] Swinburne being despised in our circles, I began to think the baron was not so *avant-garde* after all. Very soon he was boring me so much that I used to dodge him in the street. Then someone discovered that he was only an adoptive baron. Which explained his dirty fingernails, and that, of course, was that.

As the baron faded out, my Jewish friends (one of whom I afterwards married)[19] came up into the foreground with a flash of primary colours and a strong waft of *chypre*. I had never

---

[15] Walter de la Mare (1873–1956) was a prolific poet who wrote many books for children including *Peacock Pie* (1913) and the famous *Memoirs of a Midget* (1921), and compiled many anthologies, including *Come Hither* (1923). His themes of fantasy and childhood appealed to MacNeice at this time. De la Mare gave a 'paper on the craftsmanship of poetry', 6 May 1929, 'to a tightly packed audience' in MacNeice's room at Merton College: see the article 'The Poetry Society' in *Sir Galahad* (ed. MacNeice) 1: 2 (14 May 1929), 30.

[16] The Zwemmer Gallery was then at 26 Lichfield Street, London WC2.

[17] Mary Beazley and her daughter Mary Ezra: see n. 5 above.

[18] The first chorus of A. C. Swinburne's *Atalanta in Calydon* (1865).

[19] MacNeice married Mary Ezra (nn. 5, 17 above; named Mariette in *Strings*) 21 June 1930 and divorced her 2 Nov. 1936.

known any Jews, and now found that in addition to the guilt of
insularity, I ought to be ashamed of being Gentile. It was tran-
spiring that Jews were in every way far more sensitive than
other people, being all of them like the princess on the nine
mattresses. Sometimes I had doubts about this, e.g. when
Christianity was disposed of by the rhetorical question 'How
can three people be one person?' but what did strike me in the
face was a superabundant vitality. How pale, I thought, in
comparison are the Ulster curates, the Old Marlburians, the
tired dons, and the bored housewives.

Also, these people had travelled, and their memories seemed
stocked from the Arabian Nights: there were relatives in India,
jewel merchants, whose daughters spent their days on silken
cushions measuring each other's eyelashes and running the
rubies through their fingers; and there had been a pigeon
fancier in Baghdad; and balls in Bucharest; and so on and so on,
all glitter and bubble and fanfare. To me this seemed, though
later I found I was mistaken, to be the very opposite of puritanism and a marvellous escape from *petit bourgeois* mentality.

But, even while I was succumbing to these Scheherazades, I
was still keeping up with (or down? down on the earth with) the
Joneses. At one of the very few lecture courses I attended at all
regularly I was irritated by the faces of two most intense young
men who were said to be sure of their Firsts. If people who look
so boring can get Firsts, I thought, I must get one too—only I
will do it more gracefully; I will lounge my way in like Petronius
Arbiter.[20] The names of my two irritants, I discovered, were
Quintin McGarel Hogg and R. H. S. Crossman.[21]

Which brings me back to politics and to what later was called
social consciousness. Auden and Spender were at Oxford at the
time, but their poetry had barely become political. Auden
already indeed thought of modern society as diseased, and was
stressing the 'clinical' approach; flowers and such things were
vulgar or trivial and the proper study of the modern poet was

[20] Petronius' *Satyricon* (probably 1st c. AD), the satire on Roman social life, was a
favourite with MacNeice. See his *Selected Literary Criticism*, 49, 128–9, 258.

[21] Quintin M. Hogg, Baron Hailsham of St Marylebone (1907–   ), Conservative
leader in the House of Lords 1960–3; the Rt. Hon. Richard H. S. Crossman
(1907–74), member of the Labour Party Executive 1952–67. At Oxford all three—
Crossman, Hogg, and MacNeice—took firsts in Mods and firsts in Greats; all three
were undergraduate authors.

man, man being the congeries of a lot of pretty nasty *specimens*. But the specimens *could* get out of the killing-bottle (soon the escape was to be Marx-cum-Freud, then—much later—the Anglo-Catholic Church) if they took a tip from D. H. Lawrence; it was thanks to Auden that I first read Lawrence and added *The White Peacock* and *Twilight in Italy* to my short list of sacred books.[22]

It may be that Auden was already becoming Teutonically left-wing, and he had after all driven a vehicle for the strikers during the General Strike,[23] but I cannot remember him at that time doing any political propaganda; his gospel seemed to be much more the Lawrentian one of spiritual revival through instinct but qualified by the cerebral methods of the 'clinic'. The only undergraduate poet who seemed thoroughly committed to Socialism was Clere Parsons, who died soon after he left Oxford.[24] Yet Parsons's poetry, far from being political propaganda, consisted of experimental lyrics in the manner of E. E. Cummings, while as a person—and here he prefigured the 'Thirties Poets'—he did not look at all like a man who was at home with the masses. The Decadents had at least been self-consistent; their successors were to find themselves tugged at by incompatibles, feeling things they had renounced and professing beliefs they hardly felt.

Take, for instance, the question of class. There were many undergraduates like myself who theoretically conceded that all men were equal, but who, in practice, while only too willing to converse, or attempt to, with say Normandy peasants or shop-keepers, would wince away in their own college halls from those old grammar school boys who with impure vowels kept admiring Bernard Shaw or Noël Coward while grabbing their knives and forks like dumb-bells. Thus I was horrified one day to receive a letter from some Poor Relations—a middle-aged and, I suspected, ungrammatical couple—suggesting they should come to tea with me. Then I remembered I had an 'oak'. As soon as the dreaded visitors had been corralled in my rooms in college I explained to them the old Oxford custom of

[22] Lawrence's first novel (1911) and first travel book (1916).
[23] Summer 1926.
[24] Clere Parsons (1908–31): see Grigson's *Recollections* (1984) and MacNeice's *Selected Literary Criticism*, 30 with n. 60.

the two doors in the one doorway: once the outer one, the oak, had been 'sported', no one could get in from outside. 'The idea,' I said, 'is to leave one undisturbed to work.' 'Look!' I said, sporting it quickly and forgetting to open it again. The idea was to protect my snobbery from callers; and so it did, but the bad taste still recurs to me. This fear of being caught with the wrong people was constant, and the world seemed full of wrong people. Americans, however uncouth, were different: I knew a number of Rhodes Scholars who, however they dressed or spoke, could always be explained away as either exotic or comic. And all college servants, of course, were comic and usually 'period' too, straight out of Rowlandson or Cruik-shank,[25] collectors' pieces and talking points. In fact in the social game the more hayseed one's American friend, or the more illiterate one's scout, the better. Like illustrations to *Punch* they were props rather than people.

Still, people in general were a perpetual menace. At school several of us who belonged to the intellectual minority had developed elaborate and sometimes paradoxical defence mechanisms. My own was to stick my neck out. Although I disliked being stared at, when I first went up to Oxford I made a point of dressing eccentrically, growing long side-whiskers and pitching my voice up whenever my opinions were unpopular. When I got an angry reaction, such as someone calling after me in the street 'Is your name Daphne with the long hair!' I felt I had scored, even though I was embarrassed.

The absurd old Oxford antithesis of Aesthete and Hearty was still going strong. It was not only a point of honour to show which side one belonged to; it also, even at the risk of violence to one's clothes, person, or property, gave a peculiar sense of security. By my twenty-first birthday, however, I no longer felt so partisan, and I was annoyed in the following term when a very affected freshman (described by Father Knox[26] as looking like one of those insipid old-fashioned dolls which close their

[25] Thomas Rowlandson (1756–1827) and George Cruickshank (1792–1878), the English painters, illustrators, and especially caricaturists famous in the late 18th and the 19th c.

[26] The Rt. Revd Mgr. Ronald A. Knox (1888–1957), the prominent Catholic convert and author; his *Life* had just been written by Evelyn Waugh (1959). MacNeice had reviewed Knox's translation of *The New Testament* in the *Spectator* 176: 6150 (10 May 1946), 484.

eyes when you lay them on their sides) pulled out a lavatory chain, while walking with me in the Turl, and hit a large hearty across the face with it.

I was beginning to feel that provocation of people was wasteful. But this did not mean that I was drawing nearer to people. In my last year at school, when I was sharing a study with Anthony Blunt,[27] whose chief interest was already in the visual arts although he was specializing still in mathematics, I had agreed with him that People were of minor importance compared with Things. Whether I had ever completely believed this or not, I still certainly thought that a good many things were preferable to a good many people. This is perhaps why I so much enjoyed both *Ulysses* and *Mrs Dalloway*.[28] Both Poldy Bloom and Mrs Dalloway are not so much active characters as people possessed by the things that have crammed their memories and the things that impinge on their senses. If I had only come across Rilke[29] then, this further levitation of Things would have certainly made me canonize him. As it was, I spent much of my time at Oxford alone, staring at cylinders of brawn in the grocer's or at the sluices in Mesopotamia,[30] comparing the visual aspects of things and standing Plato on his head to insist that Appearance was more real than what he would have called Reality.[31]

That I had to make comparisons, to find that x looks like y, was of course a drawback; but then I was not a painter, though I often wished I was. At the age of 17 I had swallowed Clive Bell's doctrine of Significant Form,[32] at 18 I had repudiated this, but at 19, on my first visit to Paris, I had found myself

---

[27] Prof. Anthony F. Blunt (1907–83), Surveyor of the Royal Pictures 1945–72 and author of scholarly art criticism; see Dodds's index to MacNeice's *Strings*.

[28] Novels by James Joyce (1922) and Virginia Woolf (1925) respectively.

[29] Rainer Maria Rilke (1875–1926), the great modern German lyric poet, to be later translated into English verse by James Blair Leishman (1902–63) and Sir Stephen Spender (1909–   ).

[30] Popular name for an area between rivers in the University Parks, Oxford.

[31] For Plato, Reality consists of the world of Ideas or Forms of things; things themselves partake of the realm of Appearance; further, see MacNeice's article 'Plato Made Easy', *Spectator* 155: 5584 (5 July 1935), 28, para. 3. MacNeice became an Aristotelian at Oxford.

[32] A. Clive H. Bell, *Art* (1914), new edn (1949), 8: a standard slogan of the Bloomsbury Group of artists and writers, for which see MacNeice's *Selected Literary Criticism*, 83 n. 3.

saying of a bridge across the Seine 'How significant that is!', to which my companion,[33] being an incipient philosopher, replied 'Significant of what?' At 21 I still thought that the look of things—or sometimes the sound or the smell or the feel of them —could be more important than the things themselves, whatever *they* might be (though, as compared with 'people', I often tended to equate these sensible aspects of the thing with the thing itself; hence my acceptance of Blunt's schoolboy dictum). By now I had also discovered (long before Mr Aldous Huxley played about with mescalin)[34] what an ally alcohol was in these matters.

When I was drunk, I found, things could either look more so, themselves with an added emphasis, or swoop off into fantasy and look like quite other things; in either case the change seemed an improvement. I also noticed that, on a morning after, something very simple, like an earthenware pot of flowers or the clock across the quad or an earthenware pot empty, could fill my whole consciousness like a solid meal—or was this perhaps going for a ride on a tiger, was the thing perceived making a meal of *me*? So, though I had not yet read Rimbaud, I began to experiment in a certain *dérèglement des sens*.[35] Not, of course, that this was my only reason for getting drunk; it was also obviously a challenge to convention and a quick way out of the Valley of Diffidence. During this year I was to get arrested for drunkenness and spend a defiant hour or two singing in my cell to a tune of Schubert's 'That was in another country and besides the wench is dead'.[36] I had not had any wench by that date.

In my twenty-second year, then, the sheer look of things probably exercised me more than it ever has since. It was also the heyday of my bookishness; books were tokens, talismans,

[33] John R. Hilton (1908–   ), the English architect and diplomat, friend of MacNeice from Marlborough and Oxford days, who contributed a memoir to Dodds's edn of MacNeice's *Strings*, app. B, 239–84.

[34] See Huxley's *The Doors of Perception* (1954).

[35] Arthur Rimbaud's (1854–91) experimentation with evil and with self-induced states of delirium to produce a heightened poetry.

[36] The words are Marlowe's, *The Jew of Malta* 1592 (1633), 4. 1. 40–3, quoted as the epigraph to T. S. Eliot's early poem 'Portrait of a Lady' (1917). Apparently, in his drunken state, MacNeice was fitting the words to a tune that was not written for them, as Schubert never set a song to a Marlowe text.

keys to a lost kingdom. Again, of course, there was snobbery involved; just as mantelpieces had been made to prove one was invited out, bookshelves were there to show one was really *in*. While one *had* to admire *The Waste Land*, one *could* not have been seen reading Galsworthy.[37] In fact *The Waste Land* did appeal to me; I understood it much better than I did *Prufrock*, for instance, in which I completely missed the humour, as I did in much of *Ulysses*.[38] This surely is understandable. However deep one's ignorance, historically, of the Decline of the West, it has been since World War I something that must hit one in the marrow at adolescence; anyhow Waste Lands are not only community phenomena, there must be one somewhere in each individual just as everyone contains in himself those places which Spenser described as the Cave of Despair, the House of Busyrane, and, thank God, the Garden of Adonis.[39]

The Waste Land, therefore, hit me in the way a person hits one. But the bulk of my reading was not on this thou-thou plane; many books I went to not as ends but as means in a Robinson Crusoe effort to knock up my own *Weltanschauung* (I would certainly, not only for reasons of snobbery but of magic, have preferred the German word to its English equivalent). Some of these books were my prescribed texts for Greats, and among these, oddly it might seem, in view of my romantic disposition, I was beginning to prefer Aristotle to Plato. Which is perhaps not so odd after all. It was Shelley, the most Platonizing of our poets, who wrote:

> Life, like a dome of many-coloured glass,
> Stains the white radiance of Eternity,[40]

whereas people like myself must always prefer the Twopence Coloured to even the Pound Plain. For all his famous dryness, Aristotle, being among other things a zoologist, never let transcendental radiance destroy the shapes of the creatures or impose a white-out on everything.

[37] In the 1920s Eliot was avant-garde, Galsworthy arrière-garde.

[38] Cf. MacNeice's 'Eliot and the Adolescent' (Sept. 1948), in his *Selected Literary Criticism*, 148–53. MacNeice enjoyed Joyce's humour later: '*James Joyce's World* | *Letters of James Joyce*', ibid. 212–16.

[39] Locales of three episodes in Edmund Spenser's *The Faerie Queene* (1590–6), respectively, I. ix (despair), III. xi (profane love), III. vi (earthly paradise of forms).

[40] P. B. Shelley's *Adonais* (1821), st. 52. 463–4.

This is probably why I was so fascinated not only by D. H. Lawrence but by *The Dance of Life* by Havelock Ellis,[41] a book which I have not read for thirty years and which now might very well bore me. What I hankered for was unity in difference, and Ellis's not original concept of all life as a dance was so fully illustrated in the concrete and over such a wide range, from the courting ritual of birds to the virtues of aberrant spelling, that I thought 'Now I'm really getting hot!' But at the same time I found an equal, and more fashionable, satisfaction in the polemical writings of Wyndham Lewis, even though often he was attacking some of my own favourites; for instance he attacked the 'child cult'[42] for which I had a strong weakness— but here once more, no doubt, I wanted to have my cake and eat it. The two main things that appealed to me in Lewis were his destructive criticism and his constructive demands for system and firm outlines; these two came together in his eulogies of works like *Timon of Athens*.[43] I had at the time—and here my own age (for 20-year-olds have always been seduced by *Hamlet*) clicked with the period I was living in—a preference for Shakespeare at his most sombre and apparently destructive. I had already grown tired of pinprick satire, and had no wish to read *Point Counter Point* when it came out in 1928,[44] but despair and disgust in the grand manner enlivened me. I found Donne's Sermons and Jeremy Taylor's *Holy Dying* excellent for reading aloud,[45] and one of my favourite Shakespeare characters was Thersites.[46] But I was also very fond of Tchehov's short stories.

So there I was, caught between bonfires and backfires, like many of my contemporaries. Much self-deception lay ahead of me. Not long after my twenty-first birthday I became engaged to be married, which very much altered my day-to-day life in Oxford. I had less time for reading or talking with my friends

---

[41] (1923).

[42] The English satirist P. Wyndham Lewis (1884–1957) attacked the Romantic 'child cult' in *The Childermass* (1928).

[43] Lewis, *The Lion and the Fox: The Rôle of the Hero in the Plays of Shakespeare* (1927, 1951), pt. 7, chap. 3.

[44] By Aldous Huxley—a novel of social satire featuring a portrait of his friend D. H. Lawrence as the protagonist Mark Rampion.

[45] Often read for their sonorous prose, in the 17th-c. Anglican tradition.

[46] The foul-mouthed critic of war and warriors in Shakespeare's *Troilus and Cressida*, dealt with by Lewis, *The Lion and the Fox*, pt. 7, chaps. 3–4.

and was encouraged instead to listen to gramophone records of Sophie Tucker the Red-Hot Momma and Jack Smith the Whispering Baritone.[47] I even learned to foxtrot, but never, though this was its period, to Charleston. And I tried to cultivate optimism and a belief in the domestic virtues.

In the summer of 1929 I spent four weeks in the island of Achill and six weeks at St Tropez.[48] The former place was inhabited by stage patriarchs on stage donkeys, the latter by stage Frenchmen who lolled on a stage beach. People were not only a menace, they were also something of an illusion; of course in Ireland, my own country, I now felt hopelessly anglicized, and, as for Frenchmen, I could not follow what they said. In both the West of Ireland and in France my books of philosophy seemed more out of place than they had the year before in the Arctic Circle. My tutor had been a pupil of F. H. Bradley,[49] and I was very fond of Bradley's dictum that every judgement (in the logical sense of the word) is a judgement about the universe.[50] It was exciting, when I said I liked aubergine, to be saying something true about the universe—and moreover to be adding something to it; still, it did not help me to understand the Provençal woman who had cooked the aubergine and who after all was in the universe too.

When I returned to Oxford for my fourth year, many of my exact contemporaries had gone down at the end of their third and some had already got jobs. Their letters had a whiff of what reluctantly I granted were wider spheres; people in Oxford seemed to know all the questions, but earning a weekly wage was at least one answer to something. Some of my friends who had no ideas about careers used to turn to Father D'Arcy,[51] who was said to have much influence with concerns like ICI.[52] Though I admired Father D'Arcy, expert on

[47] Both American entertainers of the time.

[48] In the W. of Ireland and the S. of France, respectively.

[49] MacNeice's tutor Mure (n. 3 above) had been a disciple of the great British idealist Francis Herbert Bradley (1846–1924), about whom T. S. Eliot wrote his Ph.D. thesis.

[50] 'Judgment [of sense] is not the synthesis of ideas, but the reference of ideal content to reality': Bradley, *The Principles of Logic*, 2nd edn rev., 2 vols. (1922), i, bk. 1, chap. 2, sect. 15, p. 56; cf. MacNeice's *Strings*, 125.

[51] The Very Revd Martin C. D'Arcy (1888–1976), the prominent English Jesuit and Thomist author, then very much a presence at Campion Hall, Oxford.

[52] Imperial Chemical Industries.

Aquinas and master carver of game, as a man who had both
feet in both worlds, he too, like more secular Oxford intellectuals, seemed to bear the stamp of the Hothouse (a cliché
still used today by Oxford undergraduates of their alma
mater).

Anyhow, I joined neither ICI nor the Church of Rome, but
got married and went to live in Birmingham, thus exchanging,
at first, a public hothouse for a private one.[53] But, as the panes
of glass fell gradually out of their frames, while the plants inside
were endangered, I began to smell the life that went on outside
and to notice—but only gradually—that what had seemed
walking props were really persons like myself. All that, though,
was still in the future. I was still *in statu pupillari*, working for an
archaic examination and given to quoting from a poem in Ezra
Pound's *Cathay* (about a middle-aged Chinese who had failed
in *his* examinations): 'But all this comes to an end and is not
again to be met with.'[54] All this did. And it was high time.

[53] Cf. MacNeice's move to Birmingham, in *Strings*, chap. 25, 130 ff.

[54] Corr. 'And all this comes to an end. | And is not again to be met with': 'Exile's
Letter', ll. 58–9, *Cathay* (1915), in Ezra Pound, *Personae: Collected Shorter Poems* (1952),
146.

In Pursuit of Cuchulain[1]

Celtic Heritage. By Alwyn Rees and Brinley Rees.
(Thames and Hudson. 50s.)

The legendary Irish hero Cuchulain has a statue in the Post
Office in Dublin and five plays written about him by Yeats.[2] As
Yeats himself put it in a late poem, 'What stalked through the
Post Office?'[3] For an answer we can search in *Celtic Heritage*, a
study of 'Ancient Tradition in Ireland and Wales.'

Being of a generation that on first reading *The Waste Land*
proceeded religiously to Jessie Weston's *From Ritual to Romance*,
I still am a pushover for this sort of book but must warn those
who are not that this particular example is very much of a
banyan: it is hard to see the branches for the roots—or do I
mean the roots for the branches?

It sent me back to *At Swim-Two-Birds*, by Flann O'Brien, the
Celtic answer to Chinese boxes and a masterpiece of auto-
genocide:

> Oh mother of this herd,
> thy coat has greyed,
> no stag is following after thee
> without twice twenty points.[4]

Twice twenty points would be nothing to the Rees brothers
who can run without drawing breath to a hundred footnotes
per chapter and who warn us in their Introduction that 'In
pondering upon these fragments of tradition it is not enough for

---

[1] *Observer* 8878 (27 Aug. 1961), 19. (The signed galley proof at the HRC, Austin,
Texas, is attributed falsely thus: 'book review in *New Statesman*, 1961'.) Alwyn David
Rees (1911–74), the Welsh editor, writer, and sociologist, was Director of the Extra-
Mural Department, University College of Wales, Aberystwyth, 1949–74; Brinley
Rees was his brother: *OCLW*, 507. See *Ym Marn D. Rees*, ed. Bobi Jones (1976).

[2] The five Cuchulain plays by Yeats are: *On Baile's Strand* (1904), *The Green Helmet*
(1910), *At the Hawk's Well* (1917), *The Only Jealousy of Emer* (1919), and *The Death of
Cuchulain* (1939). See n. 17 below for Cuchulain himself.

[3] 'The Statues' (1939), st. 4. 2.

[4] 'Flann O'Brien' (pseud. of Brian O'Nolan), fantasy novel *At Swim-Two-Birds*
(1939, 1951, 1966), 113.

modern man to disabuse his mind of the preconceptions of the historian, the prejudices of the scientist, and the aestheticism of those who read the Bible "as literature". He needs all the clues he can find.'[5] The brothers have certainly proved themselves indefatigable clue-merchants and I for one, though my motives may be tainted by aestheticism, am only too willing to buy from them.

In spite of its Welsh authorship, the lion's share of this book goes to Ancient Ireland while other mythologies, especially Indian, are introduced for purposes of comparison; thus the Irish St Moling, renowned for his three enormous leaps, is compared with Vishnu the Thrice-Stepper.[6] Such comparisons aid the authors in their quest for general principles among all the undergrowth and overgrowth; they can point out for instance 'the presence both in Ireland and in India of the curious idea that social classes have to do with the points of the compass'.[7] And in their attempt to explain 'the elusive fifth' exemplified in 'the subdivision of an island [Ireland] into four parts each of which is called a fifth',[8] they are able (seventy pages later) to draw upon the knowledge that 'in Voudoun: "The figure five is as the four of the cross-roads plus the swinging of the door which is the point itself of crossing, the moment of arrival and departure."'[9]

Much is there here in fact for confusion—and for detection—and some of their conclusions as to the symbolism of the myths are magnificently sweeping. Thus they find that Taliesin, the Welsh wizard-poet, 'is everything' because 'there existed alongside the belief in individual reincarnation a doctrine that there is essentially only One Transmigrant'.[10]

To assess the correctness of these more metaphysical findings is a job for an expert—the Reeses themselves remark that there are 'unlimited opportunities for confusion in the transmission

---

[5] Rees and Rees (1961, 1973), 25.
[6] Ibid. 77–9. The Irish St Moling (d. 697), 'also known as Daircheall (and Myllin in Wales), . . . founded an abbey at Achad Cainigb . . . named Tech Moling'; 'He succeeded St Aiden as bishop of Ferns, Leinster, lived a life of great austerity'; his feast day is 17 June: John L. Delaney, *Dictionary of Saints* (1982), 412.
[7] Rees and Rees, 132.
[8] Ibid. 119.
[9] Ibid. 192.
[10] Ibid. 230.

and interpretation of a tradition which has been only partially preserved'[11] but on a lower or at least a more human plane the layman is in a position to agree with, say, the generalization that the typical Ancient Irish hero was faced with a tragic choice between evils or with the distinction drawn between the Ulster Cycle ('the apotheosis of the will' shown in solo feats of heroism) and the Fenian stories (a 'human warmth of feeling'[12] proper to more communal heroics). It is obvious why Yeats, casting his cold eye,[13] was so obsessed by Cuchulain and comparatively unconcerned with Finn.

Reverting to the aesthetic standpoint I find that this book endorses what I have always felt: that the majority of the Celtic legends are spoilt for the modern reader, except as unconscious comedy, by the proliferation of incredible detail but that at their highest moments they are as moving a tribute to the human spirit as the best hero stories from Ancient Greece or from the Norse countries.

So, while it is fun to hear of a certain Math, son of Mathonwy, who has the 'peculiarity . . . that he can live only if his feet are held in a maiden's lap'[14] or of the mad King Sweeney, who grew feathers and flew about all over Ireland perching in tree-tops,[15] Diarmuid and Grania[16] still hold their own with Tristan

---

[11] Ibid. 145.

[12] Ibid. 61, 69.

[13] 'Cast a cold eye | On life, on death': Yeats, 'Under Ben Bulben', Sept. 1938 (1939), ll. 92–3.

[14] Rees and Rees, 50. 'Math fab Mathonwy, magician and King of Gwynedd in the Fourth Branch of *Pedair Caincy Mabinogi*'; 'also mentioned in *The Book of Taliesin* where it is claimed that Math created Taliesin by Magic': *OCLW*, 388.

[15] Rees and Rees, 77. The early Irish legendary *Buile Suibhne* ('The Madness of Sweeney') 'is one of the most interesting, imaginative, and poetic of Irish tales. Incidentally it inspired *At Swim-Two-Birds* [n. 4 above] by Flann O'Brien'—*Dictionary of Irish Literature*, ed. Robert Hogan (1979), 30—as well as many other works, from T. S. Eliot's Sweeney poems (1920) and *Sweeney Agonistes* (1932) to Seamus Heaney's rendition *Sweeney Astray* (1984). Sweeney, king of Dal Araidhe, who offends the cleric Ronan, undergoes wanderings and hardships, lives in the trees as a bird, 'is eventually mortally wounded' and 'reconciled, somewhat unconvincingly, to Christianity': Ciaran Carson, '*Sweeney Astray*: Escaping from Limbo', *The Art of Seamus Heaney*, ed. Tony Curtis (1985), 142.

[16] Diarmuid and Grainne (Grania), the legendary Irish lovers, protagonists of a stage play by W. B. Yeats and George Moore 1901 (1951) and of a radio play (1950) by the Irish poet Padraic Fallon (1905–74), as well as many other works: *Dictionary of Irish Literature* (1979), 710, 230.

and Ysolde,[17] Deirdre still holds her own with Helen, and
Cuchulain,[18] when he is not too grotesquely involved in magic,
can rank with Achilles (just as his horse is as immortal as
Xanthos and Balios)[19] or with the Gunnar of the *Njal Saga*.[20]
Look at Cuchulain, for instance, when he is compelled, or
compels himself, to kill his son and throws him down before
Conchobar and his warriors: 'Here is my son for you, men of
Ulster.'[21]

[17] Tristan and Iseult are Celtic lovers of an intense and unfortunate love–death
passion—similar to that of Diarmuid and Grainne—whose tale told in medieval
romances was linked to the Arthurian cycle and is best known in Malory's *Morte
Darthur* (1485) and Wagner's opera *Tristan und Isolde* (1865). See *OCLW*, 599–600.

[18] 'The ancient Irish epic, *The Tain Bo Cuailnge*, . . . is the story of the great deeds of
Cuchulain [The Hound of Culainn]', the greatest warrior-hero in the Ulster Cycle: see
Dictionary of Irish Literature, 21–4.

[19] Achilles' pair of immortal horses (Homer, *Iliad* xvi. 149), loaned by Achilles to
Patroclus when the latter fought Hector and was slain by him.

[20] For the Icelandic hero Gunnar, fatally betrayed to his enemies by his wife, see
Brennu-Njals Saga, or *The Story of Burnt Njal*, trans. Sir George (W.) Dasent (1861, 1900,
1911), a favourite book of MacNeice: *Strings*, 98. Cf. his *Selected Literary Criticism*, xvii,
49, 233–4, 242, 257.

[21] Rees and Rees, 62.

Nine New Caps[1]

Why do people go to watch rugby matches? The England–Wales game last month provided no possible answer. The England–Ireland one last Saturday did: it was a highly enjoyable spectacle. But then England and Wales were well matched and England and Ireland were not. Could the explanation be that, to get a game worth watching, one side must be much stronger than the other? One hopes not, but one is not sure. At the same time we must ignore any canting suggestion that the players instead of playing to win should put on a pretty exhibition of 'open play'. We often hear that modern rugby is ruined by the wing forward. It was not so ruined this 10 February at Twickenham, but that may only have been because the Irish wing forwards were so inept. Sharp, the English stand-off half, played a marvellous game but then he was given more room than he can ever have prayed for.[2] Yet the answer is certainly not that wing forwards should pull their punches.

A few years ago the Welsh selectors got gassed and picked a winning side. This time the Irish selectors, after a confusing final trial, panicked and picked a losing one. '*Nine* new caps!' we all said to each other, 'There's nothing like sowing with a full sack when you don't know what the hell is in it.' Most of the Irish *aficionados* began predicting defeat—the Irish love doing this ('We'll take a terrible hammering') though some of us—we love doing this too—said: 'D'ye know, I think it will come off.' The former lot were attuned in advance to anti-climax, the latter suffered a good deal, but both lots, needless

---

[1] *New Statesman* 63: 1614 (16 Feb. 1962), 239–40. Title: nine new players selected for a national team (Ireland) in international competition (against England). The score in this game of Sat., 10 Feb. 1962, was England 16, Ireland 0: *The Times*, 11 Feb. 1962, 3c–d. Additional information in the notes to this article is taken from a copy of the programme.

[2] Richard A. W. Sharp (1938–) (Oxford Univ.), stand-off for England: *The Times*, 10 Feb. 1962, 3f. 'Sharp played the game of his life and scored 10 of England's 16 points in the process': RF Corresp., ibid., 11 Feb. 1962, 3c. Sharp made 'Remarkable International debut against Wales'; with this game he won his 2nd cap: programme note.

to say, enjoyed the frills and tangents inseparable from any international. On the eve of the match there is the preliminary talk that keeps you up late. On the day there is the getting to the ground which is usually left till the last moment and appears excitingly impossible. After which there is the sudden submersion in the monstrous crowd.

At any Twickenham international what colours the crowd is the minority. The Welsh for instance come flaunting in red, though this is not necessary: a blind man could tell who they were. The Irish supporters are a more mixed lot than the Welsh —Papish faces, Prod faces and Ascendancy faces—but they all are obviously Irish and in a love-hate relationship not only with their hosts but with each other. Thus in a jampacked nasty tunnel under the North Stand my friend from County Armagh[3] saw a Catholic priest barging and bullocking. 'Shame on you, Father,' he said. 'You're right,' replied the priest.

After the game we found ourselves, as usual, drinking down each other's necks, first in Twickenham itself where the Guinness is the flattest in the world and then at Richmond in a club bar as resonant and homey as a garage, where huge white enamel jugs of beer were passing from hand to hand and lending a clinical touch suitable to the moment of autopsy. This moment of course goes on for the rest of the day. On this occasion our findings were very roughly that the Irish selectors were mad but that Quirke, the unprecedentedly young Irish scrum half,[4] had not only come out of it alive but with credit, that Sharp was probably the finest runner with the ball playing, that the Irish covering and following up were not only bad but un-Irish, and that the Irish full back, Kiernan, was the only man in the side who showed a flair for attack.[5]

[3] For George Galway MacCann, sculptor, the great Ulster friend of MacNeice, see Barbara Coulton, *Louis MacNeice in the BBC* (1980), *passim*, from index.

[4] 'John Thornton Michael Quirke [(1944–   ), of Blackrock College, scrum-half for Ireland] is the most remarkable and controversial figure in the five nations today. At 17½ is the second youngest player ever to be capped for Ireland . . .; must be the youngest ever international scrum-half in rugby history. . . . First cap today': programme note.

[5] Thomas J. Kiernan (1939–   ), 'Rugby Union full-back for Cork Constitution, Ireland, and British Lions': *The Oxford Companion to Sports & Games*, ed. John Arlott (1975), 575. 'The best run of the day was made by Kiernan . . . with an astonishing pick-up and gallop of 80 yards': RF Corresp., *The Times*, 11 Feb. 1962, 3d.

When I do get home on these occasions my last pleasure of the day is reading or re-reading the programme of the match. On the last page this gives the record of all the matches between the two countries since 1875. Trying to remember which games I had seen myself, I enjoyed again certain notable spectacles—Kyle on his first visit to Twickenham going through the English side like a straight-backed ghost to score near the right corner flag, and an earlier Irish stand-off half, Cromey, one of the smallest ever, playing concussed through the whole second half without the English rumbling him: these were Ireland's last two wins at Twickenham.[6] I also remembered the fiasco at Lansdowne Road in 1938, the only match which I ever watched with my father,[7] who did not really understand the code. England won by 36 to 14, the whole Irish side, who for once started favourites and had previously been noted for their defence, giving up tackling altogether. My father, who was unaware that a white jersey makes you look bigger than a green one, kept saying: 'Sure, they're much bigger than our men and anyway haven't they far more to pick from!'

Last Saturday's match, though there was no doubt about the result, was at least not a fiasco. Even the Irish spectators came away happy and babbling, very unlike the crowd after the Welsh match. For we had all been suddenly reminded that rugby is a handling game. Maybe Sharp will never again be indulged in such a romp: anyone who failed to see him last Saturday missed something lyrical. The England–Wales match was not only prose but bad prose. I asked my County Armagh friend, who happens to be a sculptor,[8] for his last word on the match. He said: 'Every time Sharp had the ball I thought to myself "A terrible beauty is born."'[9] Ironic coda: as I write this I hear that a strike—the first for 200 years—is threatened in St James's brewery in Dublin.

[6] Ireland's last two wins against England at Twickenham were on Sat., 14 Feb. 1948 (Ireland 11, England 10), with John W. Kyle (1926–   ), 'the dominant figure in Irish Rugby during its successful period after the Second World War' (*OCSG*, 586); and Sat., 11 Feb. 1939 (Ireland 5, England 0: an upset victory), with G. E. Cromey. See *The Times*, 16 Feb. 1948, 2a; 13 Feb. 1939, 6a.

[7] The Rt. Revd John Frederick MacNeice (1866–1942).

[8] See n. 3 above.

[9] Refrain used 3 times in Yeats's poem 'Easter 1916'.

C'est la Terre[1]

The Furrow Behind Me. By Angus MacLellan. (Routledge. 28s.)
The Hard Road to Klondike. By Michael MacGowan. (Routledge. 25s.)
My Ireland. By Kate O'Brien. (Batsford. 25s.)

About thirty years ago there came out of the Blasket Islands off the wild coast of Kerry a Gaelic autobiography which was heralded by E. M. Forster as 'an account of neolithic civilization from the inside'.[2] *Twenty Years A-Growing* by Maurice O'Sullivan[3] was what every well-upholstered urban reader would like as his Present from the Gaeltacht: a beautiful rich 'Celtic' cake-mix of nostalgia and fantasy and humour and idyll and rhythm and image and those quaint old folk ways. Magnificent but not—not exactly—*la terre.* The balance is now redressed by the Gaelic autobiographies of Angus MacLellan and Michael MacGowan, both, by the way, of an older generation than O'Sullivan. For both these diehard old realists the Light that Never Was has been replaced by the Facts that Have to be Faced—intractable nature, poverty, hunger, disease. MacGowan was born in 1865 in County Donegal; his story was taken down by his son-in-law and translated by Valentin Iremonger. MacLellan was born in 1869 in South Uist and is still alive; his story was tape-recorded and translated by John Lorne Campbell. We should be grateful to the people who have put these human great auks on record.

MacLellan and MacGowan have much in common. To start with, for each of them his native language, whether it is Scottish Gaelic or Irish Gaelic, is practically his alter ego. MacGowan in the States found himself 'a bit unhappy . . . among people

    [1] *New Statesman* 63: 1632 (22 June 1962), 911–12.
    [2] 'Introductory Note' to the book (n. 3 below), v–vi.
    [3] Rendered from the original Irish by Moya Llewelyn Davies and George Thomson (May 1933).

who spoke only English and other foreign languages'.[4] And both had a very tough childhood with fever in the home and a hard landlord.

MacGowan at the age of 8 was hired out as a cowherd to a farmer in another district; his total wages from May to November were 30 shillings. At 15 he went looking for work in Scotland where the Irish of course were very unpopular (MacLellan gives the other side of the picture): 'it was as likely as not that we'd be attacked if we went barefoot. So we kept our boots on.'[5] MacLellan at the age of 15 was fined two pounds or fourteen days in prison for shooting a rabbit. And so both of them go forward, taking it on the chin, MacLellan into the Militia and then to serve as a ploughman under various slave-drivers on the Scottish mainland, and MacGowan shipping himself off like a beast to America, to Pennsylvania, the mines of Montana, Alaska.

There is no Celtic twilight in either of these stories. They have far more the bony quality of an Icelandic saga where a man has a right to be proud of his physical prowess but tends to understatement when he boasts of it. Of the two perhaps MacLellan's story is slightly the more impressive, just because it is less obviously sensational; it is something of a feat to interest a modern reader in the petty rivalries of these dour farm-hands of the nineteenth century. MacGowan's adventures have a more exotic and more familiar cinematic lighting. On St Patrick's Day 1897 he first heard of the Klondike gold rush; the sequel for him was blood, toil, sweat, and frostbite. He pulls an overloaded sled up a frozen mountain single-handed, he fights his way against the current up the Yukon, he pays for a drink with gold dust carried in a moose-skin purse. In the end he returns like MacLellan, to find honour in his own country.

When we turn to Miss Kate O'Brien we are back in literature, though Miss O'Brien over a certain distance could probably keep up with the MacGowans and MacLellans, perhaps partly because they would all be Roman Catholics together. Miss O'Brien dislikes some of her country's past, the part represented by the ruined Norman castles, but she is all in favour of the part represented by the ruined monasteries. At the same

---

[4] MacGowan, 60.   [5] Ibid. 42.

time she is both humane and on occasions sceptical and can take her history with a grain of salt: 'when Cromwell came he was in fact late for the true kill. He found plenty of land-robbing to arrange, and enough human blood to let and to freeze, certainly. But the golden age had got away from him, into history and legend before he could kick it.'[6]

She is good about Ireland in general because she does not try to discuss it in general; all her Ireland is particular. Thus she does not know County Donegal and does not much like County Kerry and has certain doubts about Dublin. Her great loves are Limerick and Clare and, what comes very welcome from a Catholic, she has many good words for Belfast.

[6] O'Brien, 128. Kate O'Brien (1897–1974), the Irish Catholic novelist and playwright, was noted for a prize-winning first novel *Without My Cloak* (1931), and for a Spanish romance *That Lady* (1946); she was also a journalist for the *Manchester Guardian*.

Under the Sugar Loaf[1]

'Dublin?' said a friend of mine after his first visit. 'Dublin! There's no such place. It's just one enormous pub.' This aspect of the city presses itself upon visitors thanks to traditional Irish hospitality, combined, one should add, with the pleasure of a new audience. Not all the citizens, of course, are pubgoers. AE and the late Sarah Pursar,[2] mistress of stained glass and malice, made do with their own weekly salons, while W. B. Yeats, they say, went only once into a pub and did not like it at all. But the Dublin salon is a thing of the past and the pub remains the temple of talk. There are other hard-drinking cities—New York, Edinburgh, Accra—but it is the talk in Dublin that gives the drinking its very distinctive quality. If any Dublin alcoholic were to write an autobiographical novel in answer to Malcolm Lowry's *Under the Volcano*,[3] it could well be called *Under the Sugar Loaf* (that conspicuous Wicklow mountlet): things are not going to end with an eruption, they are going to melt in the mouth.

Anyhow the pubs in Dublin were even more assertive than usual this 16 June, 'Bloomsday',[4] when some of the more intellectual and tourist-conscious Irishmen were about to open (or should we say consecrate?) the new Joyce Centre in his old Martello tower at Sandycove described in the first chapter of *Ulysses*. For me the pilgrimage began at Davy Byrne's,[5] which was Joyce's favourite pub though he might not now recognize it

---

[1] *New Statesman* 63: 1633 (29 June 1962), 948–9. Headnote: 'Louis MacNeice has just returned from a visit to Dublin. His is the first of a series of articles, *Out of London*, on rival—or provincial—cities.' The occasion: the opening, in June 1962, of the Martello Tower at Sandycove, Dublin, as a James Joyce museum.

[2] 'AE', pseud. of George William Russell (1867–1935), the mystic Irish poet, friend of Yeats; Sarah Pursar, the founder in 1902 of a co-operative society of artists known as *An Túr Gloine* (The Tower of Glass) for stained-glass design: *Encyclopaedia of Ireland*, ed. Victor Meally (1968), 339.

[3] Malcolm Lowry (1909–57), *Under the Volcano* (1947), a novel depicting the last days of a British consul in alcoholic delirium in Mexico.

[4] 'Bloomsday', 16 June 1904, the day on which the entire action of Joyce's novel *Ulysses* (1922) takes place. Its anniversary was and still is widely celebrated by Joyceans. Cf. para. 4 of the article below.

[5] The pub setting of episode 8 ('Lestrygonians') in *Ulysses*: Bloom's lunch.

with its smart modern décor and fancy murals. We met at mid-morning and, though everyone complained of being 'frail', started at once dissecting the Old Master. 'Let's face it,' someone said, 'he must have been a terrible old bore. He had no talk in him at all.' Someone else said someone was writing it all up for the *Lancet*.[6] And so on till someone said: 'What makes us a nation is we treat our heroes like human beings.' At this point who should walk in but James Joyce himself in a straw boater with a bright blue band, a spruce blue bow-tie to match, and a Charlie Chaplin walking-stick dangling from his forearm. It turned out he was a well-known promoter who happens to look like Joyce (he himself said he was the *tourist's* idea of him) and Bloomsday indeed was a promoter's dream; outside waiting for us beside the Creation Arcade were two freshly refurbished black and yellow four-wheeler horse cabs. The only difficulty was to get the jarveys to start driving.[7] It seems they were waiting for the cameramen.

The day, everyone said, was 'too bright too soon' but their fears proved unfounded; in another sense, perhaps, it lasted too bright too long. Martello towers, built to keep out the French, are like great grey stone gasometers, an apt image, I suggest, for this one at Sandycove which should certainly provide a vent for what Dublin calls 'great gas'. Yet it is to be doubted whether its high rocky perch will ever again be the setting for such a large and mixed cosmopolitan assembly, with drinks in a marquee and cameras attempting to focus and microphones thrust like carrots into reluctant faces.

All the time Dublin Bay down below us refused to look as Joyce said it did on 16 June 1904. It was neither grey nor snotgreen but obstinately and unbelievably blue, this blue being emphasized by the little white sails that littered it as though someone had been running a paper chase on the water; to the north the Hill of Howth remained as anomalous as ever. Above us on the tower was a strange flag, newly hoisted by Miss Sylvia Beach, who was naturally the heroine of the day;[8]

6 The British medical journal, founded 1823, widely read and esteemed.

7 Jarvey: a hackney-coachman, especially of an Irish car: *OED2*.

8 Sylvia Beach (1887–1962), the American proprietor of the Paris bookshop Shakespeare and Co. which became an expatriate centre, publisher of *Ulysses* (2 Feb. 1922, Joyce's 40th birthday): see her memoirs of the Joyce–Hemingway period in Paris, *Shakespeare and Company* (1959).

it had been lifted from one of the best scenes in *Ulysses*—'none of your Henry Tudor's harps, no, the oldest flag afloat, the flag of the province of Desmond and Thomond, three crowns on a blue field, the three sons of Milesius'.[9] Certainly a memorable occasion, were one only to remember the half of it. Some cynics, downing their free drinks, wrote it off as a cultural gimmick but, if it is such, it is one to be welcomed. It was time Joyce was rescued from the campus laboratories.

If Joyce might be proud of his resurrected tower, he might also be turning—with laughter—in his grave at something that had happened the day before. In Dawson Street opposite the Mansion House, a pretty white doll's house with blue facings and a cast-iron porch, something yet dollier has appeared, the Anna Livia Boutique.[10] Some years ago Sybil Connolly, by using native materials and concentrating on line, put Ireland on the couturiers' map. She has been followed by other dress designers, prominent among whom is Kay Petersen of Anna Livia who cannily timed her first showing for 'Bloomsday Eve' of this year. Her hand-out explains that 'Understated elegance is the theme carried out in the exclusive hand-woven tweeds fashioned into impeccably tailored suits.' Among those present at this excellently stage-managed performance were Sylvia Beach, Madame Eugène Jolas[11] and the Irish playwright-magistrate who was chief organizer of the Bloomsday ceremonies (another writer long ago labelled him 'that fellow whose name goes round and around—Donagh MacDonagh Mac-Donagh MacDonagh . . .');[12] there were also one English

---

[9] Quotation from *Ulysses*, episode 12 ('Cyclops'). For the flags—Renaissance invader's harp, ancient Irish crowns—see Weldon Thornton, *Allusions in Ulysses: An Annotated List* (1961, 1968), 282.

[10] The 'character' called Anna Livia Plurabelle, named after the River Liffey of Dublin, dominates Joyce's *Finnegans Wake* (1939), pt. 1, chap. 8 (The Washers at the Ford).

[11] Eugène Jolas and his wife Maria were co-founders of the European review *transition* which published chapters of *Finnegans Wake*, then called 'Work in Progress' 1927–9: see Richard Ellmann, *James Joyce* (1959, rev. edn 1982).

[12] Donagh MacDonagh (1912–68), the Irish poet, son of one of the leaders of the 1916 Rising (Thomas MacDonagh), contemporary of the Irish writer Brian O'Nolan (pseud. 'Flann O'Brien'), staged the first Irish production of T. S. Eliot's *Murder in the Cathedral*. MacDonagh was a district justice 1941–68 and 'became a popular broadcaster on Radio Eireann'—'a platform for his lifelong interest in folk ballads'. 'His most successful play was *Happy as Larry* (1946), with variations on exact rhyme and off-rhyme': *Dictionary of Irish Literature*, 391–2.

atonal composer and one English actor, while Dominic Behan got near the door but did not come in.[13]

Thirty-nine models, all 'with Joycean titles' and some, such as 'Molly Bloom', intended as 'direct interpretations of Joyce's characters'—there was never a dull garment. There were also 'jars' (of champagne) before and after, five beautiful girls to do the modelling (all swan necks and false eyelashes), a background of gramophone music and a foreground of very suave commentary. 'All you Joycean scholars,' said the lady commentator, 'will appreciate for example "Finnegan": Kay Petersen calls it her igloo outfit.' And 'Martello', the 'stylized idea' of which should be as right 'for Joyceans as for fashion people'. And 'Proteus' (with reversible cape). And 'Sylvia Silence': 'Do you see the way it *links*?' And 'Calypso': 'tweed simulating knitting and it's all hand-smocked'. 'I'm sure by now,' the commentator said, 'you're beginning to get the Anna Livia idea.' We were but it was worth it. The billing of Molly Bloom gave rise to ribald cracks in the pubs but this 'evening dress in three brilliant tweeds' *as a dress* was a sheer feat, though not everyone of course could wear it. Kay Petersen has stood the concept 'tweedy' on its head.

Dress designing is only one element in the new Dublin. Another is Irish television, pronounced tellyfish. This is partly a state affair and partly commercial and is said to be paying its way; I was surprised and impressed to hear that the well-known Irish actress Sheila Richards is in charge of religious tellyfish.[14] Certainly the forest of unusually high aerials has changed the skyline of Dublin. This new Dublin contains, compared with the old, a lower percentage of bugs and bowseys[15]

13 Dominic Behan (1928–), the younger brother of the Irish playwright Brendan Behan (1923–64) and a fellow-writer. See MacNeice's review of D. Behan's *Teems of Times and Happy Returns* in *New Statesman*, 24 Nov. 1961, 795–6.

14 Telefís Éireann (the official name of the Irish TV service) was begun at Montrose, Donnybrook, on New Year's Eve 1961: see Niall Sheridan, 'Irish Television Makes its Bow', *Spectator* 208: 6983 (27 April 1962), 550; Donagh MacDonagh, 'Donnybrook Fare: Telefís Éireann', *Contrast* 1 (Summer 1962), 250–6. Shelah (Kathleen) Richards (1903–), the first wife (1928–45) of the Irish playwright Denis W. Johnston, was an actress-producer of the Irish theatre who had acted Nora Clitheroe in the original production of Sean O'Casey's *The Plough and the Stars* (1926), and later presented Paul Vincent Carroll's *The Strings, My Lord, Are False* (1944) at the Olympia Theatre, Dublin, 'during the German bombing'. See Christopher Fitz-Simon, *The Irish Theatre* (1983), 165, 169.

15 Bowsy: 'a low gutter-snipe (Anglo-Irish), 20th c.': Eric Partridge, *A Dictionary of Slang and Unconventional English*, ed. Paul Beale (1984). See also 'bowsie man'.

and a higher percentage of smoothies. Here are the head-quarters of the people who arrange subsidies and cajole German firms into opening up industries in Ireland. This may well be necessary in Ireland's precarious economy. What is certainly undesirable and unnecessary is the commercial vandalism which is prepared, in the name of efficiency, to ruin the finest Georgian vista in the world, Fitzwilliam Street. There is also some smugness about.

Yet the old Dublin survives and still dominates, not only the astonishing light and the air that caresses and the gifts for the amateur photographer (impoverished doorways framed by Ionic pillars) and the screaming of the gulls and the newsboys and the shops of Religious Goods (Sick Call Sets included), but also—and more important—the paradoxes of the Dubliners themselves, their notorious charm, their natural courtesy and misleading bonhomie, and what Kate O'Brien[16] calls their 'cold gaiety'. They seem always to have the virtues of their vices and vices versa. Their malice in a way is innocent, except when there is a chance of litigation. Their sex life is mainly inadequate but their bawdy talk is uproarious. Their women, who seem so much put upon, have not only a great ease of manner but look happier than most Englishwomen. Among them are many good blaspheming Christians and many decent fluthered puritans.[17] They are famous wasters of time but possibly because they prefer ends to means. Above all they can mythologize and debunk themselves simultaneously.

Though I am not a Dubliner, I have always found the city a home from home. My grandfather lived there once with his family and my father and an uncle were alumni of Trinity so that, when I was first taken there as a child, even though what I chiefly noticed was a shopwindow with little souvenirs of bogoak and Connemara marble, I felt, as E. M. Forster might say, that the city and I had at least 'connected'.[18] I like it of course more than it likes me: there was a time when they sang about me,

---

[16] Kate O'Brien, in *My Ireland* (1962), 110. See MacNeice's review, 'C'est la Terre', with n. 6.

[17] Fluther, a Scoticism for 'flutter', 'to fly out in a disorderly manner, to confuse, agitate': *EDD*.

[18] 'Only connect': famous phrase of E. M. Forster, *Howards End* (1910), chap. 22, para. 3, as well as that novel's epigraph.

Let him go back and labour
For Faber and Faber

though even then I found that flattering. My memories over
the years are as mixed as sea-shells. Visits as a small boy to the
Zoo in Phoenix Park: very good lions and a voluble keeper. My
first visit to Trinity College Library: one very good book—
rhymed with bells?—and again a voluble keeper. Visits in the
early thirties to Lansdowne Road for rugby football and out to
Rathfarnham for W. B. Yeats.[19] The former kept me shouting,
the latter kept me wondering. I was there with a Professor of
Greek,[20] so Yeats talked of nothing but spirits. 'I suppose you
are like Burnet,'[21] he said, 'and think the Ionian Physicists
were physicists; they were not, of course, they were spiritual-
ists.' When challenged, he reluctantly admitted he had never
actually *seen* any spirits. Then he rallied and said: 'I have often
smelt them.'[22]

In the late Thirties I came to know Yeats's disciple, the late
F. R. Higgins,[23] who thought I was lacking in 'singing robes'
but seemed pleased to let me beguile him away from the Abbey
Theatre when he was supposed to be rehearsing the company;
we used to meet other poets and borrow odd pounds from each
other. At this period in the famous Bailey restaurant I encountered a madman in the Gents. He poured out a monologue to
which I had no reply. 'D'ye know?' he said, glaring. 'I'm like
O'Connell Bridge.' 'Why?' I said, feeling I must at last say
something. 'I get angry,' he said, 'when I'm crossed.' And
then at the end of the Thirties I remember that Third of
September when England declared war. I went to Croke Park
to see the All Ireland Hurling Final. An old woman stood near
me selling bananas. Suddenly there came thunder and a
deluge: it was like Saint Michael, with All Angels to help him,

19 For MacNeice's 1934 visit to Yeats, see *Strings*, 147–8.

20 Professor E[ric] R[obertson] Dodds (1893–1979), then (early 1930s) head of
Classics at Birmingham University, a mentor and close friend, MacNeice's first
literary executor.

21 John Burnet's well-known *Early Greek Philosophy*, 4th edn (1930), 13–15.

22 For these odours, see Yeats's 'Introduction', sect. vii, to *A Vision* (1938, 1956),
15–16.

23 F[rederick] R[obert] Higgins (1896–1941), the Irish poet, successor to Yeats at
the Abbey Theatre. See radio discussion between Higgins and MacNeice, 'Tendencies
in Modern Poetry', *Listener*, 22: 550 (27 July 1939), 185–6.

if they had been producing *King Lear*. I looked round at the old woman; her bananas had vanished into pulp. Well, I thought, Dublin may keep out of the war (and who would blame her?) but at least she's ushered it in with her well-known sense of theatre.

Such reminiscences must seem trivial but for me they add up to a chain which can lower an anchor when I need it. On this last visit I was lucky enough to stay in a farmhouse with cows just under the window and the Wicklow hills in the distance and huge poppies in the garden and laburnums weeping on the lawn: a typical Irish farmhouse and only four miles from the Pillar in O'Connell Street on which Nelson still, typically, stands. I treated the house, as they say, 'like a hotel' but my host and hostess made me feel I treated it like home. Sometimes they came into Dublin to see me and we found ourselves in a pub with the Father and Mother of All Behans (constants if ever there were such)[24] drinking cheek by jowl with teenagers. Age and youth: Dublin remains constant and constantly variable. Just before I left the wind got up and lathered the moon with clouds and tangled it and tousled it in the trees of Stephen's Green. I was taken to a final party. It was a room with the lights out and people sitting on the floor and a young man with a guitar singing with a final delicacy.

[24] Stephen Behan and Kathleen Kearney: parents of Brendan (the most important new Irish playwright of the 1950s), Dominic, Brian, and Seamus; as well as Sean and Rory Furlong, their elder step-brothers, offspring of Kathleen Kearney and Jack Furlong (d. 1917)—see Ulick O'Connor, *Brendan Behan* (1970).

The Two Faces of Ireland[1]

Brendan Behan's Island. By Brendan Behan. (Hutchinson 25s.)
West Briton. By Brian Inglis. (Faber and Faber. 25s.)

The more the Irish pour out of Ireland the more books pour out of it too. These two latest autobiographical pieces complement each other very nicely and Paul Hogarth's illustrations to Brendan Behan's book add a strong dose of atmosphere; you can almost smell these pencil drawings of pubs and peasants and slum children and bogs and curraghs and graveyards.

As for Behan's text, anyone who has read his very vivid *Borstal Boy*[2] will know what to expect: he writes like a good talker talking, with plenty of hyperbole and emphasis; this is a book who drinks may read.[3] It is of course somewhat thrown together: when he has nothing particular to say he will put in a traditional ballad or the whole of 'The Groves of Blarney'. His

---

[1] *Observer* 8935 (30 Sept. 1962), 29. The Irish dramatist Brendan Behan's (1923–64) book was published with the subtitle *An Irish Sketch-Book*, and with drawings by Paul Hogarth. 'Writing without the support of the theatrical establishment . . . Behan developed an original style that combined bawdy humour, genuine pathos, and social insight' along the lines of Sean O'Casey, 'whom Behan admired both as a playwright and as an opponent of censorship. The major influence on his plays, however, was Joan Littlewood's Theatre Workshop, which emphasized improvisational effects, songs, and contemporary allusions': *British Dramatists since World War II*, 2 parts, ed. Stanley Weintraub (1982), pt. 1, p. 71. Brian St John Inglis's (1916–) book was also published in 1962. Inglis, the Irish journalist, then editor and director of the *Spectator*, had been an outstanding squadron leader in the RAF 1940–6 (mentioned in dispatches 1944–6) and then Professor of Modern History at Trinity College Dublin. A Ph.D. and FRSL, in his later career he became a TV commentator 1956–? with programmes including 'What the Papers Say' 1956–? and 'All Our Yesterdays' 1961–73; after 1962 he wrote books on medicine, modern morality, drugs, and the paranormal: *Who's Who 1988*.

[2] *Borstal Boy* (1958) was an autobiography including Behan's joining in the IRA bomb-planting campaign (between the ages of 13 and 16), his serving a three-year sentence in a reform school in England for young offenders. For 'Borstal' see Behan's 'Glossary' in *Borstal Boy*, American edn (1959), 367.

[3] Based on 'who runs may read': 'Write the vision, and make it plain upon tables, that he may run that readeth it'—Habakkuk 2: 2; and 'There is a book [the Scriptures], who runs may read'—John Keble (1792–1866), 'Septuagesima', st. 1. 1, in *The Christian Year* (1827; many edns).

own writing shows humanity, gusto, and a formidable wit, as when he is talking about the new social climbers of Dublin:

It started off with top-hats and white ties and getting into the gentry and then to chatting about the servant problem with the Anglo-Irish Horse-Protestants (who at least were reared to it) and it went from that to late dinner and now it's Angst, no less.[4]

The best thing in this book is 'The Confirmation Suit', which, though a remembered episode, reads like a good short story. Behan in fact is much better at narrative than at exposition. Some of his comments on Ireland, however, are much to the point, as when in a chapter entitled 'The Black North' he writes:

I won't say that there's no difference between people north and south of the border, but I will say, without fear of contradiction, that there's less difference between them than there is between, say, a Yorkshireman and a Somerset man.[5]

I once expressed exactly this opinion in a pamphlet for the British Council and had a blue pencil put through it. Behan himself has far more in common with a Belfast writer like Sam Thompson[6] than either of them has with any English writer. Many people in the North, however, will find him unduly irreverent about the Orange processions:

It's a colourful show, I must admit, and I think when the country is again united, we'll keep it going under the auspices of the Tourist Board—after all, people travel to distant countries to see these tribal ceremonies and dances and, as those up here in the North are as good as any to be found, we might as well make a bit of money out of them.[7]

It is a pity that Paul Hogarth did not draw one of these processions.

While Brendan Behan's island is similar to Sam Thompson's,

---

[4] Behan, *Brendan Behan's Island* (1962), 18.

[5] Ibid. 158.

[6] Sam Thompson (1916–65) had a brilliant but short career in the Ulster theatre: *Over the Bridge* (1957), *The Evangelist* (1963), *Cemented with Love* (1966). Like Behan, he was a controversial, Irish working-class writer, a Northern Protestant, not like Behan a Southern Catholic. See obit. in *The Times*, 16 Feb. 1965, 18a, as well as MacNeice's review of *Over the Bridge* in the *Observer* (31 Jan. 1960), 23.

[7] *Brendan Behan's Island*, 162.

the one that Brian Inglis grew up in was a very different place. It now belongs to history and Dr Inglis, having the gifts of a professional historian, has done a service in preserving it. His first chapter, recounting his early years in Malahide north of Dublin, 'quite a typical English village', is entitled 'Our Set' and is a rather touching, if mildly comic, picture of the unconscious snobbery of the Irish Ascendancy; the golf club where the young Inglis spent much of his time was closed to families 'in trade' and, with a few exceptions, to Catholics. The rest of the book shows the author gradually discovering the other Ireland, the island of 'the Paddies and Bridies'[8] and, we may add, of the Behans. He met with some discomfiture on the way from the time he took a job on the *Irish Times* and, as a reporter, was forced to acknowledge to himself his own ignorance.

As an Anglo-Irishman, Brian Inglis found it difficult to carry out his wish to contribute to the new Ireland. Thus he tried joining the small Irish Labour Party, only to discover that 'all that William Norton and the other party leaders were concerned about was that the branches should not pass any resolutions that might identify the Irish Labour Party with the Labour Government in England; such resolutions might get into the papers, and make people think we were a gang of dangerous socialists'.[9]

Shortly after this, in 1950, he was sent by the Irish News Agency to Strasbourg on the occasion of the Council of Europe Assembly; for sending back a straight story about a debate in which the Irish delegates had bored everyone by 'brandishing the sore thumb',[10] i.e. the Partition issue, he much displeased the delegates, one of whom attached to him the derogatory label 'West Briton'.[11] Much of the interest in this book lies in his very honest and self-searching effort to see how far this label could generally apply to him. 'Paradoxically', he writes, 'the Protestant trying to work his passage away from being regarded as a West Briton was more likely to intrude his Ascendancy habits of mind and speech on the company, without realizing

[8] Inglis, *West Briton* (1962), 30.
[9] Ibid. 135.
[10] Ibid. 141–2.
[11] Ibid. 143.

it.'[12] In the end he seems to have decided that he could not work his passage.

West Briton is packed with information and intelligent comment. We learn, for instance, that the Irish, surrounded by their 'mackerel-crowded seas',[13] eat far less fish than most other civilized nations; Brian Inglis attributes this to the fact that the Catholic Church has made fish-eating appear a penance. And we learn that at the time of the Potato Famine it was difficult for the English to find out what was happening in Ireland because ' "potato" was not considered a polite word in early Victorian England'.[14]

Particularly penetrating is the last chapter, entitled 'Loyalties', where a conclusion is reached which no one should dispute:

If the future relationship of Church and State was sooner or later going to become the most serious political issue in Ireland, this was something that no Protestant or Anglo-Irishman could do much about.[15]

This feeling of political impotence was probably one reason why this book ends with Brian Inglis leaving Ireland. Another was the fact that the *Irish Times*[16] had never paid him a salary. Yet he remembers that peculiar paper with nostalgia and paints a warm portrait of its eccentric editor, the later Robert Smyllie,[17] who, he says, 'had done more, probably, than anybody else to persuade the Irish Unionists . . . to come to terms with the Irish Free State'.[18]

[12] Ibid. 147.

[13] Yeats, 'Sailing to Byzantium', st. 1. 4.

[14] Inglis, 200.

[15] Ibid. 208.

[16] 'Daily newspaper founded by Major Laurence E. Knox in 1859, Ireland's first penny newspaper. The unofficial organ of the (Protestant) Ascendancy for many years, it was bought by Sir John Arnott upon Knox's death in 1873. Its most famous editor (1934–54) was R[obert] M[aire] Smyllie [1893–1954]. Its Unionist attitudes have gradually changed until in more recent years it has become the principal forum for liberal views': D. J. Hickey and J. E. Doherty, *A Dictionary of Irish History since 1800* (1980), 263. Chap. 2 of Inglis's book is devoted to the *Irish Times*.

[17] Smyllie was educated at Sligo Grammar School and Trinity College, Dublin. He 'never believed in the official [Irish] policy of neutrality' during World War II: obit. in *The Times*, 13 Sept. 1954, 8e.

[18] Inglis, 53.

Gael Force at Wembley[1]

June came in like a barbecue of brides and there was I on the
top of Wembley Stadium looking down like one of the Olympians on the sports of the *barbaroi*[2]—

> For they lie beside their nectar, and the bolts are hurl'd
> Far below them in the valleys—[3]

only this time it was the *barbaroi* who were doing the hurling. As
for the nectar, the programme very properly advertised eight
Mooney's Irish Houses in London.[4] And some Irish girl
pipers, nature imitating Dagenham,[5] played 'Come back,
Paddy Reilly, to Ballyjamesduff': appropriately enough, since
that little town is in Cavan, a county which today was challenging Kerry at Gaelic football.[6] Somewhere in the huge stands
which were not more than one-third, or even one-quarter, full
but were at least four-thirds vocal, were a very fine American
actor, Burgess Meredith, and a very fine Irish actor, Jack
MacGowran, both taking time off from rehearsals for a two-
man Eugene O'Neill play about to open in Brighton.[7] When

[1] *New Statesman* 65: 1682 (7 June 1963), 876. Note the pun in the title of the article.

[2] The spectators in position among 'the gods' ('Olympians') look down on the
players below as 'foreigners' (*barbaroi*); there is also ironic word play on the Barbarian
Football Club, the [British] Rugby Union touring club, for which see *OCSG*, 54.

[3] Tennyson, 'The Lotos-Eaters' (1832), Choric Song, st. 8. 12–13. Hurling is an
Irish game resembling both hockey and lacrosse, but played with a broad-bladed,
netless stick.

[4] Irish pubs.

[5] Nature (naturally lively Irish girls) imitating art (a disciplined troop of Dagenham
girl pipers), reversing the familiar saying of Seneca—*Omnis ars naturae imitatio est* (All
art is the imitation of nature), in his *Epistles* lxv. 3—probably in recall of Oscar Wilde's
character Vivian's (devil's advocate) argument that ' "Life" [and therefore "Nature"]
imitates Art far more than Art imitates Life', in 'The Decay of Lying', 3rd last para.,
in *Intentions* (1891).

[6] Gaelic football, 'a fifteen-a-side ball-and-goal game . . . played almost exclusively
in Ireland. . . . The rules include no offside rule, and allow the players to play the ball
both on and off the ground with foot or hand': *OCSG*, 391.

[7] Burgess Meredith (1908–) played Erie Smith and Jack MacGowran (1918–73)
the hotel clerk, in the première of O'Neill's *Hughie* (first produced 1958) on tour in the
UK (with an O'Neill miscellany) in May and June 1963, opening at the Duchess
Theatre, London, 18 June: see *The Times*, 19 June 1963, 5c.

I met them just before the second final whistle (for we had a double bill, Gaelic football first and hurling second) Mr Mac-Gowran was wearing a Tipperary rosette and Mr Meredith, who has no connections with Ireland, a Cork one, Cork not being represented in either of the matches.

Mr Meredith, whom I accompanied many years ago on his first visit to a cricket match, which left him not only emotionally but physically cold, reacted very differently to these Gaelic capers in the heat; in fact they had so inspired him that he contrived, with a cloth cap and an open collar, to look more freshly (if that is the word) arrived from the bogs than the thousands of Irish exiles around him. He commented, correctly, that both these strange games seemed uncommonly fast. As well he might in view of American football with its interminable huddles and blockages. Yet who are we to speak? Latterly rugby has not been much better. Had it not been for the Calcutta Cup match,[8] which reminded us what a beautiful game rugby can be, last season's battles of giant tortoises were enough to convert one to almost any other ball game.

Before we return to the Gaels, who used to prevent the President of the Gaelic League, Mr De Valera, a rugby fan, from visiting Lansdowne Road, headquarters of the Irish Rugby Union, let us consider this present alleged malaise of rugby, notoriously exemplified in this year's match between Scotland and Wales at Murrayfield.[9] Murrayfield is the only centrally heated rugby pitch in the world but this was one kind of frost it could not thaw out. Scotland were determined to win the game defensively by working the touchline and relying on their forwards. But Wales did the same and proved slightly better at it. There was a record number of line-outs and no kind of spectacle. Of course in an international both sides

[8] 'Calcutta Cup, Rugby Union perpetual challenge trophy at issue since 1878 in the annual match between England and Scotland': *OCSG*, 154.

[9] 'Murrayfield, Edinburgh, headquarters and home ground of the Scottish Rugby Union since 1925': ibid. 705. Unexpectedly, 'Scotland [with A. R. Smith of the Edinburgh Wanderers, captain] . . . beat Wales [with Ll. H. Williams of Cardiff, captain] by a goal and a try to a dropped goal in vile weather at Cardiff Arms Park' (Wales 3, Scotland 8): *The Times*, 5 Feb. 1962, 4a. (A[rthur] R[obert] Smith (1933–), wing three-quarter, 'a strong runner and defensive player, . . . made 33 appearances for [Scotland] (a record for a Scottish back) and was captain of the British Lions touring party to South Africa in 1962': *OCSG*, 974.)

rightly play to win and the success of the Springboks' tankman-
ship on their last tour here[10] suggests that a team's best bet
today is to play it tight. So it was not surprising after the
Murrayfield boredom that people once again demanded
changes in the rules. And indeed, if one compares Rugby
Union with Rugby League, a strong case can be made for the
restriction of kicking to touch.[11] On the other hand the conservatives argue that only professionals can be fit enough to play
Rugby League and that amateur players *need* just those stop-
pages which spoil Rugby Union as a spectacle. In view of the
speed of Gaelic football, played entirely by amateurs, this
argument seems a weak one. But, whether any change is made
in the *playing* of rugby or not, it seems high time to reduce the
points awarded for a penalty goal. It has become a common
tactic, when in the enemy's twenty-five, to hold the ball in the
scrum and so entice the opposing wing-forwards into an offside
position: it seems absurd that a penalty goal thus procured
should rate as many points as a try. Here again the Gaels show
more sense. Both in their football and in hurling the goalposts
are H-shaped as in rugby and there are two kinds of score: a
'goal', below the cross-bar, rating three points, and a 'point',
above it, rating one.

Gaelic football, unlike hurling which goes back to the days of
the sagas, is something of a modern ragbag contrived to satisfy
nationalist sentiment. Still, it is a very live ragbag, full of
gibbons, eagles, eels, and all manner of other wrigglers,
leapers, and fliers. But to anyone brought up on rugby, or
American football, a handling game which uses a *round* ball

---

[10] The South African rugby touring team (Springboks: *OCSG*, 984) arrived at
Southampton, mid-Oct. 1960, to challenge UK teams—with their honorary manager
E. W. Bergh and captain A. S. Mahon of the Transvaal—until winding 'up their tour
with a match against [the] Barbarians at Cardiff', 4 Feb. 1961: *The Times*, 15 Oct.
1960, 3e. A Welsh boycott was threatened: ibid., 26 Oct., 7b. The Springboks played
Ireland in Dec.; England, Scotland, and Ulster in Jan.; the Barbarians at Cardiff; see
ibid., 19 Dec. 1960, 3a; 9 Jan. 1961, 5a; 23 Jan., 3e; 30 Jan., 3d; 6 Feb., 3c. They
won every match except the last: see the leading article 'A Broken Record', ibid.,
10 Feb., 13d.
[11] 'Rugby League differs from Rugby Union in the following main particulars:
teams are 13-a-side instead of 15; the scrum consists of 6 forwards instead of 8; a
tackled player is allowed to retain possession of the ball up to a point regulated by the
play-the-ball rule; ground gained by a kick to touch (except from a penalty award)
does not count unless the ball lands in the field of play before crossing the touch-line':
OCSG, 870.

looks rather silly; it also seems most unnatural that the man holding the ball may be obstructed but not tackled. This game has been described as a mixture of rugby and soccer but it also smacks a bit of basketball. And perhaps also of water polo played in the middle air. There is always something happening and the ball is seldom on the ground. That the game is taken very seriously is shown by the fact that Kerry, the champions, flew two men over from America for this match at Wembley. But Irish rugby fans must regret the talent drawn off from their game into the Gaelic variety: they would love to see these leaping Cuchulains let loose in the line-outs.

It must be said that rugby is a better game than Gaelic football. But, to redress the balance, hurling is a far, far better game than hockey. Just one of its many advantages is that the stick has two faces, thus allowing marvellous backhands. It was noticeable at Wembley that the hurling match, which came second, aroused more enthusiasm than its predecessor: my daughter[12] maintained that the noise was different not only in quantity but in quality. It is interesting to speculate how other nationalities would take to this magnificent game. It is played a good deal in the US but almost entirely, I believe, by Irish Americans. On the face of it, it seems as well adapted to the Irish temperament as cricket is to the English, though this does not mean that it is a sort of Donnybrook free-for-all. How one can last a game without having one's skull cracked is a puzzle: it is a puzzle solved by sheer skill. And the accuracy with which players far down the field can hit the ball through the upper part of the H makes one wonder why Irish rugby players are notoriously bad at goal-kicking. On the other hand the Irish, both amateur and professional, are pretty good at golf.

Hurling, said to be (after ice hockey) the second-fastest ball game in the world, is as airborne a sport as you can get outside a gliding club. Half the time the ball is 'a thing enskied and sainted'[13] (I am thinking of those tiny invisible saints) and the players' speed of both eye and hand suggests illusionism or even pagan magic. I have seen Jack MacGowran in a wine bar in Baker Street mime the famous Christy Ring of Cork. He

---

[12] The artist, Corinna Brigid MacNeice (1943–   ).

[13] Lucio to Isabella: 'I hold you as a thing enskied and sainted'—in Shakespeare's *Measure for Measure* I. iv. 34.

swung his non-existent stick (or hurley or caman) and everyone in the bar watched the non-existent ball soar through the wall and away into Regent's Park. But brilliant mime though MacGowran is, this is no more remarkable, and certainly less dangerous, than what a real hurling player does with a real ball. As was demonstrated on this holocaustic First of June when the champions of Ireland, Tipperary, beat the runners-up, Kilkenny. I was reminded of an All Ireland Hurling Final at Croke Park, Dublin, in which, too, if I remember correctly, Kilkenny was playing. Towards the end, when tension was high, there was a real *King Lear* thunder-and-rainstorm. An old woman behind me had been selling bananas; within a minute her stock was pulp. Catharsis, I thought: Aristotle never had it better. It was the 3rd of September, 1939.[14]

[14] Outbreak of World War II, with the declaration of war by Britain and France on this date. Cf. 'Under the Sugar Loaf' (June 1962) above, penult. para.

Great Summer Sale[1]

The isle was full of Garda.[2] In the Black North the Orangemen were so anxious not to discuss the President's visit (he, it was implied, having slighted the Six Counties)[3] that they found themselves reduced to discussing the election of the Pope.[4] The northern Catholics on the other hand, who felt equally slighted, were pondering the Irish Derby.[5] I had lunch in Belfast with a Monsignor, all of whose three brothers are old IRA men, while his mother is the best preserved 93-year-old I have yet met: we talked about modern poetry. And so to Dublin and the bunting and the loud speakers.

In this country, which is not without a record of violence, nobody had ever seen such a display of 'security': Queen Victoria must have been turning in her grave with envy. It was rumoured that for the progress of the 'motorcade' between Dublin Airport and Dublin the Americans, not content with their own 280 security men, had asked for the loan of more native police than the whole Garda Síochána in the Republic could muster.[6] It was also rumoured that the individual who drove behind the President in a car with the door ajar was such a virtuoso that he could jump out while the car was moving at 25 m.p.h., take just two paces and start shooting. Some of the Irish, to start with, were piqued by all this. By the end of the visit, however, they were beginning to feel sorry for the security

---

[1] *New Statesman* 66: 1686 (5 July 1963), 10, 12. The US President John F[itzgerald] Kennedy's (1917–63) European tour to Germany, Ireland, England, and Italy, without visiting Ulster, Scotland, or Wales, included a highly publicized visit to the Irish Republic, 26–28 June, on much of which MacNeice reported here. See *The Times*, 6 May 1963, 10b; 8 June, 10g; 29 June, 8e; 1 July, 9a; 3 July, 9e.

[2] See para. 2 below with n. 6.

[3] Northern Ireland.

[4] Pope John XXIII, who had summoned the Second Vatican Council (1962–5), died 3 June 1963; Pope Paul VI was elected 21 June.

[5] The Irish Sweeps Derby was held the weekend of 29–30 June 1963; the favourite was the colt Relko; the winner, however, was Ragusa: *The Times*, 26 June 1963, 3f; 1 July, 5a.

[6] *An Garda Síochána*, 'The Civil Police' in the Irish Republic: *English-Irish Dictionary*, ed. Tomás de Bhaldraithe (1959), 538.

men. 'The poor fellows!' one said, 'sure they almost forgot themselves and waved. And anyhow, one thing in their favour, they failed in their task, which was to cut him off from humanity.' 'Security men,' another said, 'are like Presbyterian ministers. It takes them some time to relax.'

The first motorcade (an ugly word[7] which we all enjoyed, and which sounds especially good in a low-Dublin adenoidal accent) I watched from the window of a small hotel in Parnell Square: there were several nobs present, including the surviving editor of *The Oxford Book of Irish Verse*.[8] After the vanguard of motor bicycles, Kennedy himself glided past, standing in an open car and looking just like himself but, we were glad to observe, more so. Or more so at least than his many pictures which plastered O'Connell Street as far as the Bridge. Interspersed with the legend 'Cead Mile Failte', which, as Kennedy himself later explained to a Galwegian audience, means '100,000 welcomes'. One large shop said: 'Cead Mile Failte! Great Summer Sale!' A building opposite said: 'Bingo Nightly'. Left behind in the window, we agreed that the man had a presence. Then we made plans for the morrow and how wrong we were.

I turned up, not too sharp, with my friend D.B.[9] to keep an appointment 'at 8 a.m. sharp' outside Jury's Hotel in College Green: we were to be driven in a high-powered car to the ancestral Kennedy territory in New Ross, Co. Wexford, nearly 100 miles away.[10] But our driver had overslept. After waiting half an hour D.B. said: 'Let's go to the Gresham, we'll get it all fixed there.' We went to a bedroom in the Gresham and found one heavy-lidded American reporter and one heavy-lidded American cameraman. They were wearing aggressive pyjamas. We asked for seats in a helicopter, but they said that couldn't be and offered us a drink instead. Keeping up with the President, they explained, was tiring—well, kind of tiring. Now the German visit, they said, they could see the point of that—kind

---

[7] The word 'motorcade' was introduced into American English 1913; into British English 1924: *OED2*.

[8] The surviving editor was Donagh MacDonagh (1912–68); his co-editor E. S. Lennox Robinson (1886–1958) had died 5 years before. The full title reads: *The Oxford Book of Irish Verse, 17th Century–20th Century* (1958).

[9] An Irish friend, probably Dominic Behan (1928–   ).

[10] Due S. of Dublin, on St George's Channel.

of high policy and strategy and things—but this Irish trip—
they'd gotten the idea the President was out to enjoy himself. It
would be nice to have time off, they said, but sooner in Frank-
furt than in Dublin: 'What the hell can a man do in Dublin?'

They left to catch their helicopter and we went downstairs
and got a breakfast-time drink. An Irishman connected with
the Press Centre began to give us the dope. 'A hundred and
four of their own,' he said, 'and about 70 foreign reporters.
And would you believe it, last night when he arrived, there
were only four messages went out through the Centre. The
boys had pre-filed their stories. It's only natural of course.'
D.B. looked up contemplatively at a huge chandelier. 'D'ya
know,' he said, 'that thing has 96 pieces missing.' 'How do you
know?' we naturally asked. 'Because,' he said, 'I was employed
one time to wash it. Ammonia it was we washed it with and we
had to take it apart. Well, when we came to put it together
again, there were these 96 pieces that just wouldn't fit.' And
he sang:

> We had wine, porter, and Jameson,
> We had cocktails and cocoa and all . . .

Somebody else said: 'Isn't it terrible hard on John Fitzgerald
Kennedy that he has to be tethered all the time to the telephone?
Even up there in his helicopter sittin' at his walnut writing
desk. But that's the American constitution. Suppose now some
place like Alabama was to forget itself? Wherever he was, say
at his cousin Mrs Ryan's in Dunganstown,[11] he'd have to quell
the problem from there.'

The official hand-out had said: '12 noon Lounge Suit
Thursday, June 27. President Kennedy arrives at Kennedy
homestead, Dunganstown, where he will be a guest at a tea
given by Mrs Mary Ryan . . . She has invited 13 other distant
relatives to the tea.' We missed it, of course, and the following
day's visit to Cork—where the Radio Eireann commentator
was so carried away, so his colleagues tell me, by the rapturous
crowd that, remembering his race meetings, he said: 'President
Kennedy is now well out in front.'

---

[11] See photo in *The Times*, 28 June 1963, 14c–d, of Kennedy having tea with his
distant cousin Mrs Mary Ryan of Dunganstown, Co. Wexford. Dunganstown is near
the W. border of Co. Wexford, due W. of the capital Wexford.

Instead, I got in a train for Galway and read the papers. The Irish *Evening Herald* said helpfully in a special article: 'The role of the President in the USA falls somewhere between that of An t-Uachtaran and the Taoiseach in Ireland.'[12] In the same number were tributes in verse that reminded one that Ireland could always hold her own with England in the broadsheet class:

> Heaven direct you safely, and guide you and yours on
>   an even keel,
> Never has America had one like you before, you have
>   great appeal . . .
> Never despondent, never depressed, never ill at ease;
> Nicely illustrating true manhood in the skies, on land,
>   and on seas.

While I was indulging myself with such light reading in the train, Kennedy was laying a wreath on the graves of the 1916 martyrs,[13] addressing a joint sitting of the Houses of Parliament and receiving honorary degrees from both University and Trinity Colleges.[14] Of the latter (so long regarded as a Protestant and Saxon garrison) an old man said to me that evening: 'I've just had a terrible shock listening to the radio—beautiful Latin pouring out, better even than you hear from the priests, and, would you believe it, it was Trinity College, Dublin!'

In Galway, Your Man, as they would call him, came down again from the overcast skies, and at last I heard him speak. But not till several dignitaries had spoken at length in the Gaelic. Kennedy replied in the English and did it with wit and charm. Something like this, as he pointed towards Galway Bay: 'If the day were a little bit clearer and you went down there and your eyesight was good enough, you would see Boston, Massachusetts, and all your relatives working there.' The crowd liked this very much. I decided that Your Man was a fine showman, but also, and more important, happy to be

---

[12] 'Between that of "The President" and the "Prime Minister" in Ireland': *English-Irish Dictionary* (1959), 549, 552.

[13] Burial plot in Glasnevin (officially titled Prospect) Cemetery, Dublin.

[14] On 28 June Kennedy 'received the honorary degrees of Doctor of Laws of the National University from Mr [Eamon] de Valera' (1882–1975), the university chancellor, and of (Trinity College) 'Dublin University, from Lord Rosse' (6th Earl of Rosse, L. M. H. Parsons, 1906–79): *The Times*, 29 June 1963, 8e.

there. *Of course* this was a sentimental visit: you can't have power politics all the time.

When he had helicoptered away I walked round the capital of the Gaeltacht to look at the decorations. Two of them I found original. The usual brace of flags but apparently made of rough bathroom towelling: I crossed the street and found they were made of carnations, all except the stars in Old Glory which were made of cornflowers. But what about the yellows and greens in the tricolour? 'Ah, those ones are dyed,' said the girl in the flower-shop; 'anyhow they're all imported from Holland.' A little further on, in Dominick Street Lower, there was a window full of toys and among them a donkey with a creel of turf on each side of him; out of one stuck the Stars and Stripes and out of the other the Tricolour. But the point was this was a mechanized donkey: he kept nodding his head, but very slowly, like an oriental holy man. It was only later that I remembered that in the US the donkey is the emblem of the Democratic Party.

'Go on!' I said to myself. 'Can't *you* ever say Yes too?' When I got back to Dublin a Dubliner said to me: 'I hope you're not going to send this whole thing up.' When a Dubliner says that, it means his heart has for once got in front of his mind. Well out in front, like the President himself.

Autobiographical Talk: Childhood Memories

[I've been asked to give a few reminiscences of my childhood, in Carrickfergus. I'm afraid I've not written these out, so don't expect the exact word. But I hope it'll be interesting for subject matter. Now,] although my earliest memories are of Carrickfergus, I was, in fact, born in Belfast. But my father was appointed rector of Carrickfergus when I was still almost an infant. My first memories are, in fact, of living in a house which was not a rectory, which we couldn't enter at the time because the retiring rector was still there on his deathbed. So we were put in a house that looked over the harbour. I still have [for this reason] an affection for this really rather drab-looking harbour. [It was very muddy and a rather peculiar shape. But I remember very well there were three piers: two great long ones, the one on the right-hand side we knew as a coal pier, because it was black with coal dust, and the one on the left-hand side was a salt pier, because in those days they used to export salt from the salt mines; this has long since finished, but you had the black pier and the glycerine pier—and then, at right angles to the salt pier, or before you came to the salt pier proper, was the pier King William landed at, which was a

---

¹ This unscripted talk was pre-recorded by MacNeice for his friend John Boyd at BBC Belfast, 2 July 1963, and later posthumously broadcast in the Third Programme, 29 Nov. (MacNeice died of pneumonia 3 Sept.). The transcription under the title 'Autobiographical Talk' is now housed at the BBC Written Archives Centre, Reading. It was cut and re-titled 'Childhood Memories' for publication in the *Listener* 70: 1811 (12 Dec. 1963), 990, by the literary editor K. W. Gransden (1925-   ), successor to J. R. Ackerley (retired 1959). (For Gransden, see Ackerley, *The Letters*, ed. Neville Braybrooke (1975), 142, 157, 163.) The complete talk is printed here to give some sense of MacNeice's speaking voice and to include further details of biographical and historical interest. Square brackets indicate those portions cut for publication in the *Listener*. Cf. MacNeice's earlier childhood reminiscences in *Strings*, 1940–1, chaps. 4–9, 36–63, and in the poems 'Carrickfergus' (1937) and 'Carrick Revisited' (1945) in *Collected Poems*, 69–70, 224–5.

glamorous piece of history impressed on me very strongly at a very early date.]²

[Now,] a[n odd] thing that I remember about living in that house was—[of course there were far more] sailing boats on Belfast Lough [in those days—and] these affected me in quite a sentimental way: almost 'red sails in the sunset'.³ And, for some odd reason, [some sort of] a, perhaps, Jungian archetypal reason, I assumed that these sailing boats were moving in a westward direction, which meant going towards the head of the Lough, towards Belfast itself, would be going on forever in that direction, like Columbus. I didn't realize, being only about 2 or 3, that the Lough came to an end and they couldn't sail on forever. [And I always found it extremely exciting to watch these little boats. However, I don't know how long we lived there, I only remember very few other details about it, such as a very old-fashioned red rope bell pull, dangling beside the bed. And there was a coal yard, somewhere in the back, which made a great deal of noise.]

[But] in due course, we moved into the rectory; [and I remember we had been taken up several times to see the rectory, or at any rate the garden, before we moved in. And] the first time I ever saw a lot of apple trees in blossom was there, and it made a terrific impact on me. A lot of these things I have woven into poems here and there. [Anyhow, the second house, which is] the rectory, was a red-brick house [with the whole ground on which it stands, garden, the whole lot is about an acre]—not, in fact, architecturally very beautiful; and it was not an old house, but it was [of course, being one's own house,] the centre of a great deal of mythology—private mythology—which still affects me in dreams. I quickly gave names to every corner of the garden; every little clump of shrubbery was given its special name. And there were all sorts of fantasies my sister⁴

---

² 'On the old pier below the castle walls, William of Orange landed with a Dutch and English Army. He was proclaimed King in the ancient Parish Church, sitting in a chair that is still preserved in the nave': Denis O'D. Hanna, *The Face of Ulster* (1952), 46—a book reviewed by MacNeice in 'About Ireland' (May 1952), above.

³ English popular song 1935 (words: James Kennedy; music: Will Grosz) which also became very popular in the USA.

⁴ (Caroline) Elizabeth, Lady Nicholson (1903–81). For an account of MacNeice at her wedding (autumn 1928), see *Strings*, 118, para. 1 of chap. 22. Cf. her account of their childhood in Carrickfergus, 'Trees Were Green', *Time Was Away* (1974), 11–20.

and I wove around it. [As I say, I lived there from then until I grew up.]

My sister was a good deal older than me, but we did a lot of playing together. We didn't really meet [very] many other children when I was small. In fact, we didn't meet so [very] many other people at all—we were rather sequestered, and I think sometimes, probably, very lonely. [But,] in a way this, of course, encouraged one to develop one's imagination. But [the few people,] the few regulars, the people who worked for the house, became very important *dramatis personae*. There was a wonderful cook we had, who, in fact, I now realize was only in her teens, but of course I thought of her as quite old. She came from County Tyrone, and she was a Catholic. Another woman [who worked], described as a 'mother's help', was a Calvinist, and, between them, they made for very lively conversation in the kitchen, where I spent a great deal of my time. The one from County Tyrone had a number of ghost stories and rather racy line of talk. [She was the first person I heard mention John Jameson[5]—bit of advertising. There sometimes were arguments, of course nearly always on religious and political grounds, but it was all great fun in the kitchen.]

We also had a most remarkable, ancient, very rheumatic gardener, called Archie White, of whom I have very fond recollections. He was regarded very much as a 'character', he was illiterate, he was a passionate Orangeman, and he was a great [kind of a] one for the make-believe. In fact, he was ideal company for someone about the age of 5 or 6 or 7. Across the garden hedge, at the far end, there was a graveyard[;] and [there was] the hawthorn hedge, [and it] used to be allowed to grow up quite high; and then he would cut it, which was a very cumbersome process as, because of his rheumatism, he had to rig up a huge contraption with a step-ladder at one end and boxes at the other, and a great long plank laid across them, and he would, very slowly, move along this plank, cutting the hedge. When he cut the hedge that divided us from the grave-yard, in my earliest days I found this very frightening because there were two or three sorts of obelisks made of shining grey, I suppose Aberdeen granite, and these would be obscured

---

[5] An Irish whiskey.

when the hedge was high. But, when he cut it, you would see their heads looking over, and the old gardener used to treat them himself in his talk [and] he would say, 'look at that oul' fellow, there.' And sometimes he would take up his stick and pretend to shoot him, shoot the obelisk. And I took this, to start with, rather seriously—I really [couldn't,] didn't like the look of these granite creatures at all.

There were a number of very exciting things to go and see in Carrick. In particular, as my father was the Church of Ireland rector, there was the church, which, whether one liked it or not, one had to go to from an early age. In fact, I liked it, because the Church of St Nicholas, [as you know,] in Carrickfergus, is one of the most historic churches in the country and it has all sorts of quaint things about it which I like to ponder on.[6]

At the same time, on my earliest visits to the church there were things in it that frightened me. There's a transept called the Chichester Transept[7] on the north side, up some steps. The rector's pew was put in such a position, where the arms of the cross met, that from our pew you couldn't see this properly when you were sitting down, but when you were standing up, you could. And, if you looked, you would see, high up, this huge Elizabethan monument to the Chichesters; but above this, right up under the roof, on one side there was an old coat-of-arms hanging—and, again, I thought of this anthropomorphically. I thought of this coat-of-arms as a sort of evil man, looking at me, and whenever I had to stand up, I tried not to look in that direction, but some compulsion came over me and I always did.

I was between two fires[8] because, on the other side, looking up towards the chancel, a bit to the right, there was a reading desk and behind that there was a pew, and in this pew every Sunday morning there used to be a rich old lady who was a widow. [In fact, I know very well who she was—needn't go

---

[6] For another account of Carrickfergus Parish Church, see Hanna, 46–7, with a para. on MacNeice near the top of 47.

[7] For the Arthurs Chichester—the Lord Chichester of Belfast (1563–1625) and the first Earl of Donegal (1606–75), both governors of Carrickfergus and both buried in Carrickfergus Parish Church, see *DNB*. Cf. MacNeice's poem 'Carrickfergus', st. 5: 'I was the rector's son, born to the anglican order, | Banned for ever from the candles of the Irish poor; | The Chichesters knelt in marble at the end of a transept | With ruffs about their necks, their portion sure.'

[8] i.e. between two discharges of fire-arms: *OED*, 'fire' *v*.[14].

into that.] And [when she was sitting down,] when we were sitting down I couldn't see her because the reading desk screened her. But when she got up, I could see her. Now she, in fact, was [a very composed and] in every way an able old lady, but she always dressed in an old-fashioned widow's weeds, completely in black, and in my simple-minded way at that age, I assumed this meant she must be blind. I had an absolutely sort of savage, primitive fear of blindness for some reason. There were some real blind people one used to meet around Carrick, and I was always scared when I met them; I thought, [so to speak,] because their eyes were sightless, they were also evil, that they could put a kind of evil spell on one. [So those are the frightening things about the church but, as I say, I enjoyed it too, and I very much enjoyed my father reading the lesson because, unlike many Anglican clergymen I came across since, he could deliver the English language with rhythm and dignity.]

[Then, of course, there was also the Castle which was very exciting and which is, as you know, one of the best preserved Norman castles in these islands.[9] We were only taken over it once and away, but it was a great expedition.]

[Then we were taken for walks and, at one time, the lady who took us for walks got in her head we mustn't go through the town because the town was full of germs and we'd catch something. So, that period was rather boring, for you always did the same walks every day—up the same road which led, if you went far enough, to Lough Mourne, which was an exciting lake because it had legends attached to it.]

There were various houses we used to visit: [a couple of big houses, you know, the sort of house with loggias and that was all very glamorous indeed; and some other] one just up the road, that was a smallish house where a widow lived. She had a live parrot to whom I wrote an ode at about the age of seven; and a stuffed monkey to whom I wrote another ode, beginning, 'Oh, monkey, though now thou art stuffed | Thou hast very often roughed | A night out in the wild forest.'[10] It had to be

---

9 For Carrickfergus castle, see Hanna, 47, with mention of MacNeice; photograph in fig. 24 facing 45.

10 For the poem on a live parrot, see MacNeice's *Modern Poetry*, 39–40; his 'Ode to a Stuffed Monkey' is quoted in *Zoo*, 69; for both odes see also *Strings*, 59.

pronounced for-*est* because it was going to rhyme with something. The parrot ode was rather a neat job of work, I think.

This writing of odes reminds me that while, in a way, my childhood was rather lonely, [and incidentally, at one period I had a lot of nightmares and all that, there are various unhappy things in the background; on the other hand] this loneliness did encourage one to read a lot. My father had a great many books, not all to my taste, I must admit. Very early on, in the stock way, I fell, like so many little boys, for Macaulay's 'Lays of Ancient Rome', which was in a book by itself.[11] And then I thought, 'Well, this man Macaulay is the tops. I must see if my father has any more by him.' And, sure enough, he had two great volumes of collected essays.[12] So I started in on Macaulay's account of the trial of Warren Hastings.[13] This is when I had only been able to read for about a year. I'm afraid I didn't get through it.

Apart from all that, there were several public events which made a great impact on me as a small child, one of the very earliest ones being the maiden trip of the *Titanic*,[14] which I actually saw passing down the Lough. And then, of course, the outbreak of World War I, when I was getting on for 7. [And] that I was very conscious of, because of the huge camp of soldiers just across the way from us, in a place called Sunnylands, which is now, I think, a housing estate. [But] we used to hear these soldiers practising, [we used to] see them doing

[11] T. B. Macaulay's (1800–59) *Lays of Ancient Rome* (1842) included such famous ballads as 'Horatius' on the defence of the bridge to Rome against the Tuscans.

[12] *Critical and Historical Essays, Contributed to the Edinburgh Review*, 2 vols. (1856, many edns; Everyman 2-vol. edn, 1907).

[13] Macaulay's long essay 'Warren Hastings' (Oct. 1841) reviewed 'three big bad volumes, full of undigested correspondence and undiscerning panegyric', i.e. Revd G. R. Gleig's 3-vol. edn *Memoirs of the Life of Warren Hastings, First Governor-General of Bengal* (1841). Macaulay wrote from personal experience of service in India: 'His famous Minutes on Law and Education had a decisive influence on the development of the sub-continent': *OCEL*, 5th edn, 598.

[14] The famous British luxury passenger liner the RMS *Titanic* sank on 14–15 April 1912, on her maiden voyage, after she struck an iceberg about 95 miles S. of the Grand Banks of Newfoundland. 1,522 lives were lost. The wreck was discovered 1 Sept. 1985, more than two miles deep, by Robert D. Ballard of Woods Hole Oceanographic Institution and a joint US-French expedition—reported by Ballard in 'How we Found *Titanic*', *National Geographic Magazine*, 168 (Dec. 1985), 696–719. A return trip the next summer yielded dramatic colour photographs by Ballard and Bowen in Ballard's 'A Long Last Look at *Titanic*', op. cit. 170 (Dec. 1986), 698–727. The full story is told in Ballard's *The Discovery of the* Titanic: *Exploring the Greatest of All Lost Ships*, illus. (1987).

bayonet practice, and we were very conscious of their presence all through the war. [Incidentally, there were some soldiers even living in Carrickfergus Castle during that war. This, of course, has long since stopped, but, in a way, I rather regret it, although the Castle, museum-wise as they say, is much better now. But it was rather nice that people should still be using it for some practical purpose.]

The war years themselves were, I suppose, what they call, for me formative years. I was much more conscious by the end, naturally, than by the beginning, because during the war my mother died, towards the end of the war my father married again, and before it was finished, I was sent to school in England, which, [naturally,] for me, marked the end of a period.

A Bibliography of Short Prose
by Louis MacNeice[1]

'The Story of the "Great Triobal Clan" as Created by Mr Schinabel', *Marlburian* 59: 854 (23 Oct. 1924), 135-6.

'The Four Ends of the World', *Marlburian* 60: 860 (28 May 1925), 65-6.

'The Devil' [Mr Schinabel, Part 2], *Marlburian* 60: 863 (22 Oct. 1925), 117-18.

'Windows in the Ink' [Mr Schinabel, Part 3], *Marlburian* 61: 867 (10 March 1926), 34-5.

'Jam of Aganippe', *Marlburian* 61: 868 (29 March 1926), 54.

'Apollo on the Old Bath Road (A School Serial)' I-II, *Marlburian* 61: 869 (26 May 1926), 65.

'Miss Ambergris & King Perhaps', *Marlburian* 61: 869 (26 May 1926), 66-7.

'Apollo on the Old Bath Road' II-V, *Marlburian* 61: 870 (23 June 1926), 90-1.

'Apollo on the Old Bath Road' VI-X, *Marlburian* 61: 871 (26 July 1926), 118-19.

'Fires of Hell', *Cherwell*, NS, 18: 7 (4 Dec. 1926), 251.

Collected Poems, by James Stephens; *Transition*, by Edwin Muir, *Cherwell* 18: 8 (11 Dec. 1926), 329.

Autobiographies, by W. B. Yeats; *Human Bits*, by Hildegarde Hume Hamilton, *Cherwell* 19: 1 (29 Jan. 1927), 28.

Christopher Marlowe, by U. M. Ellis Fermor, *Cherwell* 19: 4 (19 Feb. 1927), 129.

A Drunk Man Looks at the Thistle, by Hugh MacDiarmid, *Cherwell* 19: 6 (5 March 1927), 168.

Duncan Dewar's Accounts: A Student of St Andrew's 100 Years Ago, *Cherwell* 20: 3 (21 May 1927), 88.

'The Front Door of Ivory', *Cherwell* 20: 6 (11 June 1927), 185-6.

---

[1] Items from the *Marlburian* were verified by John Hilton, Anthony Blunt, and the Marlborough librarian E. G. H. Kempson; those from *Radio Times*, *London Calling*, and *Time & Tide* were researched in the main by Martin Lubowski of London; one item from the *Morning Post* (on Stephen MacKenna) and one from the *Observer* (on Sam Thompson) were discovered by Dr Peter McDonald of Cambridge; and one item from the *Observer* (on the novel in general, Sept. 1954) by David Pascoe of Oxford.

'American Universities (as gathered from *The Michigan Daily*, 8 pages, price 5 cents)', *Cherwell* 20: 8 (25 June 1927), 230.

The Enormous Room, by E. E. Cummings, *Oxford Outlook* 10: 47 (Nov. 1928), 171–3.

The Venture, edited by Anthony Blunt, H. Romilly Fedden, and Michael Redgrave: No. 1, Cambridge, Nov. 1928, *Oxford Outlook* 10: 47 (Nov. 1928), 184–5.

The Trial of Socrates, by Coleman Phillipson, *University News* (Oxford) 1: 7 (1 Dec. 1928), 253.

'Garlon and Galahad', *Sir Galahad* 1: 1 (21 Feb. 1929), 15.

'Foreword' to his *Blind Fireworks* (London: Gollancz, March 1929), 5–6.

'Our God Bogus', *Sir Galahad* 2 (14 May 1929), 3–4.

Poems, by W. H. Auden, *Oxford Outlook* 11: 52 (March 1931), 59–61.

The Lysis [by Plato], translated by K. A. Matthews and illustrated by Lynton Lamb, *Oxford Outlook* 11: 55 (June 1931), 146–7.

Deserted House—a Poem-Sequence, by Dorothy Wellesley; *Dear Judas*, by Robinson Jeffers; *This Experimental Life*, by Royall Snow; *The Signature of Pain*, by Alan Porter, *Oxford Outlook* 11: 55 (June 1931), 147–9.

'Miss Riding's "Death"' (*The Life of the Dead*, by Laura Riding), *New Verse*, no. 6 (Dec. 1933), 18–20.

'Poems by Edwin Muir' (*Variations on a Time Theme*, by Edwin Muir), *New Verse*, no. 9 (June 1934), 18, 20.

Reply to 'An Enquiry', *New Verse*, no. 11 (Oct. 1934), 2, 7.

The Domain of Selfhood, by R. V. Feldman, *Criterion* 14: 54 (Oct. 1934), 160–3.

'Greek Classical Writers' (*A History of Classical Greek Literature*, by T. A. Sinclair), *Spectator* 154: 5559 (11 Jan. 1935), 58–9.

'Plato on Knowledge' (*Plato's Theory of Knowledge*, by F. M. Cornford), *Spectator* 154: 5571 (5 April 1935), 575–6.

'A Comment' [on G. M. Hopkins], *New Verse*, no. 14 (Hopkins Issue: April 1935), 26–7.

'A Brief for Cicero' (*Cicero: A Study*, by G. C. Richards), *Spectator* 154: 5574 (26 April 1935), 700.

'Modern Writers and Beliefs' (*The Destructive Element*, by Stephen Spender), *Listener* 13: 330 (8 May 1935), suppl. xiv.

'Translating Aeschylus' (Aeschylus: *The Seven Against Thebes*, translated by Gilbert Murray), *Spectator* 154: 5576 (10 May 1935), 794.

'Plato Made Easy' (*The Argument of Plato*, by F. H. Anderson), *Spectator* 155: 5584 (5 July 1935), 28.

'Fata Vocant' (*Religion in Virgil*, by Cyril Bailey), *Spectator* 155: 5589 (9 Aug. 1935), 231–2.

'Mr Empson as a Poet' (*Poems*, by William Empson), *New Verse*, no. 16 (Aug.–Sept. 1935), 17–18.

'Poetry To-day', *The Arts To-Day*, edited by Geoffrey Grigson (6 Sept. 1935), 25–67.

'On All Souls' Night' (*The Dark Glass*, by March Cost; *The Lion Beats the Unicorn*, by Norah C. James; *Don Segundo Sombra*, by Ricardo Guiraldes; *Richard Savage*, by Gwyn Jones), *Morning Post*, 10 Sept. 1935, 14.

'Town and Country in America' (*Summer in Williamsburg*, by Daniel Fuchs; *He Sent Forth a Raven*, by Elizabeth Madox Roberts; *Two Walk Together*, by Barbara Cooper; *The Collected Ghost Stories of Oliver Onions*), *Morning Post*, 17 Sept. 1935, 14.

'The Russian Mind and Plato: A Curious Blend' (*Plato*, by Vladimir Solovyev), *Morning Post*, 20 Sept. 1935, 14.

'A Story of the "Wrong Generation"' (*A Life's Journey*, by Hermynia Zur Muhlen; *Idle Hands*, by Edward Charles; *Derby and Joan*, by Maurice Baring; *Blow for Balloons*, by W. J. Turner), *Morning Post*, 24 Sept. 1935, 14.

'The Modern Short Story: Too Much Restraint, Too Little Verve' (*The Best Short Stories, 1935*, edited by E. J. O'Brien; *Moving Pageant*, by L. A. Pavey; *Round Up*, by Ring W. Lardner; *15 Odd Stories*, by Shane Leslie), *Morning Post*, 1 Oct. 1935, 14.

'Strange Tale of a Bad Hat: Mr Thompson's Novel of Nonconformity' (*Nottke the Thief*, by Sholem Asch; *It Cannot be Stormed*, by Ernest von Salomon; *Introducing the Arnisons*, by Edward Thompson; *Odd John*, by Olaf Stapledon), *Morning Post*, 8 Oct. 1935, 14.

'Mr David Garnett's Tale of a Tramp' (*Beaney-Eye*, by David Garnett; *River Niger*, by Simon Jesty; *Portrait of the Bride*, by Betty Miller; *On Approval*, by Dorothy Whipple), *Morning Post*, 15 Oct. 1935, 16.

'Another Tolstoy and His Fine Novel' (*Darkness and Dawn*, by Alexei Tolstoy; *Life Begins*, by Christa Winsloe; *Tomorrow is Also a Day*, by Romilly Cavan; *Hallelujah Chorus*, by Chris Massie), *Morning Post*, 29 Oct. 1935, 14.

'Sinclair Lewis Imagines Fascism in America' (*It Can't Happen Here*, by Sinclair Lewis; *The Asiatics*, by Frederic Prokosch; *Once We Had a Child*, by Hans Fallada), *Morning Post*, 5 Nov. 1935, 16.

'"The Green Child" and Another Poet's Novel' (*The Green Child*, by Herbert Read; *King Coffin*, by Conrad Aiken; *Girl of Good Family*, by Lucian Wainwright; *Cut and Come Again*, by H. E. Bates), *Morning Post*, 12 Nov. 1935, 14.

'Charlatan-Chasing: How We Live and How We Think: A World-Famous Book Translated' (*The Mind and Society*, by Vilfredo Pareto: edited by Arthur Livingston), *Morning Post*, 15 Nov. 1935, 6.

'The American World, and a Tale from Trinidad' (*Eclipse*, by Dalton Trumbo; *The Sun Sets in the West*, by Myron Brinig; *Quagmire*, by Henry K. Marks; *Black Fauns*, by Alfred H. Mendes), *Morning Post*, 19 Nov. 1935, 15.

'A Vast Novel Which Is Not a Bore' (*Summer Time Ends*, by John Hargrave; *Deep Dark River*, by Robert Ryles; *Out for a Million*, by V. Krymov; *Dust Over the Ruins*, by Helen Ashton), *Morning Post*, 26 Nov. 1935, 14.

'Ireland—a Tragic, Realistic Presentation' (*Holy Ireland*, by Norah Hoult; *Till She Stoop*, by Morna Stuart; *Swami and Friends*, by R. J. Narayan; *Tortilla Flat*, by John Steinbeck), *Morning Post*, 3 Dec. 1935, 14.

'Plato and Platonists' (*Plato's Thought*, by G. M. A. Grube; *Plato*, by Vladimir Solovyev), *Spectator* 155: 5608 (20 Dec. 1935), 1037-8.

'Some Notes on Mr Yeats' Plays', *New Verse*, no. 18 (Dec. 1935), 7-9.

Letter, in reply to St John Ervine's articles 'Our Peevish Poets' [in preceding issues], *Observer* 7549 (2 Feb. 1936), 13.

The Achievement of T. S. Eliot, by F. O. Mathiessen [unsigned review], *Listener* 15: 372 (26 Feb. 1936), 414.

'The Newest Yeats' (*A Full Moon in March*, by W. B. Yeats), *New Verse*, no. 19 (Feb.-March 1936), 16.

Lysistrata, Aristophanes: *A new English version by Reginald Beckwith and Andrew Cruickschank* (Gate), *Time & Tide* 17: 12 (21 March 1936), 422.

'Sir Thomas Malory', *The English Novelists*, ed. Derek Verschoyle (30 April 1936), 17-28.

'The Passionate Unbeliever' (*Lucretius, Poet and Philosopher*, by E. E. Sikes), *Spectator* 156: 5628 (8 May 1936), 846.

'Fiction' (*I'd Do It Again*, by Frank Tilsley; *The Queen's Doctor*, by Robert Neumann; *Overture, Beginners!*, by John Moore; *A Week by the Sea*, by Bryan Guiness; *To the Mountain*, by Bradford Smith; *Please Don't Smile*, by Johann Rabener), *Spectator* 156: 5631 (29 May 1936), 994.

Collected Poems, 1909-1935, by T. S. Eliot [unsigned review], *Listener* 15: 388 (17 June 1936), 1175.

Longinus on the Sublime, by Frank Granger, *Criterion* 15: 61 (July 1936), 697-9.

'Fiction' (*Farewell Romance*, by Gilbert Frankau; *Standing Room Only*, by Walter Greenwood; *Fifty Roads to Town*, by Frederick Nebel; *Spring Storm*, by Alvin Johnson; *Rising Tide*, by Elisaveta Fen), *Spectator* 157: 5639 (24 July 1936), 156.

Love's Labour's Lost (Old Vic), *Time & Tide* 17: 38 (19 Sept. 1936), 1294.

Charles the King, Charles Colbourne (Lyric), *Time & Tide* 17: 42 (17 Oct. 1936), 1458.

Plot Twenty-One, Ronald Ackland (Embassy), *Time & Tide* 17: 43 (24 Oct. 1936), 1494.

Dramatis Personae, by W. B. Yeats, *Criterion* 16: 62 (Oct. 1936), 120–2.

'Preface', *The Agamemnon of Aeschylus*, translated by MacNeice (Oct. 1936), 7–9.

'Translator's Note' [on production of his Aeschylus' *Agamemnon*], theatre programme, Westminster Theatre, 1 and 8 Nov. 1936.

Till the Cows Come Home, Geoffrey Kerr, *Time & Tide* 17: 45 (7 Nov. 1936), 1562.

'The "Agamemnon" of Aeschylus' [letter, in reply to reviewer of Group Theatre production], *The Times*, 12 Nov. 1936, 10c.

Muted Strings, Arthur Watkyn (Daly's), *Time & Tide* 17: 46 (14 Nov. 1936), 1616.

Letter [on review of *Agamemnon* production on 7 Nov.], *Time & Tide* 17: 47 (21 Nov. 1936), 1632.

The Housemaster, Ian Hay (Apollo), *Time & Tide* 17: 47 (21 Nov. 1936), 1646.

'Extracts from a Dialogue on the Necessity for an Active Tradition and Experiment' [by Louis MacNeice and Rupert Doone], *Group Theatre Paper*, no. 6 (Dec. 1936), 3–5.

'Stephen MacKenna: A Writer Who Had the Courage of His Instincts' (*Journals and Letters of Stephen MacKenna*, edited with a memoir by E. R. Dodds), *Morning Post*, 4 Dec. 1936, 19.

'Letter from Louis MacNeice', *Cherwell* 48: 8 (5 Dec. 1936), 190.

Look, Stranger! Poems, by W. H. Auden [unsigned review], *Listener* 16: 416 (30 Dec. 1936), 1257.

'Subject in Modern Poetry', *Essays and Studies* by Members of the English Association, coll. Helen Darbishire, 22, [Dec.] 1936 (1937), 144–58.

'A Parable' [concl. to 'A Dialogue' in preceding number], *Group Theatre Paper*, no. 7 (Jan. 1937), 2–3.

Your Number's Up, Diana Morgan, Robert MacDermot, and Geoffrey Wright (Gate), *Time & Tide* 18: 1 (2 Jan. 1937), 24.

'Pax Romana' (*The Cambridge Ancient History*, volume xi: *The Imperial (Peace)*, *Spectator* 158: 5663 (8 Jan. 1937), 54–5.

'Jean Cocteau in English' (*The Infernal Machine*, by Jean Cocteau: English Version and Introductory Essay by Carl Wildman), *London Mercury* 35: 208 (Feb. 1937), 430–1.

'Fiction' (*Invasion '14*, by Maxence van der Meersch: translated by

Gerard Hopkins; *Three Bags Full*, by Roger Burlinghame; *The Sisters*, by Myron Brinig; *The Porch*, by Richard Church; *Olive E*, by C. H. B. Kitchin; *Women Also Dream*, by Ethel Mannin; *Spring Horizon*, by T. C. Murray), *Spectator* 158: 5669 (19 Feb. 1937), 330.

'Fiction' (*Devil Take the Hindmost*, by Frank Tilsley; *One Life, One Kopeck*, by Walter Duranty; *The Other Side*, by Stephen Hudson; *The Moon in the South*, by Carl Zuckmayer; *Hallelujah, I'm a Bum*, by Louis Paul; *Perilous Sanctuary*, by D. J. Hall), *Spectator* 158: 5671 (5 March 1937), 422.

'Fiction' (*Very Heaven*, by Richard Aldington; *Time to be Going*, by R. H. Mottram; *The Dance Goes On*, by Louis Golding; *The Picnic*, by Martin Boyd; *At Last We Are Alone*, by F. Sladen-Smith; *The Tomato-Field*, by Stuart Engstrand), *Spectator* 158: 5673 (19 March 1937), 550, 552.

'Fiction' (*A Trojan Ending*, by Laura Riding; *Spanish Fire*, by Hermann Kesten; *Golden Peacock*, by Gertrude Atherton; *Maiden Castle*, by John Cowper Powys; *A Bridge to Divide Them*, by Goronwy Rees; *The Paradoxes of Mr Pond*, by G. K. Chesterton), *Spectator* 158: 5675 (2 April 1937), 632.

The Tobacco Road, Jack Kirkland: *Based on the novel by Erskine Caldwell* (Gate), *Time & Tide* 18: 22 (29 May 1937), 738.

'The Bradfield Greek Play: *Oedipus Tyrannus*', *Spectator* 158: 5687 (25 June 1937), 1187.

The Note-Books and Papers of Gerard Manley Hopkins, edited with Notes and a Preface by Humphry House, *Criterion* 16: 65 (July 1937), 698–700.

The Disappearing Castle, by Charles Madge; *Poems*, by Rex Warner; *The Fifth Decad of Cantos*, by Ezra Pound [unsigned review], *Listener* 18: 451 (1 Sept. 1937), 467.

Bonnet Over the Windmill, Dodie Smith (New), *Time & Tide* 18: 38 (18 Sept. 1937), 1247.

'The Hebrides: A Tripper's Commentary', *Listener* 18: 456 (6 Oct. 1937), 718–20.

Lament for the Death of a Bullfighter and Other Poems, by Federico Garcia Lorca: translated by A. L. Lloyd [unsigned review], *Listener* 18: 456 (6 Oct. 1937), 744, 747.

'Chinese Poems' (*The Book of Songs*, translated from the Chinese by Arthur Waley), *Listener* 18: 457 (13 Oct. 1937), suppl. viii.

'With the Kennel Club', *Night and Day* 1: 16 (14 Oct. 1937), 40.

The Joy of It, by Littleton Powys [unsigned review], *Listener* 18: 462 (17 Nov. 1937), 1094.

'Letter to W. H. Auden', *New Verse*, nos. 26–7 (Auden Double Issue: Nov. 1937), 11–13.

Brief statement, in *Authors take sides on the Spanish War* (London: Left Review, Dec. 1937), unpaginated.

'In Defence of Vulgarity', *Listener* 18: 468 (29 Dec. 1937), 1407-8.

'The Play and the Audience', *Footnotes to the Theatre*, edited by R. D. Charques (1938), 32-43.

'Letter to the Editor', *New Verse*, no. 28 (Jan. 1938), 18.

The Best Poems of 1937, selected by Thomas Moult; *New Oxford Poetry 1937*, edited by Nevill Coghill and Alistair Sandford [unsigned review], *Listener* 19: 469 (5 Jan. 1938), 45-6.

It's Perfectly True and Other Stories, by Hans Christian Andersen [unsigned review], *Listener* 19: 472 (26 Jan. 1938), 207-8.

No More Peace, by Ernst Toller; *The Fall of the City*, by Archibald MacLeish; *Four Soviet Plays* [unsigned review], *Listener* 19: 474 (9 Feb. 1938), 321.

'Recantation' [early draft of chapter 5 of *Zoo*, August 1938 (November 1938)], in *The Honest Ulsterman*, no. 73, Louis MacNeice Number (Sept. 1983), 4-9.

'A Statement', *New Verse*, nos 31-2 (Autumn 1938), 7.

The Oxford Book Of Light Verse, chosen by W. H. Auden [unsigned review], *Listener* 20: 514 (17 Nov. 1938), 1079.

On the Frontier, by W. H. Auden and Christopher Isherwood, *Spectator* 161: 5760 (18 Nov. 1938), 858.

'A Brilliant Puritan' [in reference to Graves] (*Collected Poems*, by Robert Graves; *Collected Poems of Hart Crane*; *Tender Only to One*, by Stevie Smith), *Listener* 20: 517 (8 Dec. 1938), suppl., viii.

'Today in Barcelona', *Spectator* 162: 5769 (20 Jan. 1939), 84-5.

'The *Antigone* of Sophocles', *Spectator* 162: 5776 (10 March 1939), 404.

[Prefatory] Note, March 1939, to *Autumn Journal* 1938 (May 1939), in *Collected Poems*, edited by E. R. Dodds (1966, 1979), 101.

Of Mice and Men, John Steinbeck (Gate), *Time & Tide* 20: 16 (22 April 1939), 528. [Produced by Norman Marshall.]

Letter 'Painters and Poets' [on William Coldstream], *New Verse*, NS, 1: 2 (May 1939), 58-61.

'Original Sin' (*The Family Reunion*, by T. S. Eliot), *New Republic* 98: 1274 (3 May 1939), 384-5.

'Four Contemporary Poets' (*Dead Reckoning*, by Kenneth Fearing; *M.1000 Autobiographical Sonnets* by Merrill Moore; *In Dreams Begin Responsibilities*, by Delmore Schwartz; *Mirrors of Venus: Sonnets*, by John Wheelwright), *Common Sense* 8: 6 (June 1939), 23-4.

'Tendencies in Modern Poetry: Discussion between F. R. Higgins and Louis MacNeice, broadcast from Northern Ireland', *Listener* 22: 550 (27 July 1939), 185-6.

Letter, in reply to Peter Fleming's article 'Pax Bloomsburiana' in preceding issue, *Spectator* 168: 5811 (10 Nov. 1939), 652.

'A Bran Tub' (*The Christmas Companion*, edited by John Hadfield), *Listener* 22: 569 (7 Dec. 1939), suppl. xv.

'The Poet in England Today', *New Republic* 102: 13 (25 March 1940), 412–13.

'Not Tabloided in Slogans' (*Another Time: Poems*, by W. H. Auden), *Common Sense* 9: 4 (April 1940), 24–5.

'Housman in Retrospect' (*The Collected Poems of A. E. Housman*), *New Republic* 102: 18 (29 April 1940), 583.

'Yeats's Epitaph' (*Last Poems and Plays*, by W. B. Yeats), *New Republic* 102: 26 (24 June 1940), 862–3.

'American Letter' [to Stephen Spender], *Horizon* 1: 7 (July 1940), 462, 464.

'Oxford in the Twenties', *Partisan Review* 7: 6 (Nov.-Dec. 1940), 430–9.

'John Keats', *Fifteen Poets: Chaucer Spenser Shakespeare Milton Dryden Pope Cowper Coleridge Wordsworth Shelley Byron Keats Browning Tennyson Arnold* (Oxford: The Clarendon Press, Jan. 1941), 351–4.

'Scottish Poetry' (*A Golden Treasury of Scottish Poetry*, selected and edited by Hugh MacDiarmid), *New Statesman and Nation*, NS, 21: 517 (18 Jan. 1941), 66.

'London Letter: Blackouts, Bureaucracy & Courage', 1 Jan., *Common Sense* 10: 2 (Feb. 1941), 46–7.

Freedom Radio [film review], *Spectator* 166: 5875 (31 Jan. 1941), 116.

Quiet Wedding—The Mark of Zorro [film review], *Spectator* 166: 5876 (7 Feb. 1941), 143.

'Through Stained Glass' (*Some Memories of W. B. Yeats*, by John Masefield), *Spectator* 166: 5876 (7 Feb. 1941), 152.

Tin Pan Alley—Arise my Love—Arizona [film review], *Spectator* 166: 5877 (14 Feb. 1941), 172.

'Acknowledgement' and 'Foreword' to *Poems 1925-1940* (17 Feb. 1941), v and xiii.

'Traveller's Return', *Horizon* 3: 14 (Feb. 1941), 110–17.

'London Letter: Anti-Defeatism of the Man in the Street', 1 March, *Common Sense* 10: 4 (April 1941), 110–11.

'Touching America', *Horizon* 3: 15 (March 1941), 207–12.

Angels Over Broadway—The Trail of the Vigilantes [film review], *Spectator* 166: 5882 (21 March 1941), 307.

Spare a Copper—The Ghost Train [film review], *Spectator* 166: 5883 (28 March 1941), 343.

'Acknowledgements', *Plant and Phantom* (April 1941), 11.

Victory—Mr and Mrs Smith [film review], *Spectator* 166: 5884 (4 April 1941), 371.

'The Way We Live Now: IV', *Penguin New Writing*, no. 5 (April 1941), 9-14.

'Cook's Tour of the London Subways' (radio feature condensed), *Listener* 25: 640 (17 April 1941), 554-5.

'London Letter: War Aims; the New Political Alignment', 1 April, *Common Sense* 10: 5 (May 1941), 142-3.

'The Tower that Once', *Folios of New Writing* 3 (Spring 1941), 37-41.

'The Morning after the Blitz', *Picture Post* 2: 5 (3 May 1941), 9-12, 14.

'U.S.A.' (*Who are the Americans?* by William Dwight Whitney), *New Statesman and Nation* 21: 532 (3 May 1941), 466-7.

'Autobiographies' (*In Search of Complications*, by Eugene de Savitsch; *King's Messenger, 1918-1940*, by George P. Antrobus; *Pioneering Days*, by Thomas Bell), *New Statesman and Nation* 21: 534 (17 May 1941), 512-13.

'London Letter: Democracy versus Reaction & Luftwaffe', 1 May, *Common Sense* 10: 6 (June 1941), 174-5.

'London Letter: Reflections from the Dome of St Paul's', 2 June, *Common Sense* 10: 7 (July 1941), 206-7.

'"The Third Christmas"', *Radio Times* 73: 951 (19 Dec. 1941), 7.

Autobiographical sketch, in *Twentieth Century Authors: A Biographical Dictionary of Modern Literature*, edited by Stanley J. Kunitz and Howard Haycraft (1942), 888-9.

'Broken Windows or Thinking Aloud', *c.*1941-2, *Poetry Review*, 78: 2 (Summer 1988), 4-6.

'Our Fourth Wartime Christmas', *London Calling*, 18 Dec. 1942, 4-5.

'Introduction: Some Comments on Radio Drama', *Christopher Columbus* (March 1944), 7-19.

'Oddity of "The Golden Ass"' [comment on his adaptations of Apuleius' *The Golden Ass, Cupid and Psyche*], *Radio Times* 85: 1100 (27 Oct. 1944), 5.

'Note', *Springboard: Poems 1941-1944* (Dec. 1944), 7.

'"The Golden Ass" or "Metamorphoses" of Apuleius: adapted by Louis MacNeice' [comment on the rebroadcast], *Radio Times* 86: 1114 (2 Feb. 1945), 8.

'The Elusive Classics' (Virgil: *The Eclogues and Georgics*, translated into English Verse by R. C. Trevelyan), *New Statesman and Nation* 29: 724 (5 May 1945), 293.

'"The Hippolytus" of Euripides' [comment on radio adaptation of Gilbert Murray's translation], *Radio Times* 89: 1148 (28 Sept. 1945), 4.

'Mr O'Casey's Memoirs' (*Drums Under the Windows*, Sean O'Casey), *Time & Tide* 26: 45 (10 Nov. 1945), 942.

'L'Écrivain britannique et la guerre', *La France libre* 11: 62 (15 Dec. 1945), 103–9.

'Introduction' to *The Golden Ass of Apuleius*, translated by William Adlington 1566 (London: John Lehmann, 1946), v–ix.

'The Knox New Testament' (*The New Testament*, newly translated into English, by Ronald Knox), *Spectator* 176: 6150 (10 May 1946), 484.

'Pindar: A New Judgment' (*Pindar*, by Gilbert Norwood), *New Statesman and Nation* 31: 795 (18 May 1946), 362.

'*Enter Caesar*' [comment on his play], *Radio Times* 92: 1198 (13 Sept. 1946), 5.

'"Sin and Divine Justice"' [comment on radio adaptation of his translation of Aeschylus' *Agamemnon*], *Radio Times* 93: 1204 (25 Oct. 1946), 13.

'A Greek Satirist who is Still Topical' [comment on his *Enemy of Cant*, radio panorama of Aristophanic comedy], *Radio Times* 93: 1209 (29 Nov. 1946), 5.

'The Traditional Aspect of Modern English Poetry', *La Cultura nel Mondo* (Rome), Dec. 1946, 220–4.

'Scripts Wanted!', *BBC Year Book 1947*, 25–8.

'The Saga of Burnt Njal' [comment on his adaptation of *Njal's Saga* in two parts—*The Death of Gunnar* and *The Burning of Njal*], *Radio Times* 94: 1221 (7 March 1947), 4.

'General Introduction' to his *The Dark Tower and Other Radio Scripts* (May 1947), 9–17.

'Rome: Where History Plays Leap-frog' [comment on his feature *Portrait of Rome*], *Radio Times* 95: 1236 (20 June 1947), 13.

'The English Literary Scene Today: A Return to Responsibility Features the Approach to the Present Crisis', *New York Times Book Review*, 28 Sept. 1947, 1, 34.

'In the Beginning was the Word' [comment on the spoken and the sung word], printed programme note for 'A Recital of Song and Verse by Hedli Anderson, Cyril Cusack, Louis MacNeice': Wigmore Hall, London W1, Sun., 22 Feb. 1948 at 3 p.m., [2].

'An Alphabet of Literary Prejudices', *Windmill* 3: 9 (March 1948), 38–42.

'India at First Sight' [1] [radio panorama, broadcast 13 March 1948], a portion cut for publication as 'The Crash Landing', *Botteghe Oscure* 4 (1949), 378–85.

'Indian Art' (*Indian Art; The Vertical Man*, by W. G. Archer), *New Statesman and Nation* 35: 888 (13 March 1948), 218.

'Acknowledgement' and 'Note' [on 'The Streets of Laredo'], *Holes in the Sky: Poems 1944-1947* (7 May 1948), 7 and 12.

'*The Two Wicked Sisters*' [comment on his play], *Radio Times*, TV edn, 100: 1292 (16 July 1948), 7.

'Psycho-Moralities and Pseudo-Moralities' [comment on the re-broadcast of his play *The Careerist*, along with its parody *The Life of Subhuman* by Laurence Kitchin], *Radio Times*, TV edn, 100: 1301 (17 Sept. 1948), 7.

'Eliot and the Adolescent', *T. S. Eliot: A Symposium*, comps. M. J. Tambimuttu and Richard March (Sept. 1948), 146-51.

'English Poetry Today' [his broadcast on BBC Eastern Service], *Listener* 40: 1023 (2 Sept. 1948), 346-7.

'*Trimalchio's Feast*' [comment on his adaptation from Petronius' *Satyricon*], *Radio Times* 101: 1314 (17 Dec. 1948), 10.

'Westminster Abbey' [his overseas broadcast], *London Calling*, 23 Dec. 1948, 16-18.

'Experiences with Images', *Orpheus* 2 (1949), 124-32.

'Poets Conditioned by their Times' [broadcast of his lecture], *London Calling*, 10 Feb. 1949, 12, 19.

'Portrait of a Modern Man' [comment on his revised play *He Had a Date*], *Radio Times*, TV edn, 102: 1322 (11 Feb. 1949), 7.

'An Irish Proletarian' (*Inishfallen, Fare Thee Well*, by Sean O'Casey), *New Statesman and Nation* 37: 937 (19 Feb. 1949), 184-5.

'Preface' (? Spring 1949) to *Collected Poems 1925-1948* (Sept. 1949), 8, in *Collected Poems*, edited by E. R. Dodds (1966, 1979), xiv.

'Listeners are Warned . . . "a Study in Evil"' [comment on his play *The Queen of Air and Darkness*], *Radio Times* 102: 1328 (25 March 1949), 9.

'An Indian Ride' (*At Freedom's Door*, by Malcolm Lyall Darling), *New Statesman and Nation* 37: 943 (2 April 1949), 334.

'Heart of Byron' (*Don Juan*, by Lord Byron: with an Introduction by Peter Quennell), *Observer* 8235 (3 April 1949), 3.

Letter [correction of Horace quotation in his Byron article in the preceding issue], *Observer* 8236 (10 April 1949), 5.

'Betjeman' (*Selected Poems*, by John Betjeman: chosen with a Preface by John Sparrow), *Poetry* (London), 4: 15 (May 1949), 23-5.

'A Guide-Book for the Educated' (*Fabled Shore*, by Rose Macaulay), *New Statesman and Nation* 37: 953 (11 June 1949), 618.

'The Critic Replies' [comment on Christopher Fry's comedy *The Lady's Not for Burning*], *World Review*, NS, no. 4 (June 1949), 21-2.

'India at First Sight' [2] [article of 1949, pendant to a series of radio programmes on India and Pakistan 1948], *BBC Features*, edited by Laurence Gilliam (1950), 60-4.

'Poetry, the Public and the Critic', *New Statesman and Nation* 38: 970 (8 Oct. 1949), 380-1.

'On Making a Radio Version of *Faust*' [comment on his adaptation of Goethe's *Faust* in six programmes], *Radio Times* 105: 1359 (28 Oct. 1949), 5, 7.

'And so to *Faust*, Part Two', *Radio Times* 105: 1360 (4 Nov. 1949), 6.

'A Poet's Play' (*The Cocktail Party*, by T. S. Eliot), *Observer* 8292 (7 May 1950), 7.

'Great Riches' (*Collected Poems of W. B. Yeats*), *Observer* 8308 (27 Aug. 1950), 7.

'Landscape and Legend' (*The Dreaming Shore*, by Olivia Manning), *Observer* 8311 (17 Sept. 1950), 7.

'Introduction' to *Goethe's Faust, Parts I and II: An Abridged Version*, translated by MacNeice (July 1951), 9-10.

'Athens—City of Contrasts' [comment on his feature *Portrait of Athens*], *Radio Times* 113: 1462 (16 Nov. 1951), 5.

'The Olympians' (*The Gods of the Greeks*, by C. Kerényi; *Greeks and Trojans*, by Rex Warner), *Observer* 8377 (23 Dec. 1951), 7.

'The Real Mixer' (*Chiaroscuro: Fragments of Autobiography*, by Augustus John), *New Statesman and Nation* 43: 1100 (5 April 1952), 408.

'The Faust Myth' (*The Fortunes of Faust*, by E. M. Butler), *Observer* 8393 (13 April 1952), 7.

'About Ireland' (*Dublin*, by Maurice Craig; *Ireland and the Irish*, by Charles Duff; *The Emerald Isle*, by Geoffrey Taylor; *The Face of Ulster*, by Denis O'D. Hanna; *Connacht: Galway*, by Richard Hayward), *New Statesman and Nation* 43: 1106 (17 May 1952), 590, 592.

'Sharks Ltd.' (*Harpoon at a Venture*, by Gavin Maxwell), *New Statesman and Nation* 43: 1109 (7 June 1952), 681.

'Notes on the Way', Part 1, *Time & Tide* 33: 26 (28 June 1952), 709-10.

[Acknowledgments], *Ten Burnt Offerings* (11 July 1952), 10.

'Notes on the Way', Part 2, *Time & Tide* 33: 28 (12 July 1952), 779-80.

'Hatred and Love' (*Rose and Crown*, by Sean O'Casey), *Observer* 8406 (13 July 1952), 7.

'The Bardic Strain' (*Heroic Poetry*, by C. M. Bowra), *New Statesman and Nation* 44: 1121 (30 Aug. 1952), 242.

'Wedding of Simon Karras' [comment on his recordings of a Byzantine wedding ceremony 1950, in the monastery church of Daphni, Greece], *Radio Times* 116: 1504 (5 Sept. 1952), 13.

'Books in General' (*A Reading of George Herbert*, by Rosemond Tuve), *New Statesman and Nation* 44: 1123 (13 Sept. 1952), 293-4.

'A Poet's Choice' (*Poets of the English Language*, edited by W. H. Auden and Norman Holmes Pearson, 5 volumes), *Observer* 8416 (21 Sept. 1952), 8.

'Spenser's Symbolic World' [comment on 12 programmes of *The Faerie Queene*: readings chosen by C. S. Lewis], *Radio Times* 116: 1507 (26 Sept. 1952), 15.

'Yeats's Plays' (*Collected Plays*, by W. B. Yeats), *Observer* 8422 (2 Nov. 1952), 8.

'Portrait of a Would-Be Hero' [comment on his play *One Eye Wild*], *Radio Times* 117: 1513 (7 Nov. 1952), 6.

Letter, 'Literature and the Lively Arts', *TLS*, 21 Nov. 1952, 761, in reply to an article in *TLS* of 14 Nov. 1952, 749.

Second letter, 'Literature and the Lively Arts', *TLS*, 19 Dec. 1952, 837, in reply to the writer of the article, 5 Dec. 1952, 797.

Untitled article, in *This I Believe*, foreword by Edward Murrow, edited by Edward P. Morgan (1953), 64–5.

'The Sideliner' (*Edward Lear's Indian Journal 1873–1875*, edited by Ray Murphy), *New Statesman and Nation* 45: 1152 (4 April 1953), 402.

'Words Are Things Which Ring Out: The Strange, Mighty Impact of Dylan Thomas' Poetry' (*The Collected Poems of Dylan Thomas*), *New York Times Book Review*, 5 April 1953, 1, 17.

'A Greek Story of a Family Curse' [comment on rebroadcast of his adaptation of his translation of Aeschylus' *Agamemnon*], *Radio Times* 119: 1546 (26 June 1953), 21.

'A Poet's Progress' (*W. B. Yeats: Letters to Katharine Tynan*, edited by Roger McHugh), *Observer* 8458 (12 July 1953), 7.

Letter, 'Gordon Her[r]ickx', *New Statesman and Nation* 46: 1168 (25 July 1953), 104.

'Poetry Needs to be Subtle and Tough', *New York Times Book Review*, 9 Aug. 1953, 7, 17.[2]

'A Plea for Sound', *BBC Quarterly* 8: 3 (Autumn 1953), 129–35.

'The Other Island' (*Mind You, I've said Nothing!*, by Honor Tracy; *The Silent Traveller in Dublin*, by Chiang Yee), *New Statesman and Nation* 46: 1183 (7 Nov. 1953), 570, 572.

Letter, 'Dylan Thomas Memorial Fund', *The Times* 52788 (25 Nov. 1953), 9d, signed by T. S. Eliot, Peggy Ashcroft, Kenneth Clark, *et al.*, including MacNeice; same letter in *TLS*, 7 Nov. 1953, 762; in *New Statesman and Nation* 46: 1187 (5 Dec. 1953), 719; in *Encounter* 2: 1 (Jan. 1954); and elsewhere.

---

[2] The original title: 'What Makes a Good Poet'—according to a *New York Times* payment voucher, 11 Aug. 1953, in the possession of Mrs Hedli MacNeice.

'He Weeps by the Side of the Ocean' (*Teapots & Quails*, by Edward Lear), *New Statesman and Nation* 46: 1187 (5 Dec. 1953), 721.

'Dramatising a Tale of a Giant' [comment on his play *The Heartless Giant*], *Radio Times* 122: 1573 (1 Jan. 1954), 4.

'Dylan Thomas: Memories and Appreciations III', *Encounter* 2: 1 (Jan. 1954), 12–13; reprinted in *Dylan Thomas: The Legend and the Poet*, edited by E. W. Tedlock (London: Heinemann, 1960), 85–7, and in *A Casebook on Dylan Thomas*, edited by John Malcolm Brinnin (New York: Crowell, 1960), 282–4.

Note [on *Autumn Sequel*, Canto xviii], *London Magazine* 1: 1 (Feb. 1954), 104.

Introduction to 'A Dylan Thomas Award', *Dock Leaves* 5: 13 (Dylan Thomas Number, Spring 1954), 6–7 [the prize-winning poem: Anthony Conran, 'For Dylan Thomas (On hearing he was dead)'].

'Round and About Milk Wood' (*Under Milk Wood, The Doctor and the Devils*, by Dylan Thomas), *London Magazine* 1: 3 (April 1954), 74–7.

'Greece and the West' (*Fair Greece, Sad Relic*, by Terence Spencer), *New Statesman and Nation* 47: 1210 (15 May 1954), 636.

'In the Grand Manner' (*The English Epic and its Background*, by E. M. W. Tillyard), *New Statesman and Nation* 47: 1215 (19 June 1954), 804.

George Herbert, by Margaret Bottrall; *George Herbert*, by Joseph H. Summers, *London Magazine* 1: 7 (Aug. 1954), 74–6.

'Is The Novel Dead? A Poet's View', *Observer* 8520 (19 Sept. 1954), 11.

The People of the Sea, by David Thomson, *London Magazine* 1: 9 (Oct. 1954), 94, 96.

'Endless Old Things' (*The Letters of W. B. Yeats*, edited by Allan Wade), *New Statesman and Nation* 48: 1230 (2 Oct. 1954), 398.

Prefatory Note to *Autumn Sequel* 1953 (12 Nov. 1954), in *Collected Poems*, edited by E. R. Dodds (1966, 1979), 329.

'I Remember Dylan Thomas', *Ingot* (Steel Co. of Wales), Dec. 1954, 28–30.

'Sometimes the Poet Spoke in Prose: From Squib to Satire—a Collection of the Varied Writing of Dylan Thomas' (*Quite Early One Morning*, by Dylan Thomas), *New York Times Book Review*, 19 Dec. 1954, 1.

Autobiographical sketch, in *Twentieth Century Authors: First Supplement*, edited by Stanley J. Kunitz and Vineta Colby (1955), 624–5.

'Tunnelling into Freedom' [comment on rebroadcast of his play *Prisoner's Progress*], *Radio Times* 126: 1626 (7 Jan. 1955), 5.

'Told in Monologues' [comment on his adaptation of Virginia Woolf's *The Waves* in two programmes], *Radio Times* 126: 1635 (11 March 1955), 5.

Quite Early One Morning, by Dylan Thomas; *The Poetry of Dylan Thomas*, by Elder Olson; *Dylan Thomas*, by Derek Stanford, *London Magazine* 2: 5 (May 1955), 106–9.

'Journey up the Nile' [comment on his feature *The Fullness of the Nile*], *Radio Times* 128: 1651 (1 July 1955), 7.

'The River Nile' [comment on rebroadcast, in series on Africa], *London Calling*, 28 July 1955, 5.

Letter to the Editor, *London Magazine* 2: 9 (Sept. 1955), 69–70, in reply to J. C. Hall's review of *Autumn Sequel*, ibid., 2: 6 (June 1955), 95–7.

Poetry and the Age, by Randall Jarrell; *Inspiration and Poetry*, by C. M. Bowra, *London Magazine* 2: 9 (Sept. 1955), 71–4.

'What Vomit Had John Keats?' (*Dylan Thomas in America*, by John Malcolm Brinnin), *New Statesman and Nation* 51: 1310 (21 April 1956), 423–4.

'The Sound of Bow Bells' [comment on his feature *Bow Bells*], *Radio Times* 131: 1701 (15 June 1956), 5.

'Historic Rouen: a City of Contrasts' [comment on his feature *Spires and Gantries*], *Radio Times* 132: 1707 (27 July 1956), 5.

The Russet Coat [on Robert Burns], by Christina Keith; *John Clare*, by John and Anne Tibble, *London Magazine* 3: 8 (Aug. 1956), 59–62.

'Ghana: The Birth of an African State' [comment on his feature *The Birth of Ghana*], *Radio Times* 134: 1736 (15 Feb. 1957), 27.

'Indian Approaches' (*Expedition Tortoise*, by Pierre Rambach, Raoul Jahan, and F. Hébert-Stevens; *The Ride to Chandigarh*, by Harold Elvin; *Goa, Rome of the Orient*, by Rémy), *New Statesman and Nation* 53: 1357 (16 March 1957), 346–7.

'Lost Generations?' (*Poetry Now*, edited by G. S. Fraser; *Mavericks*, edited by Howard Sergeant and Dannie Abse), *London Magazine* 4: 4 (April 1957), 52–5.

'Acknowledgements' [with notes on five poems], *Visitations* (10 May 1957), 9.

'Louis MacNeice Writes . . .' [on his *Visitations*], *Poetry Book Society Bulletin* 14 (May 1957), [1].

'Nuts in May' [comment on his play], *Radio Times* 135: 1750 (24 May 1957), 7.

'Fragments I Have Shored' (*Leftover Life to Kill*, by Caitlin Thomas), *New Statesman and Nation* 53: 1369 (8 June 1957), 741.

'*The Stones of Oxford*' [comment on his feature], *Radio Times* 136: 1767 (20 Sept. 1957), 27.

James Joyce's World, by Patricia Hutchins; *Letters of James Joyce*, edited by Stuart Gilbert, *London Magazine* 4: 11 (Nov. 1957), 73–5.

'Irish Pack Quell the Uppercuts', *Observer* 8690 (19 Jan. 1958), 24.

'A Light Touch under the Stars' [comment on his script for *son et lumière* at Cardiff Castle], *Daily Telegraph*, 9 Aug. 1958, 6.

'Introduction' to *New Poems 1958* [a PEN anthology], edited by Bonamy Dobrée, Louis MacNeice, Philip Larkin (10 Nov. 1958), 9-10.[3]

The Variorum Edition of the Poems of W. B. Yeats, edited by Peter Allt and Russell K. Alspach, *London Magazine* 5: 12 (Dec. 1958), 69, 71, 73, 75.

'Foreword' to *Eighty-Five Poems* (13 Feb. 1959), 7.

'Talking about Rugby', *New Statesman* 57: 1459 (28 Feb. 1959), 286, 288.

'Modern Greeks' (*The Flight of Ikaros*, by Kevin Andrews), *Observer* 8748 (1 March 1959), 19.

'The Battle of Clontarf' [comment on his play *They Met on Good Friday*], *Radio Times* 145: 1882 (4 Dec. 1959), 6.

'A *Mosaic of Youth*' [comment on his feature], *Radio Times* 145: 1885 (25 Dec. 1959), 37.

'Twin to Drink?' (*Report on Rugby*, by W. John Morgan and Geoffrey Nicholson), *New Statesman* 59: 1505 (16 Jan. 1960), 80.

'Being Simple' (*Poetry of This Age: 1908-1958*, by J. M. Cohen), *Spectator* 204: 6868 (12 Feb. 1960), 225-6.

'Eighty Years of Tragi-Comedy' (*Sean O'Casey: The Man and his Work*, by David Krause), *Observer* 8804 (27 March 1960), 23.

J. M. Synge, by David H. Greene and Edward M. Stephens; *The Masterpiece and the Man: Yeats as I Knew Him*, by Monk Gibbon, *London Magazine* 7: 8 (Aug. 1960), 70-3.

'*Another Part of the Sea*' [comment on his TV play adapted from his stage play *Traitors in Our Way*], *Radio Times* 148: 1921 (2 Sept. 1960), 2.

'Out of Ugliness' (*Wilfred Owen*, by D. S. R. Welland), *New Statesman* 60: 1545 (22 Oct. 1960), 623-4.

'A Modern Odyssey' (*Poems*, by George Seferis, translated by Rex Warner), *New Statesman* 60: 1553 (17 Dec. 1960), 978-9.

'When I Was Twenty-One: 1928', *The Saturday Book 21*, edited by John Hadfield (1961), 230-9.

'Out of the Deadpan' (Sam Thompson, *Over the Bridge*, Empire Theatre, Belfast), *Observer* 8796 (31 Jan. 1960), 23.

'Louis MacNeice Writes . . .' [on his *Solstices*], *Poetry Book Society Bulletin* 28 (Feb. 1961), [2].

---

[3] This introduction was drafted by Larkin and Dobrée only, though signed 'B.D. / P.A.L. / L.MacN.': B. C. Bloomfield, *Philip Larkin: A Bibliography 1933-1976* (1979), 63-4.

'That Chair of Poetry', *New Statesman* 61: 1561 (10 Feb. 1961), 210, 212.

'Note', *Solstices* (10 March 1961), 11.

'Growing Up in Ireland' (*An Only Child*, by Frank O'Connor; *Kings, Lords, and Commons*, by Frank O'Connor), *Observer* 8869 (25 June 1961), 25.

'Godot on TV', *New Statesman* 62: 1582 (7 July 1961), 27-8.

'Look at the Faces' [TV review], *New Statesman* 62: 1584 (21 July 1961), 95.

'I Got Those Cathode Blues' [TV review], *New Statesman* 62: 1586 (4 Aug. 1961), 164.

'Pleasure in Reading: Woods to Get Lost In', *The Times* 55162 (17 Aug. 1961), 11b-c.

'Roll on Reality' [TV review], *New Statesman* 62: 1588 (18 Aug. 1961), 225-6.

'In Pursuit of Cuchulain' (*Celtic Heritage*, by Alwyn Rees and Brinley Rees), *Observer* 8878 (27 Aug. 1961), 19.

'Snow and Rock' [TV review], *New Statesman* 62: 1590 (1 Sept. 1961), 284.

'Two Plays, and Spike' [TV review], *New Statesman* 62: 1592 (15 Sept. 1961), 358.

'Pins and Needles' [TV review], *New Statesman* 62: 1594 (29 Sept. 1961), 450-1.

'One-Eyed Hero' [comment on his revised play *One Eye Wild*], *Radio Times* 153: 1983 (9 Nov. 1961), 30.

'Come in, Dominic' (*Teems of Times and Happy Returns*, by Dominic Behan), *New Statesman* 62: 1602 (24 Nov. 1961), 795-6.

'A Fleet Street Chronicle' [comment on his play *Let's Go Yellow*], *Radio Times* 153: 1988 (14 Dec. 1961), 26.

Letter ' "Let's Go Yellow" ', *Listener* 67: 1710 (4 Jan. 1962), 33.

'Quiet Irish Charm' (*Twice Round the Black Church*, by Austin Clarke), *Sunday Telegraph*, 4 Feb. 1962, 7.

'Nine New Caps' [rugby], *New Statesman* 63: 1614 (16 Feb. 1962), 239-40.

'Goethe's *Faust*' [comment on his adaptation abridged], *Radio Times* 154: 2000 (8 March 1962), 50.

'*The Mad Islands*' [comment on his play], *Radio Times* 154: 2003 (29 March 1962), 39.

'C'est la terre' (*The Furrow Behind Me*, by Angus MacLellan; *The Hard Road to Klondike*, by Michael MacGowan; *My Ireland*, by Kate O'Brien), *New Statesman* 63: 1632 (22 June 1962), 911-12.

'Under the Sugar Loaf' [Dublin], *New Statesman* 63: 1633 (29 June 1962), 948-9.

'The Two Faces of Ireland' (*Brendan Behan's Island*, by Brendan Behan; *West Briton*, by Brian Inglis), *Observer* 8935 (30 Sept. 1962), 29.

'Blood and Fate' (*The Odyssey*, translated by Robert Fitzgerald; *Patrocleia*, Book XVI of Homer's *Iliad*, adapted by Christopher Logue), *Listener* 68: 1749 (4 Oct. 1962), 527.

A Preface to 'The Faerie Queene', by Graham Hough, *Listener* 69: 1766 (31 Jan. 1963), 213.

'Yeats at Work' (*Between the Lines*, by Jon Stallworthy), *Listener* 69: 1773 (21 March 1963), 521.

'The Ould Opinioneer' (*Under a Colored Cap*, by Sean O'Casey), *New Statesman* 65: 1677 (3 May 1963), 678-9.

'Gael Force at Wembley' [hurling and Gaelic football], *New Statesman* 65: 1682 (7 June 1963), 876.

'William Empson', *The Concise Encyclopedia of English and American Poets and Poetry*, edited by Stephen Spender and Donald Hall (1963), 127-8.

The Saga of Gisli, translated by George Johnston, *Listener* 69: 1787 (27 June 1963), 1083.

'Great Summer Sale' [report on President Kennedy's visit to Ireland], *New Statesman* 66: 1686 (5 July 1963), 10, 12.

'Frost' (*The Poetry of Robert Frost*, by Reuben Brower), *New Statesman* 66: 1687 (12 July 1963), 46.

'*Persons from Porlock*' [comment on his play], *Radio Times* 160: 2076 (22 August 1963), 44.

'Louis MacNeice Writes . . .' [on his *The Burning Perch*], *Poetry Book Society Bulletin* 38 (Sept. 1963), [1].

'Introduction' to his *Christopher Columbus*, Faber school edition (25 Sept. 1963), 7-10.

'Childhood Memories', from an unscripted talk [recorded in Belfast, July 1963] on the Third Programme, *Listener* 70: 1811 (12 Dec. 1963), 990.

'Introduction' to his *The Mad Islands* and *The Administrator* (13 March 1964), 7-9.

'Notes' to his *One for the Grave* (29 Jan. 1968), 13-14.

Index

Entries in this index are both topical (e.g. on art, religion, politics, nationalities, and the like) and personal, including most names and many recurrent subjects in the text and the footnotes. To cut overall length of the index, there are *no* entries for names in the Bibliography: these may be found in the companion volume, *Selected Literary Criticism of Louis MacNeice* (1987), entries for 249–66.

LaVergne, TN USA
12 October 2009
160640LV00002B/19/A